DI022675

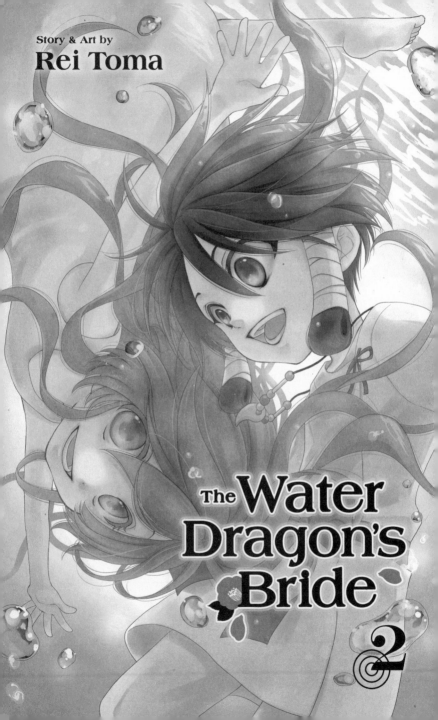

Story & Art by
Rei Toma

The **Water Dragon's Bride**

2

The Water Dragon's Bride

CHARACTER INTRODUCTIONS

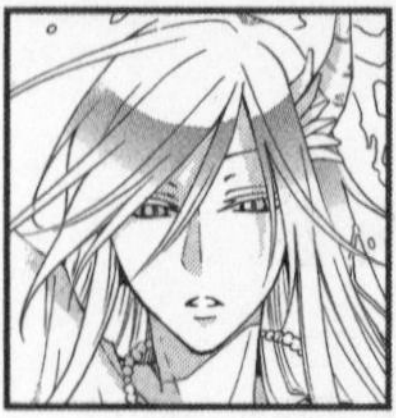

The Water Dragon God

The god who rules over the waters. Though he hates humans, he seems to be intrigued by Asahi.

Asahi

A girl who has suddenly been flung into another world. She is sacrificed to the water dragon god by Subaru's mother.

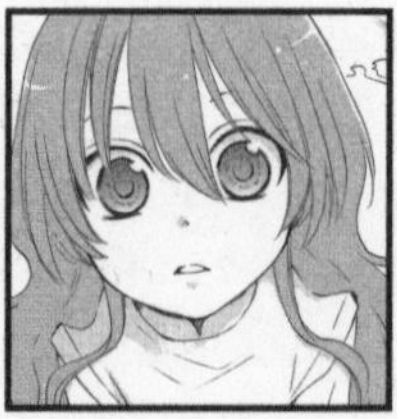

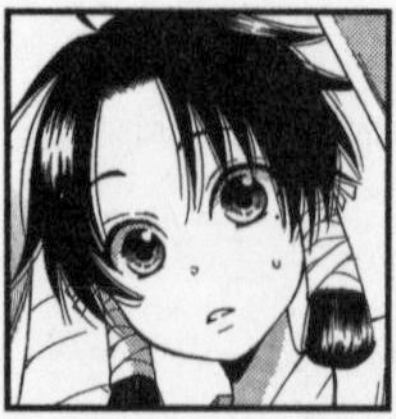

Subaru

A boy who saves Asahi. He is drawn to Asahi and has resolved to protect her from both the water dragon god and his own mother.

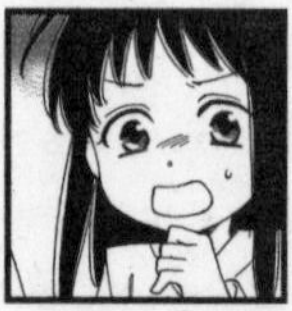

Shiina

Subaru's sister.
She thinks Asahi is weird and frightening.

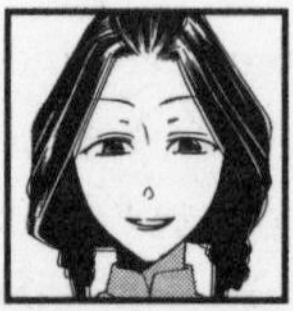

Subaru's Mother

She hates Asahi and has attempted to have her killed.

STORY THUS FAR

◎ Asahi is living a normal, sheltered life when she suddenly gets pulled into a pond and is transported to a strange new world. She meets Subaru, the son of the most prominent family in his village, and he helps her and brings her home. Subaru's mother dislikes Asahi, however, and plots to sacrifice her as a bride to the water dragon god in the Great Lake.

◎ Asahi plunges into the lake, and the water dragon god appears. He proposes that she become his wife, but she refuses. The god becomes vexed and steals Asahi's voice away from her. Asahi is terrified not knowing what her fate will be... But unbeknownst to her, Subaru trusts that she is still alive and attempts to rescue her.

◎ The two reunite despite interference from the water dragon god, and they escape safely back to the village. But when Subaru's mother learns that Asahi is alive, she plots to have her killed. She inflicts a terrible burn on Asahi, who now hovers between life and death. The water dragon god appears before Asahi, but she fearfully rejects him. Seeing that she asks nothing of him even though she is suffering and near death, the water dragon god surprisingly extends his hand... to help?!

The Water Dragon's Bride

2

CONTENTS

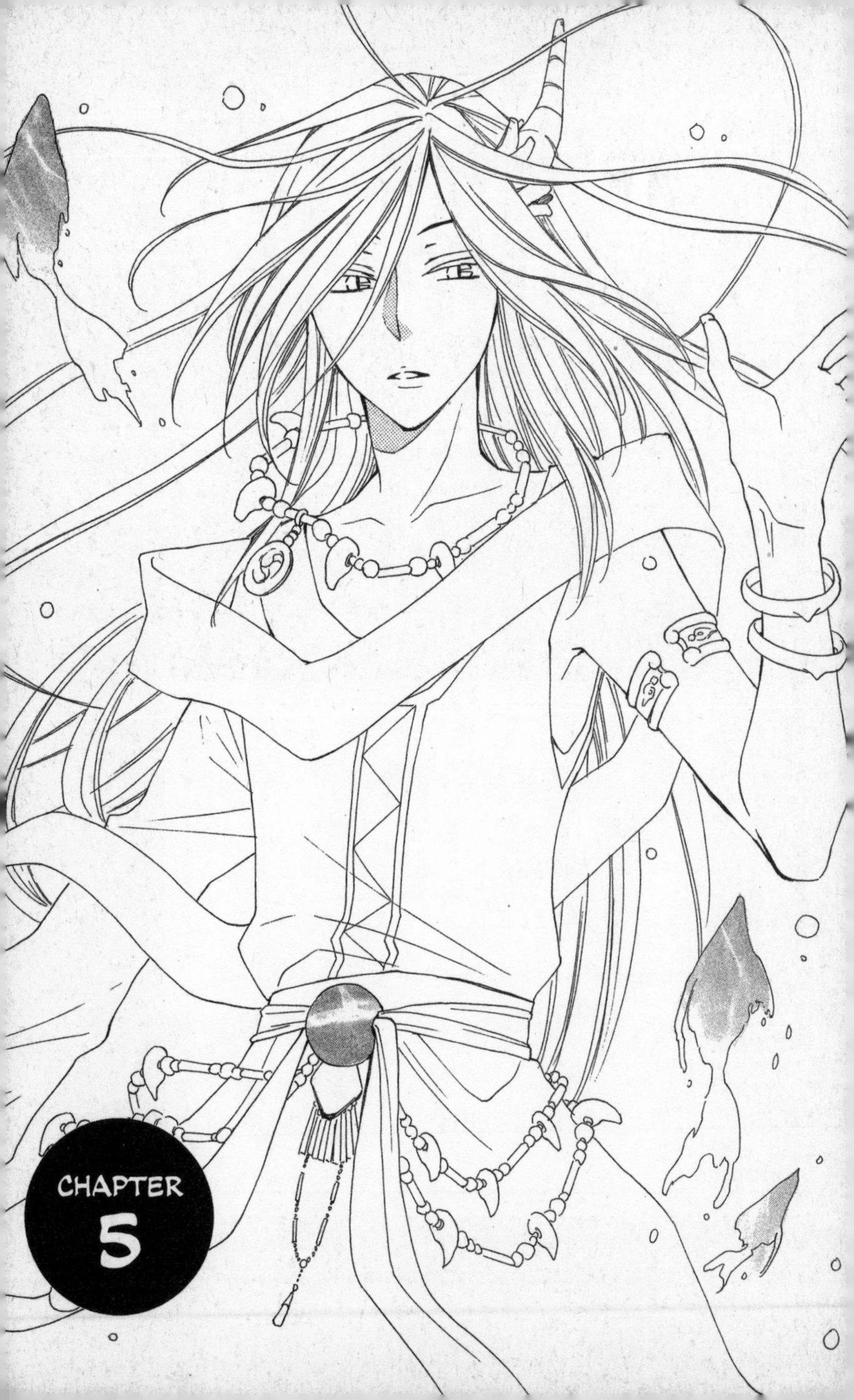
CHAPTER
5

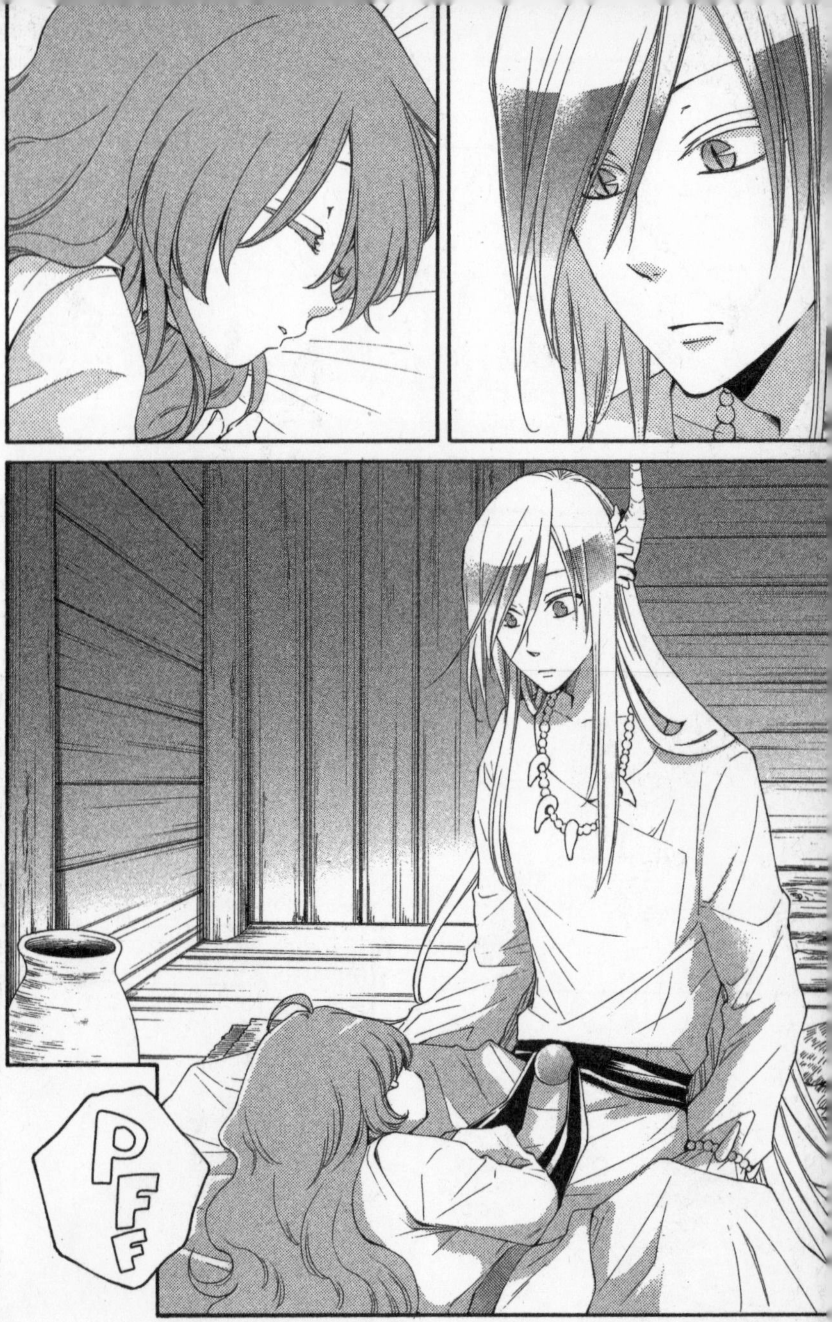
PFF

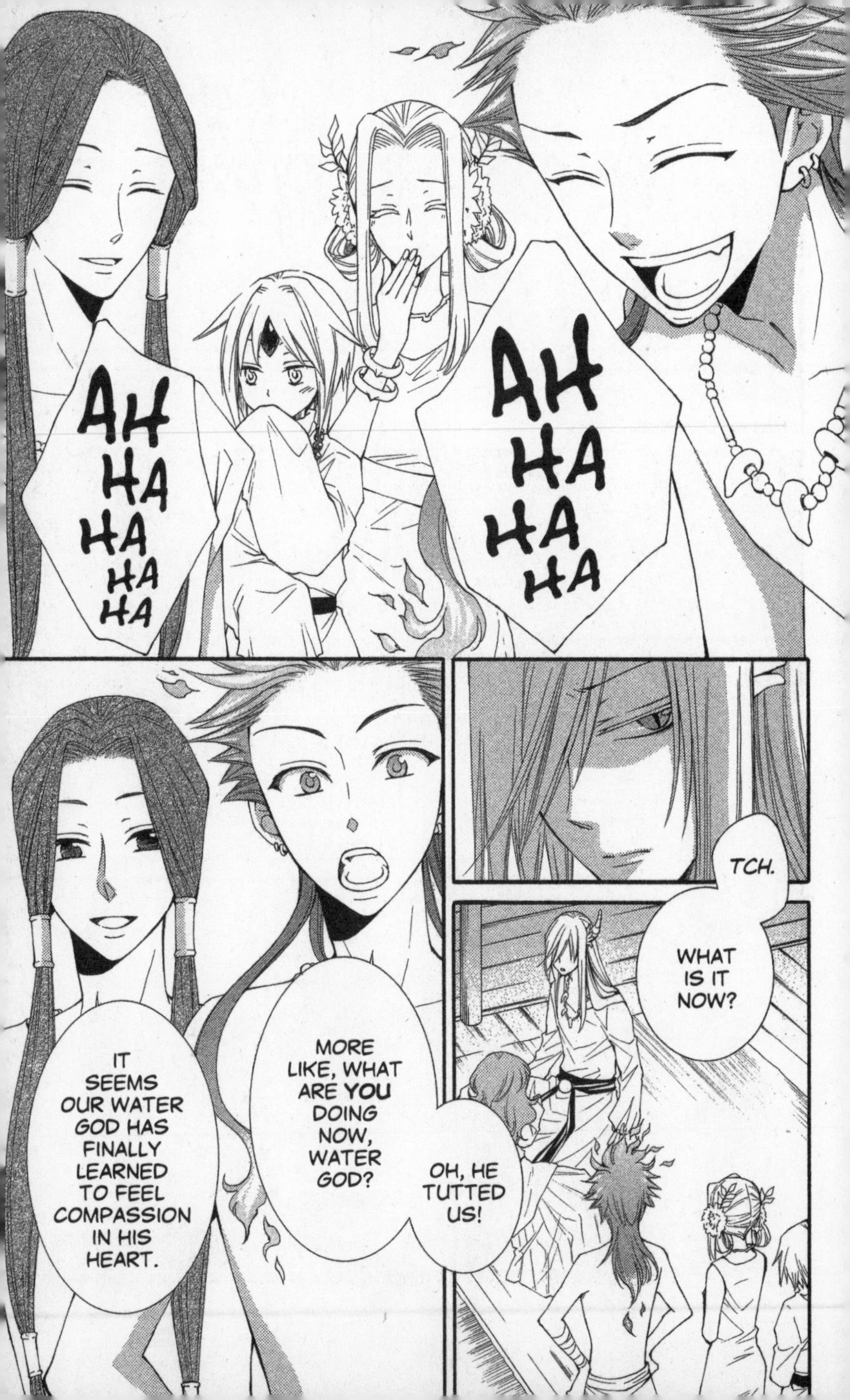
AH HA HA HA
AH HA HA HA HA
TCH.
WHAT IS IT NOW?
OH, HE TUTTED US!
MORE LIKE, WHAT ARE YOU DOING NOW, WATER GOD?
IT SEEMS OUR WATER GOD HAS FINALLY LEARNED TO FEEL COMPASSION IN HIS HEART.

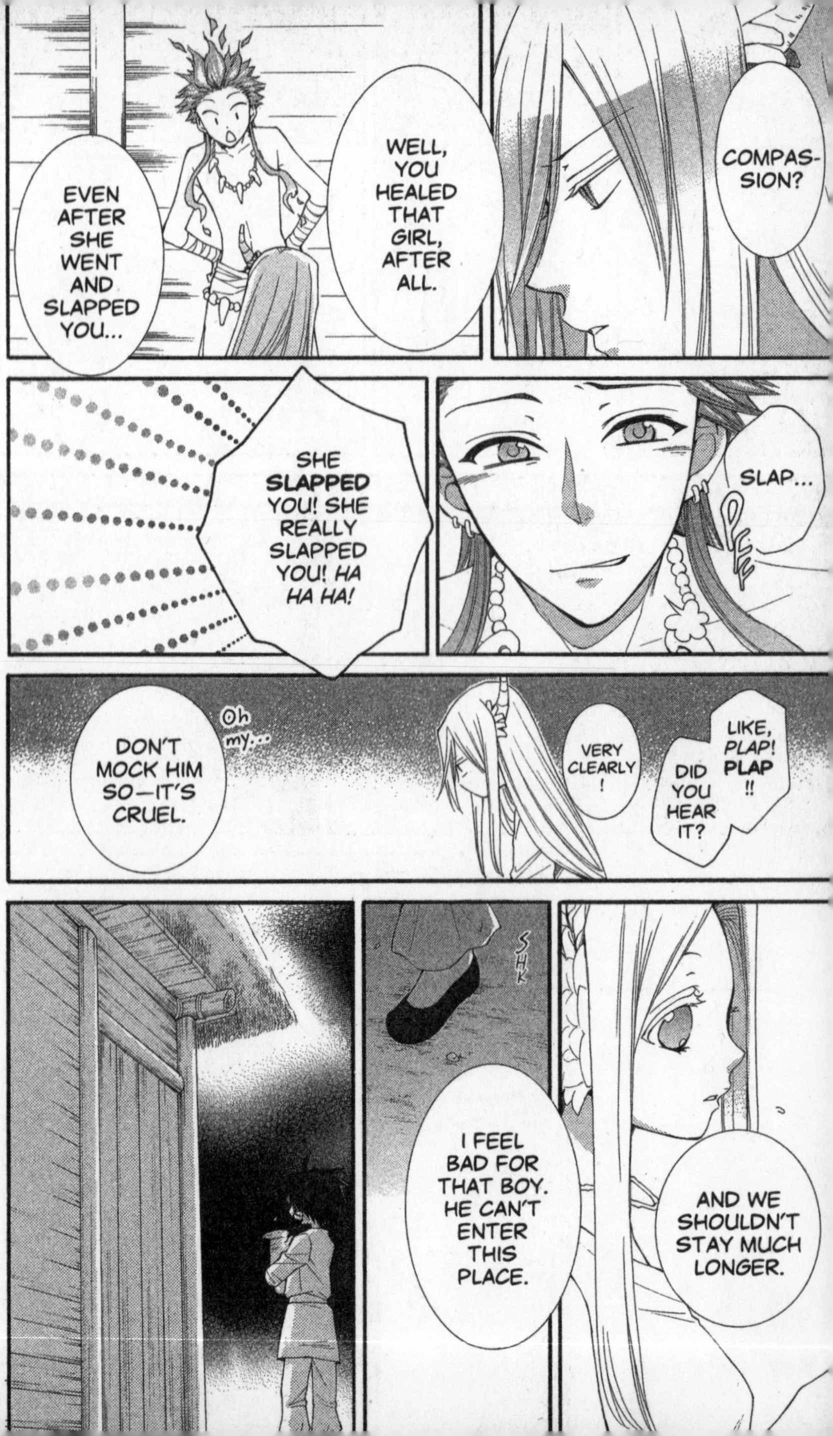
COMPASSION?
WELL, YOU HEALED THAT GIRL, AFTER ALL.
EVEN AFTER SHE WENT AND SLAPPED YOU...
SLAP...
SHE **SLAPPED** YOU! SHE REALLY SLAPPED YOU! *HA HA HA!*
LIKE, *PLAP!* **PLAP** !!
DID YOU HEAR IT?
VERY CLEARLY !
Oh my...
DON'T MOCK HIM SO—IT'S CRUEL.
I FEEL BAD FOR THAT BOY. HE CAN'T ENTER THIS PLACE.
AND WE SHOULDN'T STAY MUCH LONGER.
SHK

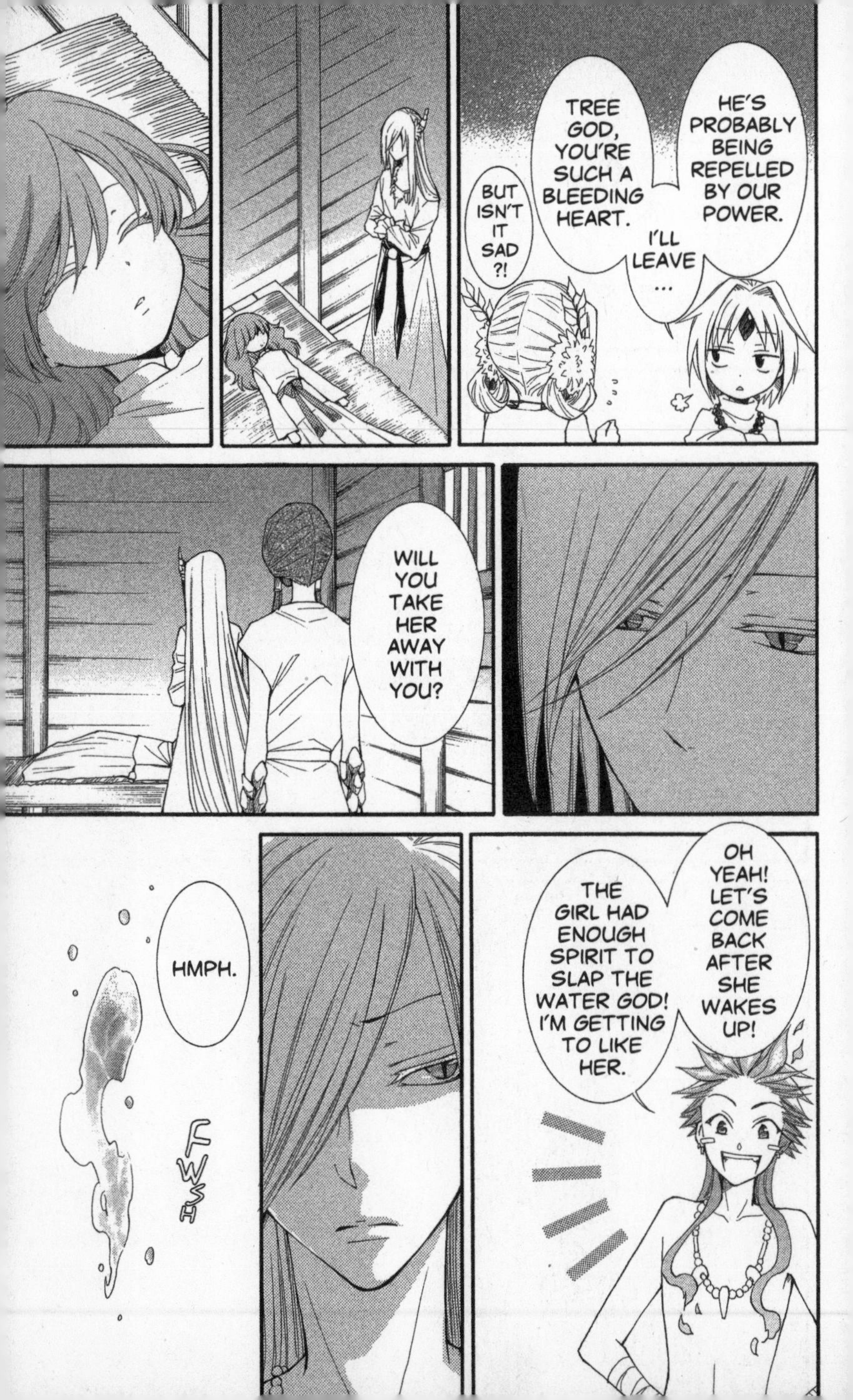
HE'S PROBABLY BEING REPELLED BY OUR POWER.
TREE GOD, YOU'RE SUCH A BLEEDING HEART.
I'LL LEAVE ...
BUT ISN'T IT SAD ?!
WILL YOU TAKE HER AWAY WITH YOU?
OH YEAH! LET'S COME BACK AFTER SHE WAKES UP!
THE GIRL HAD ENOUGH SPIRIT TO SLAP THE WATER GOD! I'M GETTING TO LIKE HER.
HMPH.
FWSH

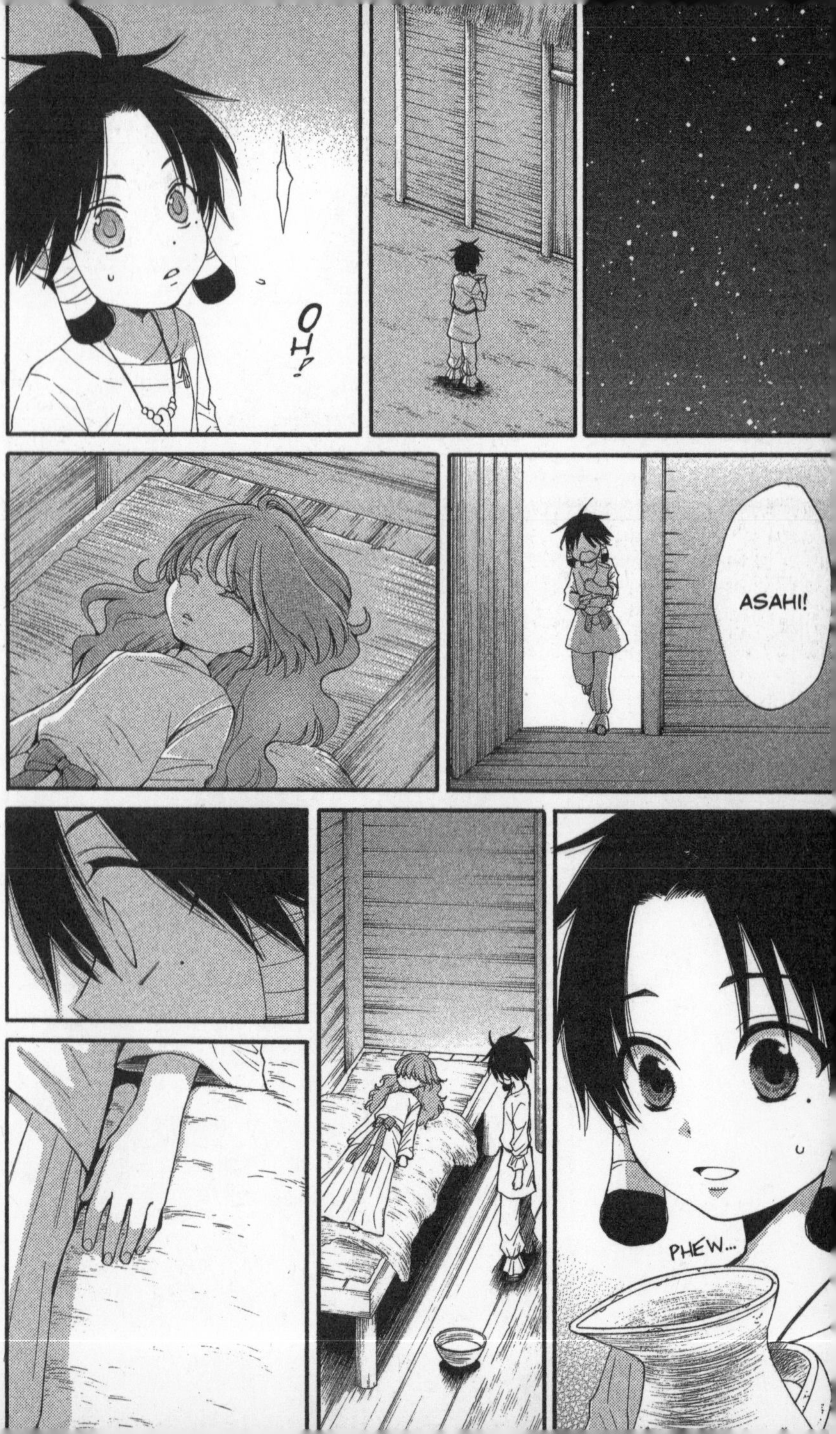

OH!
ASAHI!
PHEW...

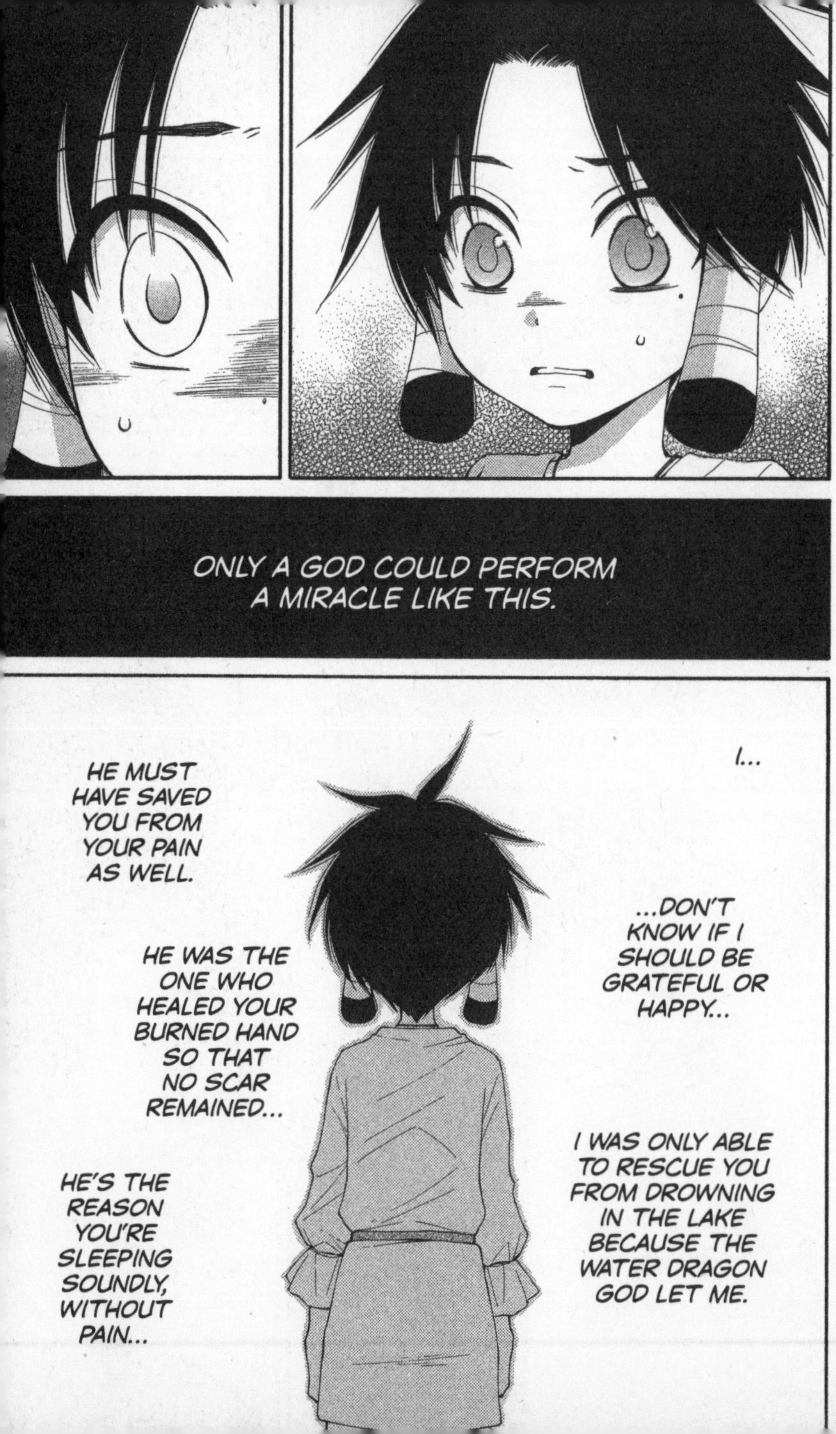
ONLY A GOD COULD PERFORM A MIRACLE LIKE THIS.
I...
HE MUST HAVE SAVED YOU FROM YOUR PAIN AS WELL.
...DON'T KNOW IF I SHOULD BE GRATEFUL OR HAPPY...
HE WAS THE ONE WHO HEALED YOUR BURNED HAND SO THAT NO SCAR REMAINED...
I WAS ONLY ABLE TO RESCUE YOU FROM DROWNING IN THE LAKE BECAUSE THE WATER DRAGON GOD LET ME.
HE'S THE REASON YOU'RE SLEEPING SOUNDLY, WITHOUT PAIN...

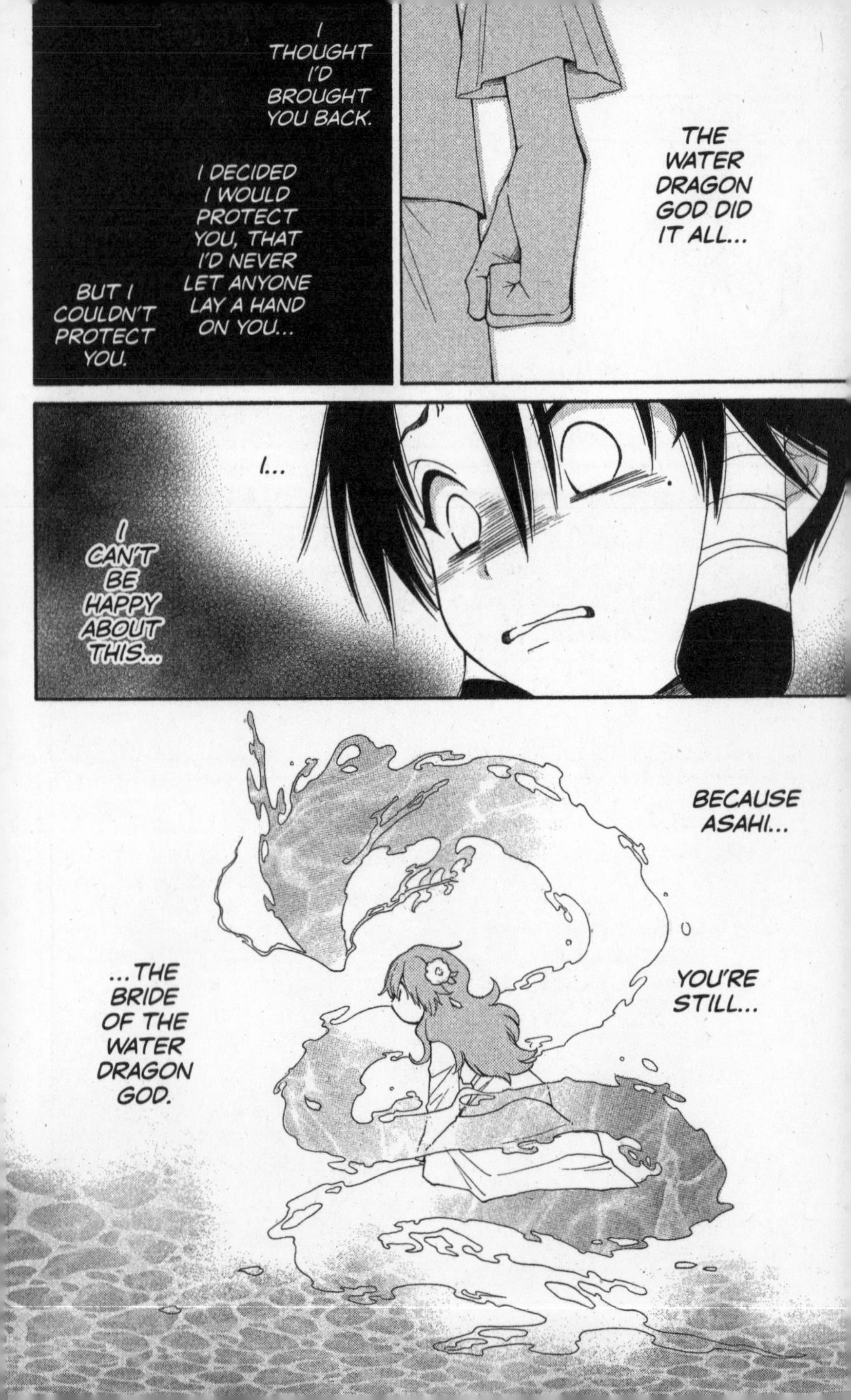
THE WATER DRAGON GOD DID IT ALL...
I THOUGHT I'D BROUGHT YOU BACK.
I DECIDED I WOULD PROTECT YOU, THAT I'D NEVER LET ANYONE LAY A HAND ON YOU...
BUT I COULDN'T PROTECT YOU.
I...
I CAN'T BE HAPPY ABOUT THIS...
BECAUSE ASAHI...
YOU'RE STILL...
...THE BRIDE OF THE WATER DRAGON GOD.

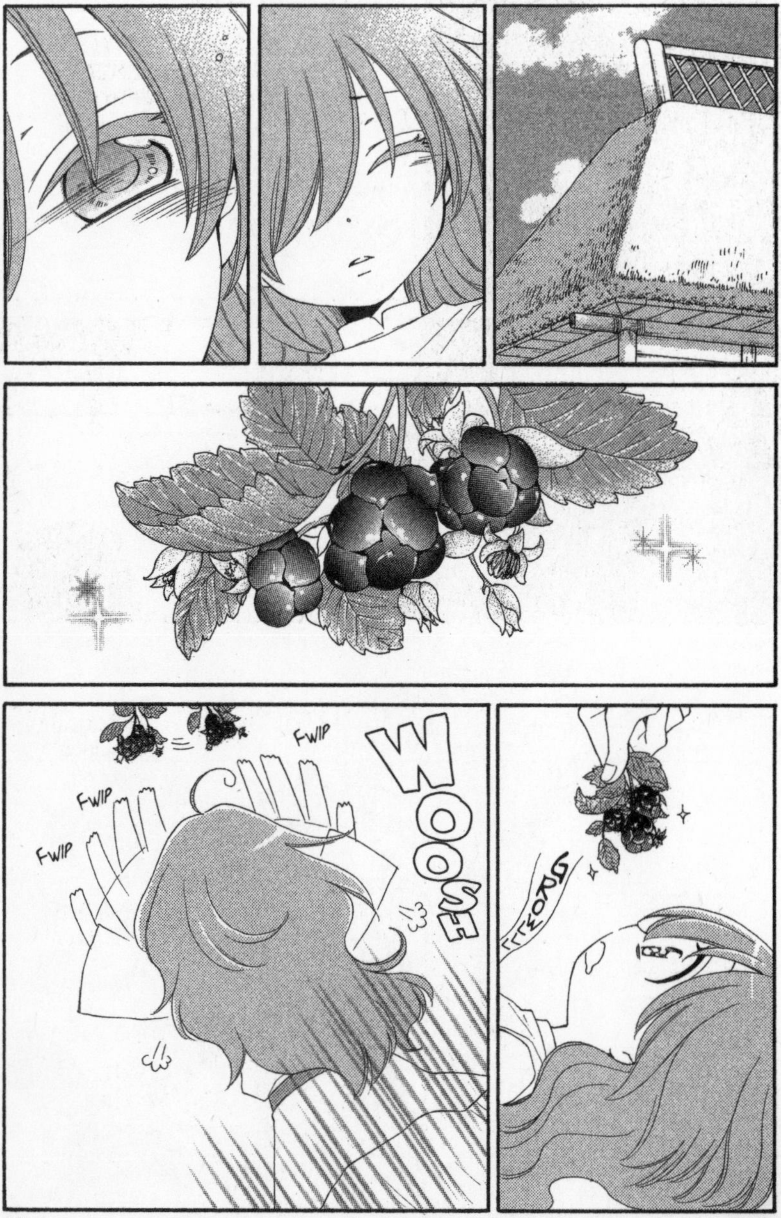
GROW
WOOSH
FWIP
FWIP
FWIP

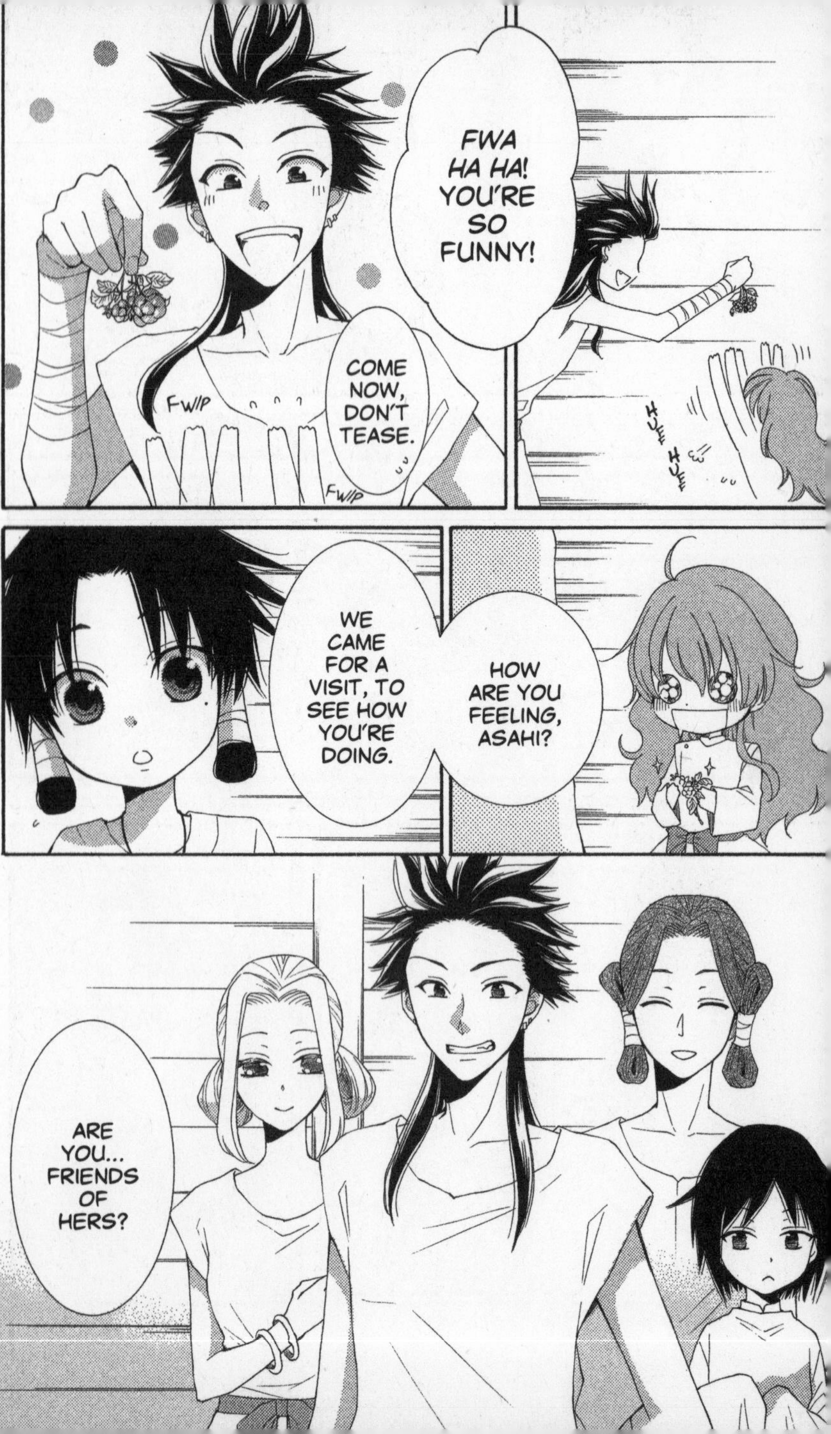

FWA HA HA! YOU'RE SO FUNNY!
HUFF HUFF
COME NOW, DON'T TEASE.
FWIP
FWIP
HOW ARE YOU FEELING, ASAHI?
WE CAME FOR A VISIT, TO SEE HOW YOU'RE DOING.
ARE YOU... FRIENDS OF HERS?

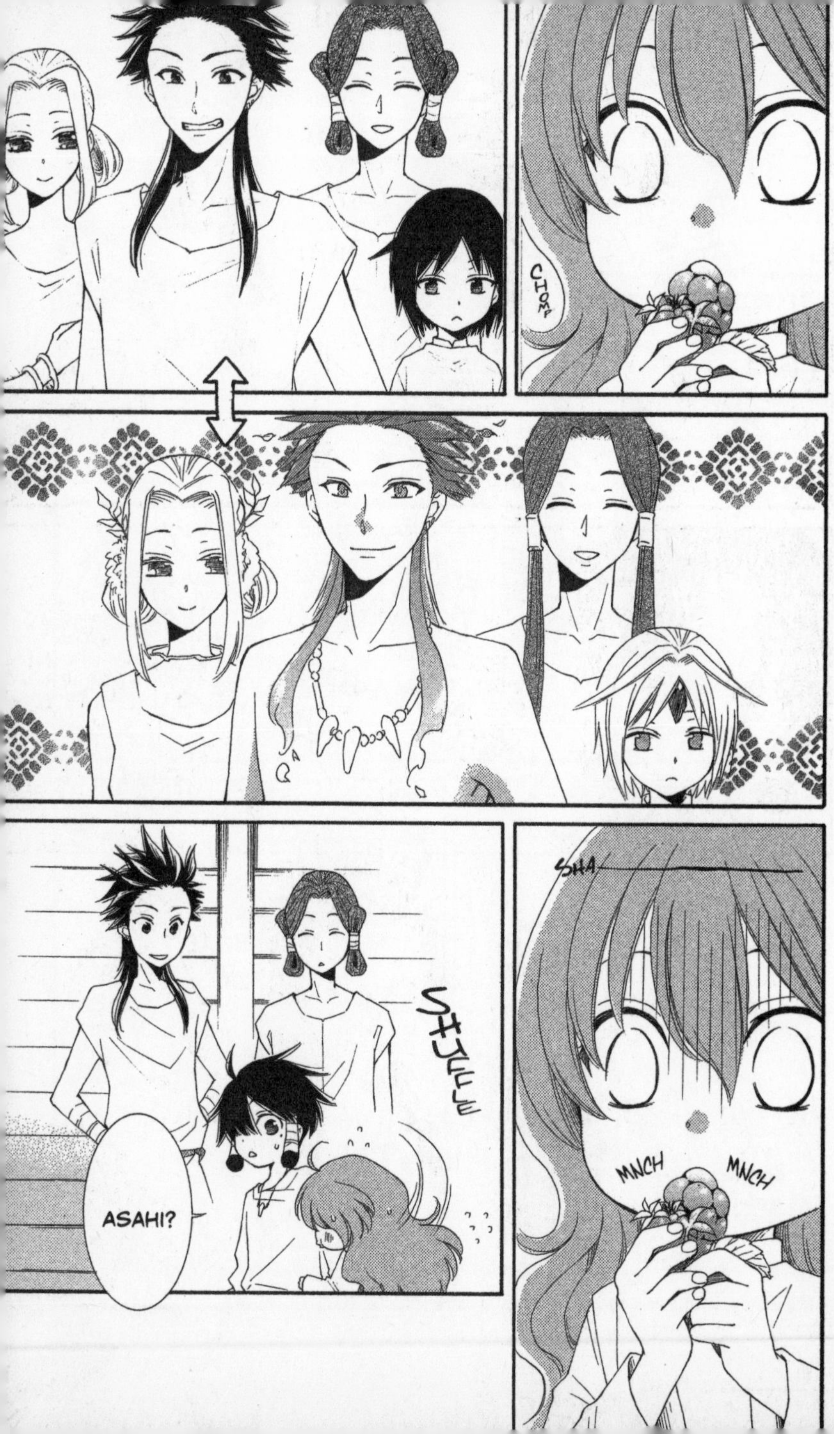
CHOMP
SHA
MNCH MNCH
SHUFFLE
ASAHI?

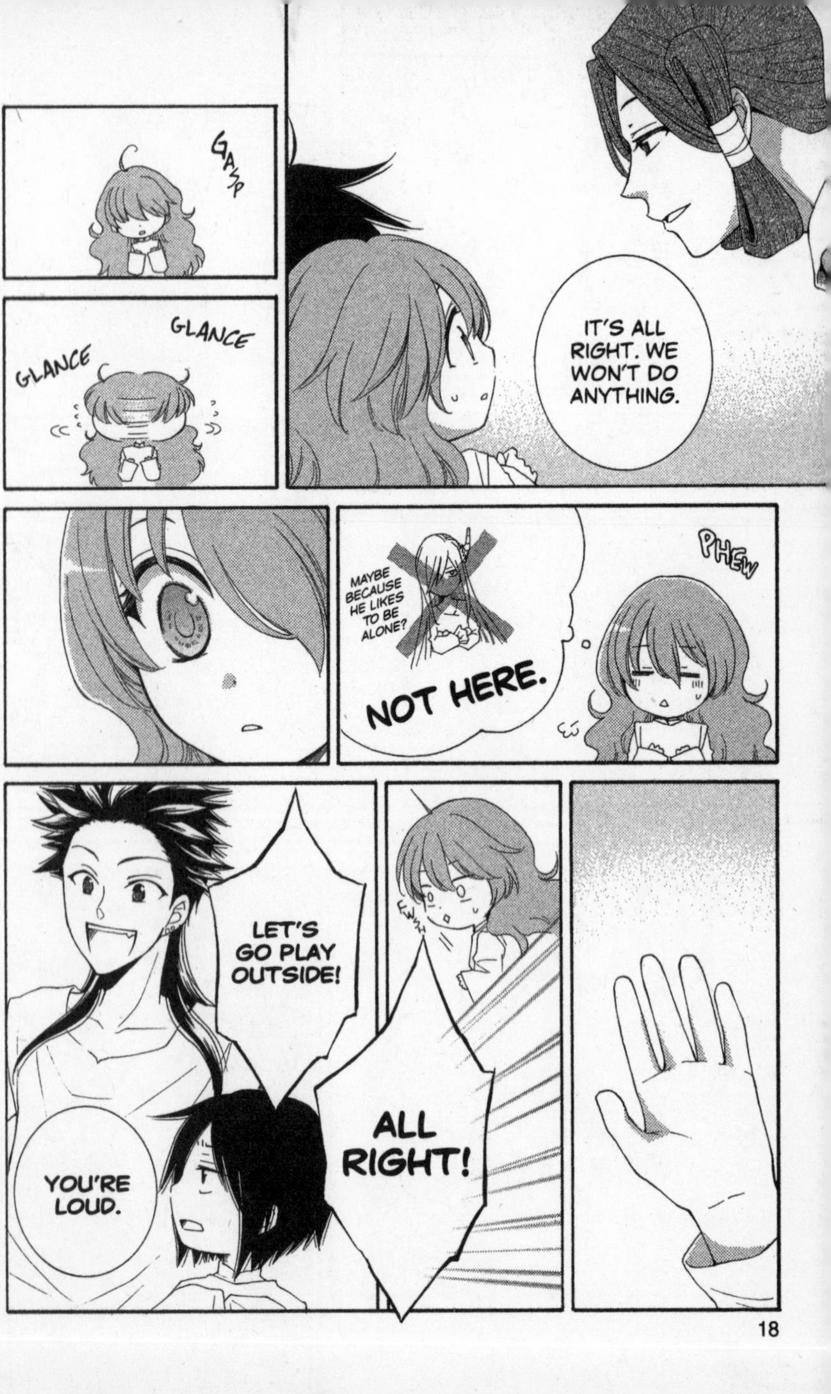
IT'S ALL RIGHT. WE WON'T DO ANYTHING.
GASP
GLANCE
GLANCE
PHEW
NOT HERE.
MAYBE BECAUSE HE LIKES TO BE ALONE?
LET'S GO PLAY OUTSIDE!
ALL RIGHT!
YOU'RE LOUD.

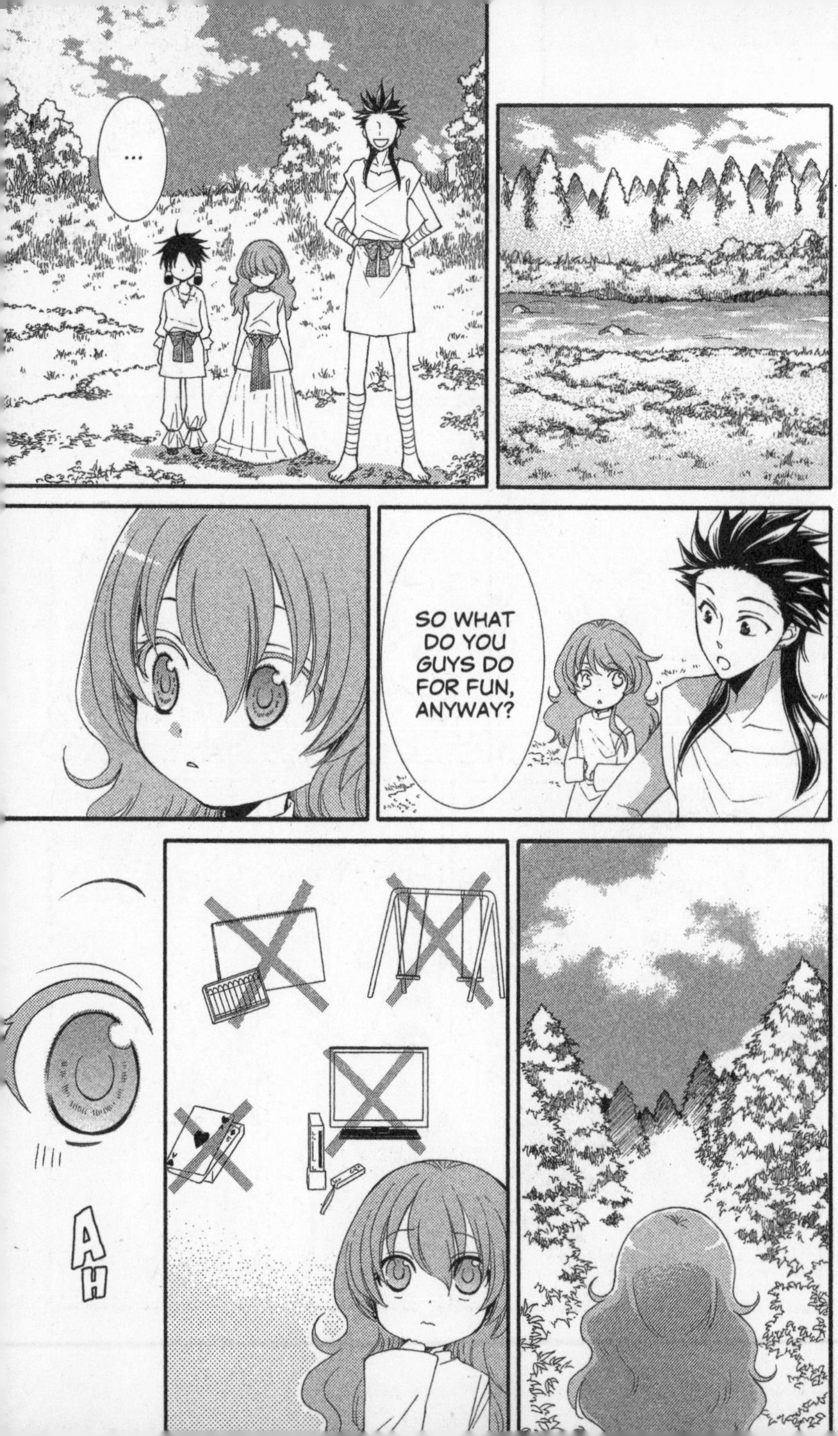
...
SO WHAT DO YOU GUYS DO FOR FUN, ANYWAY?
AH

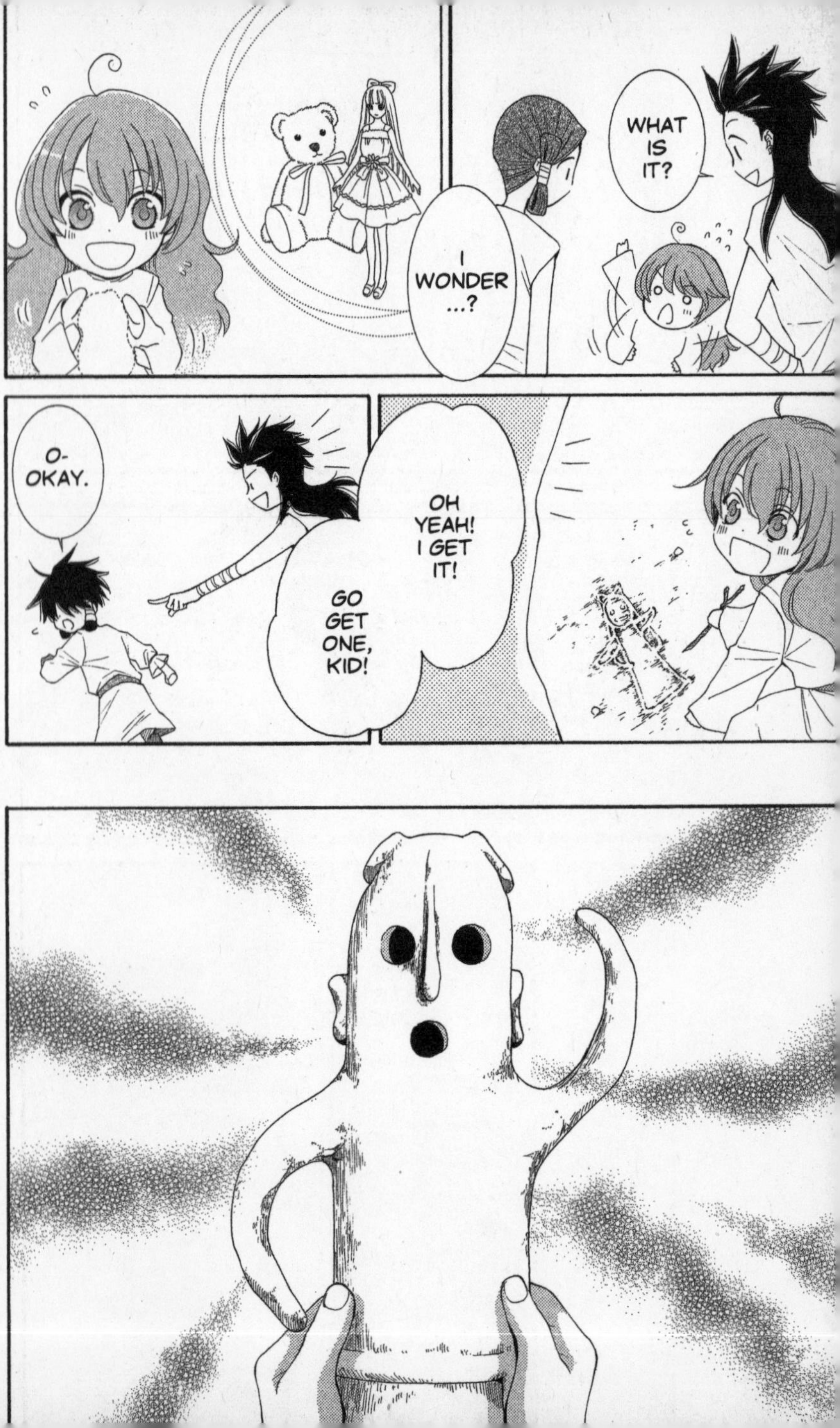
WHAT IS IT?
I WONDER ...?
OH YEAH! I GET IT!
GO GET ONE, KID!
O-OKAY.

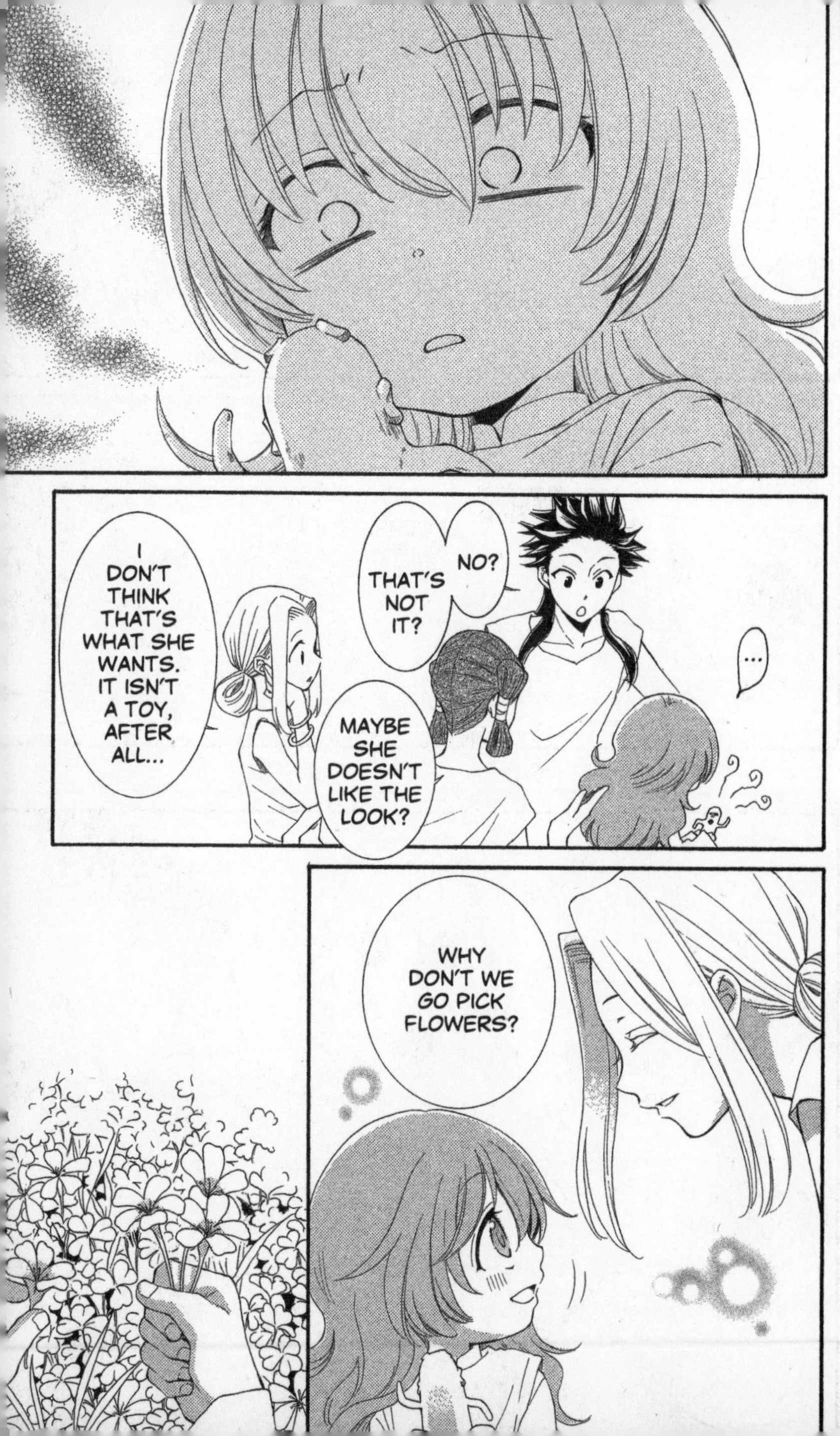
NO? THAT'S NOT IT?
...
MAYBE SHE DOESN'T LIKE THE LOOK?
I DON'T THINK THAT'S WHAT SHE WANTS. IT ISN'T A TOY, AFTER ALL...
WHY DON'T WE GO PICK FLOWERS?

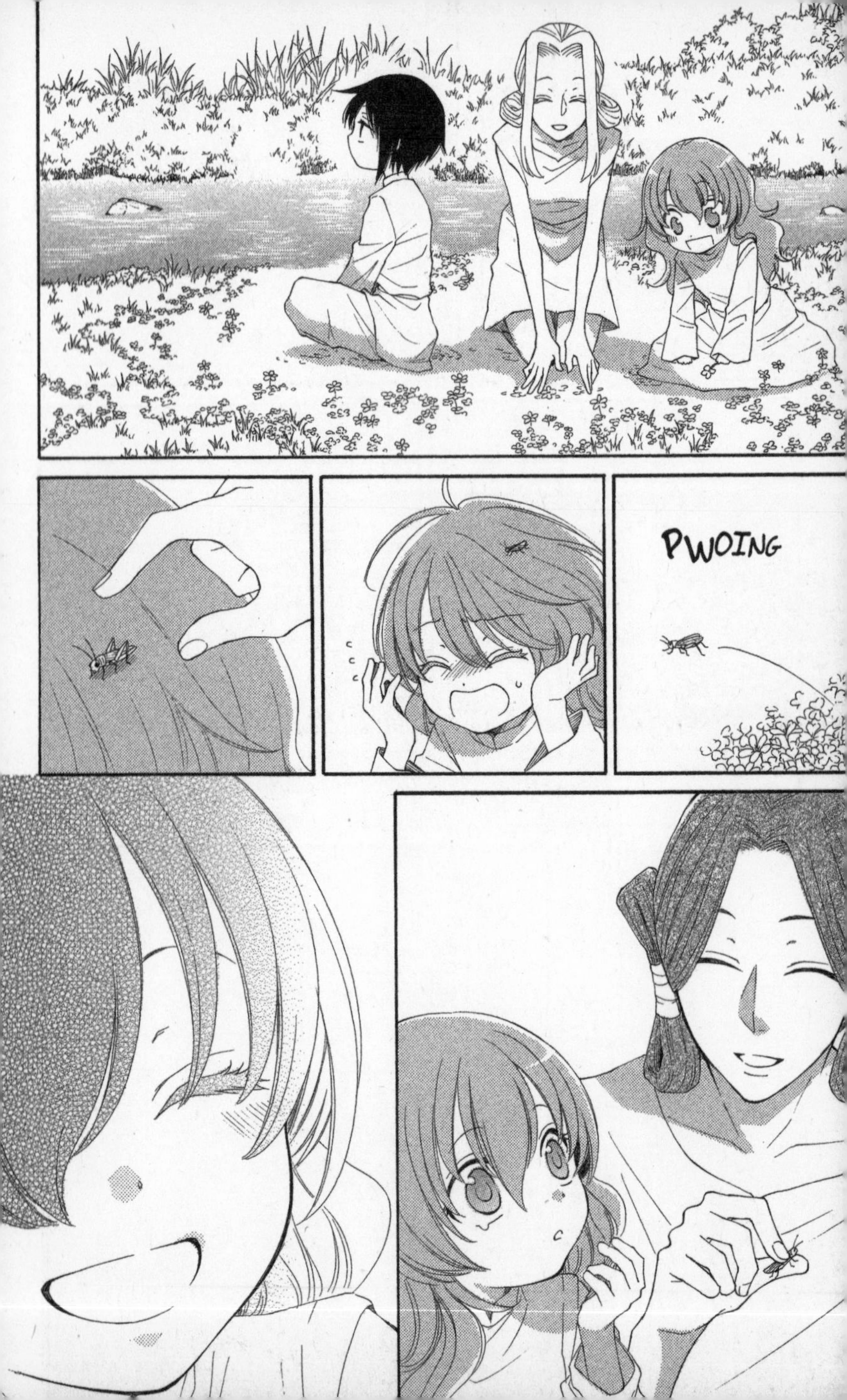
PWOING

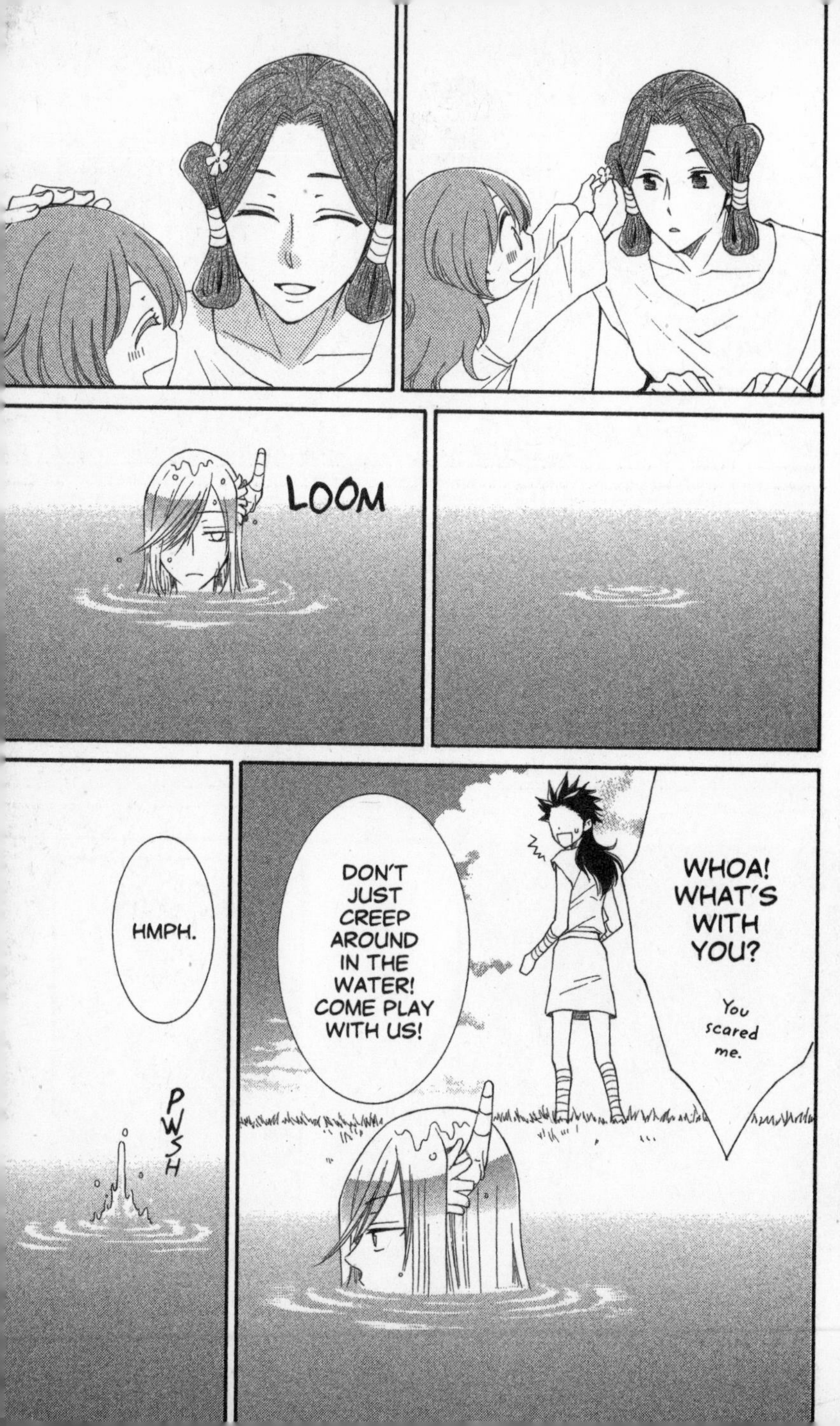
LOOM
WHOA! WHAT'S WITH YOU?
You scared me.
DON'T JUST CREEP AROUND IN THE WATER! COME PLAY WITH US!
HMPH.
PWSH

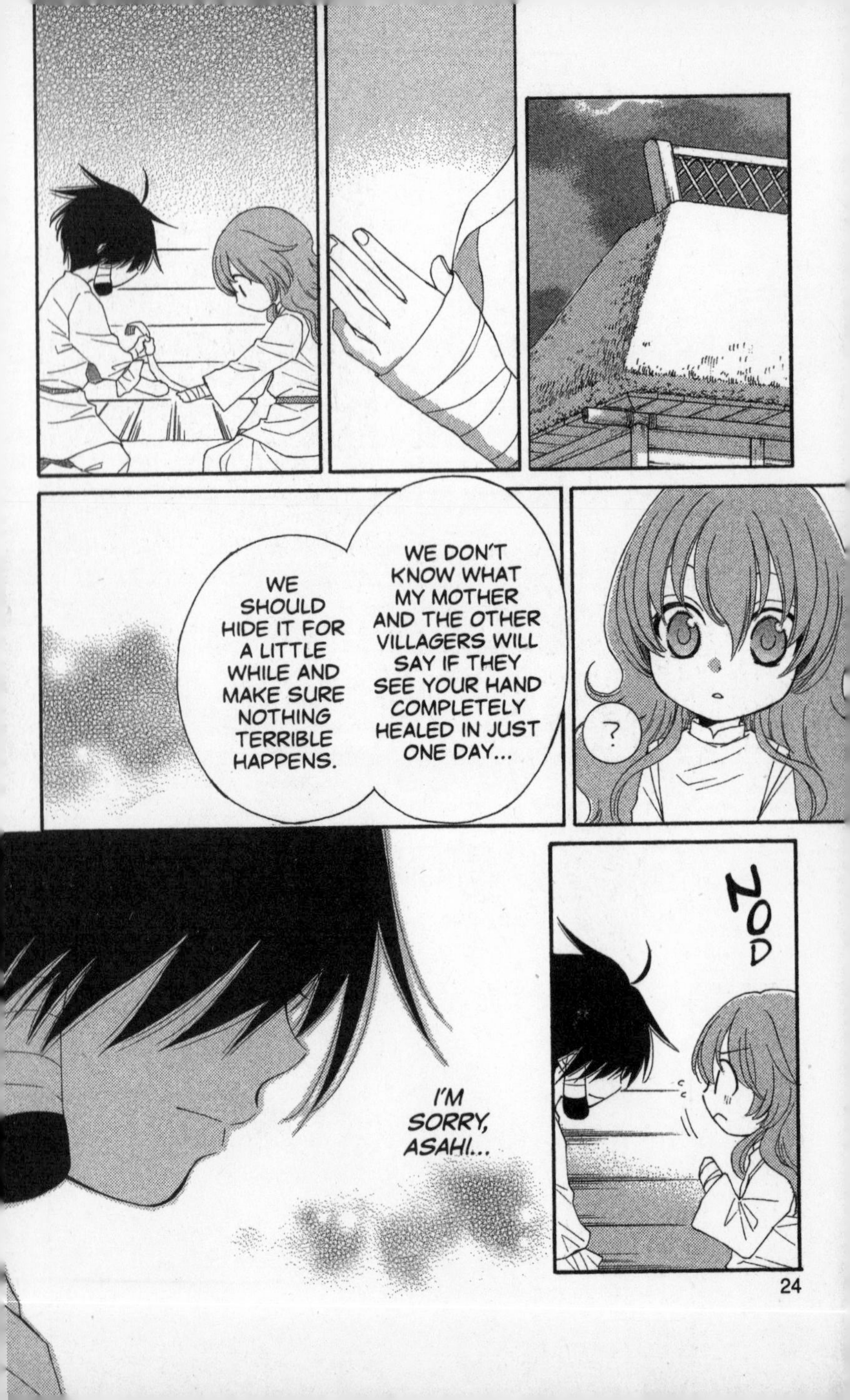
?
WE DON'T KNOW WHAT MY MOTHER AND THE OTHER VILLAGERS WILL SAY IF THEY SEE YOUR HAND COMPLETELY HEALED IN JUST ONE DAY...
WE SHOULD HIDE IT FOR A LITTLE WHILE AND MAKE SURE NOTHING TERRIBLE HAPPENS.
NOD
I'M SORRY, ASAHI...

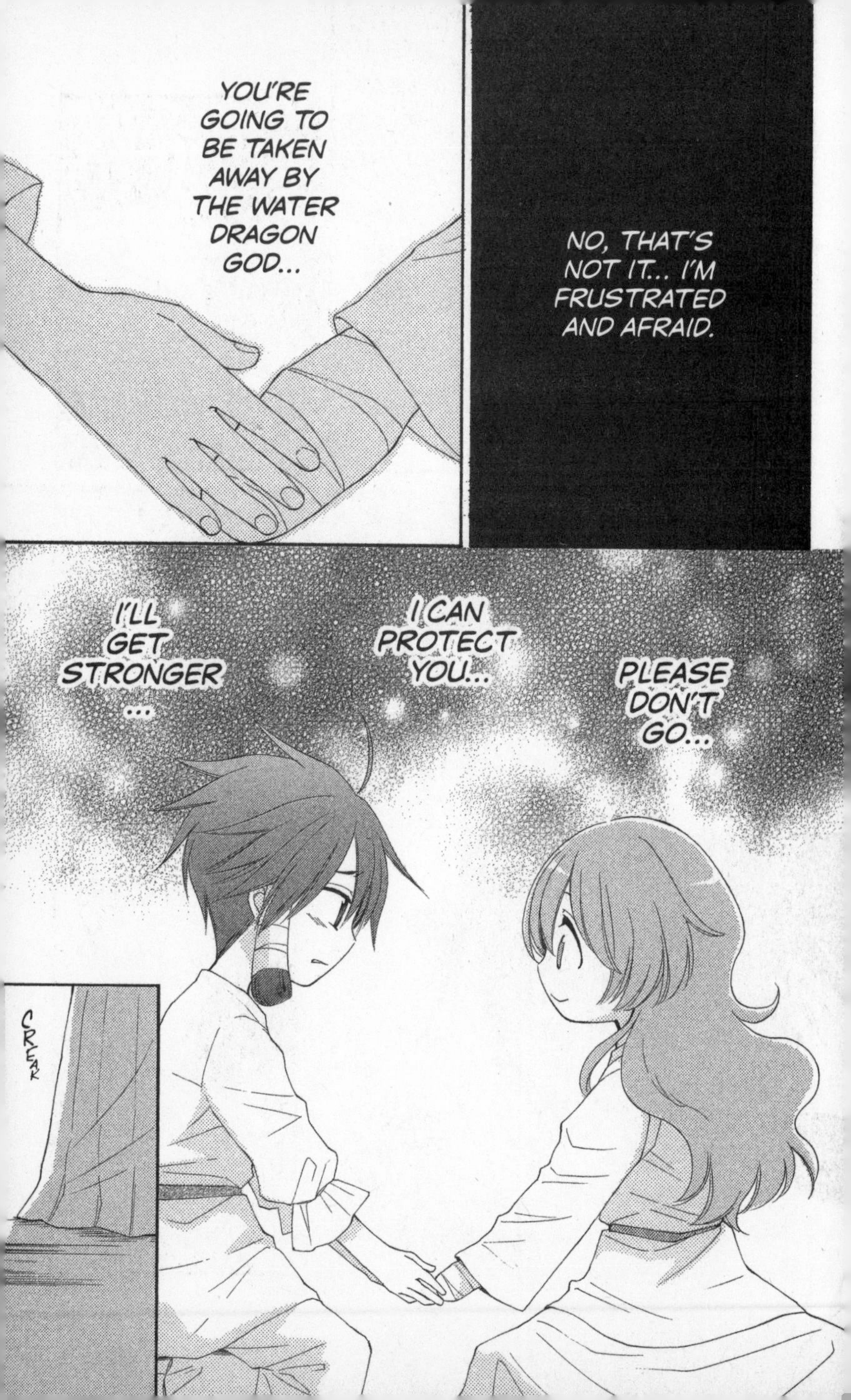
NO, THAT'S NOT IT... I'M FRUSTRATED AND AFRAID.
YOU'RE GOING TO BE TAKEN AWAY BY THE WATER DRAGON GOD...
PLEASE DON'T GO...
I CAN PROTECT YOU...
I'LL GET STRONGER ...
CREAK

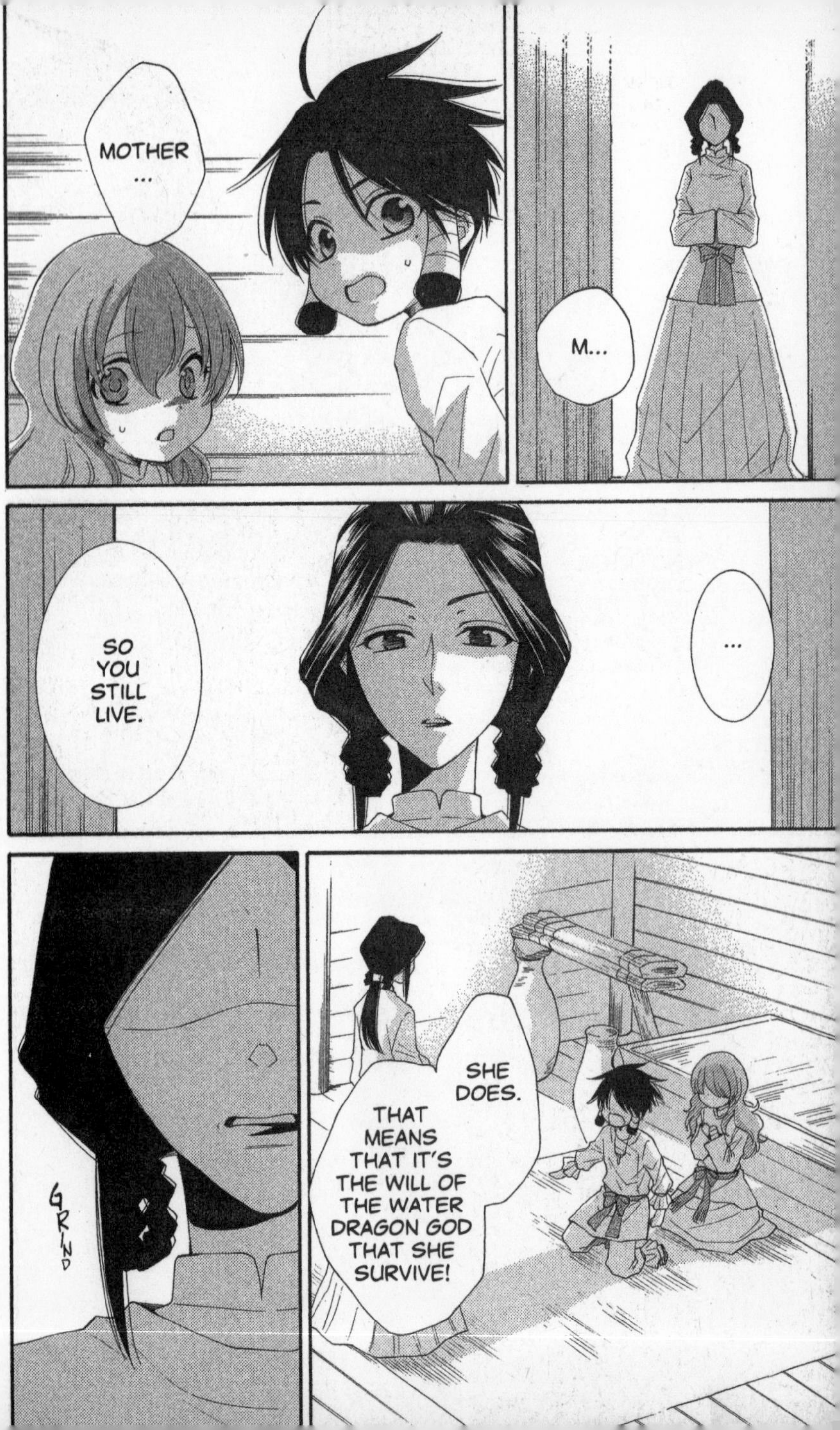
M...
MOTHER ...
...
SO YOU STILL LIVE.
SHE DOES.
THAT MEANS THAT IT'S THE WILL OF THE WATER DRAGON GOD THAT SHE SURVIVE!
GRIND

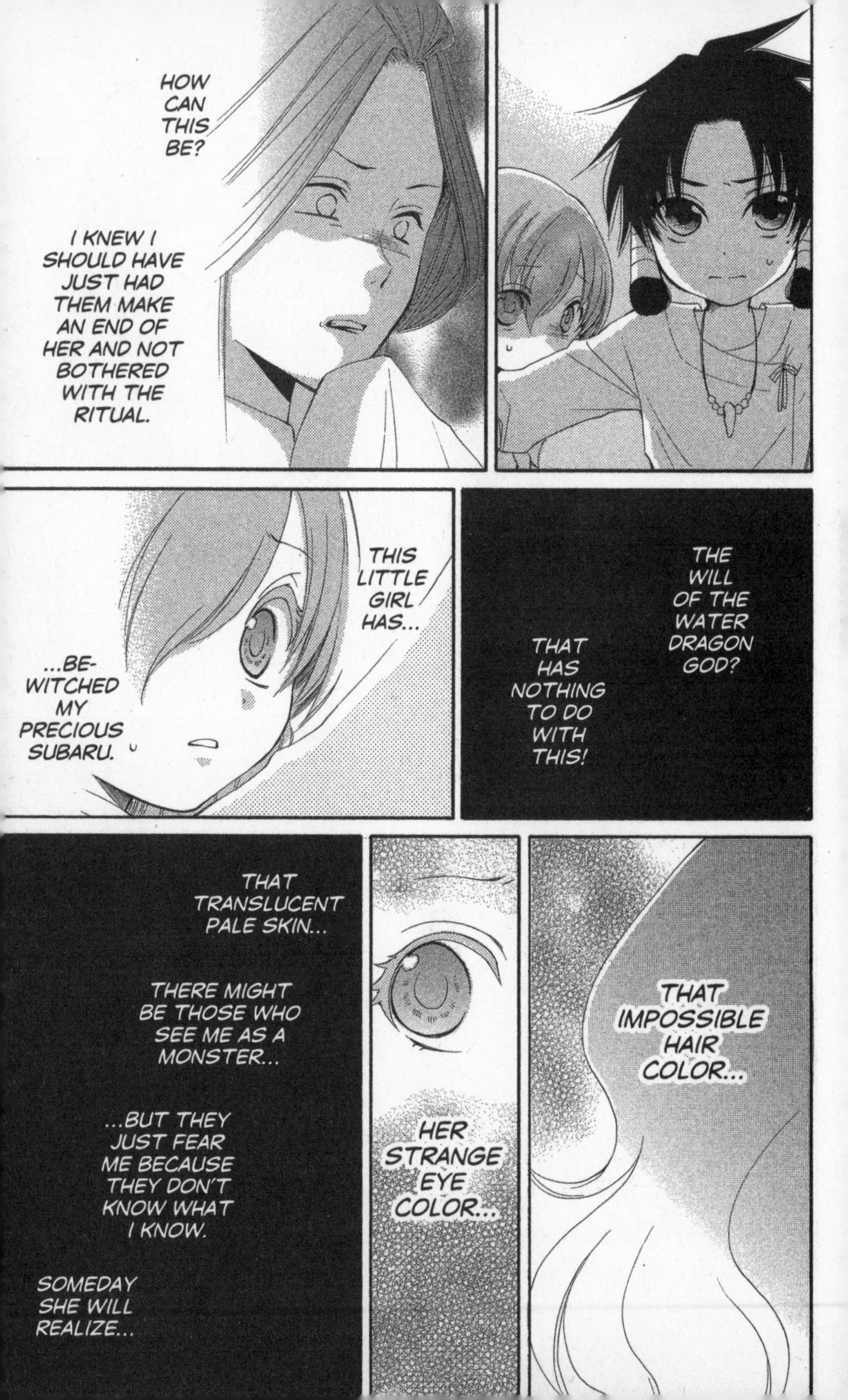
HOW CAN THIS BE?
I KNEW I SHOULD HAVE JUST HAD THEM MAKE AN END OF HER AND NOT BOTHERED WITH THE RITUAL.
THE WILL OF THE WATER DRAGON GOD?
THAT HAS NOTHING TO DO WITH THIS!
THIS LITTLE GIRL HAS...
...BE-WITCHED MY PRECIOUS SUBARU.
THAT IMPOSSIBLE HAIR COLOR...
HER STRANGE EYE COLOR...
THAT TRANSLUCENT PALE SKIN...
THERE MIGHT BE THOSE WHO SEE ME AS A MONSTER...
...BUT THEY JUST FEAR ME BECAUSE THEY DON'T KNOW WHAT I KNOW.
SOMEDAY SHE WILL REALIZE...

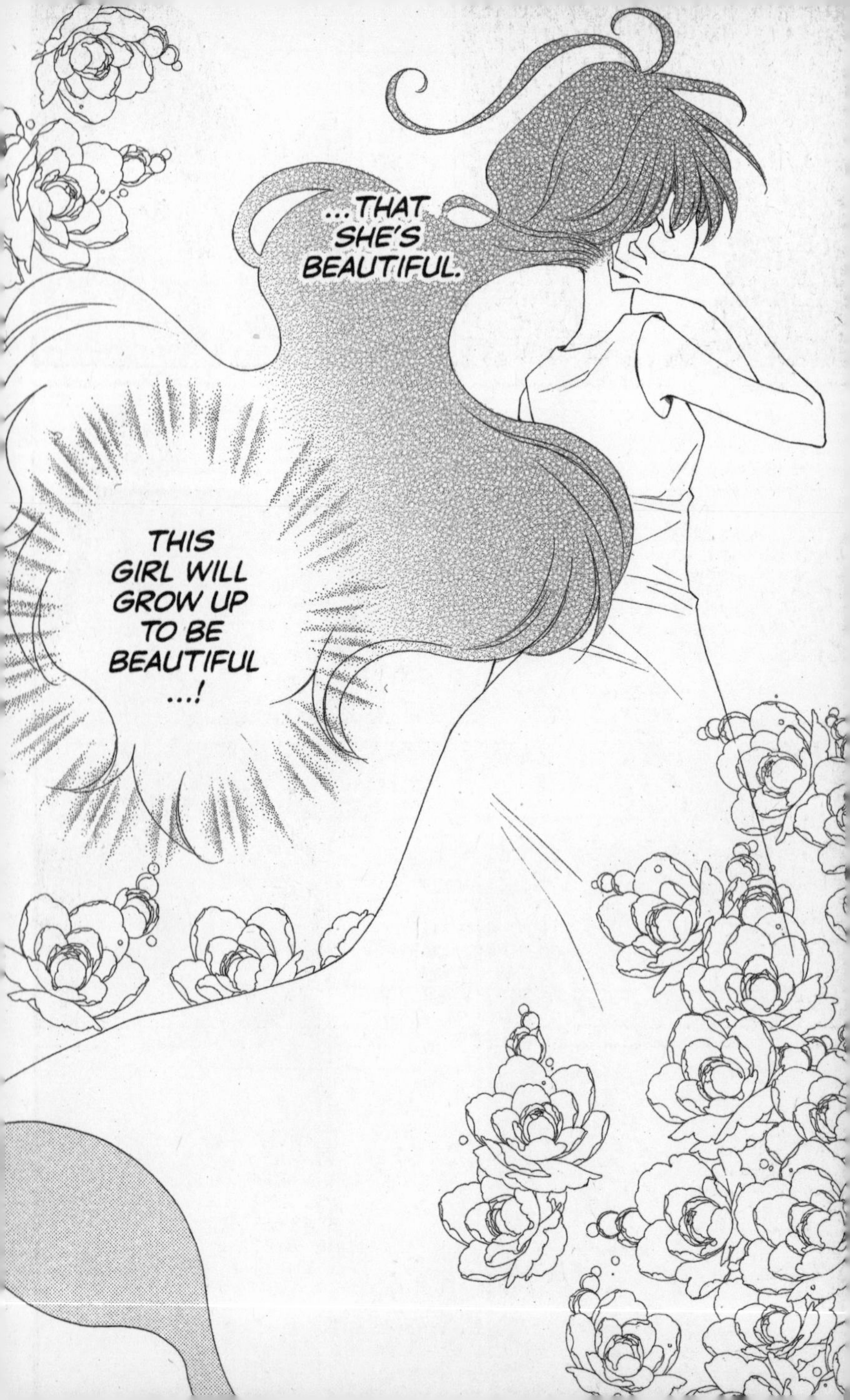
...THAT SHE'S BEAUTIFUL.
THIS GIRL WILL GROW UP TO BE BEAUTIFUL ...!

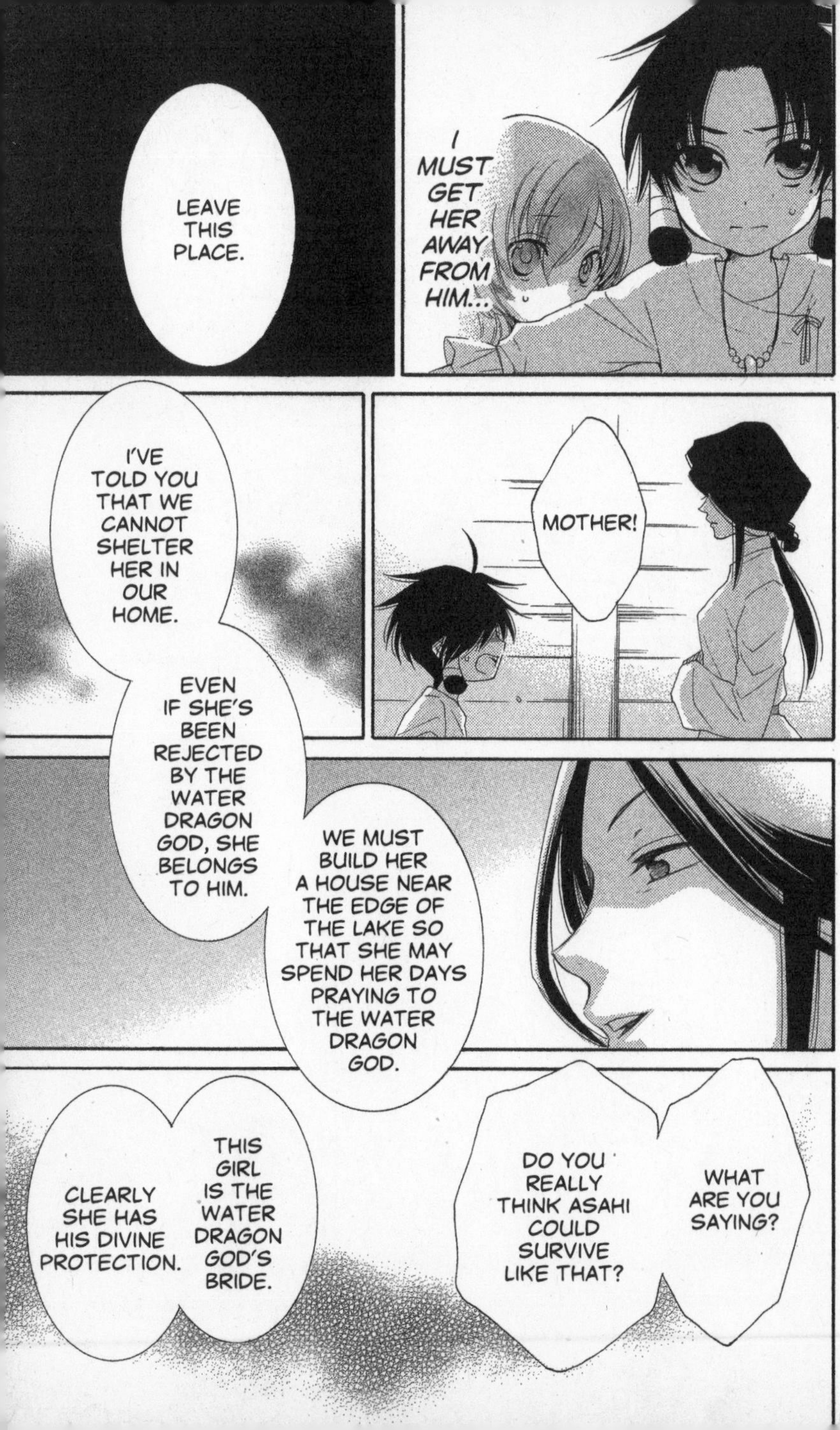
I MUST GET HER AWAY FROM HIM...
LEAVE THIS PLACE.
MOTHER!
I'VE TOLD YOU THAT WE CANNOT SHELTER HER IN OUR HOME.
EVEN IF SHE'S BEEN REJECTED BY THE WATER DRAGON GOD, SHE BELONGS TO HIM.
WE MUST BUILD HER A HOUSE NEAR THE EDGE OF THE LAKE SO THAT SHE MAY SPEND HER DAYS PRAYING TO THE WATER DRAGON GOD.
WHAT ARE YOU SAYING?
DO YOU REALLY THINK ASAHI COULD SURVIVE LIKE THAT?
THIS GIRL IS THE WATER DRAGON GOD'S BRIDE.
CLEARLY SHE HAS HIS DIVINE PROTECTION.

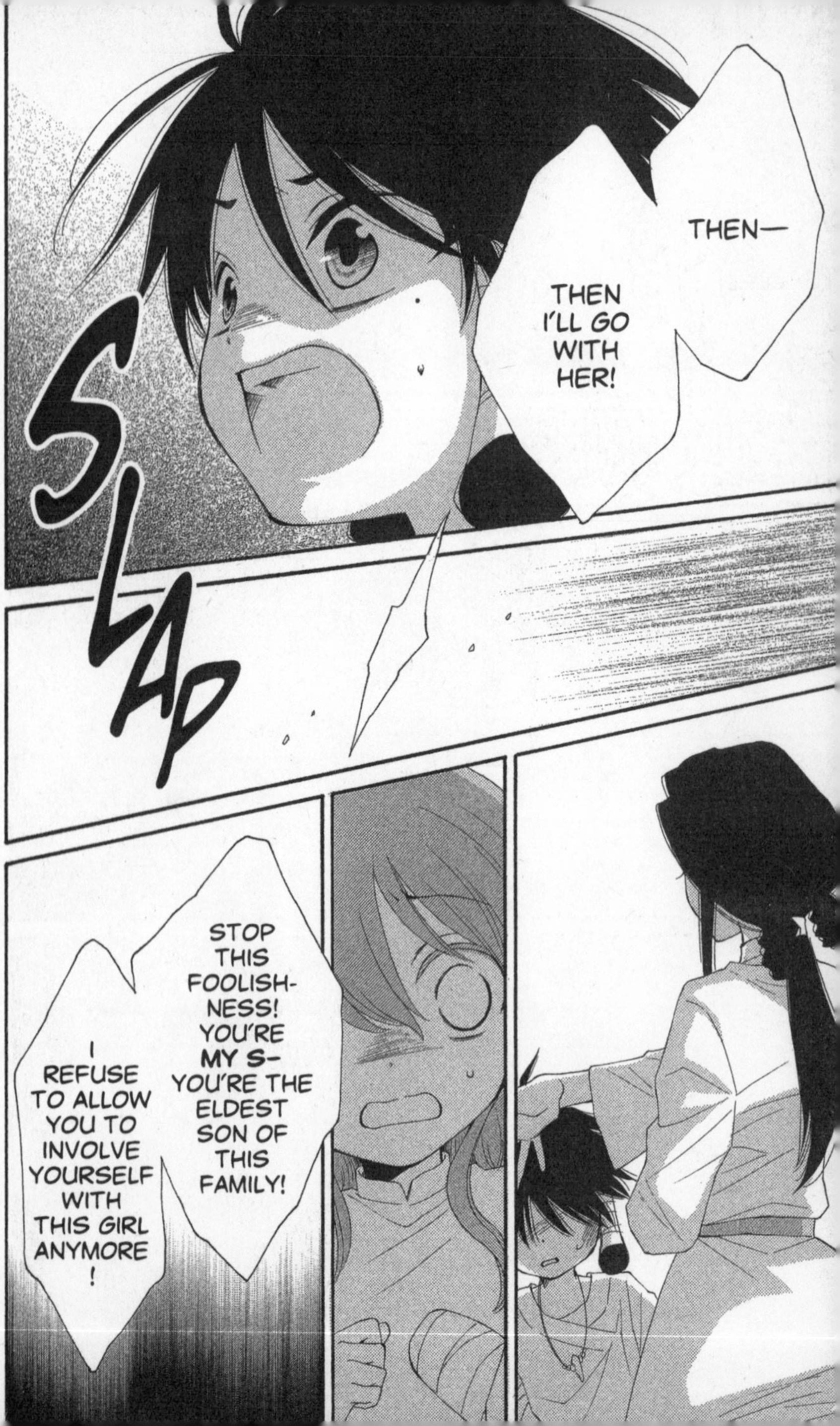
THEN—
THEN I'LL GO WITH HER!
SLAP
STOP THIS FOOLISH-NESS! YOU'RE **MY S–** YOU'RE THE ELDEST SON OF THIS FAMILY!
I REFUSE TO ALLOW YOU TO INVOLVE YOURSELF WITH THIS GIRL ANYMORE!

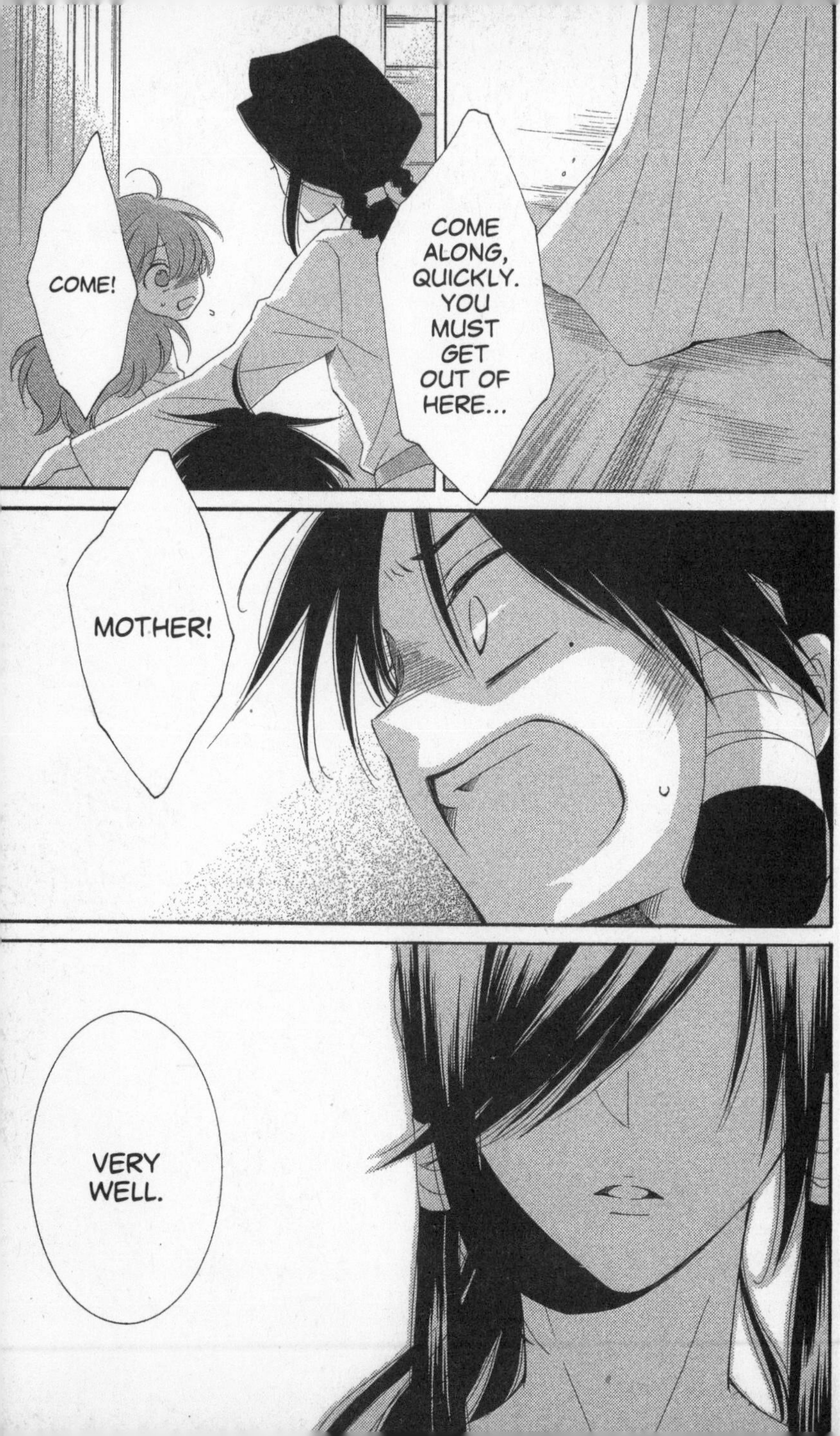
COME ALONG, QUICKLY. YOU MUST GET OUT OF HERE...
COME!
MOTHER!
VERY WELL.

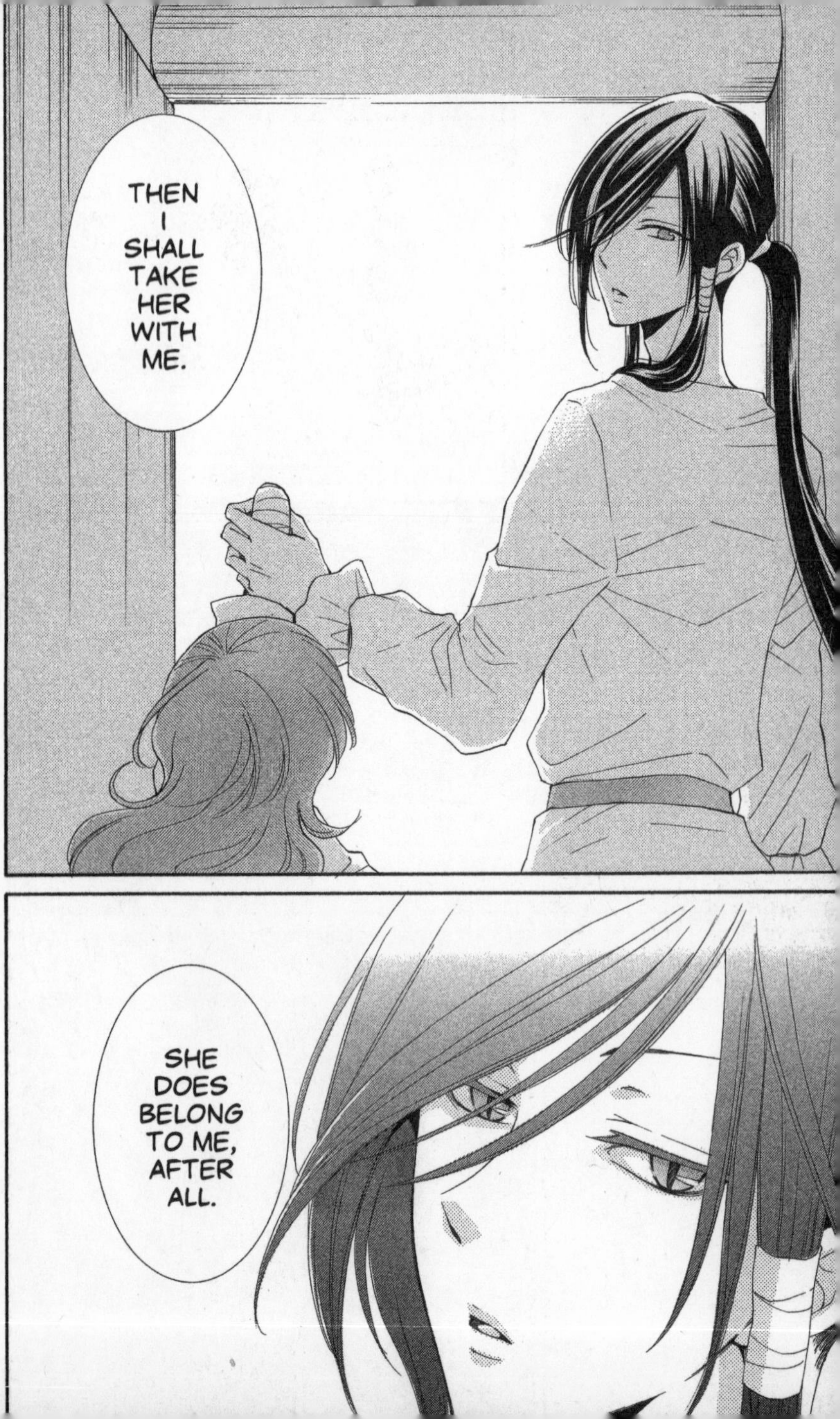
THEN I SHALL TAKE HER WITH ME.
SHE DOES BELONG TO ME, AFTER ALL.

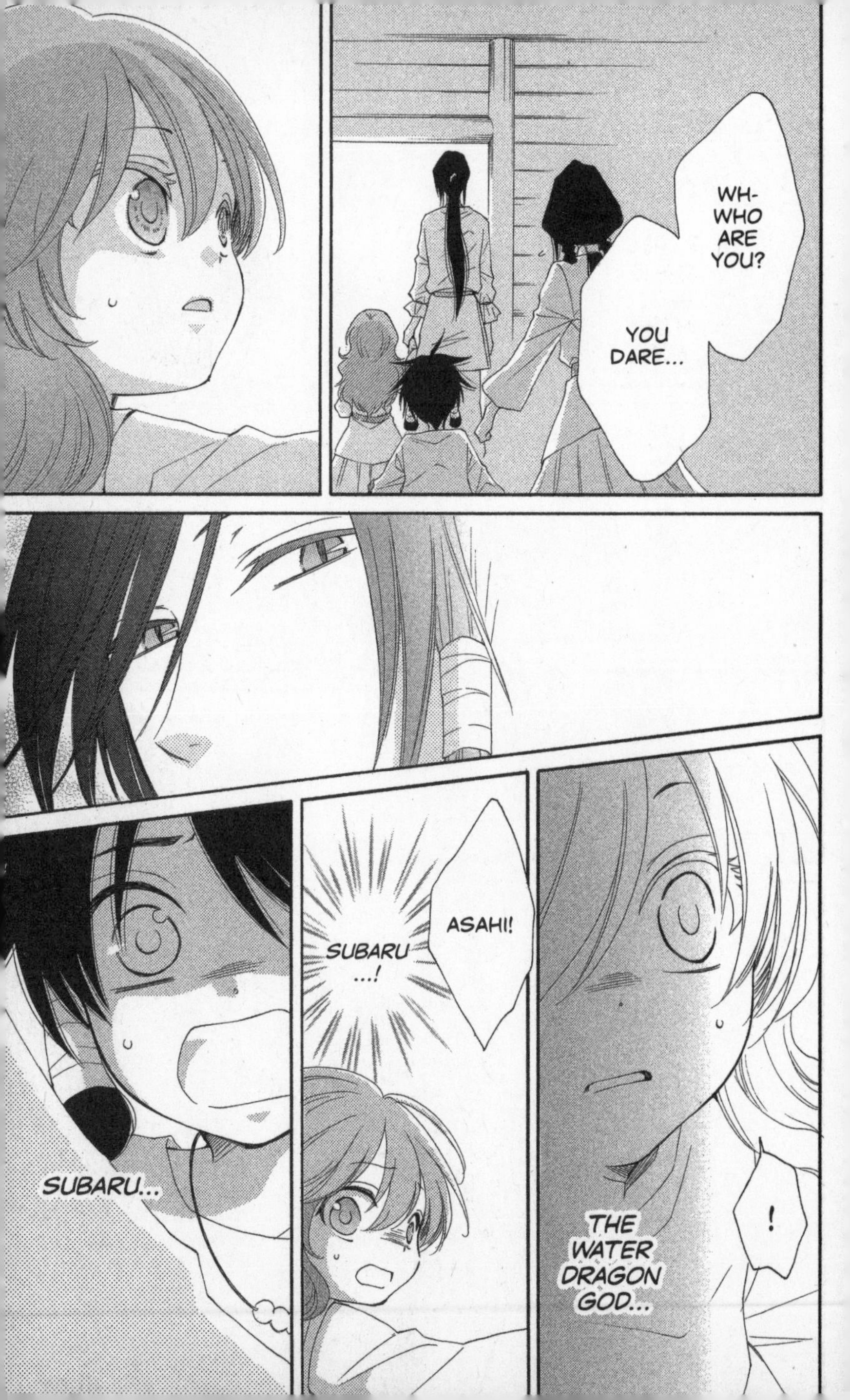
WH- WHO ARE YOU?
YOU DARE...
!
THE WATER DRAGON GOD...
ASAHI!
SUBARU ...!
SUBARU...

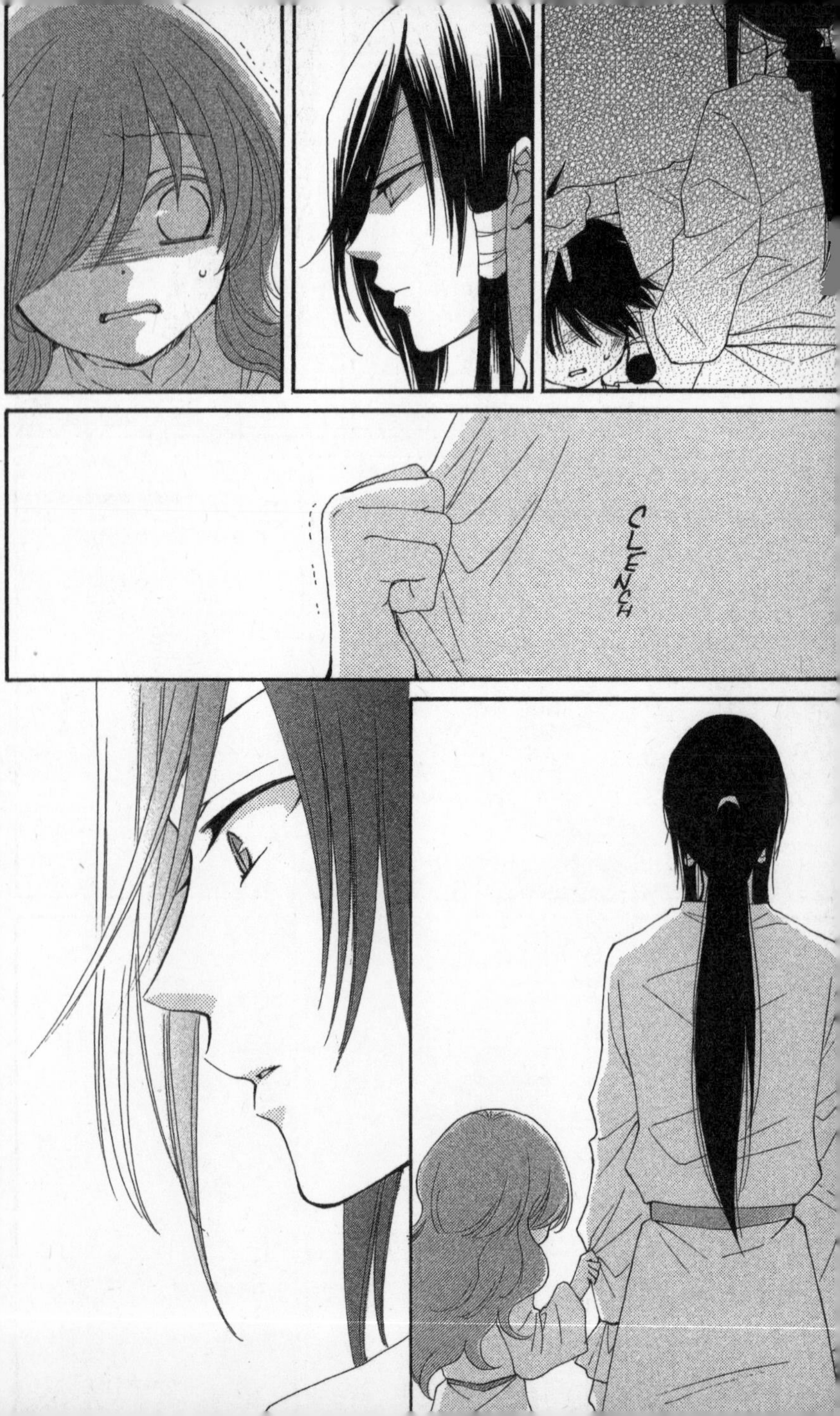
CLENCH

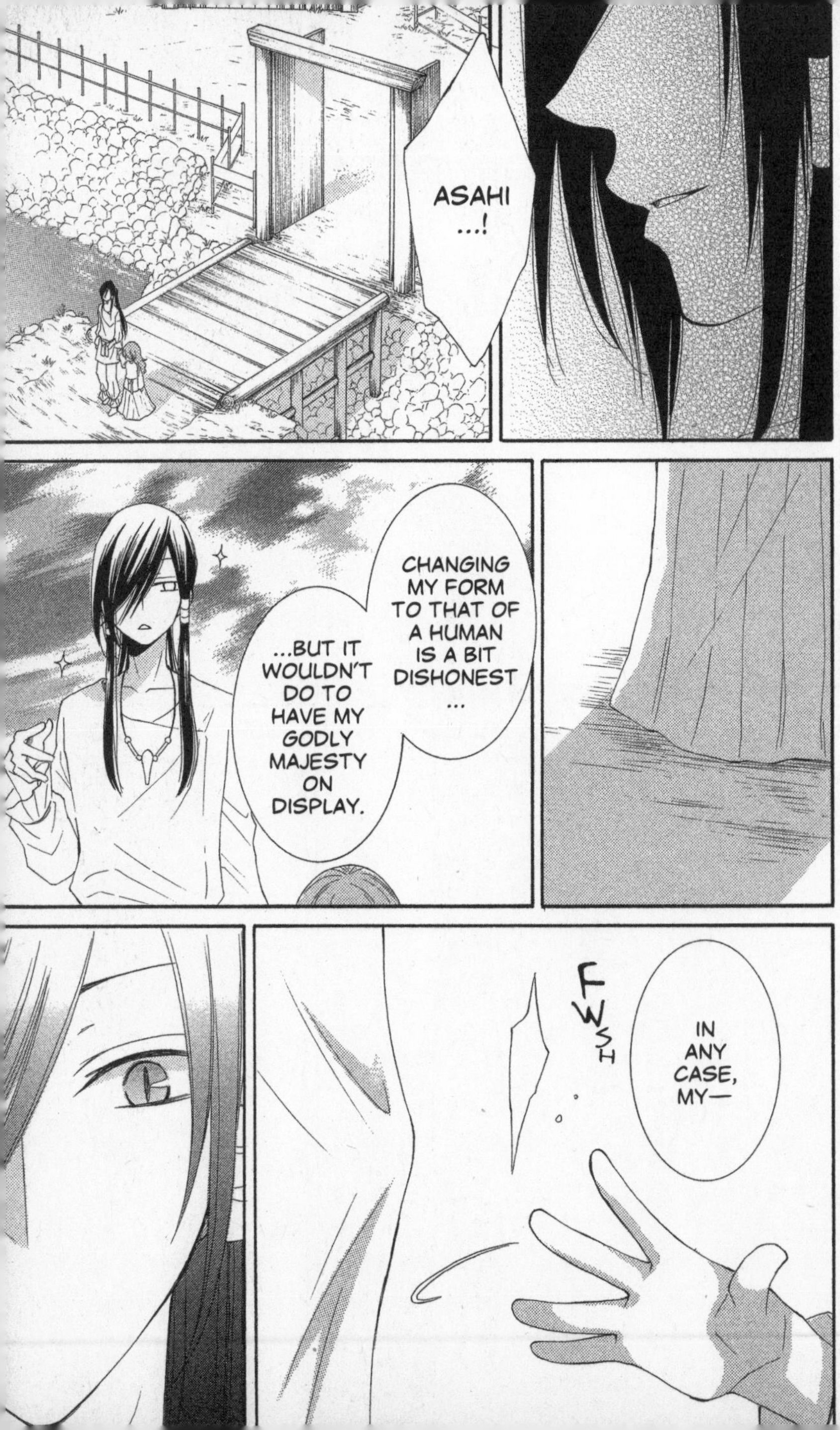
ASAHI ...!
CHANGING MY FORM TO THAT OF A HUMAN IS A BIT DISHONEST ...
...BUT IT WOULDN'T DO TO HAVE MY GODLY MAJESTY ON DISPLAY.
IN ANY CASE, MY—
FWSH

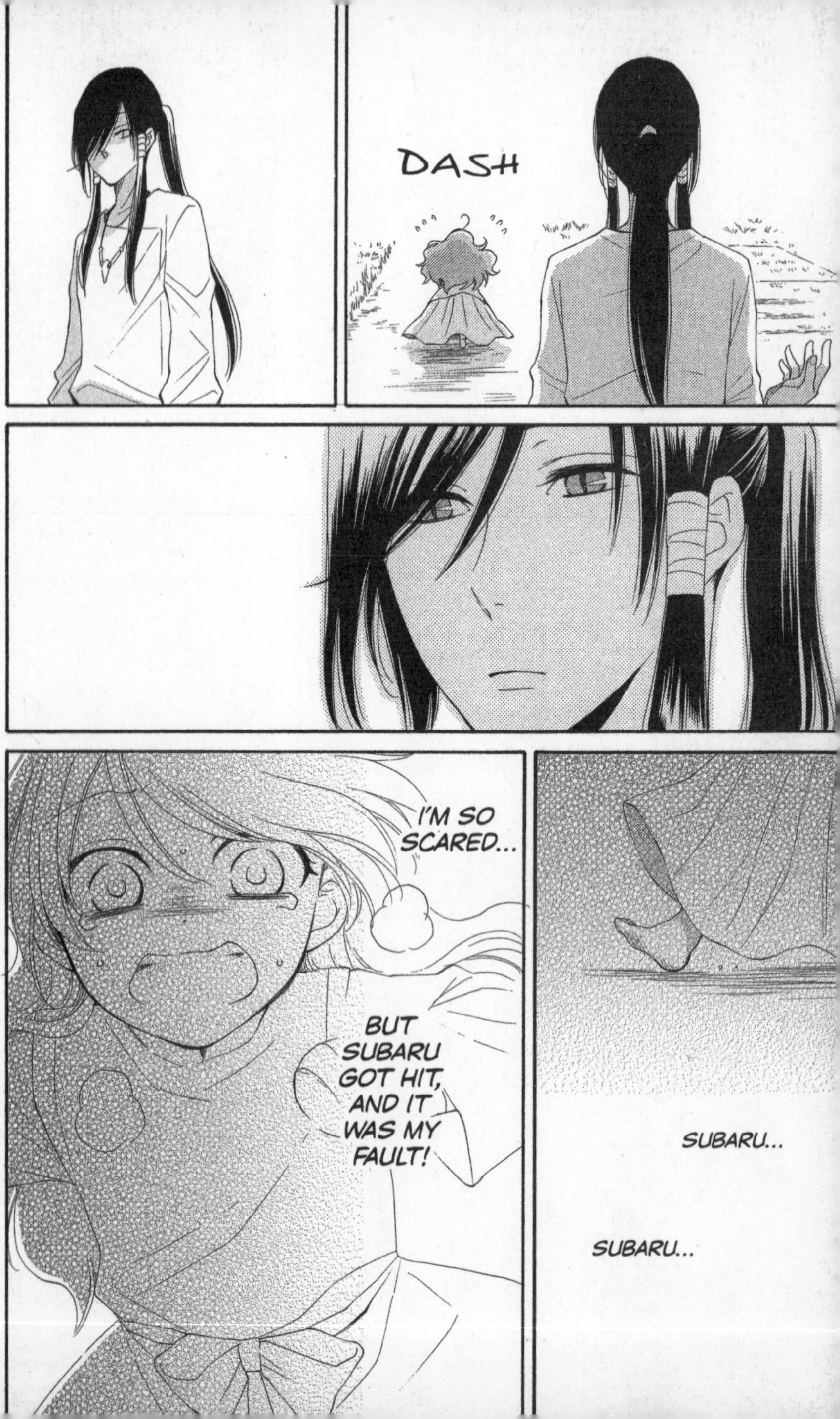
DASH
SUBARU...
SUBARU...
I'M SO SCARED...
BUT SUBARU GOT HIT, AND IT WAS MY FAULT!

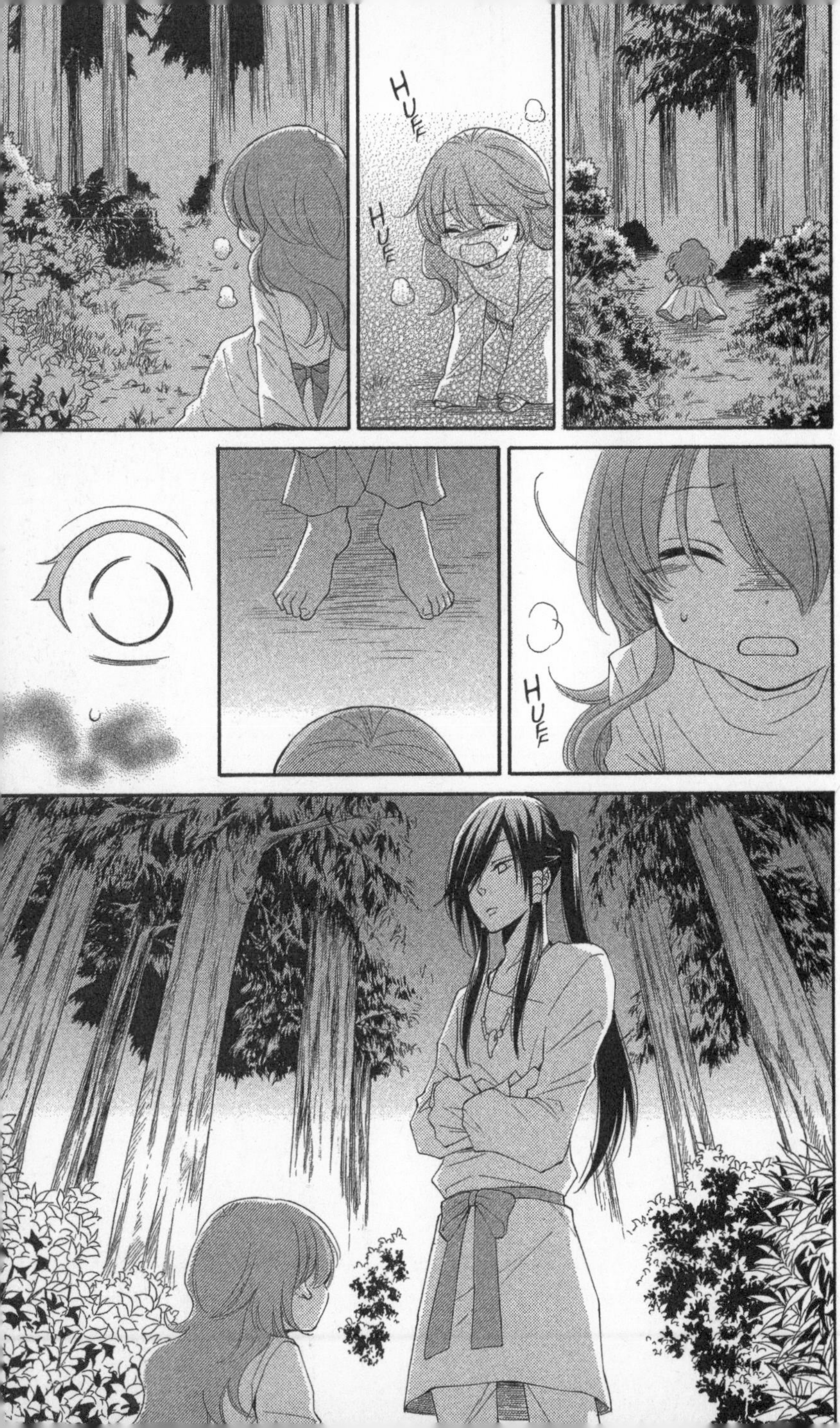
HUFF
HUFF
HUFF

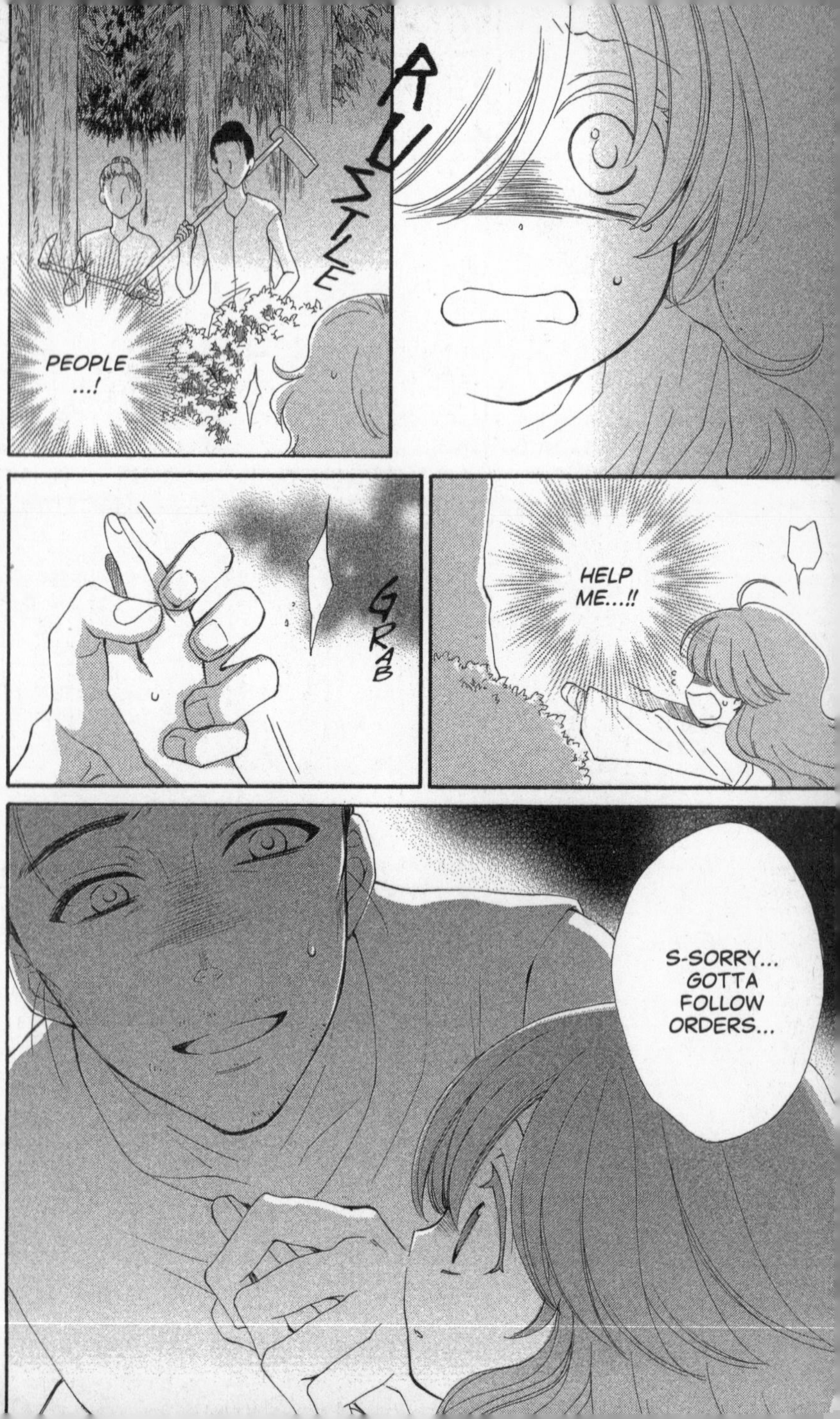
RUSTLE
PEOPLE ...!
HELP ME...!!
GRAB
S-SORRY... GOTTA FOLLOW ORDERS...

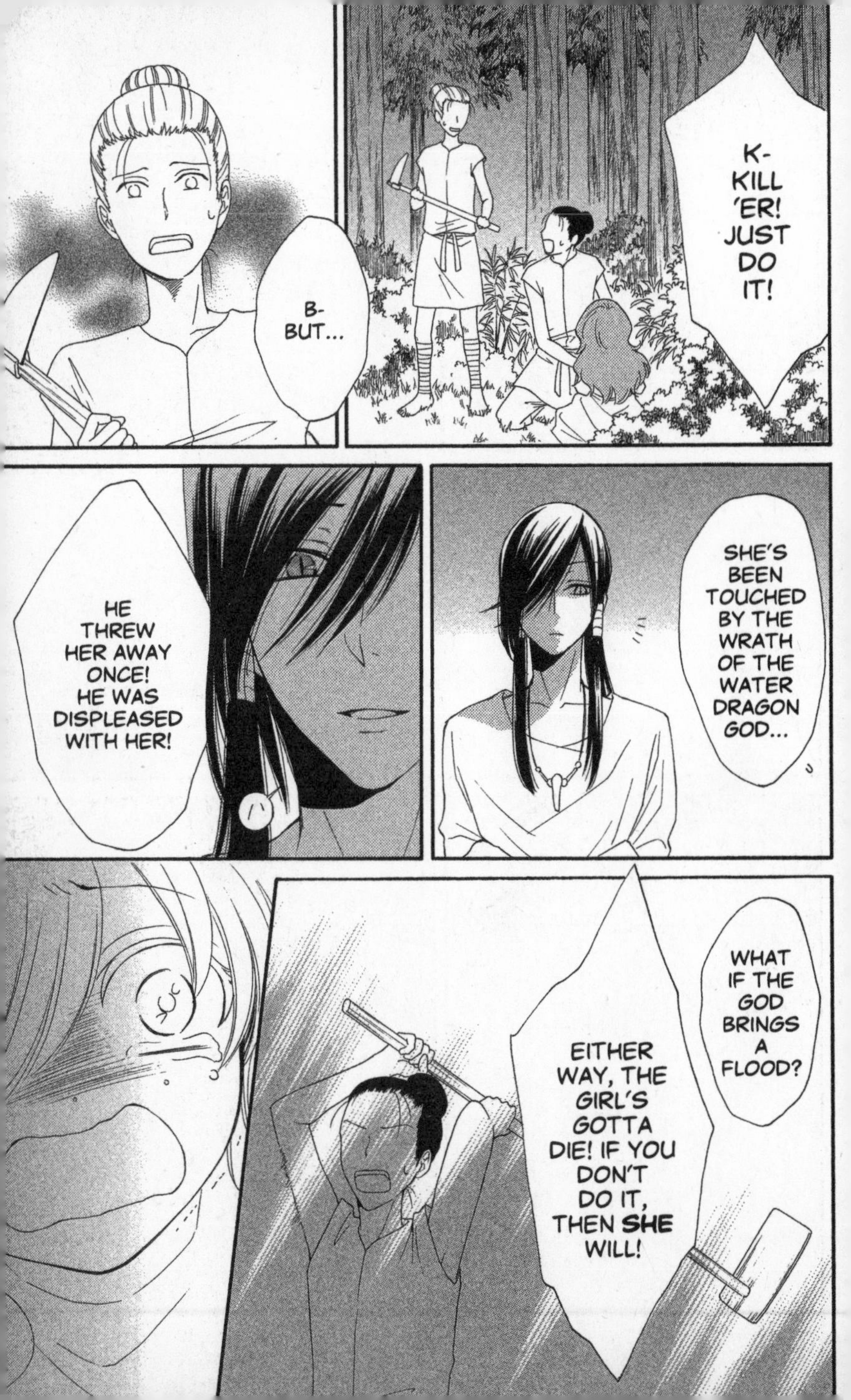
K-KILL 'ER! JUST DO IT!
B-BUT...
SHE'S BEEN TOUCHED BY THE WRATH OF THE WATER DRAGON GOD...
HE THREW HER AWAY ONCE! HE WAS DISPLEASED WITH HER!
WHAT IF THE GOD BRINGS A FLOOD?
EITHER WAY, THE GIRL'S GOTTA DIE! IF YOU DON'T DO IT, THEN **SHE** WILL!

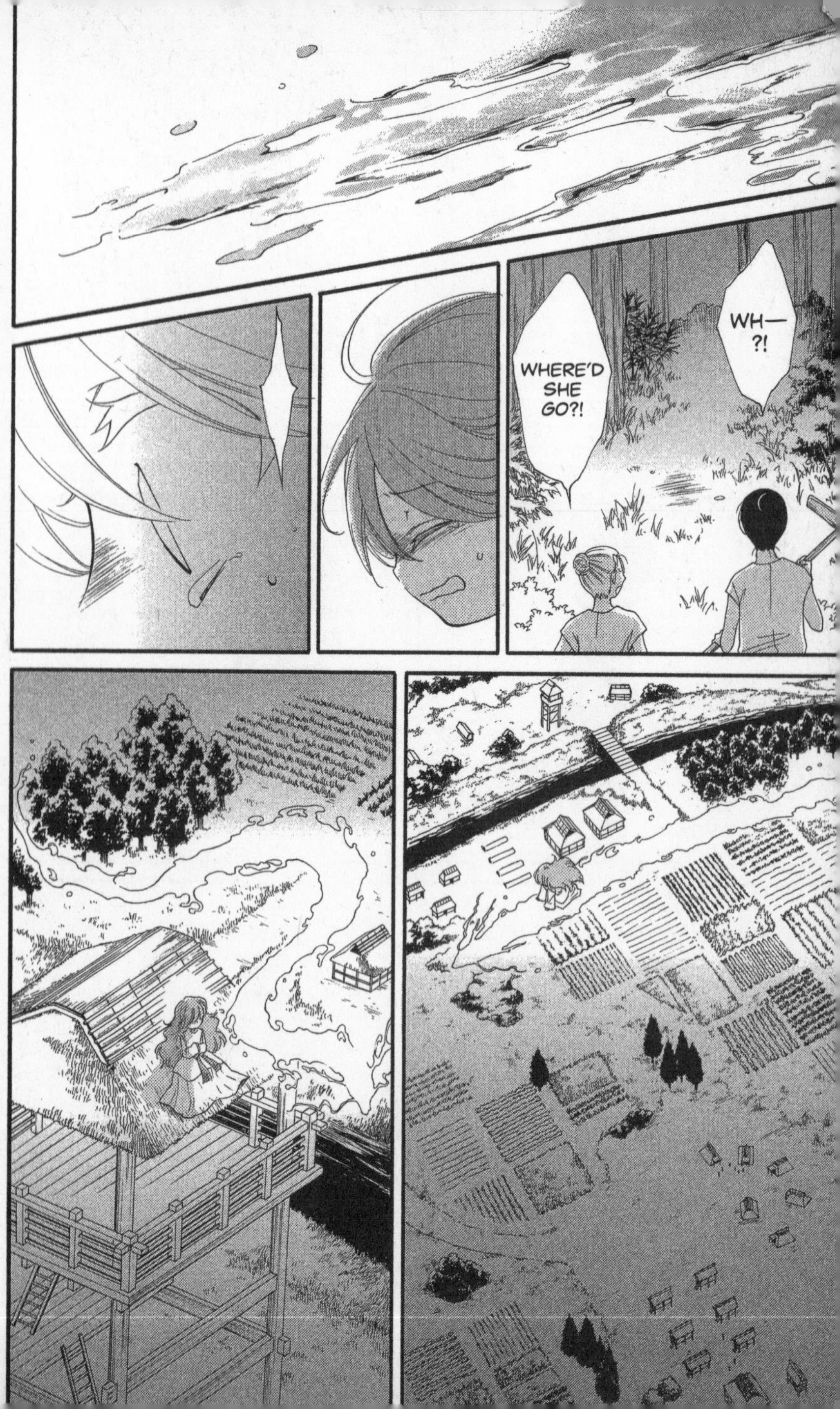
WH—
?!
WHERE'D
SHE
GO?!

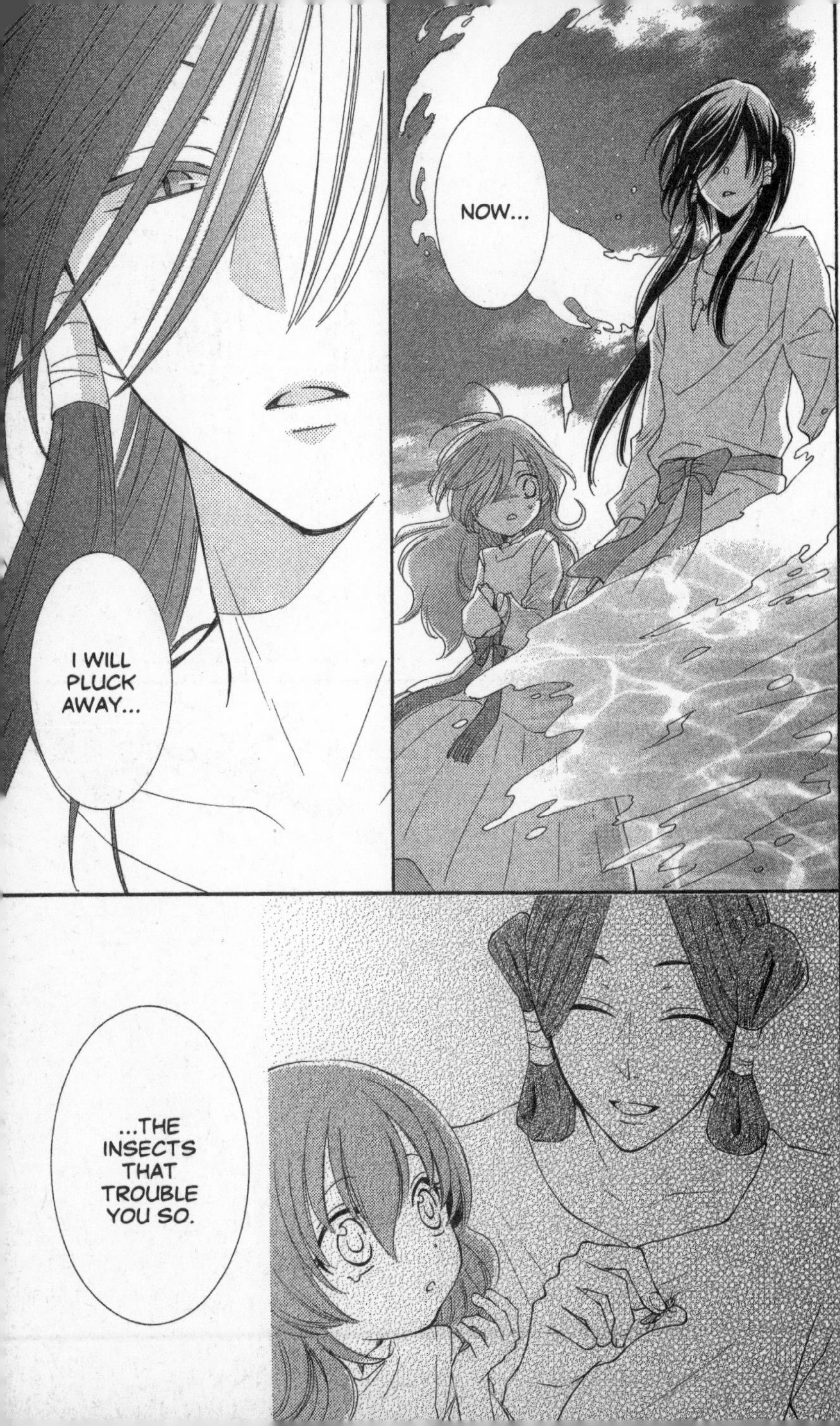
NOW...
I WILL PLUCK AWAY...
...THE INSECTS THAT TROUBLE YOU SO.

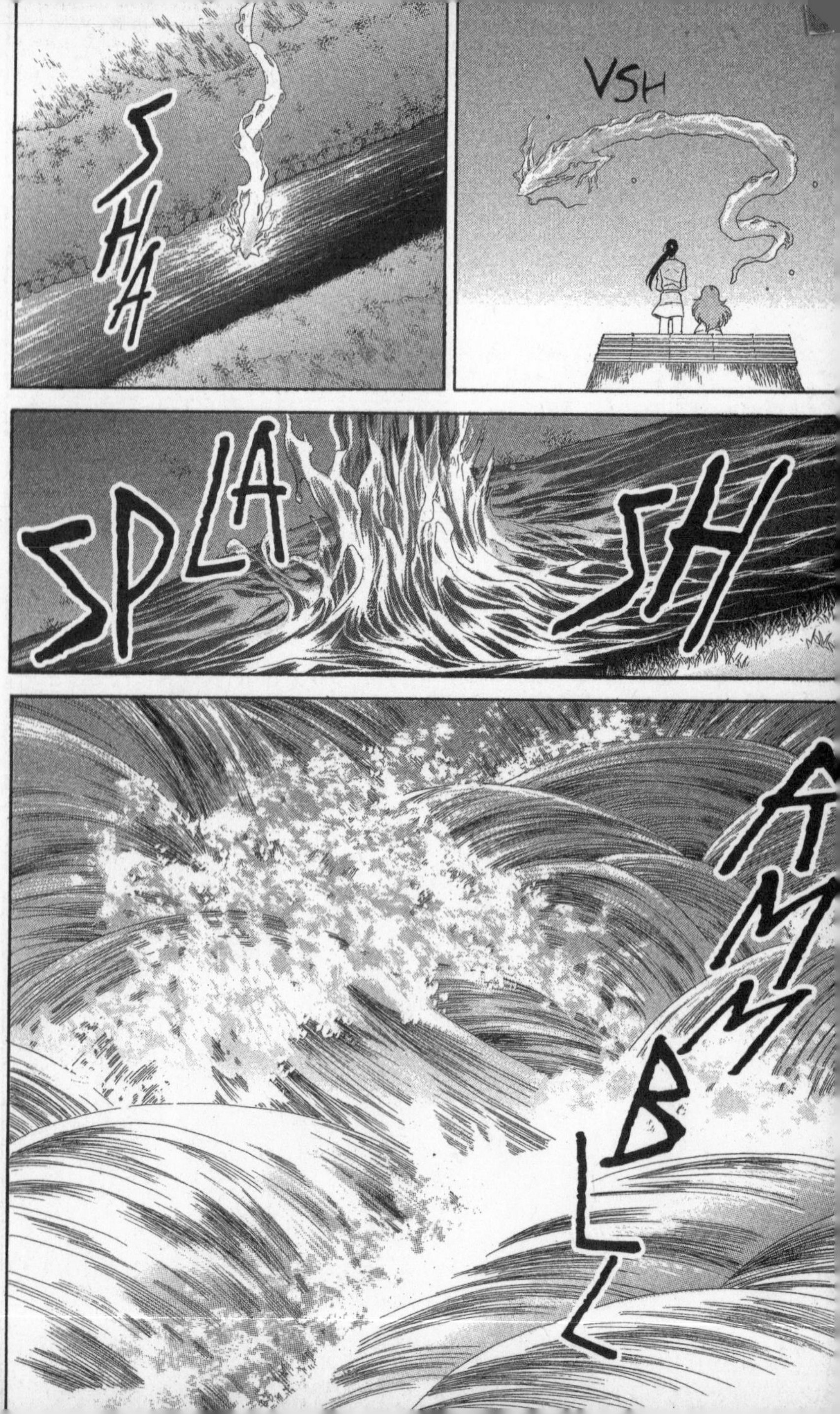
VSH
SHA
SPLASH
AMMBLL

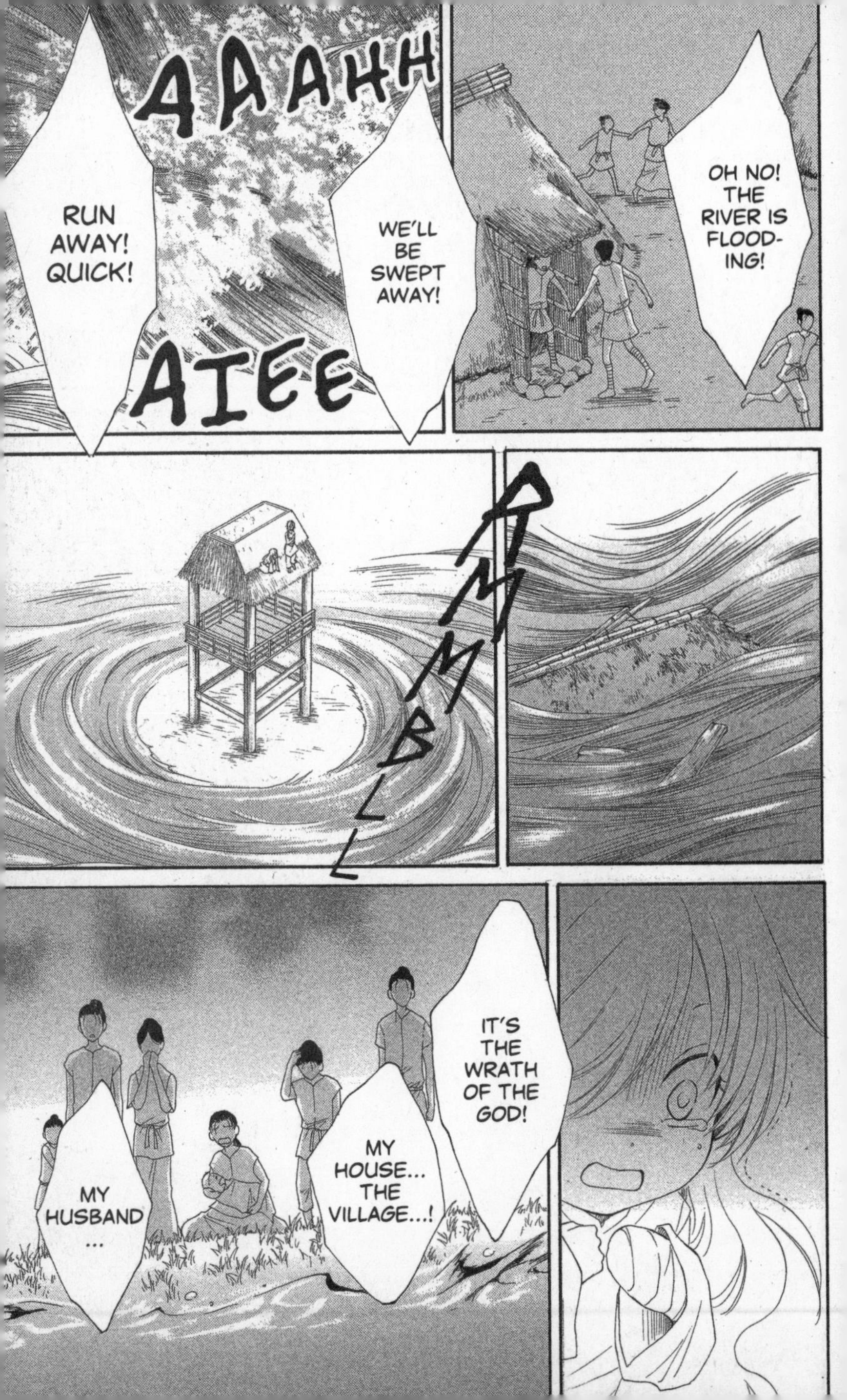

OH NO! THE RIVER IS FLOOD-ING!
AAAHH
WE'LL BE SWEPT AWAY!
RUN AWAY! QUICK!
AIEE
RMMBLL
IT'S THE WRATH OF THE GOD!
MY HOUSE... THE VILLAGE...!
MY HUSBAND ...

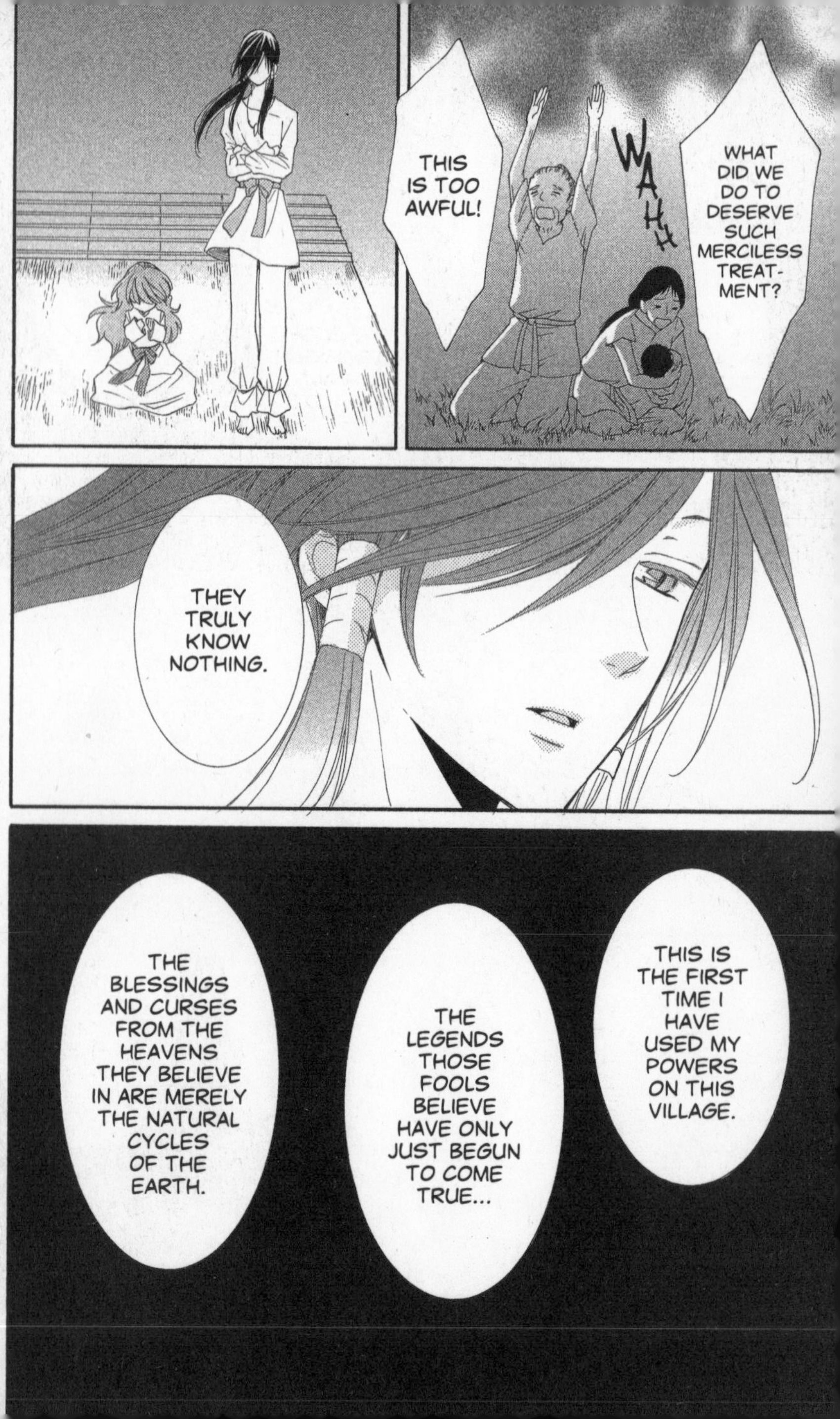
WHAT DID WE DO TO DESERVE SUCH MERCILESS TREAT-MENT?
WAHHH
THIS IS TOO AWFUL!
THEY TRULY KNOW NOTHING.
THIS IS THE FIRST TIME I HAVE USED MY POWERS ON THIS VILLAGE.
THE LEGENDS THOSE FOOLS BELIEVE HAVE ONLY JUST BEGUN TO COME TRUE...
THE BLESSINGS AND CURSES FROM THE HEAVENS THEY BELIEVE IN ARE MERELY THE NATURAL CYCLES OF THE EARTH.

WHY DO THEY BELIEVE THAT THE GODS WOULD MOVE FOR THE SAKE OF HUMANS?
WHY DO THEY BELIEVE THAT IT IS THE DUTY OF THE GODS TO DO WHAT HUMANS CANNOT?
WHAT WOULD MAKE THEM THINK THAT JUST BECAUSE THEY CANNOT DO SOMETHING, SOMEONE ELSE CAN?
WHY THESE EXPECTA-TIONS...
WHY DO THEY WANT SO MUCH MORE?
DO THEY BELIEVE GODS WILL HEED THE WISHES OF MERE HUMANS?
THEY BELIEVE THAT THE WRATH OF THE GODS WILL BRING DISASTER UPON THEM...
SO WHY DO THEY PERSIST IN ANGERING ME?

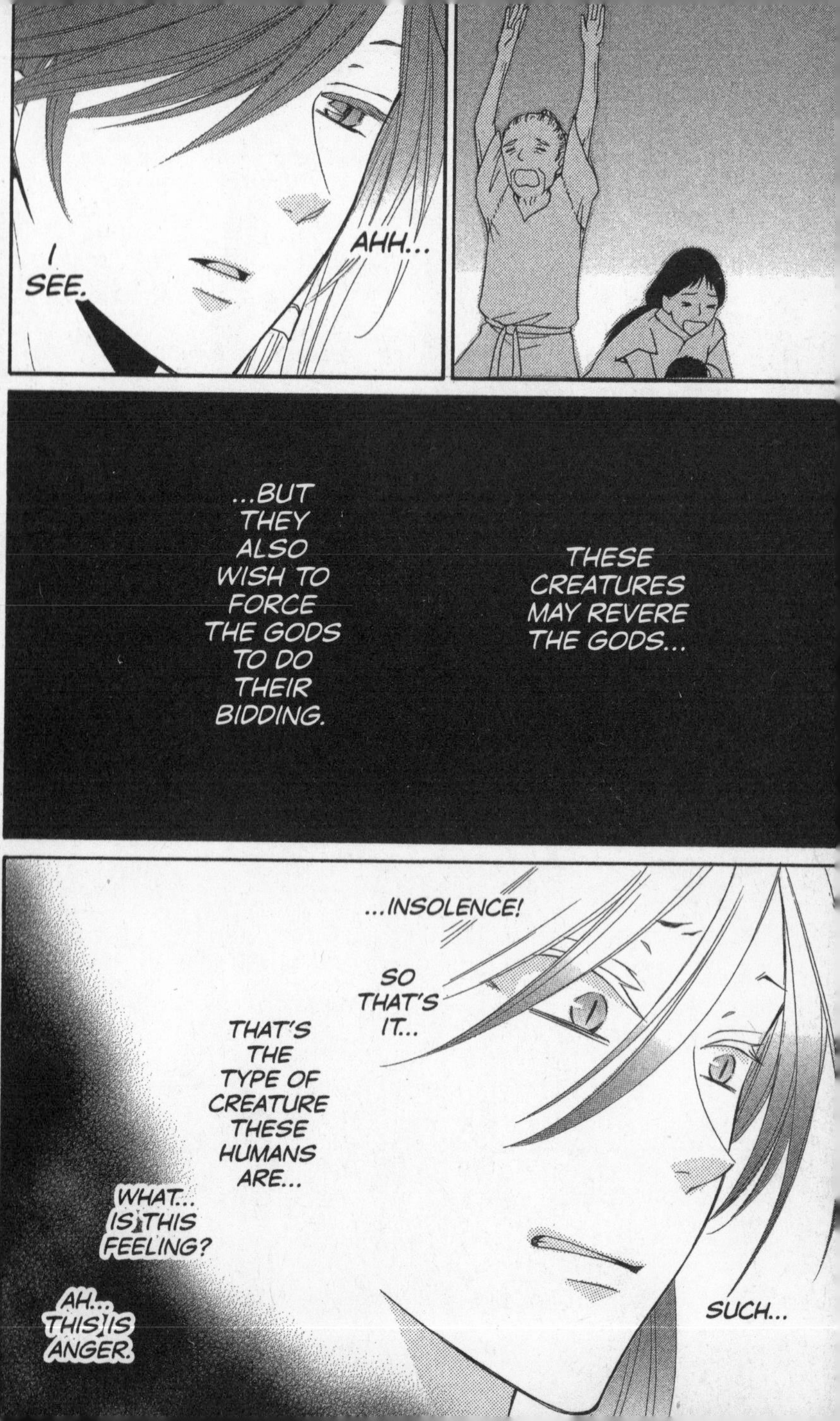
AHH...
I SEE.
THESE CREATURES MAY REVERE THE GODS...
...BUT THEY ALSO WISH TO FORCE THE GODS TO DO THEIR BIDDING.
SUCH...
...INSOLENCE!
SO THAT'S IT...
THAT'S THE TYPE OF CREATURE THESE HUMANS ARE...
WHAT... IS THIS FEELING?
AH... THIS IS ANGER.

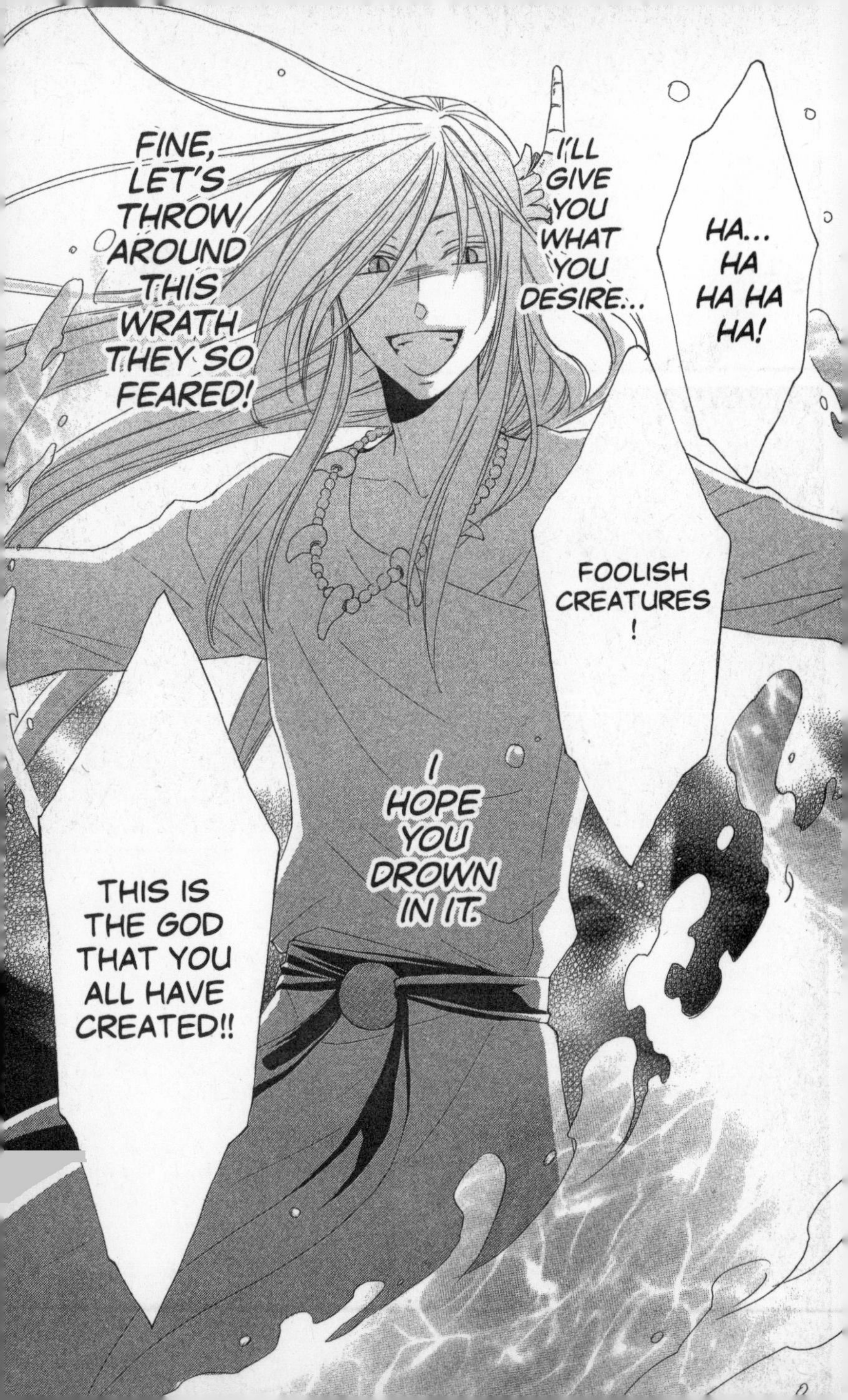
HA... HA HA HA HA!
I'LL GIVE YOU WHAT YOU DESIRE...
FINE, LET'S THROW AROUND THIS WRATH THEY SO FEARED!
FOOLISH CREATURES!
I HOPE YOU DROWN IN IT.
THIS IS THE GOD THAT YOU ALL HAVE CREATED!!

Hello! It's Rei Toma. This is volume 2 of *The Water Dragon's Bride*. This time I decided to draw Asahi and Subaru for the cover. When I work on a comic, I always have cover designs in mind that I secretly want to use. I give them to the graphic designer, who adds the title and logo and all the decorations that make it a beautiful book cover. This time, the designer who planned the cover was the same one who did the covers for *Dawn of the Arcana*, Master Chikada. I call the cover designer "Master" because my editor at the time did, and from then on I just called Chikada-san that in my head. In Japan, there's something like a little sash that wraps around the cover with more art on it. Whenever we need one of these sashes, Master Chikada makes it look amazing too. The first volume had a very thin sash made with white paper with a lovely texture. The cover itself had very faint colors, so Master Chikada was very particular about choosing a paper that looked almost as if it was see-through. Keep in mind the care taken in choosing everything when you see each new volume. Even I don't know what it'll look like at that point, so I'm looking forward to it too.

I've been stressing out about the colors for the printing, but in the end I just went with blue. The light-blue parts look a little more yellow than they did on my computer monitor though. I also had this problem when I was working with a lot of blue on my series *Rokka Melt*. I knew this series would probably also have a lot of blue in it, so I figured I'd spend a lot of time worrying about the colors. I'm always worrying about the color balance and making tons of color patterns and working over my illustrations till the very end, but somehow they always end up getting finished. (Laughs) There have been a lot of times when I'm stressed out about stuff like making the colors lighter or darker, and I keep tweaking stuff and zoning out and all of a sudden I look up and I'm like, well, that looks about right! Actually, now that I say it I feel like that might be bad...

CHAPTER 6

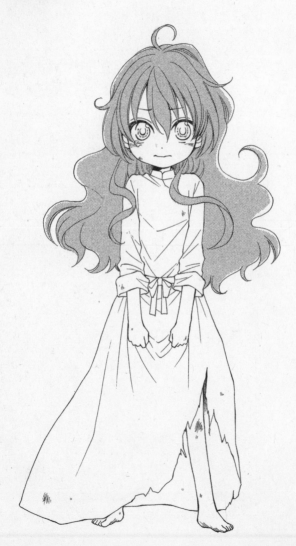

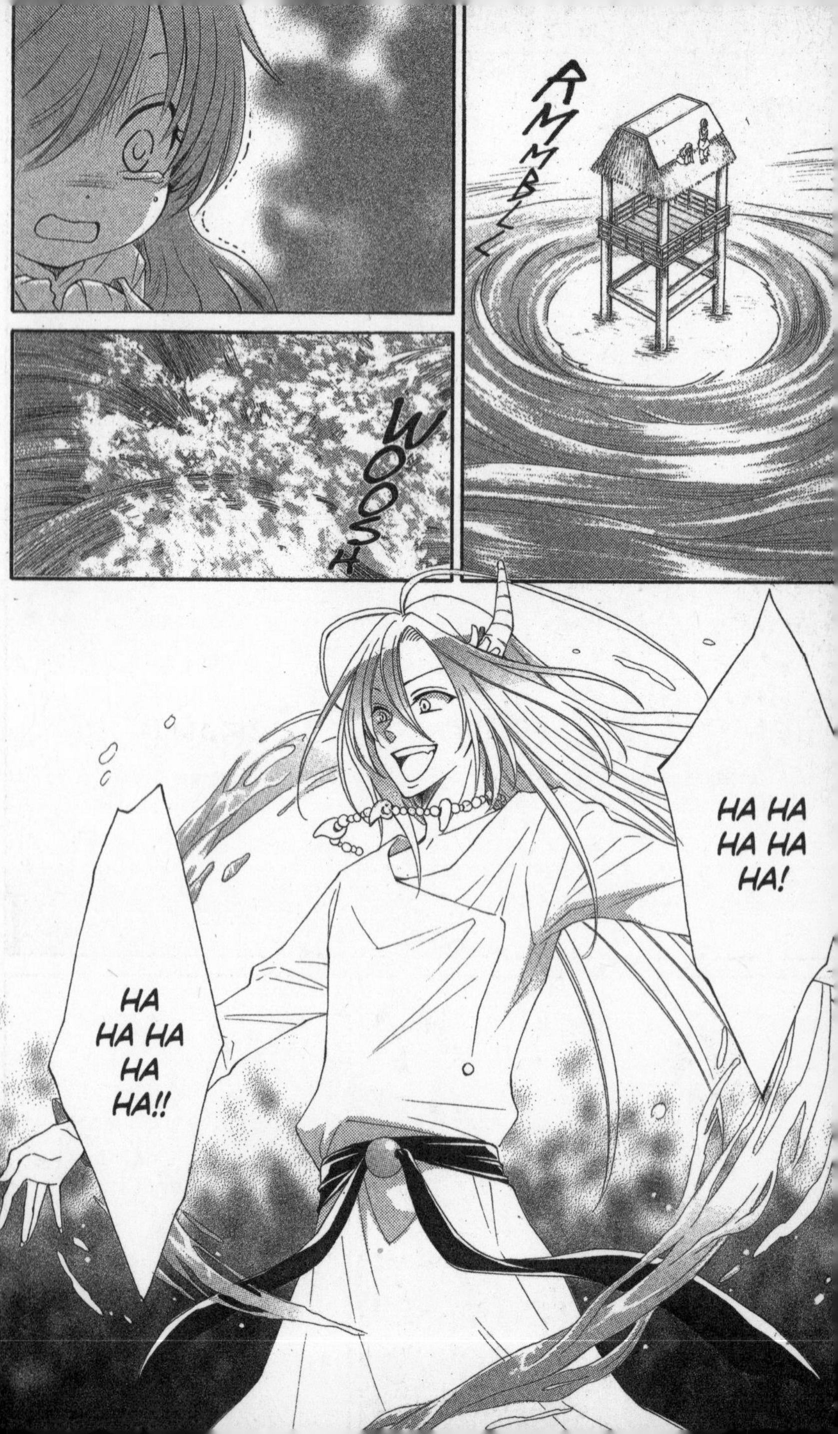
RAMMBLL
WOOSH
HA HA HA HA HA HA!
HA HA HA HA HA HA!!

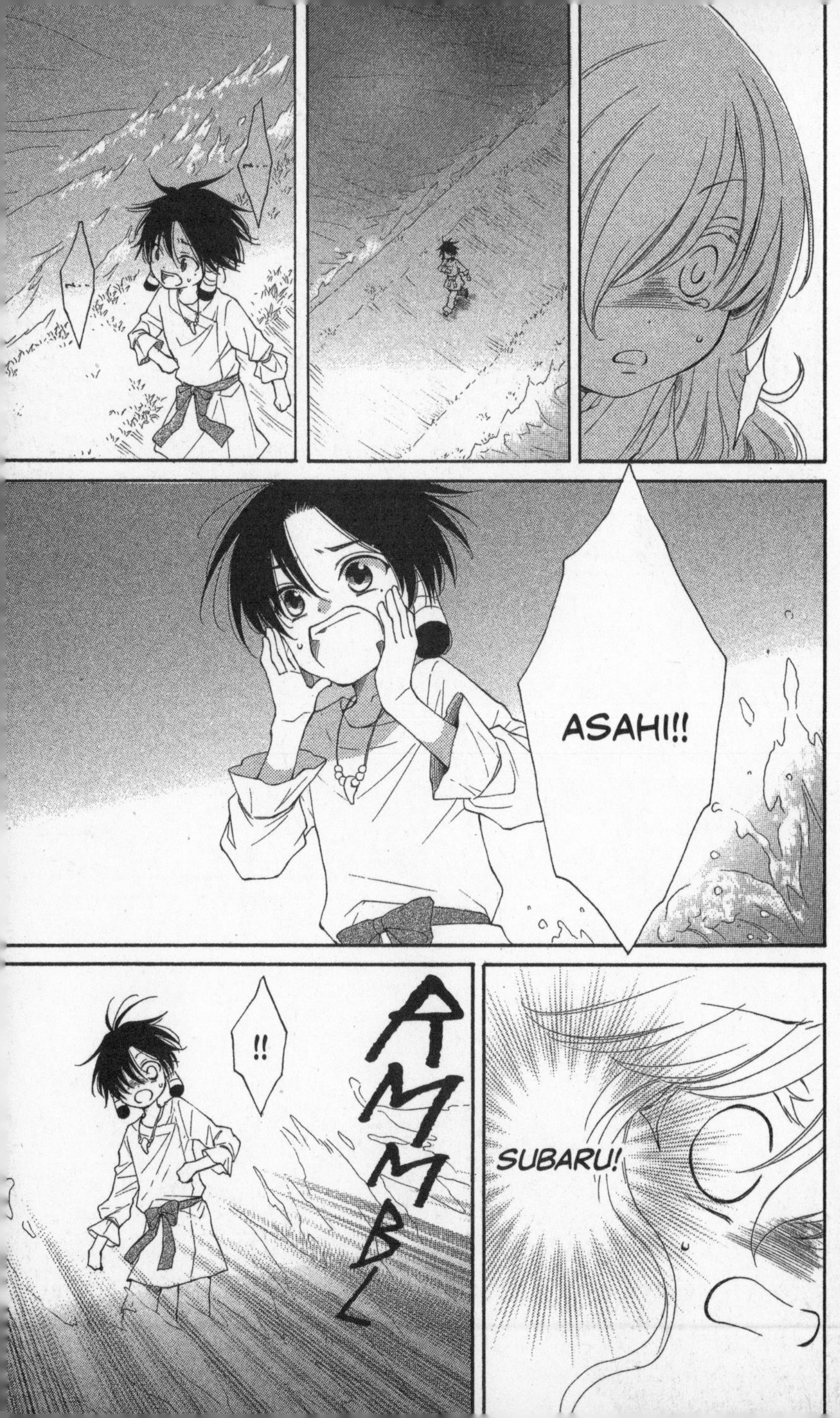
ASAHI!!
SUBARU!
!!
AMMBL

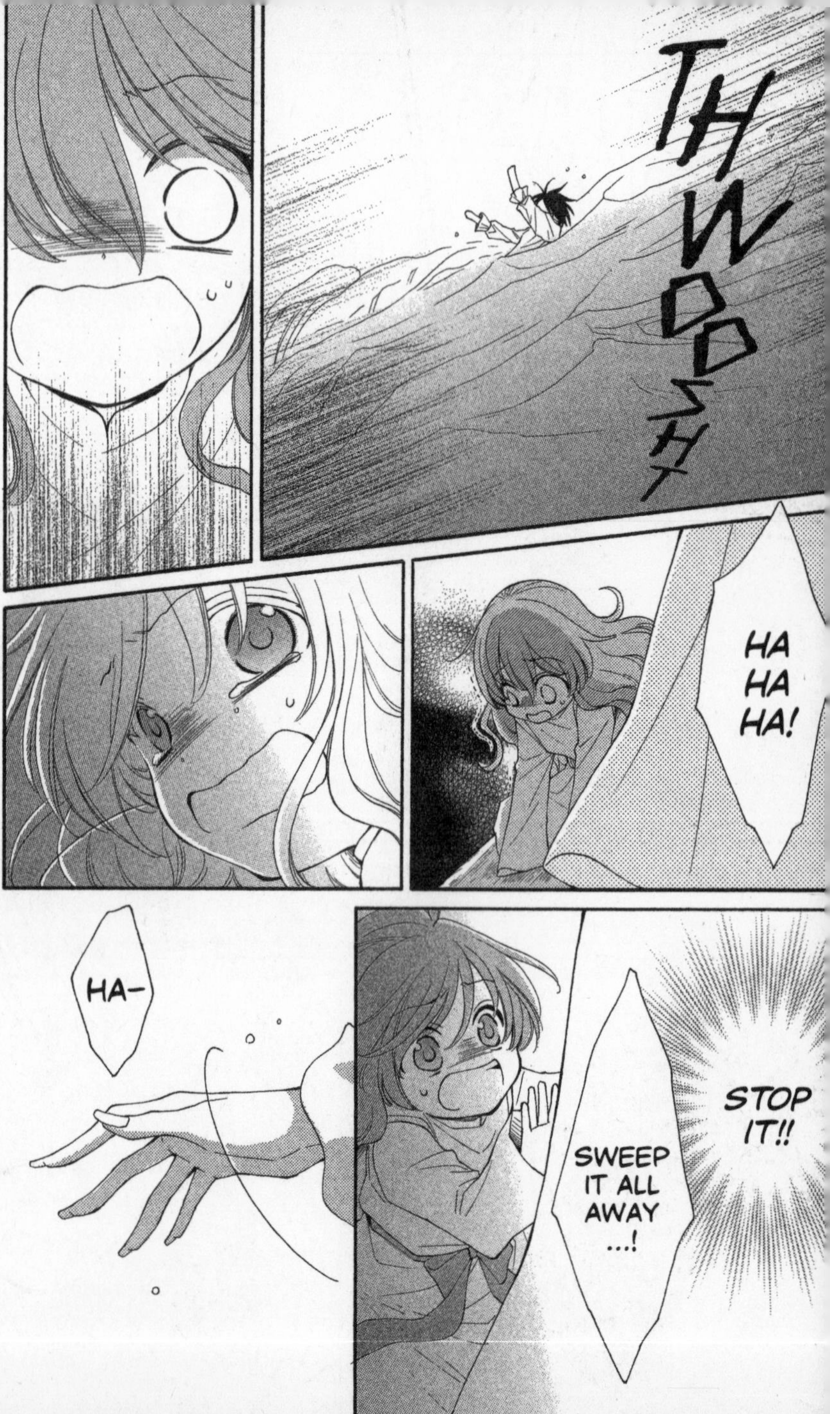
THWOOSH
HA HA HA!
STOP IT!!
SWEEP IT ALL AWAY ...!
HA-

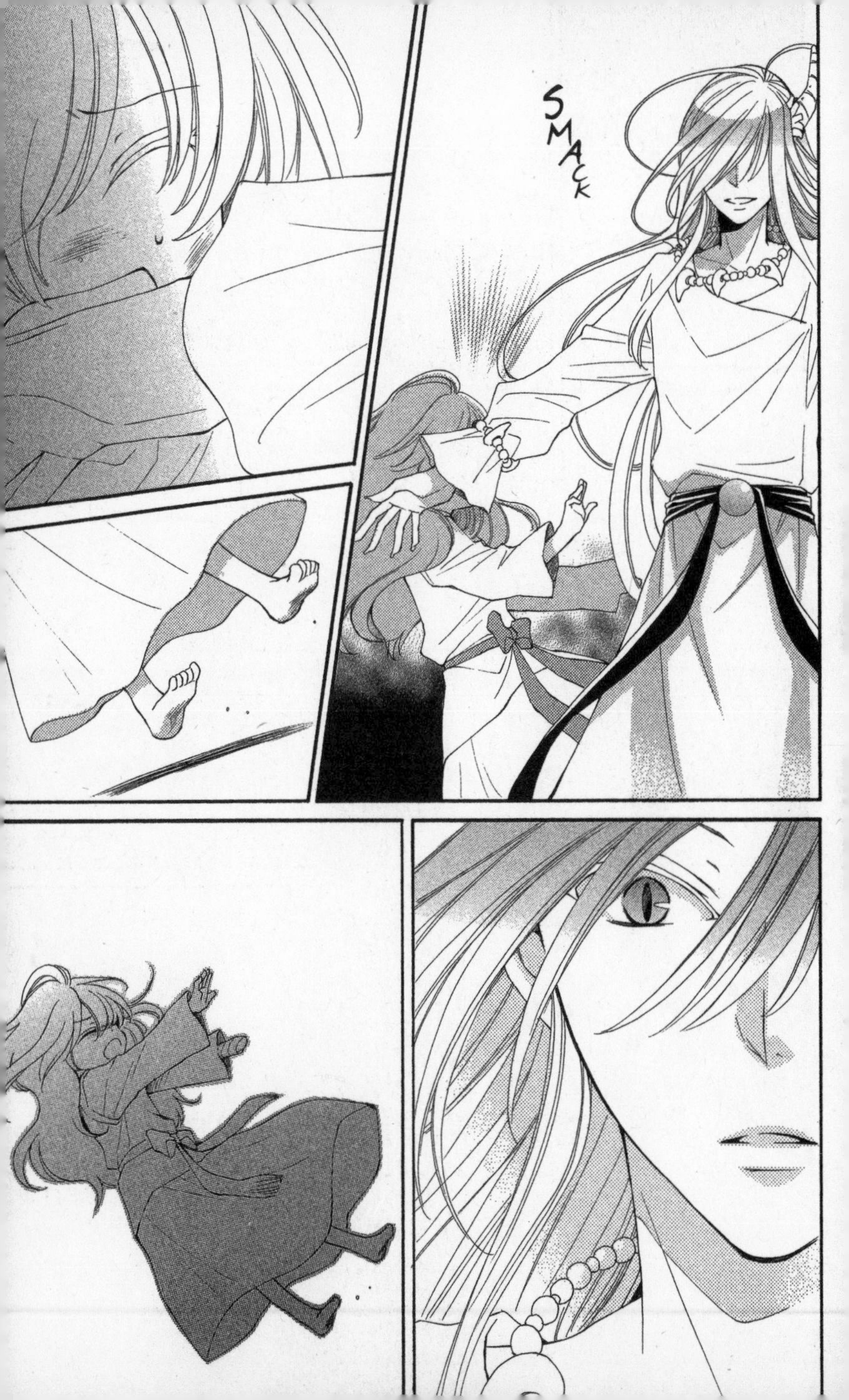
SMACK

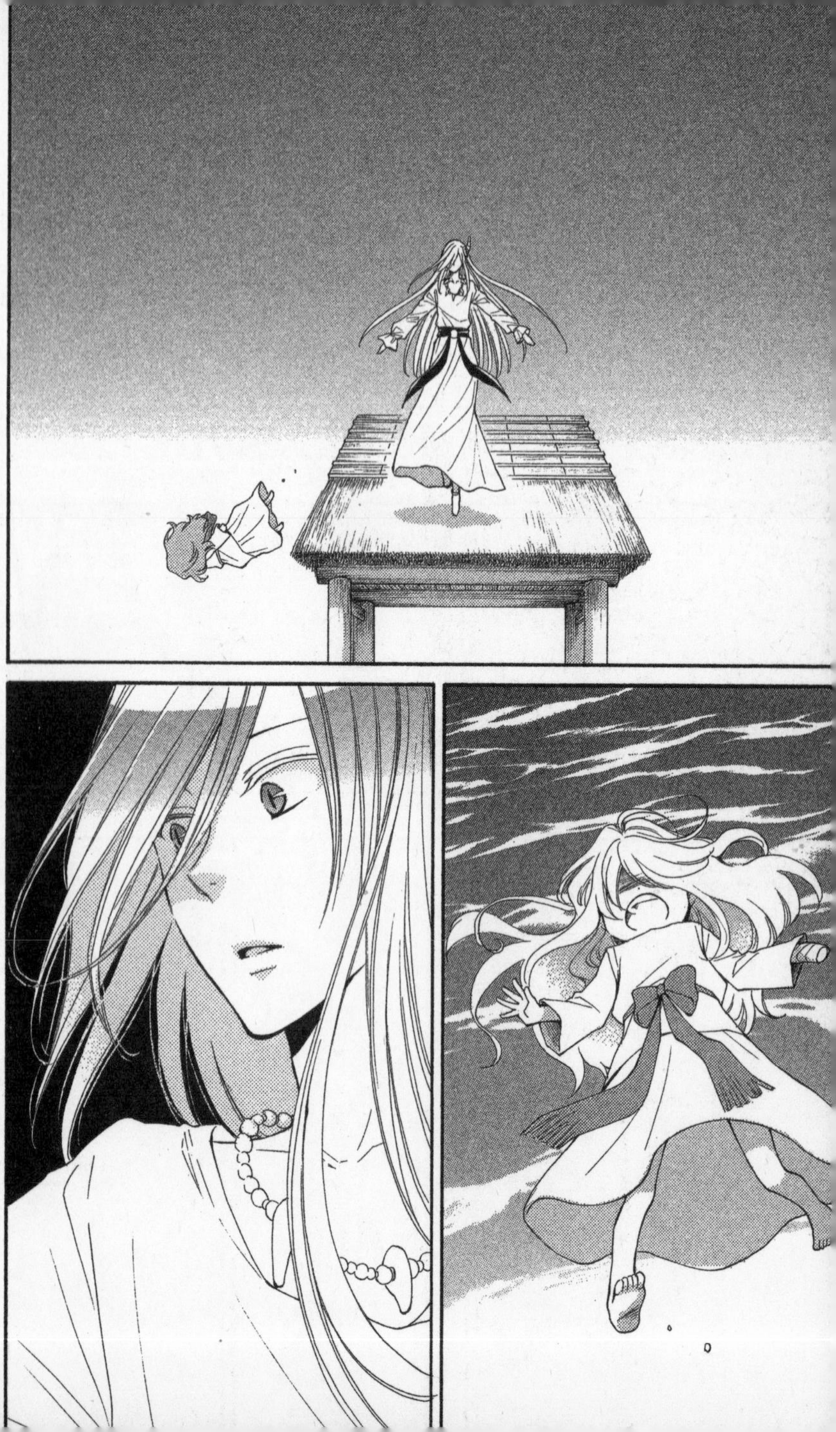

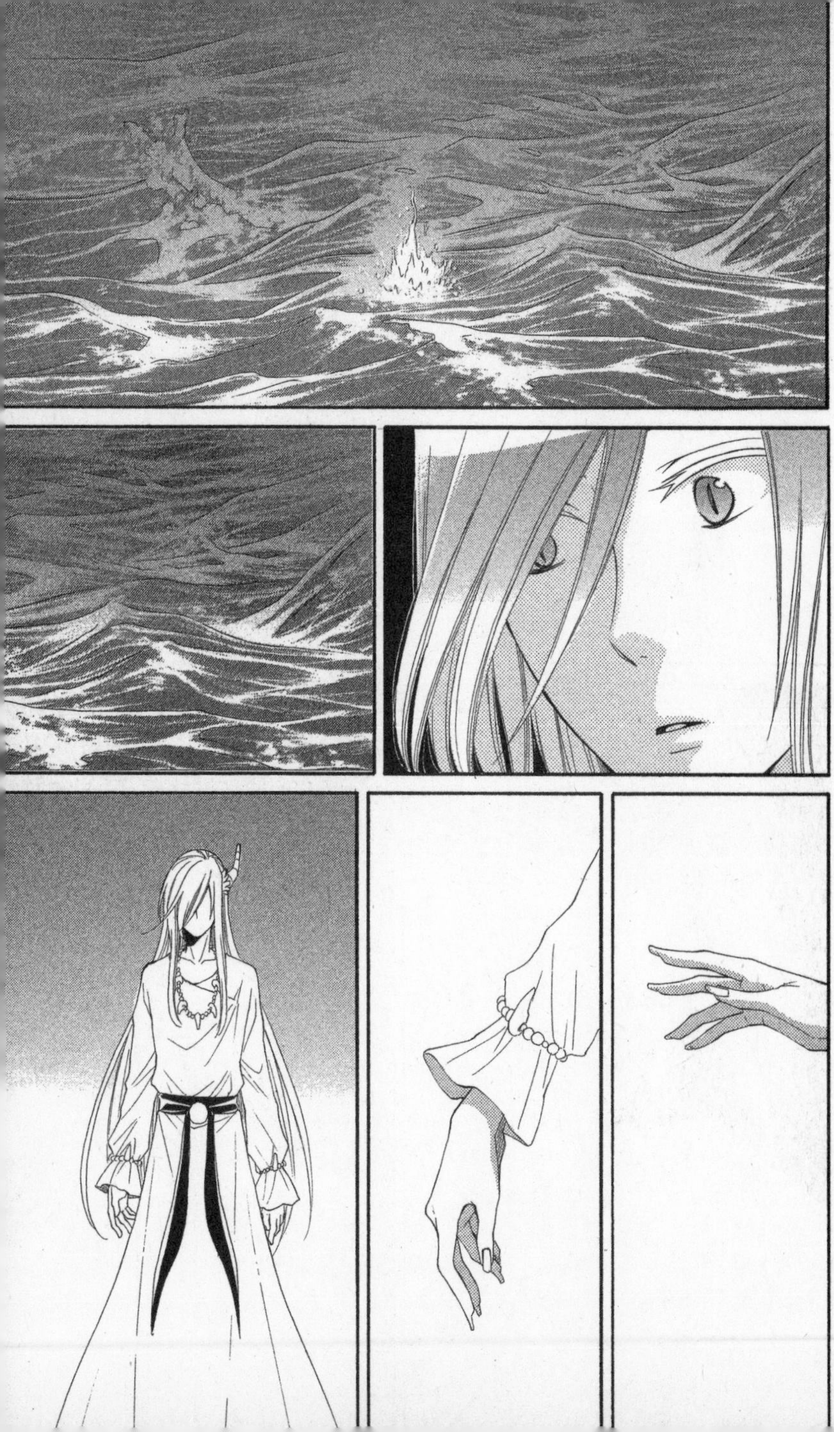

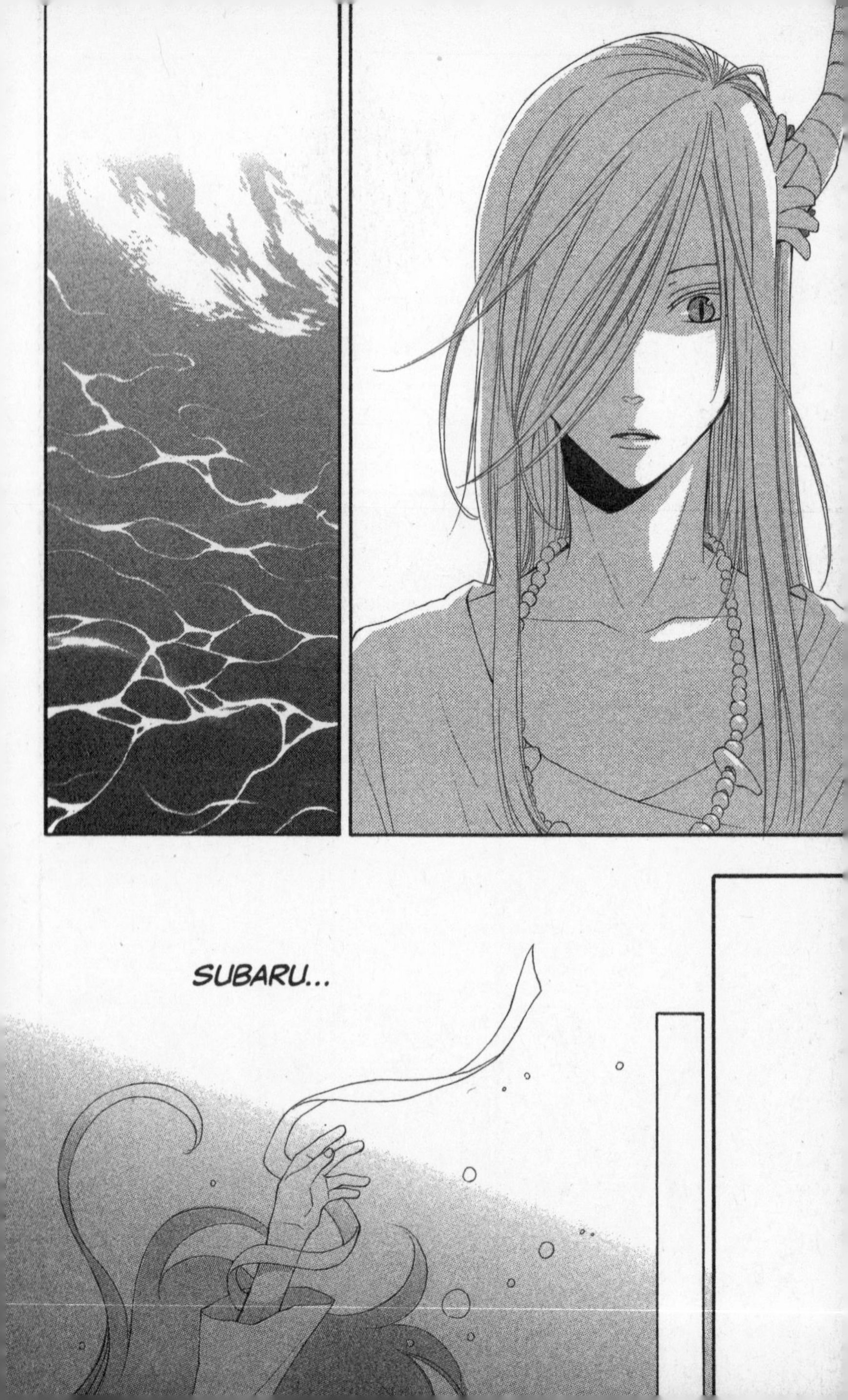
SUBARU...

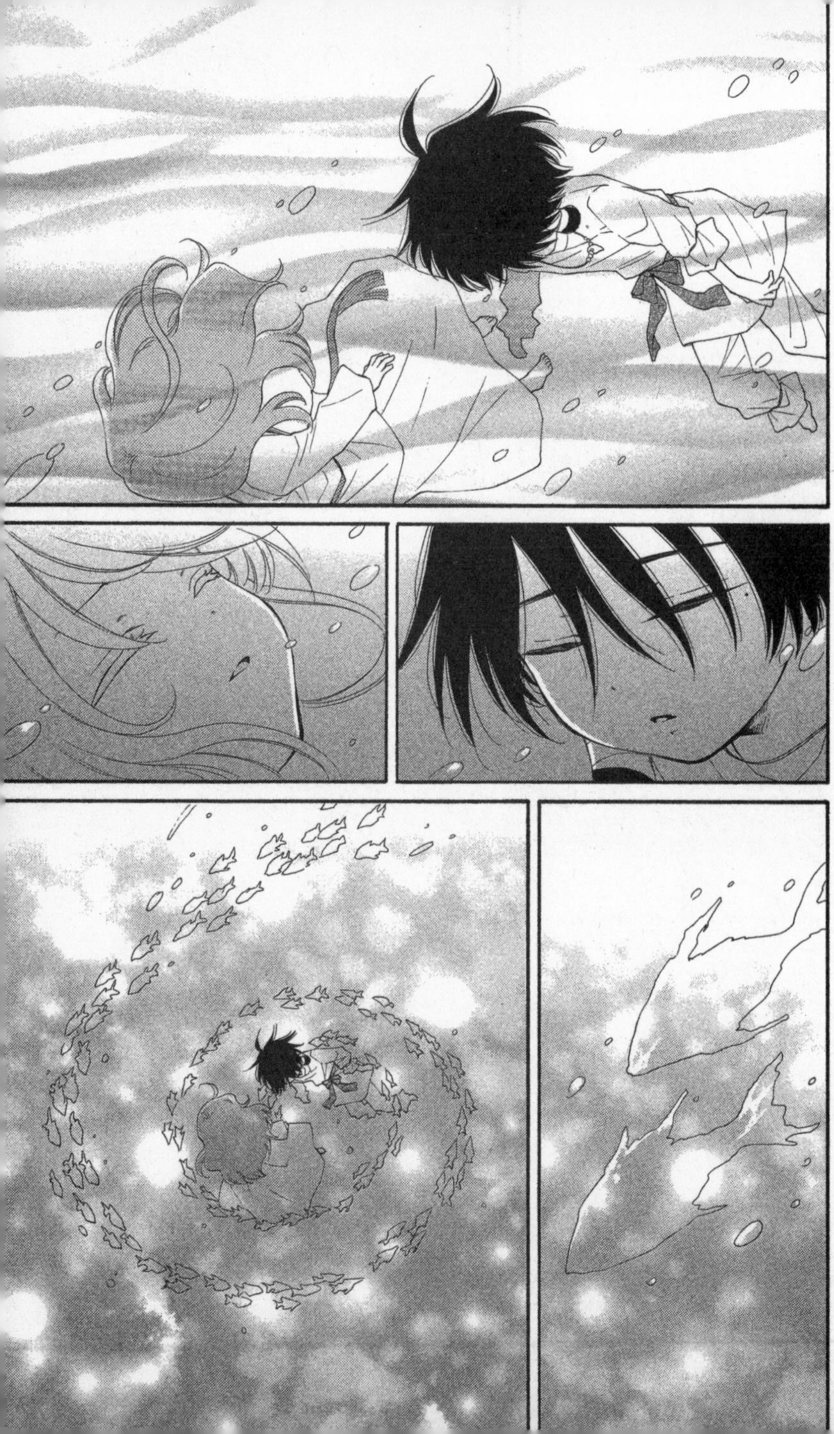

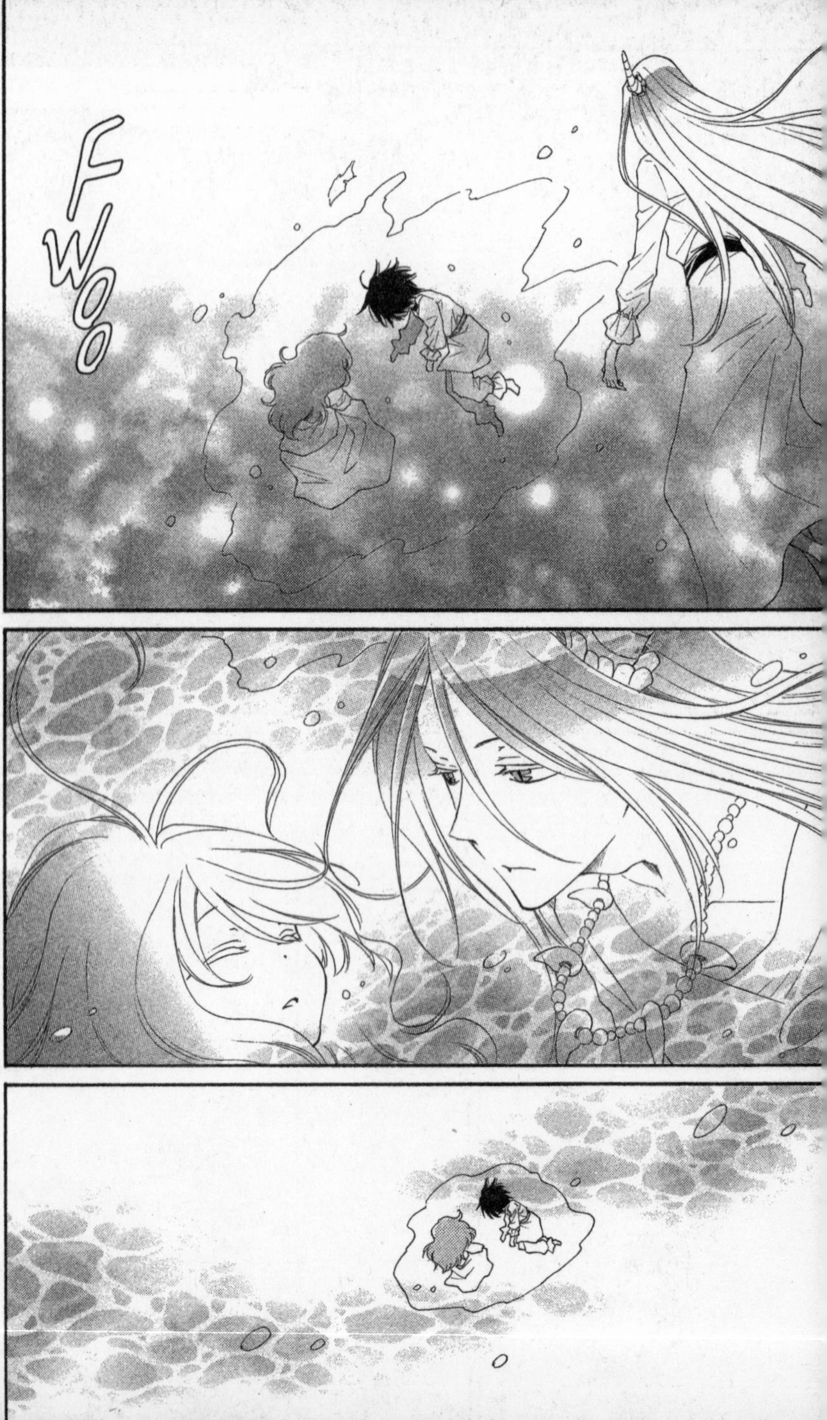
FWOO

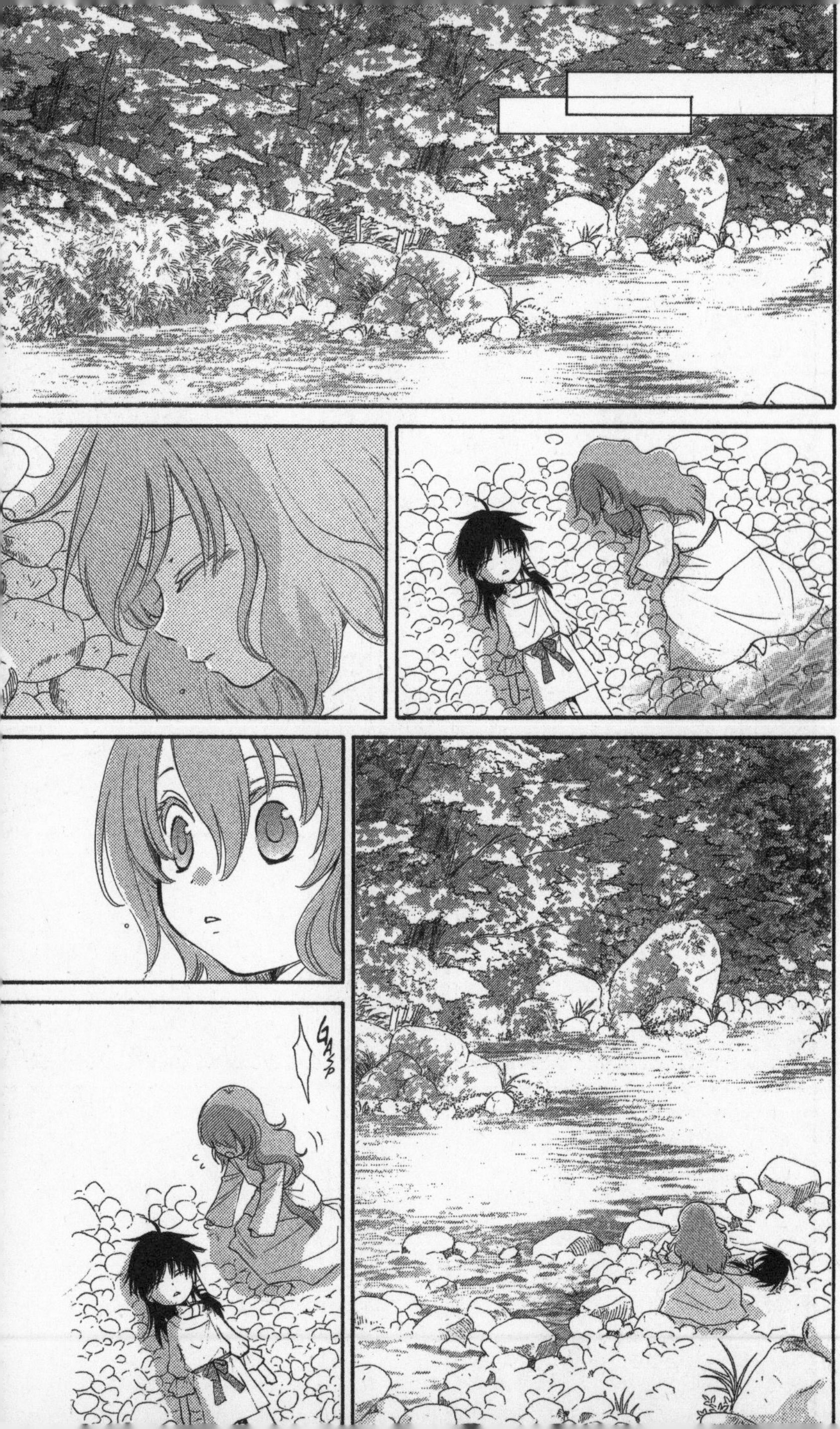
GASP

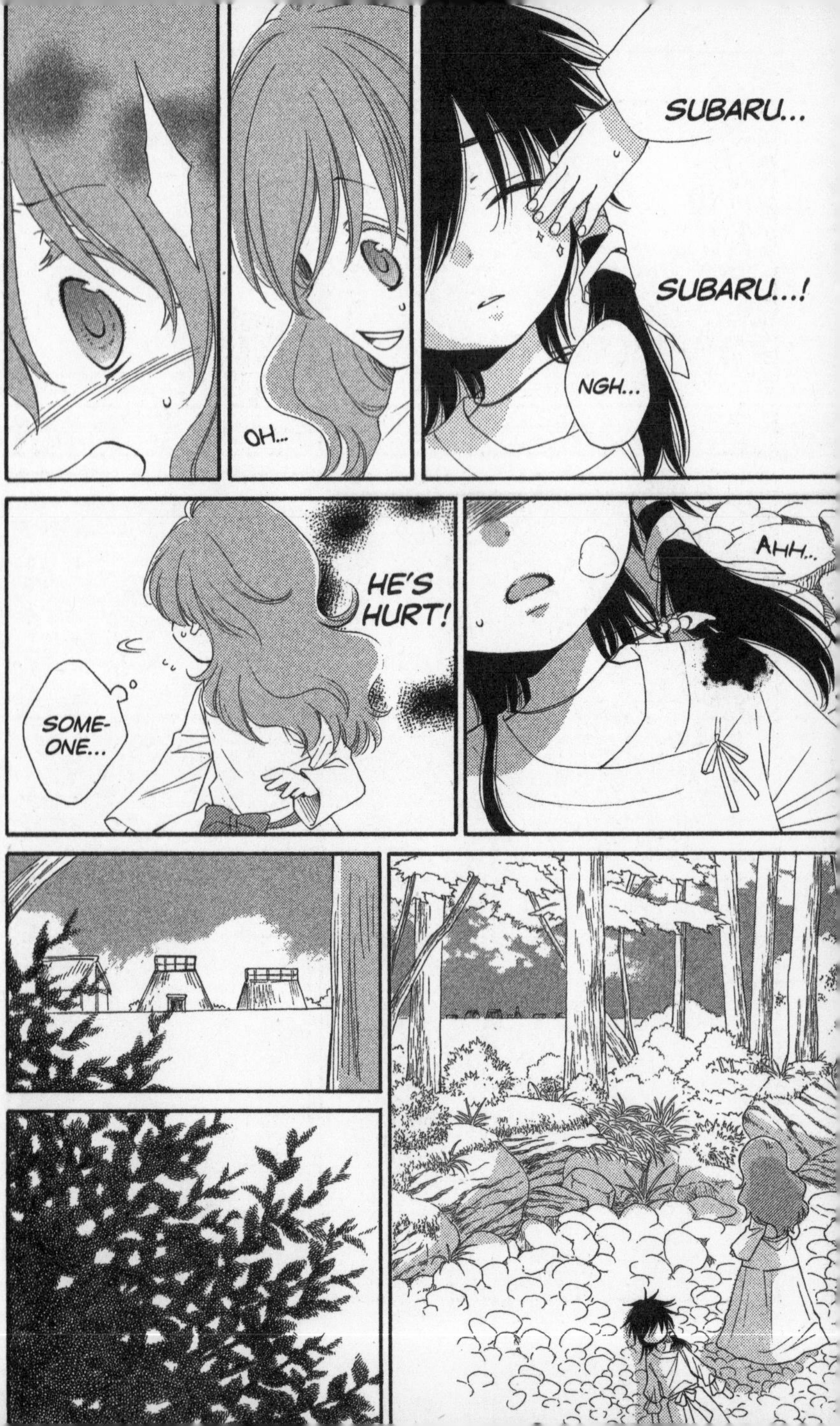
SUBARU...
SUBARU...!
NGH...
OH...
AHH...
HE'S HURT!
SOME-ONE...

HNNGH

RRRNGH

WOBBLE

JUST WAIT HERE, SUBARU...

I'LL GO GET SOMEBODY.

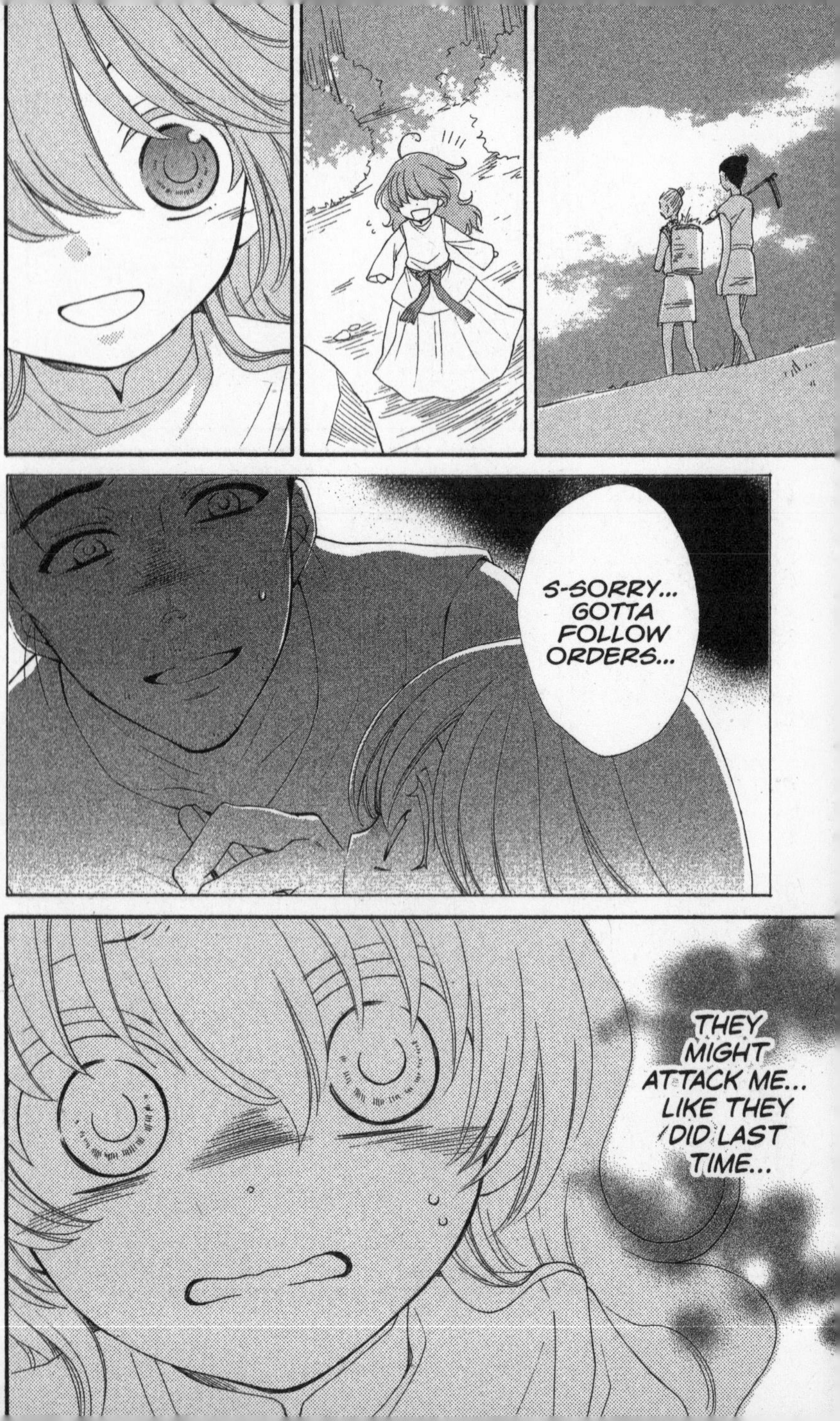
S-SORRY... GOTTA FOLLOW ORDERS...
THEY MIGHT ATTACK ME... LIKE THEY DID LAST TIME...

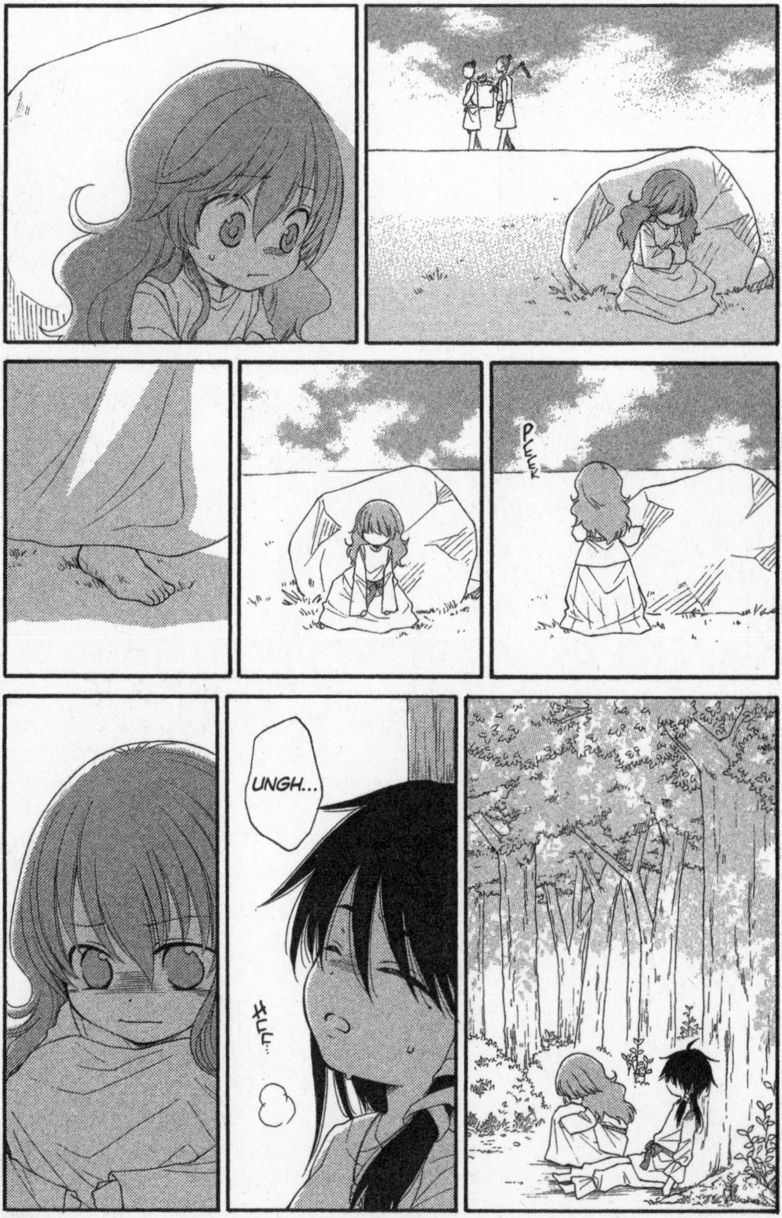
PEEK
UNGH...
HUU...

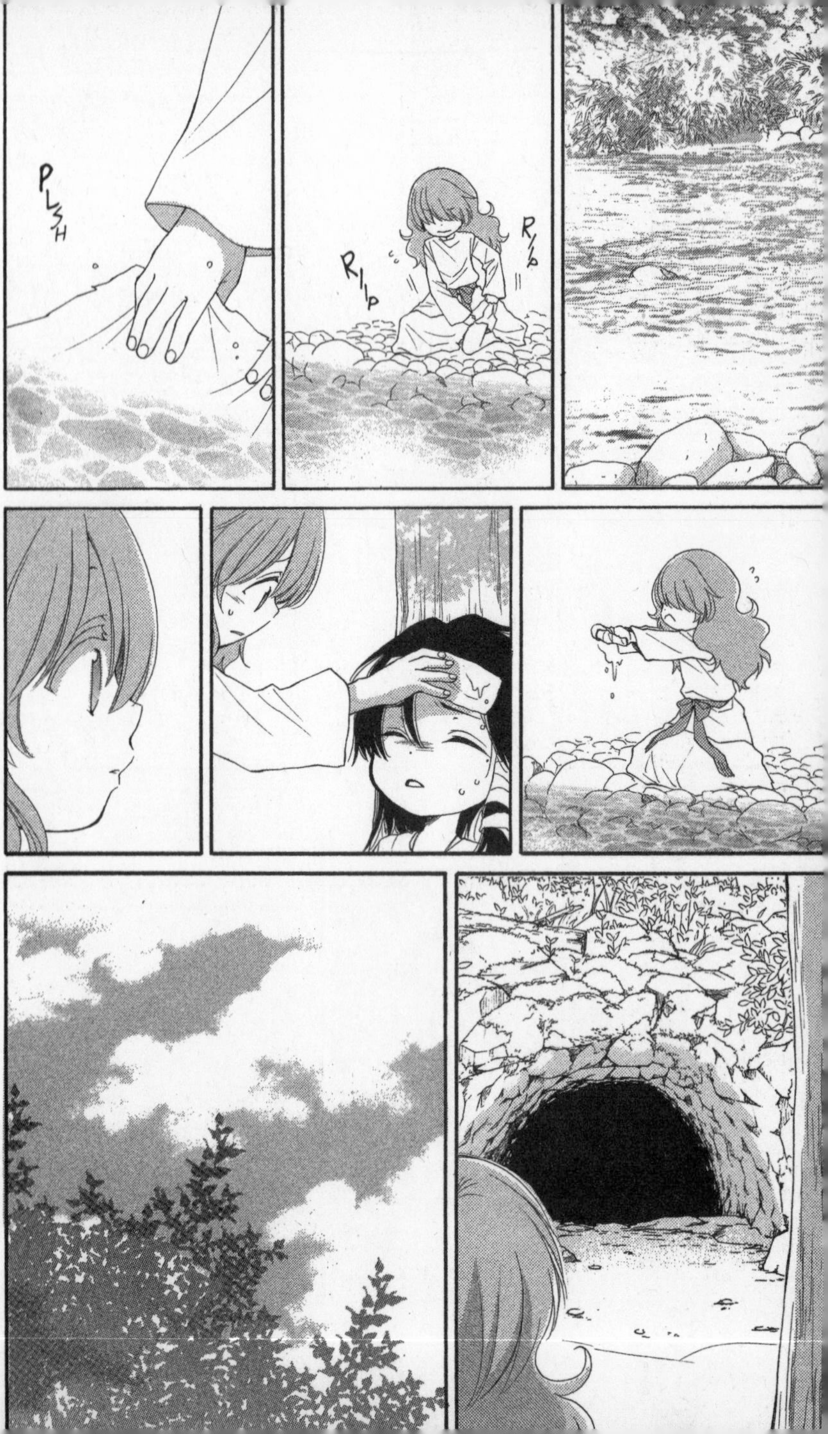
RIP
RIIP
PLSH

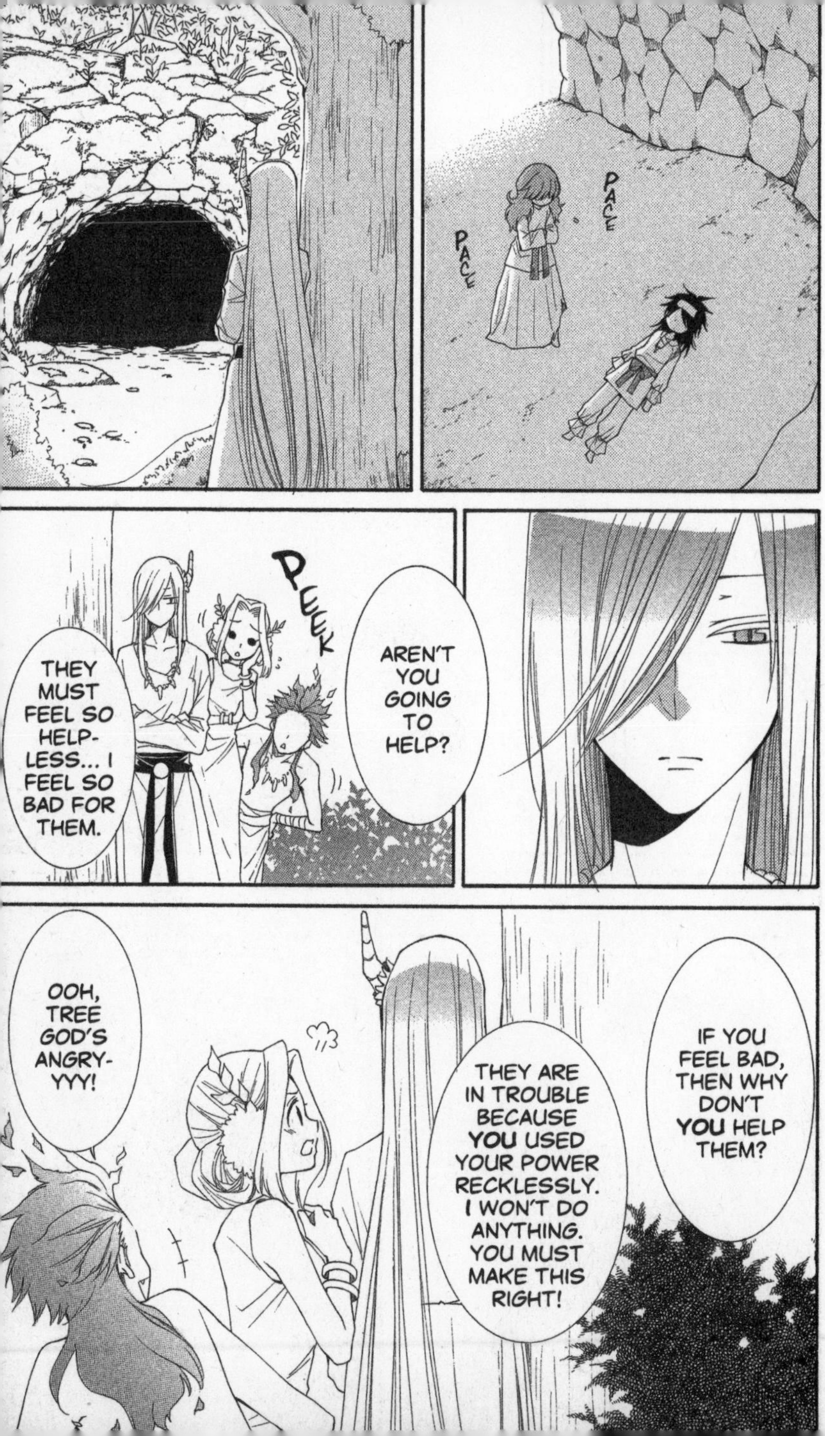
PACE
PACE
PEEK
AREN'T YOU GOING TO HELP?
THEY MUST FEEL SO HELP-LESS... I FEEL SO BAD FOR THEM.
IF YOU FEEL BAD, THEN WHY DON'T **YOU** HELP THEM?
THEY ARE IN TROUBLE BECAUSE **YOU** USED YOUR POWER RECKLESSLY. I WON'T DO ANYTHING. YOU MUST MAKE THIS RIGHT!
OOH, TREE GOD'S ANGRY-YYY!

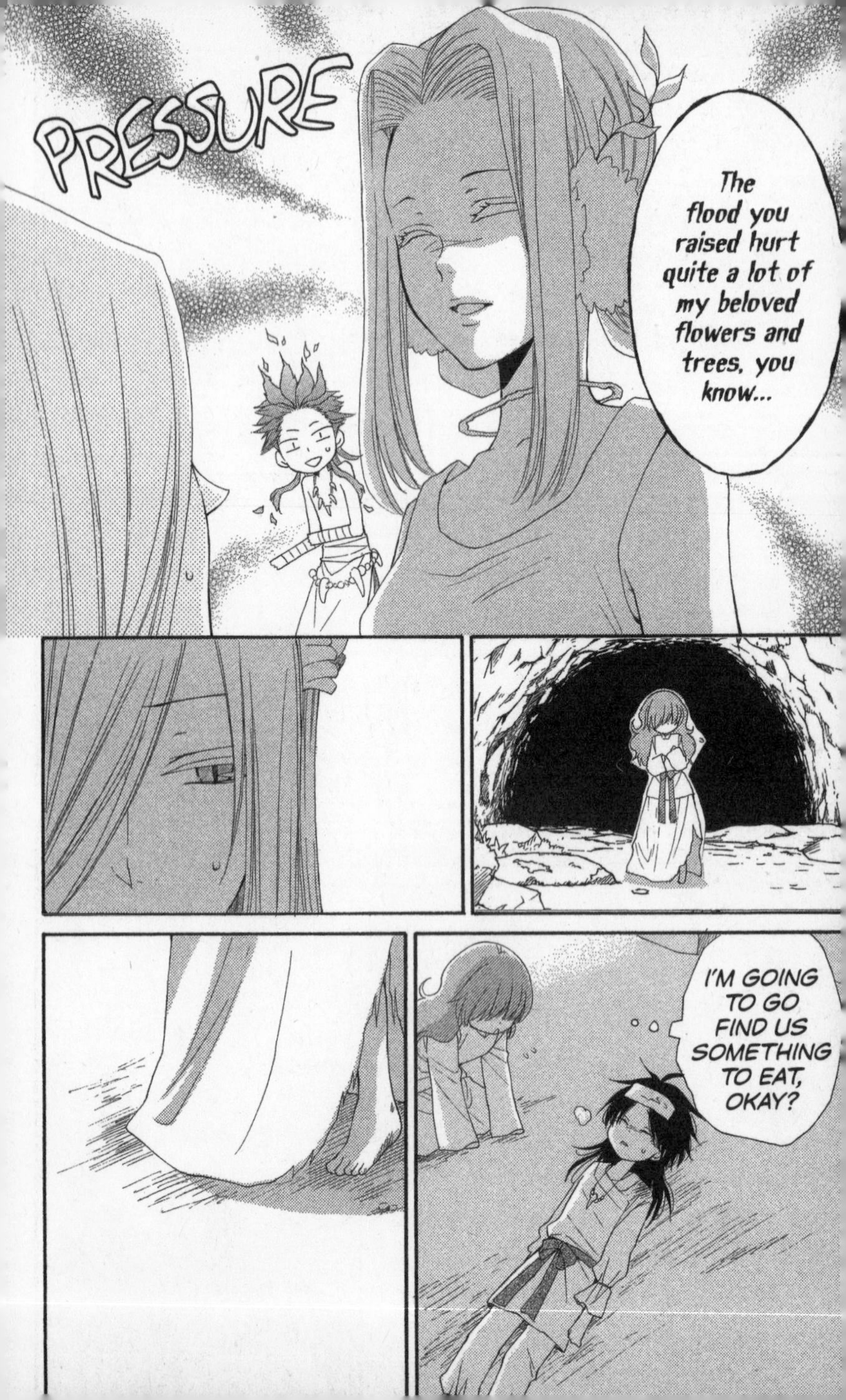
The flood you raised hurt quite a lot of my beloved flowers and trees, you know...
PRESSURE
I'M GOING TO GO FIND US SOMETHING TO EAT, OKAY?

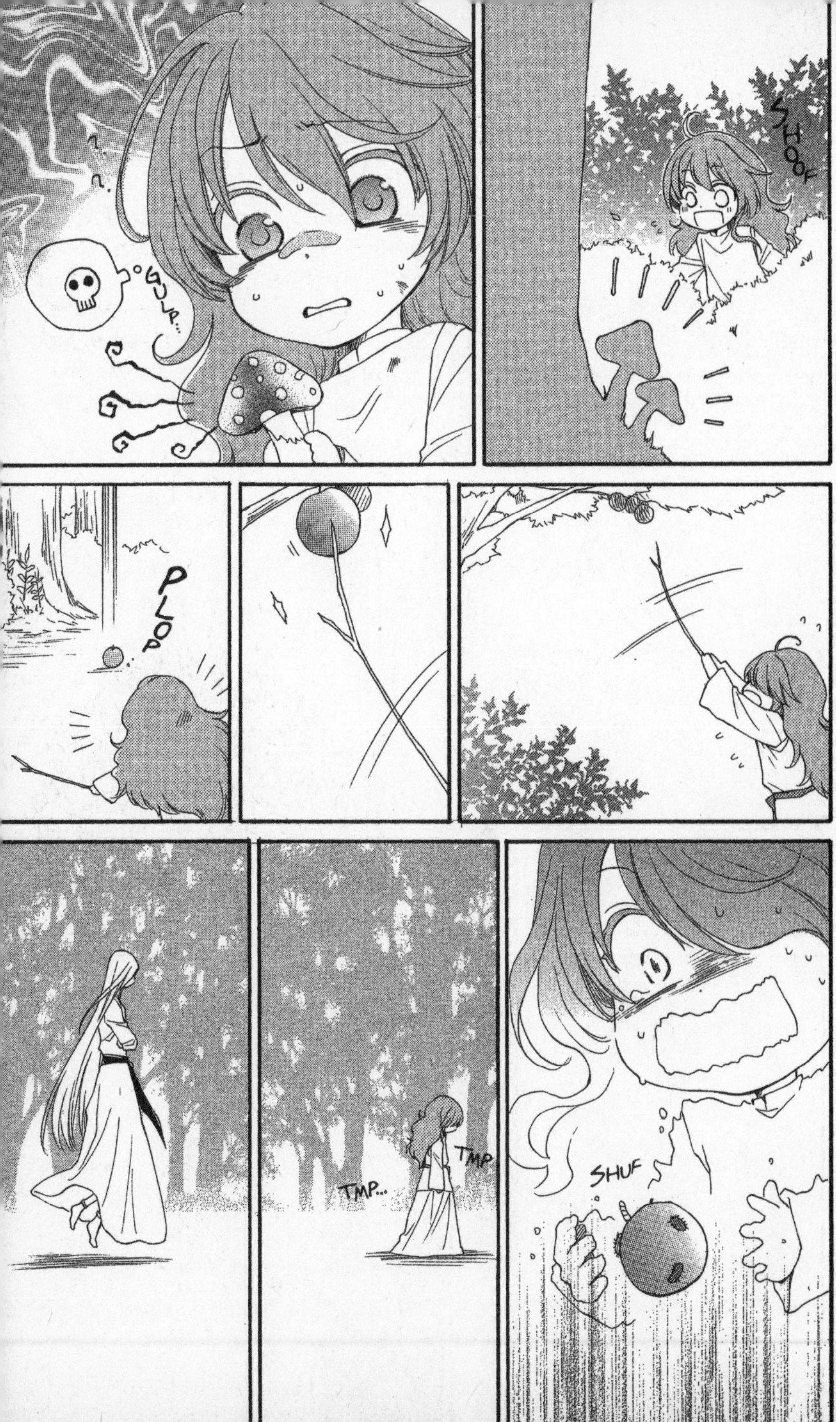
SHOOF
GULP...
PLOP
SHUF
TMP
TMP...

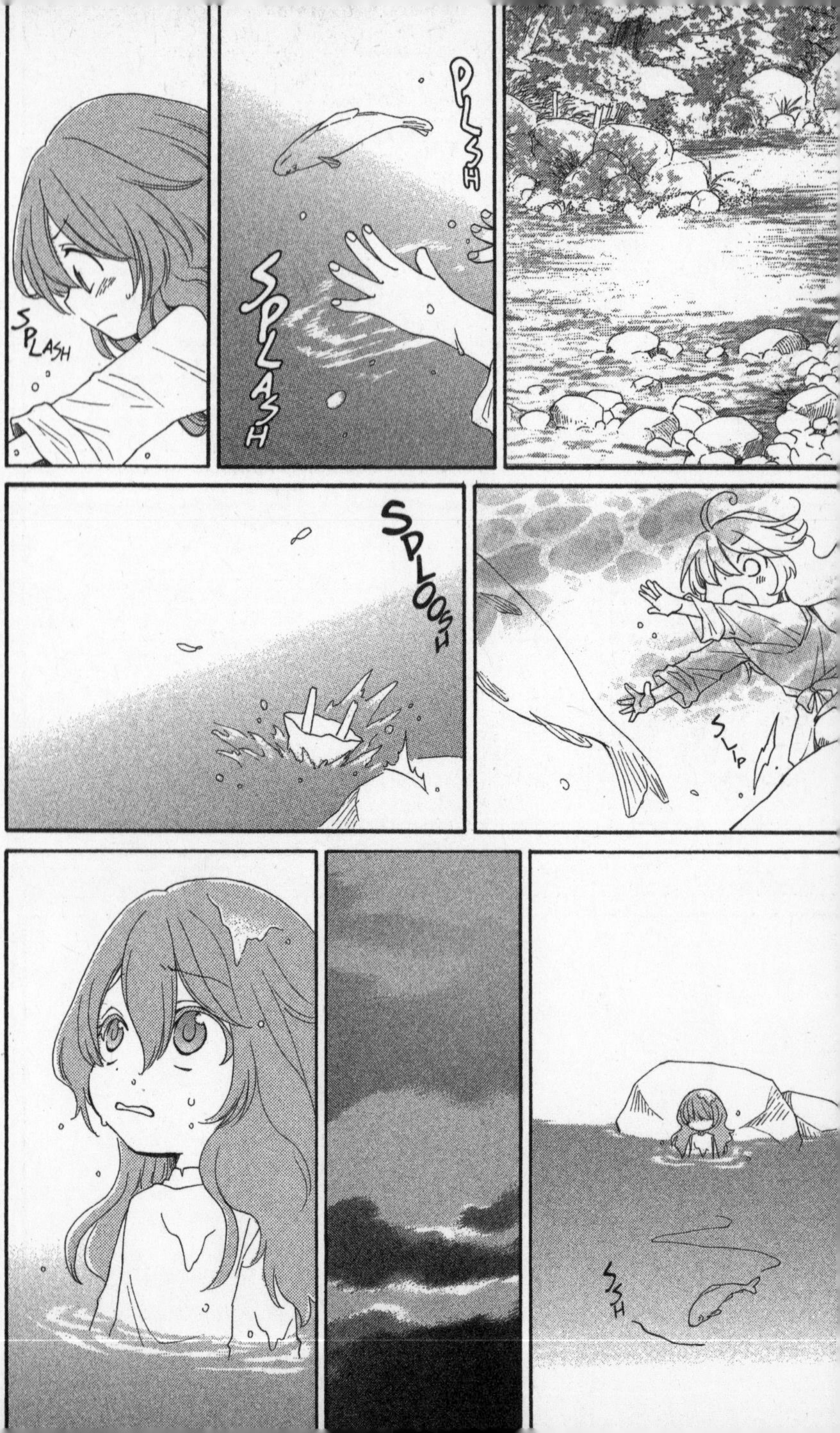
PLSH
SPLASH
SPLASH
SLIP
SPLOOSH
SSSH

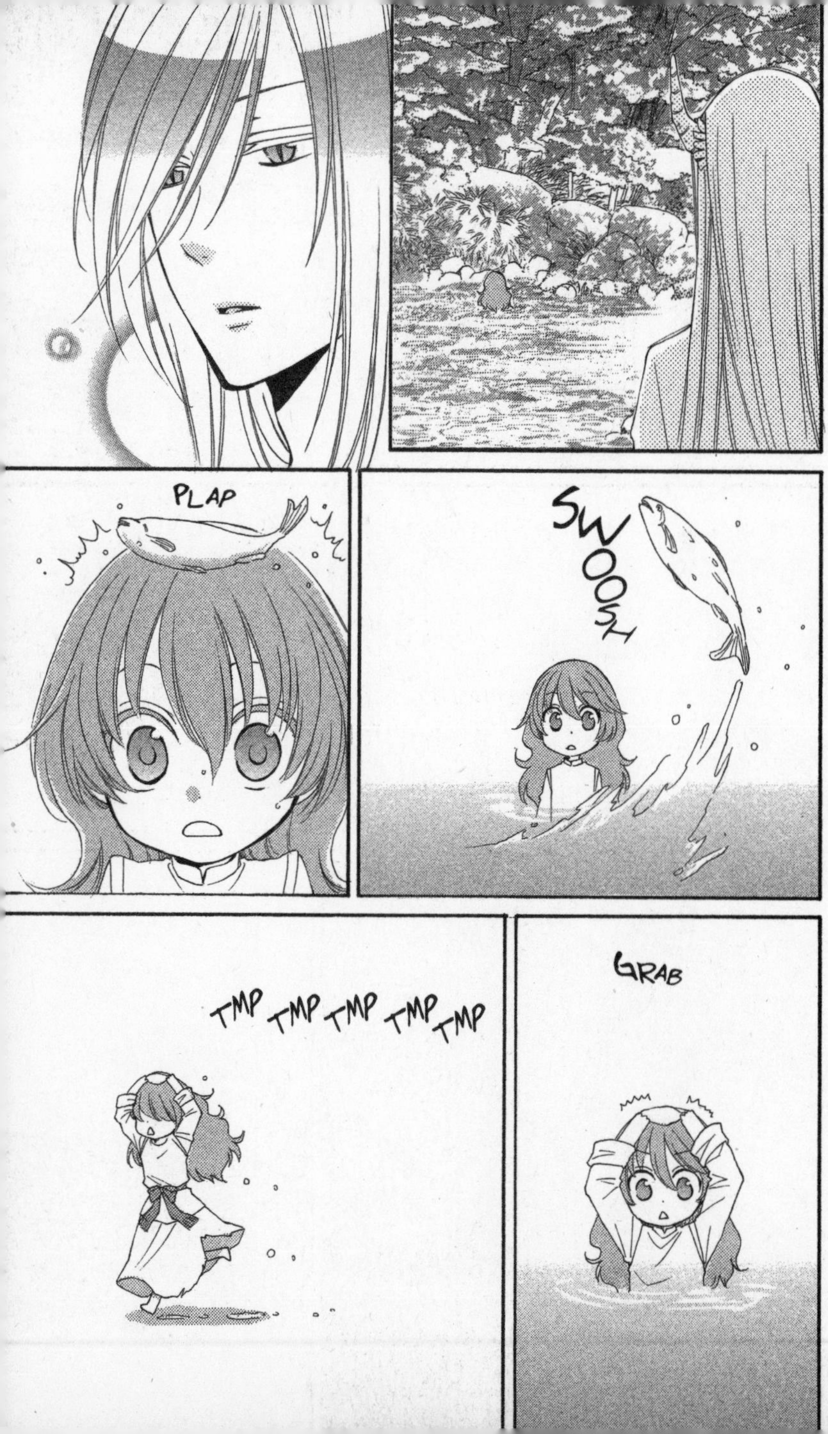
SWOOSH
PLAP
GRAB
TMP TMP TMP TMP TMP

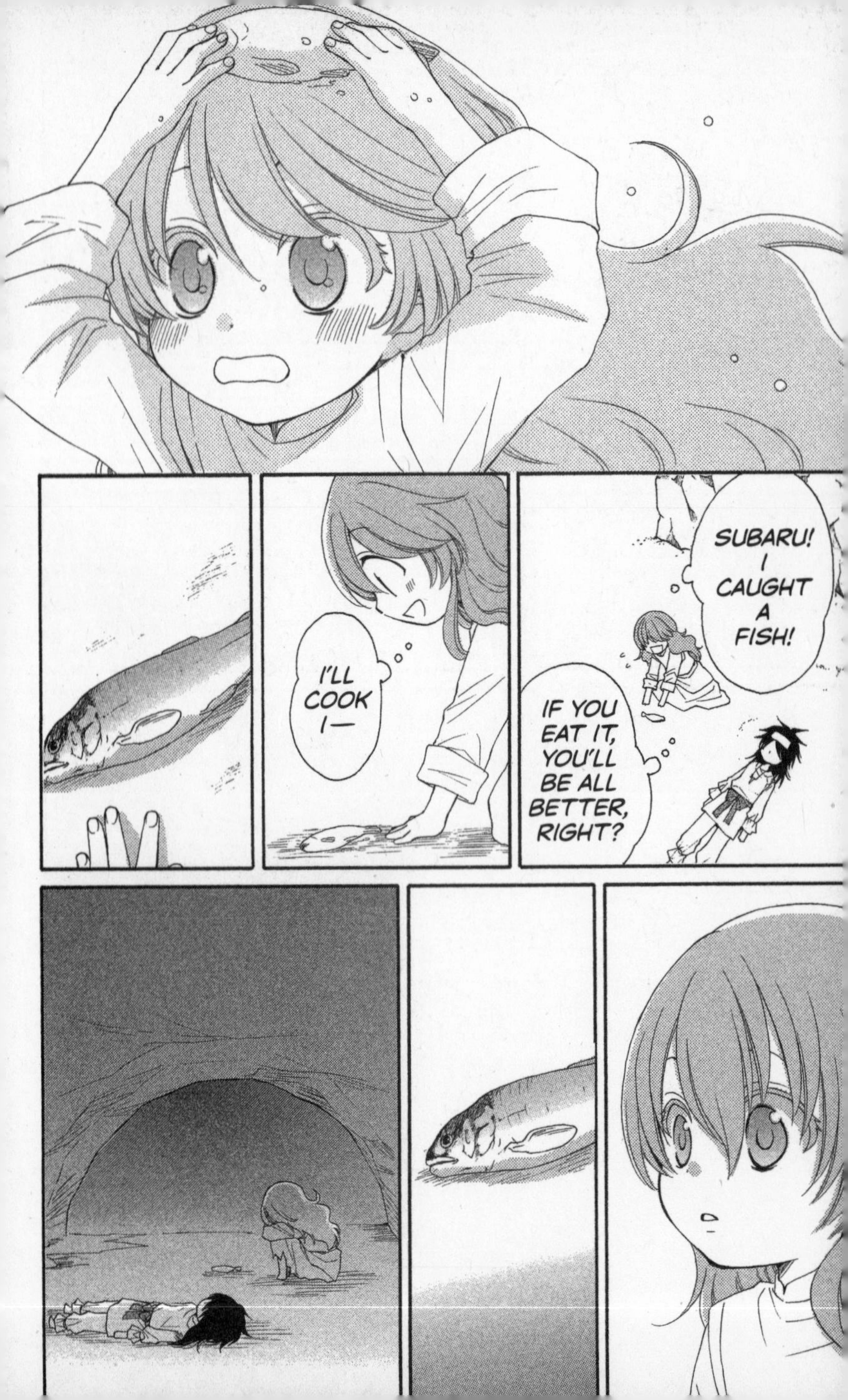
SUBARU! I CAUGHT A FISH!
IF YOU EAT IT, YOU'LL BE ALL BETTER, RIGHT?
I'LL COOK I—

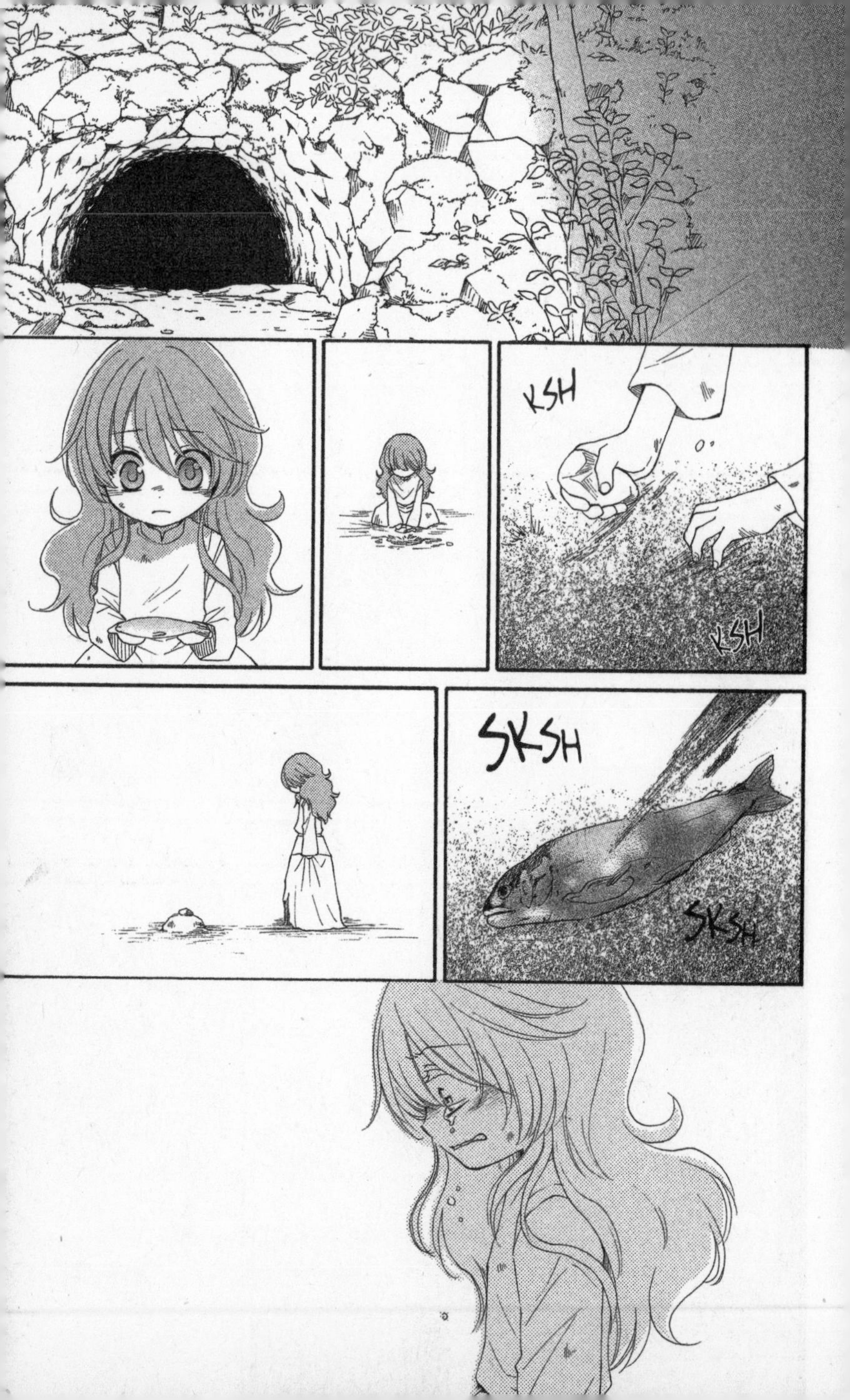
KSH
KSH
SKSH
SKSH

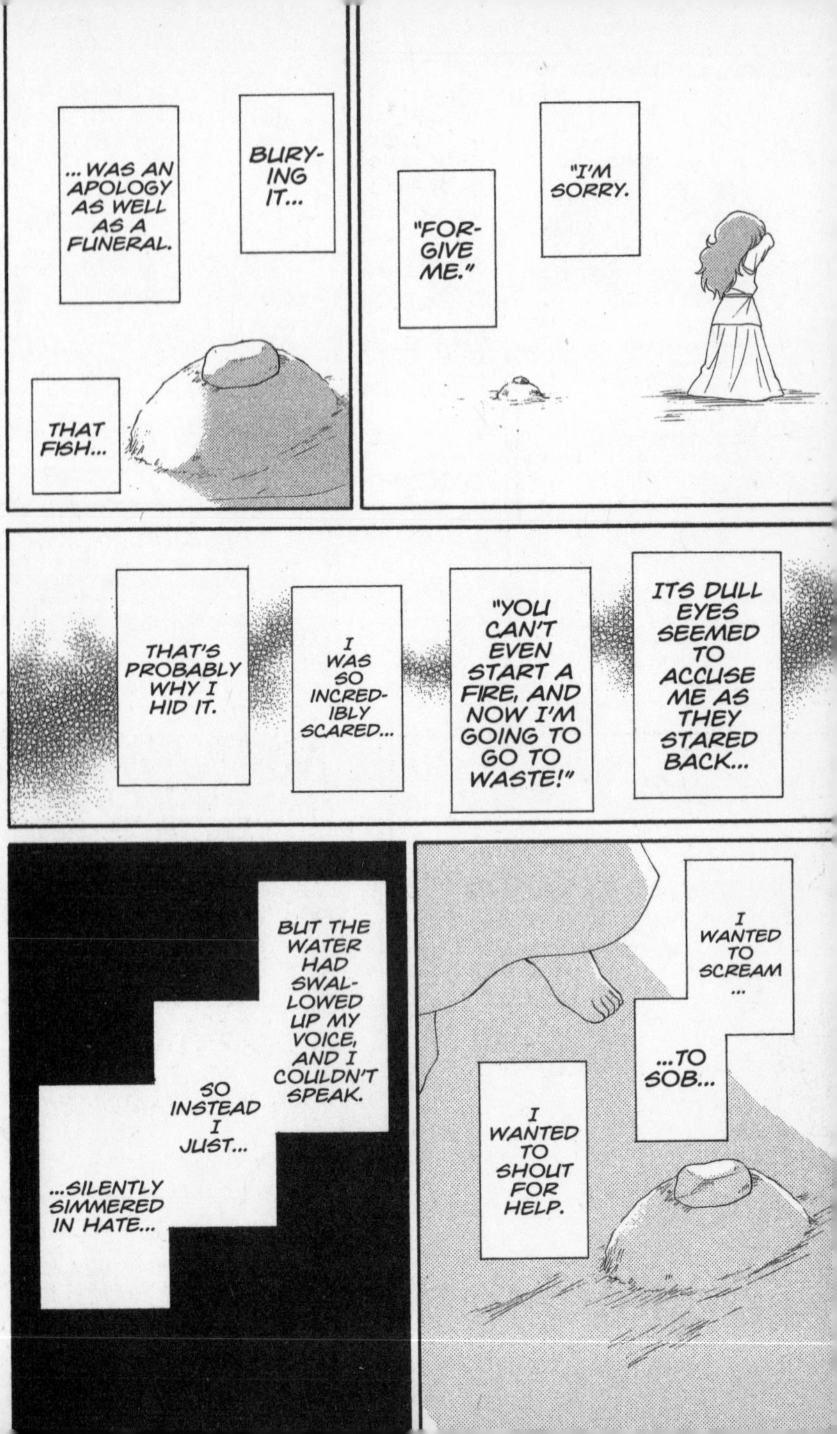
"I'M SORRY.
"FORGIVE ME."
BURYING IT...
...WAS AN APOLOGY AS WELL AS A FUNERAL.
THAT FISH...
ITS DULL EYES SEEMED TO ACCUSE ME AS THEY STARED BACK...
"YOU CAN'T EVEN START A FIRE, AND NOW I'M GOING TO GO TO WASTE!"
I WAS SO INCREDIBLY SCARED...
THAT'S PROBABLY WHY I HID IT.
I WANTED TO SCREAM...
...TO SOB...
I WANTED TO SHOUT FOR HELP.
BUT THE WATER HAD SWALLOWED UP MY VOICE, AND I COULDN'T SPEAK.
SO INSTEAD I JUST...
...SILENTLY SIMMERED IN HATE...

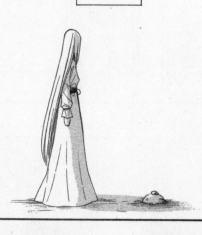

...FOR THE WATER DRAGON GOD.

WHAT YOU NEED IS THIS!! THE NO-FUSS, NO-HASSLE SOLUTION! SO SIMPLE A CHILD COULD DO IT!! SO CONVENIENT!! THE MR. FIRESTARTER!!

YOU CAN DO ANYTHING WITH THIS! ☆

TA DA

DUM

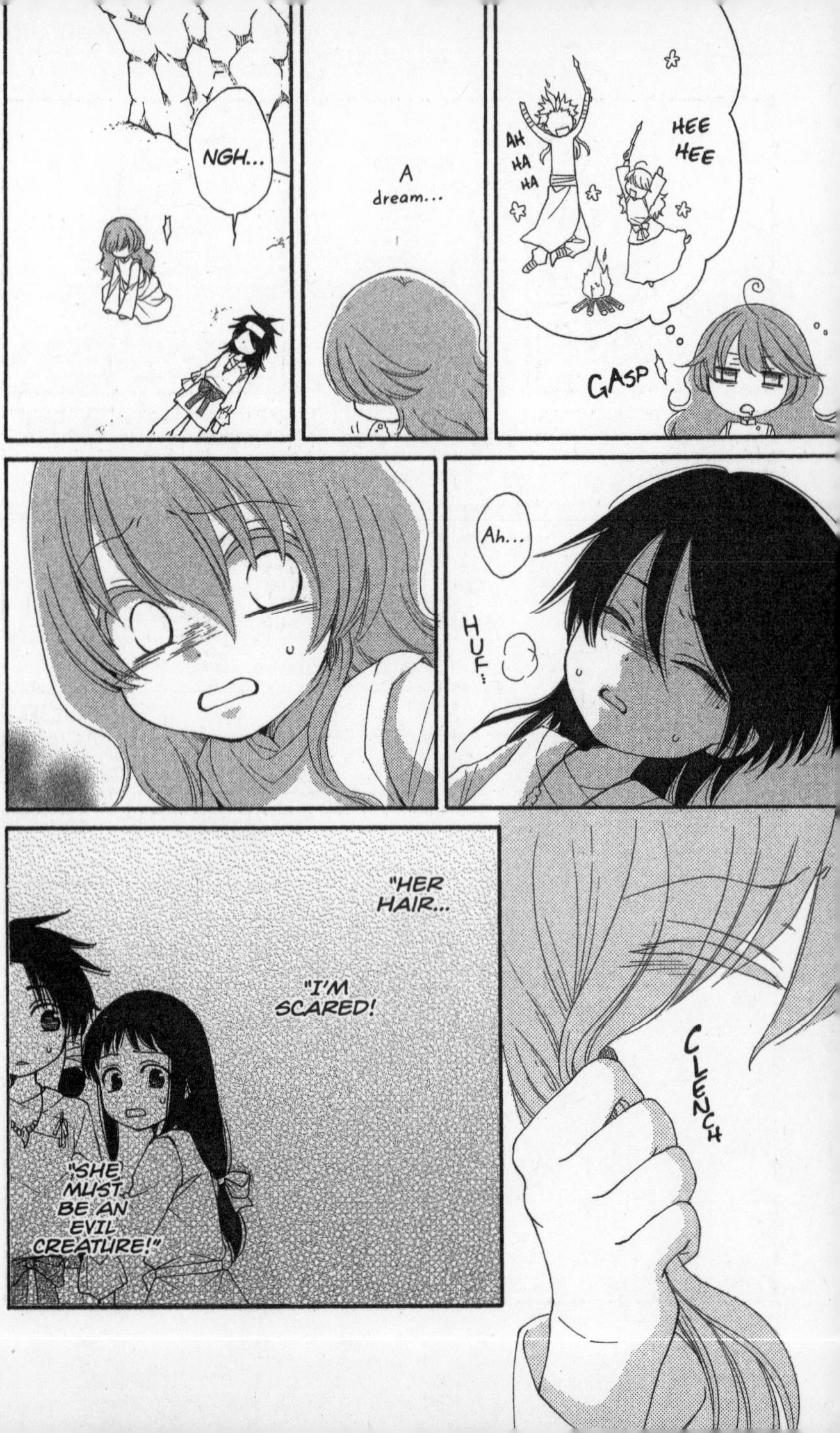
HEE HEE
AH HA HA
GASP
A dream...
NGH...
Ah...
HUF...
CLENCH
"HER HAIR...
"I'M SCARED!
"SHE MUST BE AN EVIL CREATURE!"

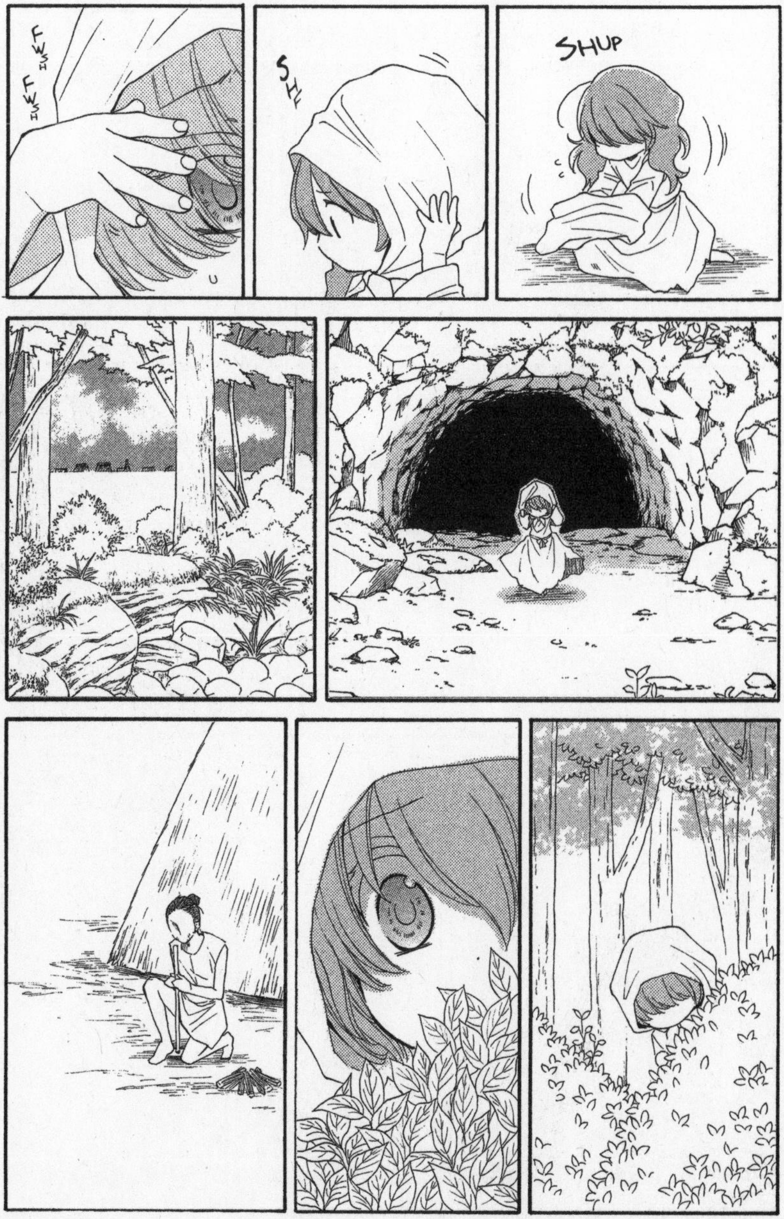
SHUP
SHH
FWSH
FWSH

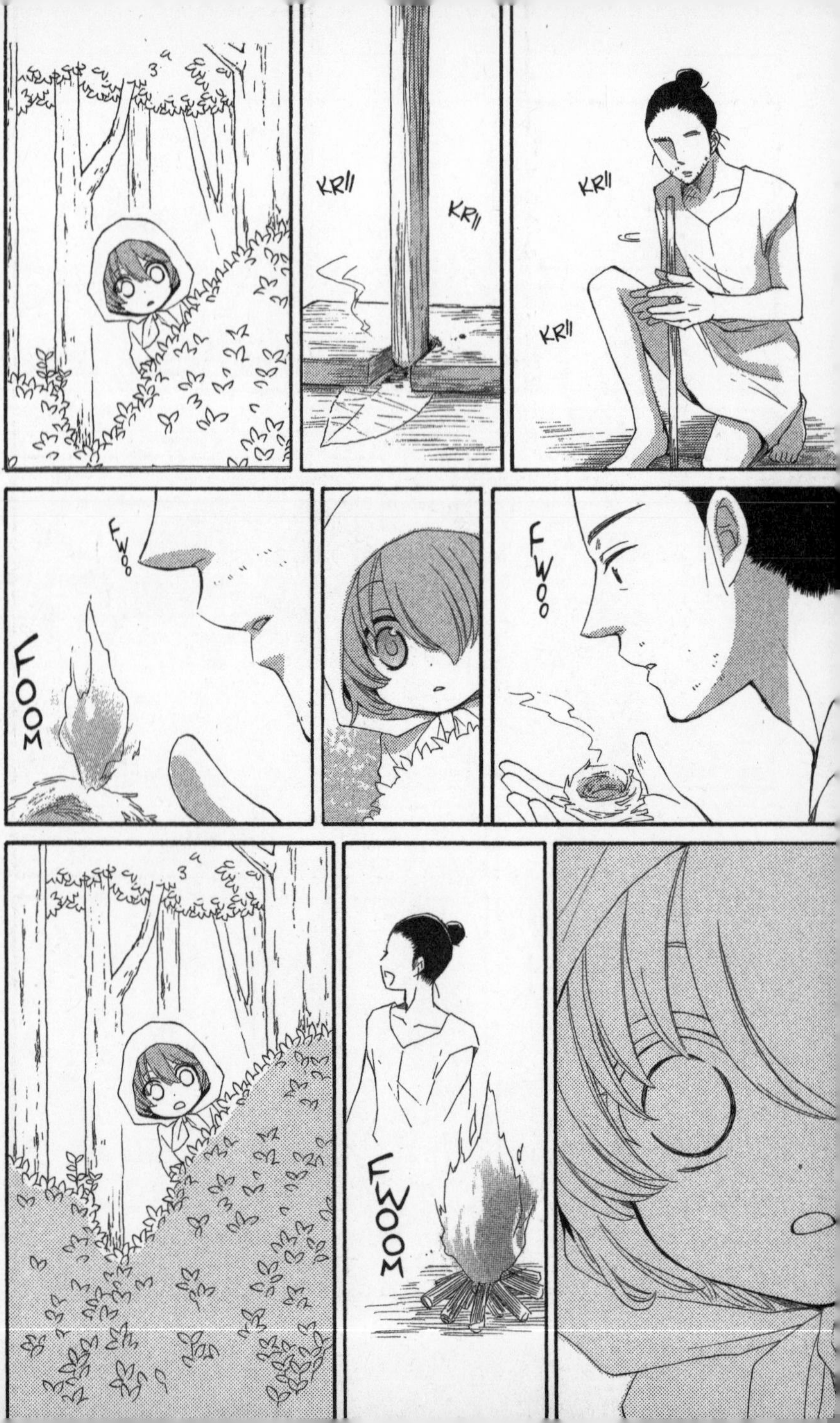
KRII
KRII
KRII
KRII
FWOO
FWOO
FOOM
FWOOM

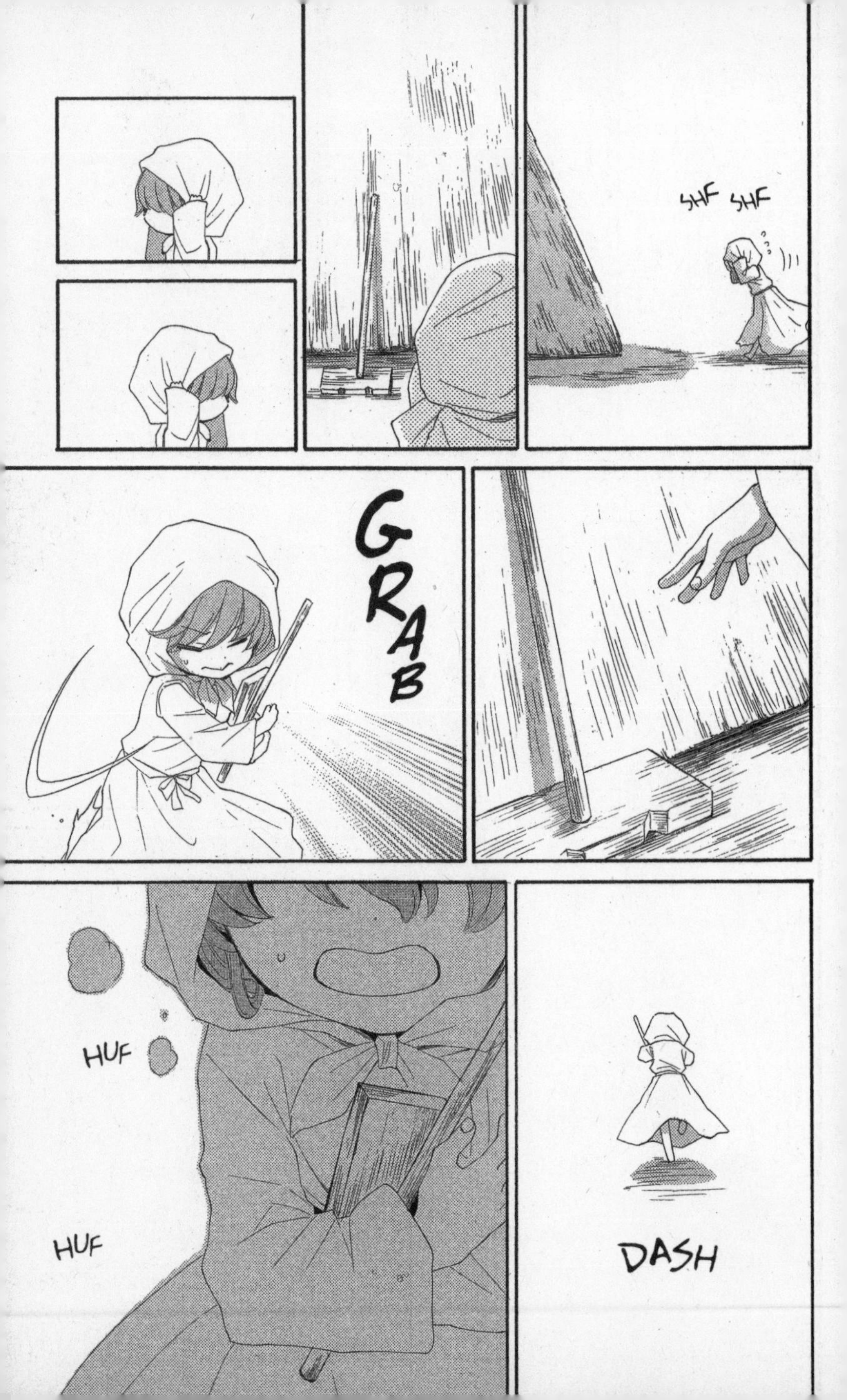
SHF SHF
GRAB
DASH
HUF
HUF

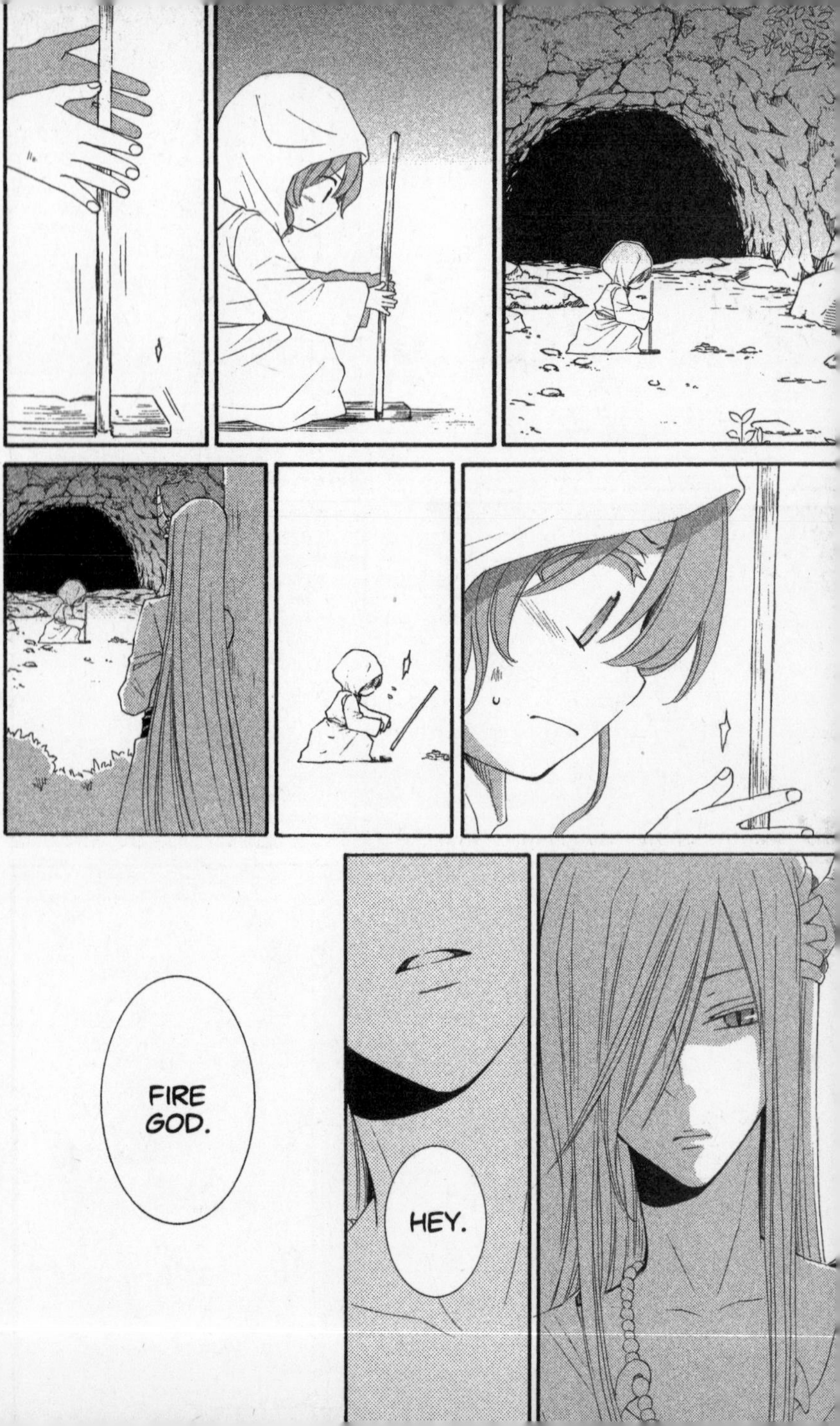
HEY.
FIRE GOD.

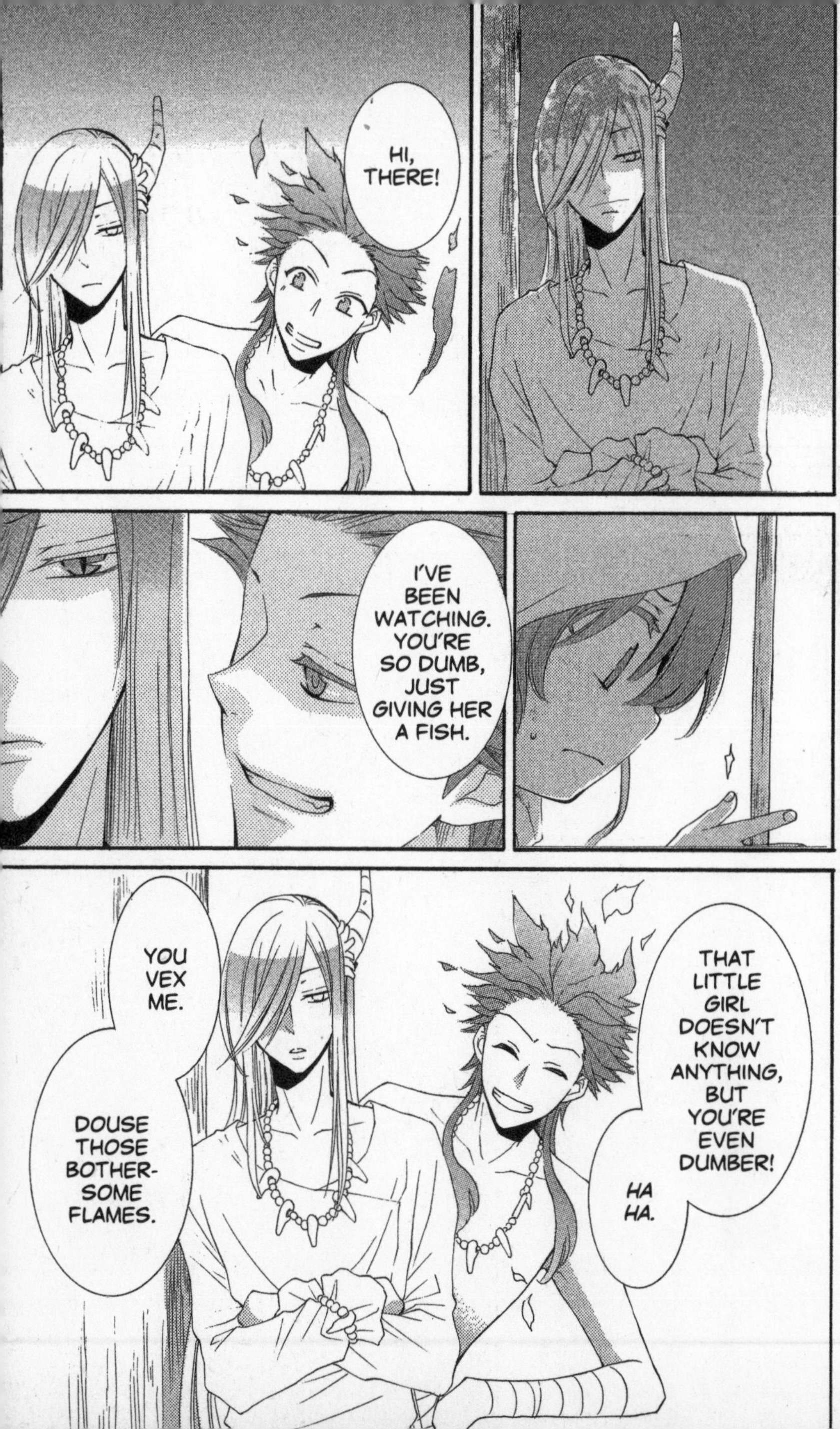
HI, THERE!
I'VE BEEN WATCHING. YOU'RE SO DUMB, JUST GIVING HER A FISH.
THAT LITTLE GIRL DOESN'T KNOW ANYTHING, BUT YOU'RE EVEN DUMBER!
HA HA.
YOU VEX ME.
DOUSE THOSE BOTHER-SOME FLAMES.

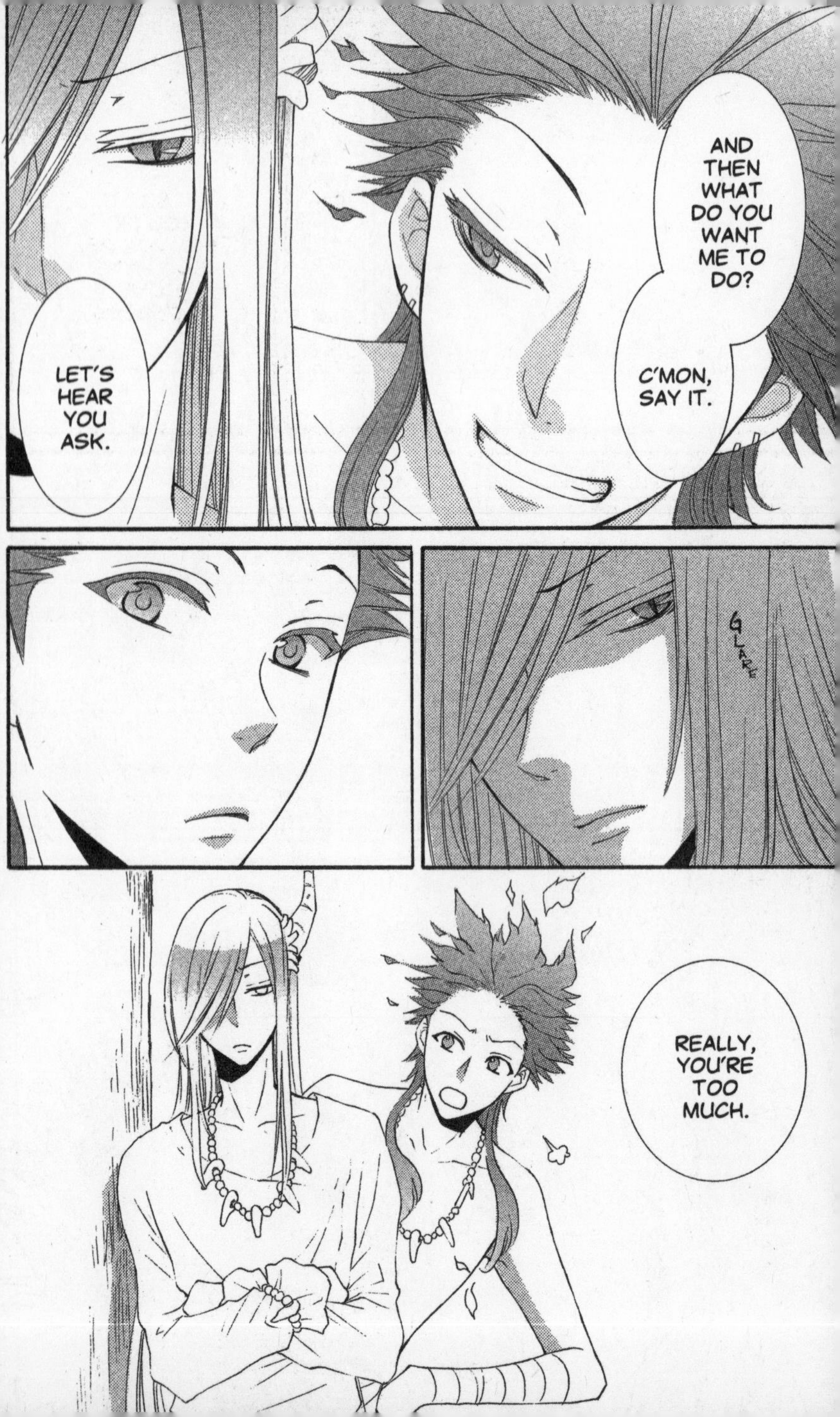
AND THEN WHAT DO YOU WANT ME TO DO?
C'MON, SAY IT.
LET'S HEAR YOU ASK.
GLARE
REALLY, YOU'RE TOO MUCH.

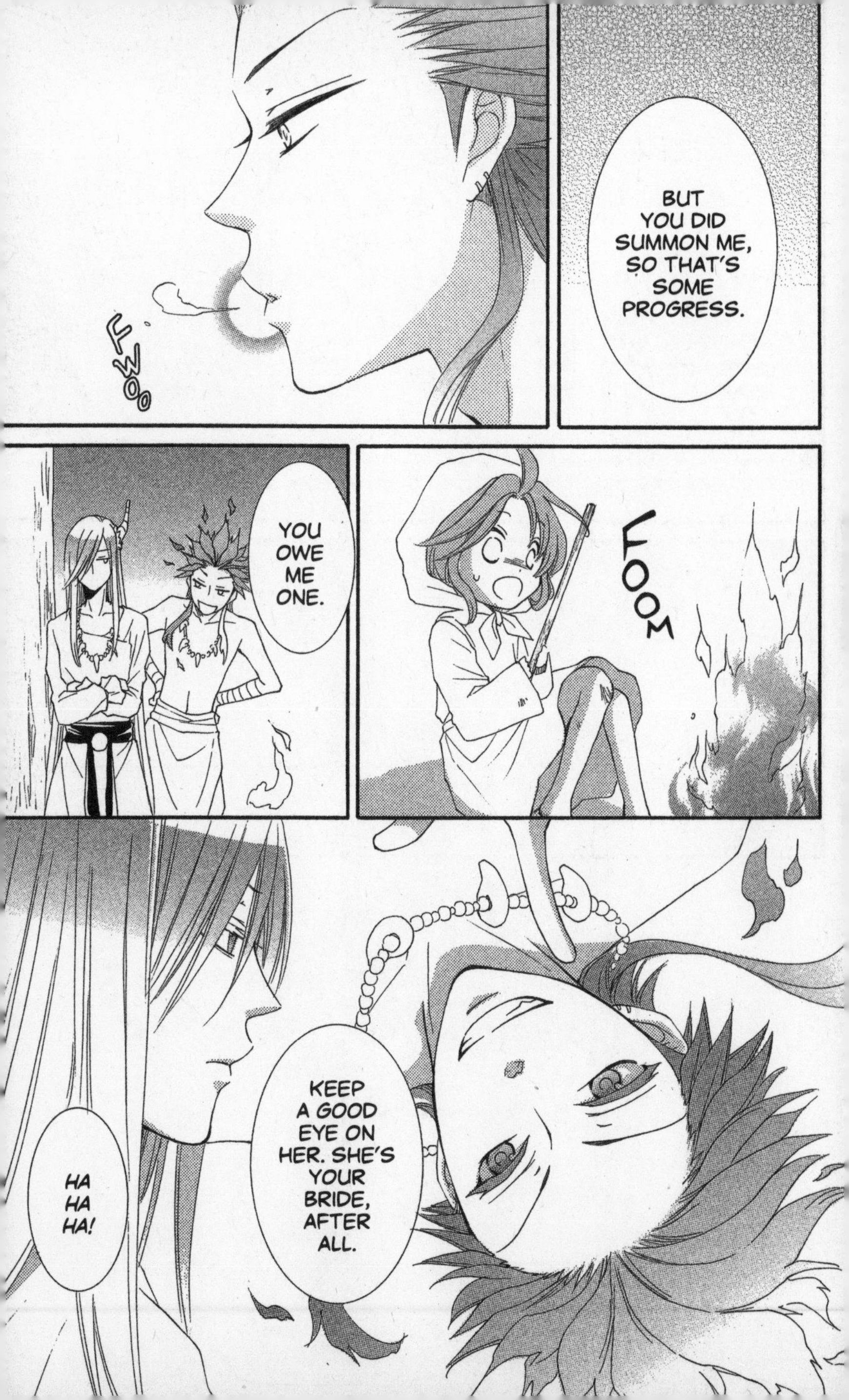
BUT YOU DID SUMMON ME, SO THAT'S SOME PROGRESS.
FWOO
FOOM
YOU OWE ME ONE.
KEEP A GOOD EYE ON HER. SHE'S YOUR BRIDE, AFTER ALL.
HA HA HA!

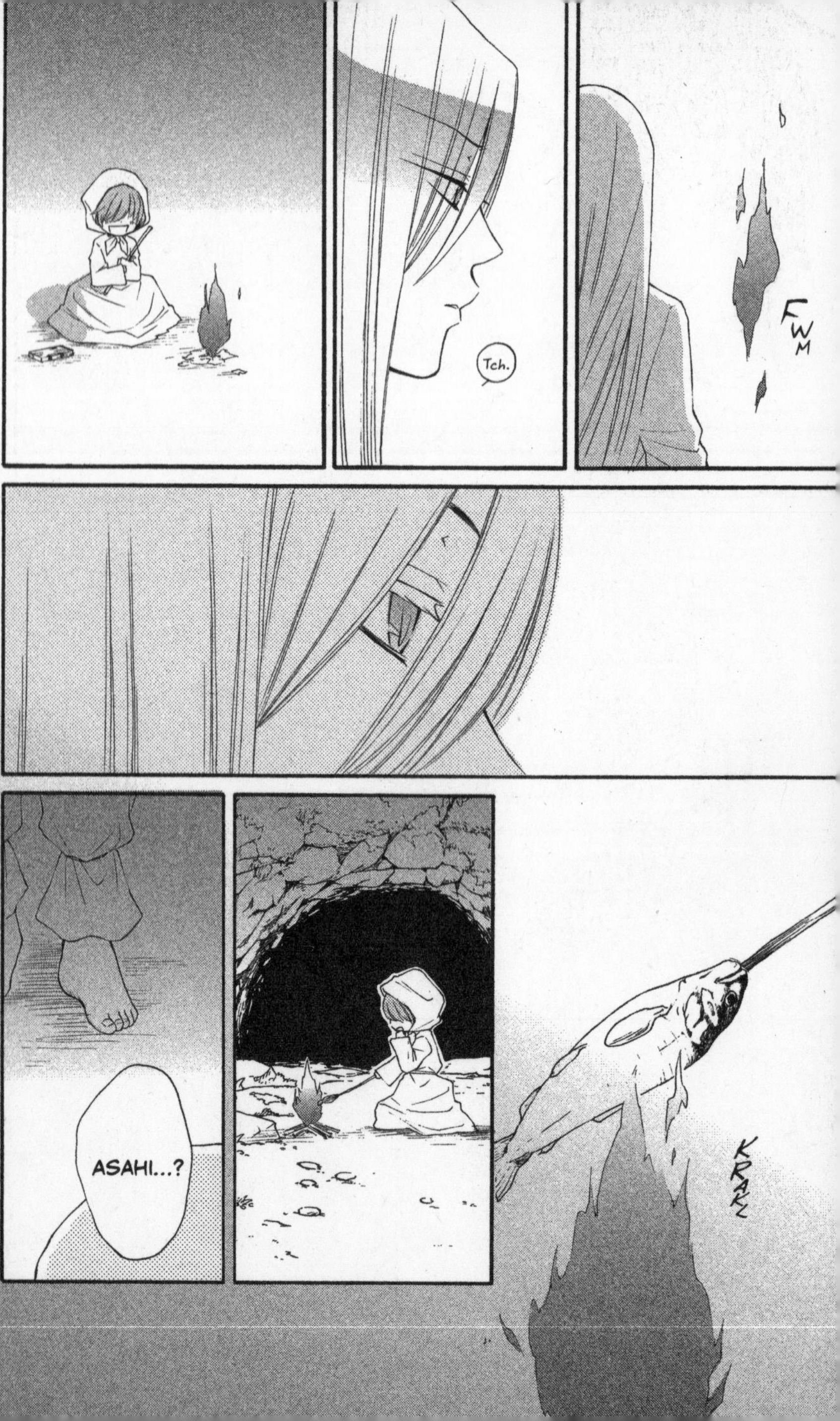
FWM
Tch.
KRAKL
ASAHI...?

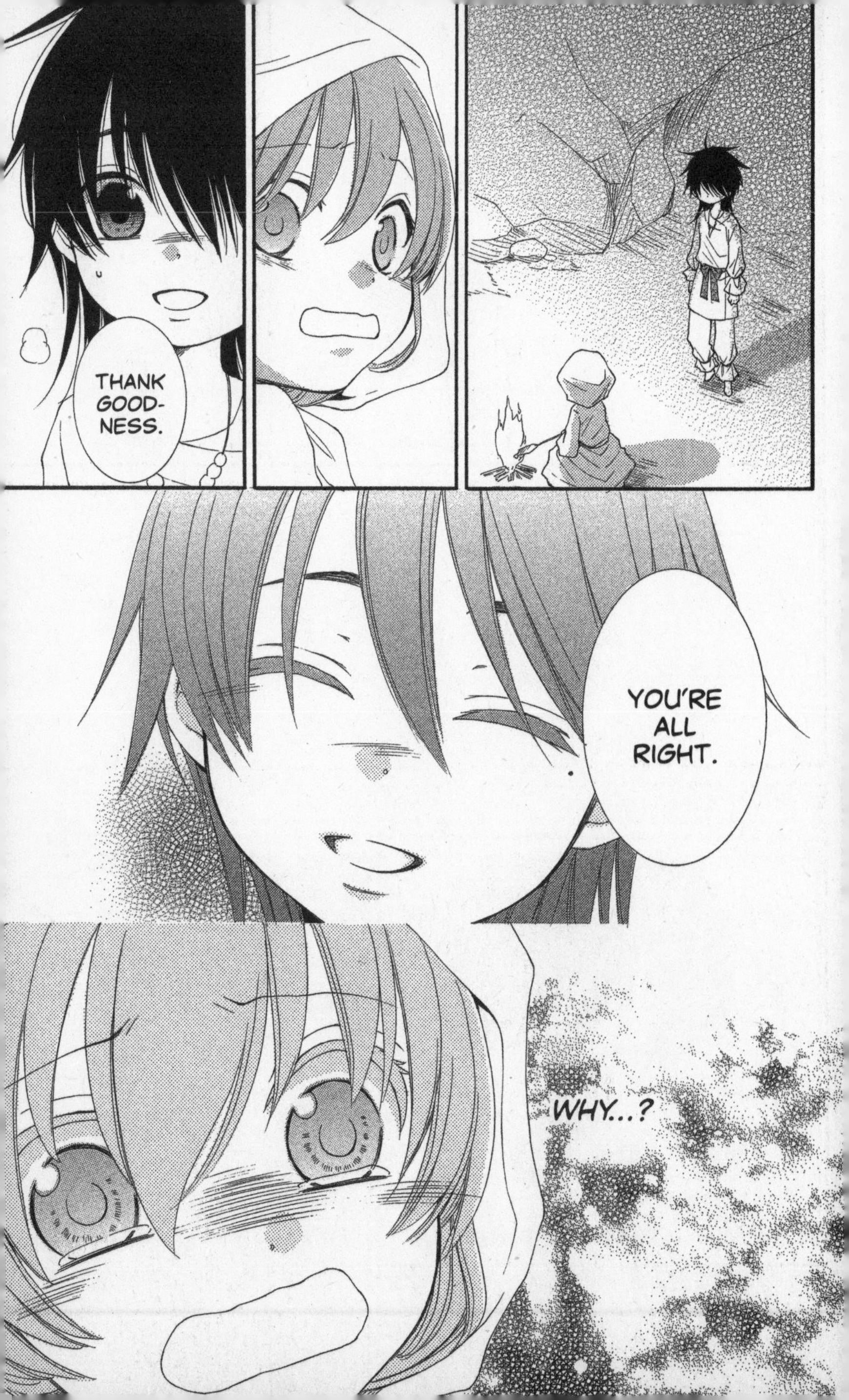
THANK GOOD-NESS.
YOU'RE ALL RIGHT.
WHY...?

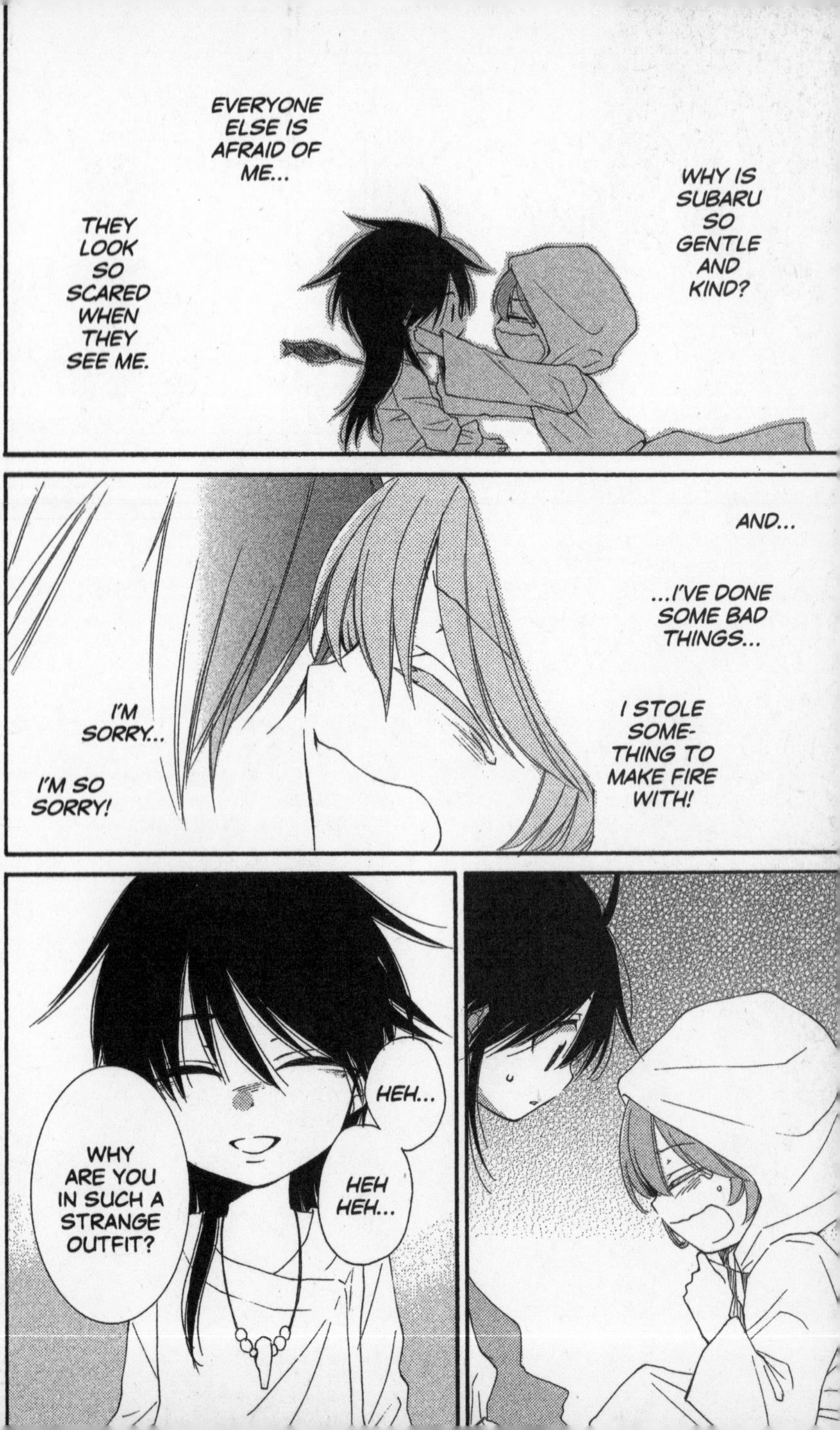
WHY IS SUBARU SO GENTLE AND KIND?
EVERYONE ELSE IS AFRAID OF ME...
THEY LOOK SO SCARED WHEN THEY SEE ME.
AND...
...I'VE DONE SOME BAD THINGS...
I STOLE SOME-THING TO MAKE FIRE WITH!
I'M SORRY...
I'M SO SORRY!
HEH...
HEH HEH...
WHY ARE YOU IN SUCH A STRANGE OUTFIT?

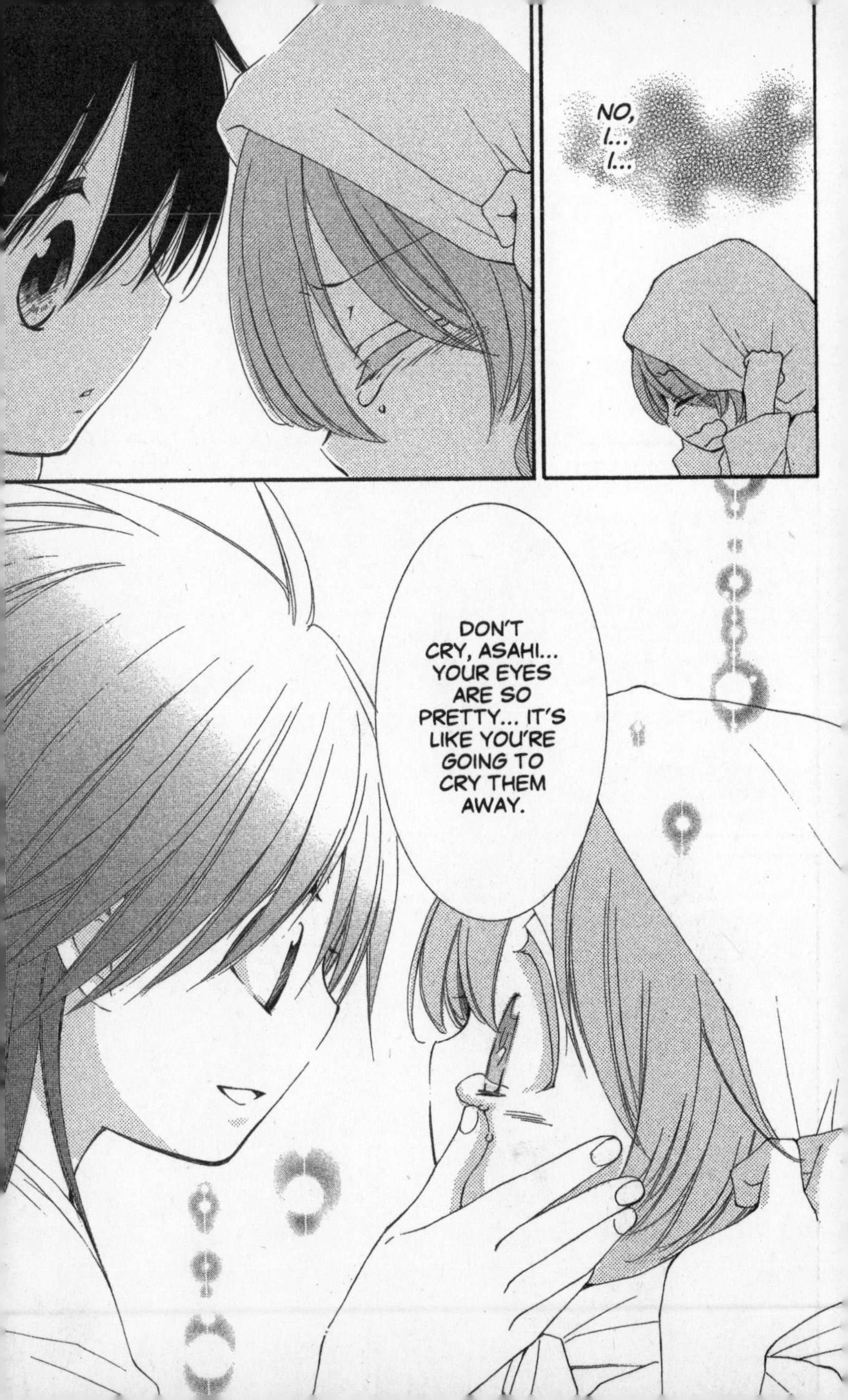
NO, I... I...
DON'T CRY, ASAHI... YOUR EYES ARE SO PRETTY... IT'S LIKE YOU'RE GOING TO CRY THEM AWAY.

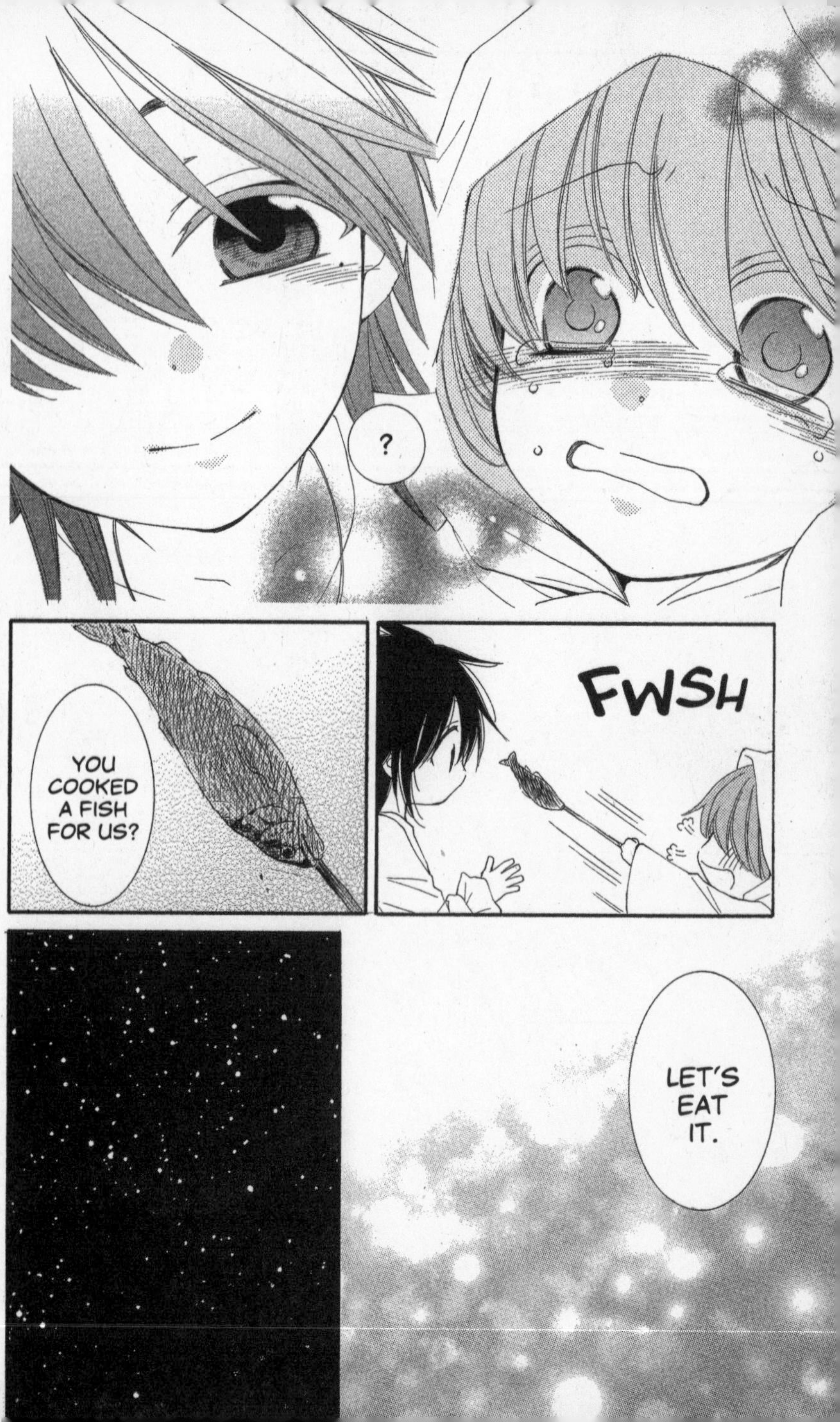
?
FWSH
YOU COOKED A FISH FOR US?
LET'S EAT IT.

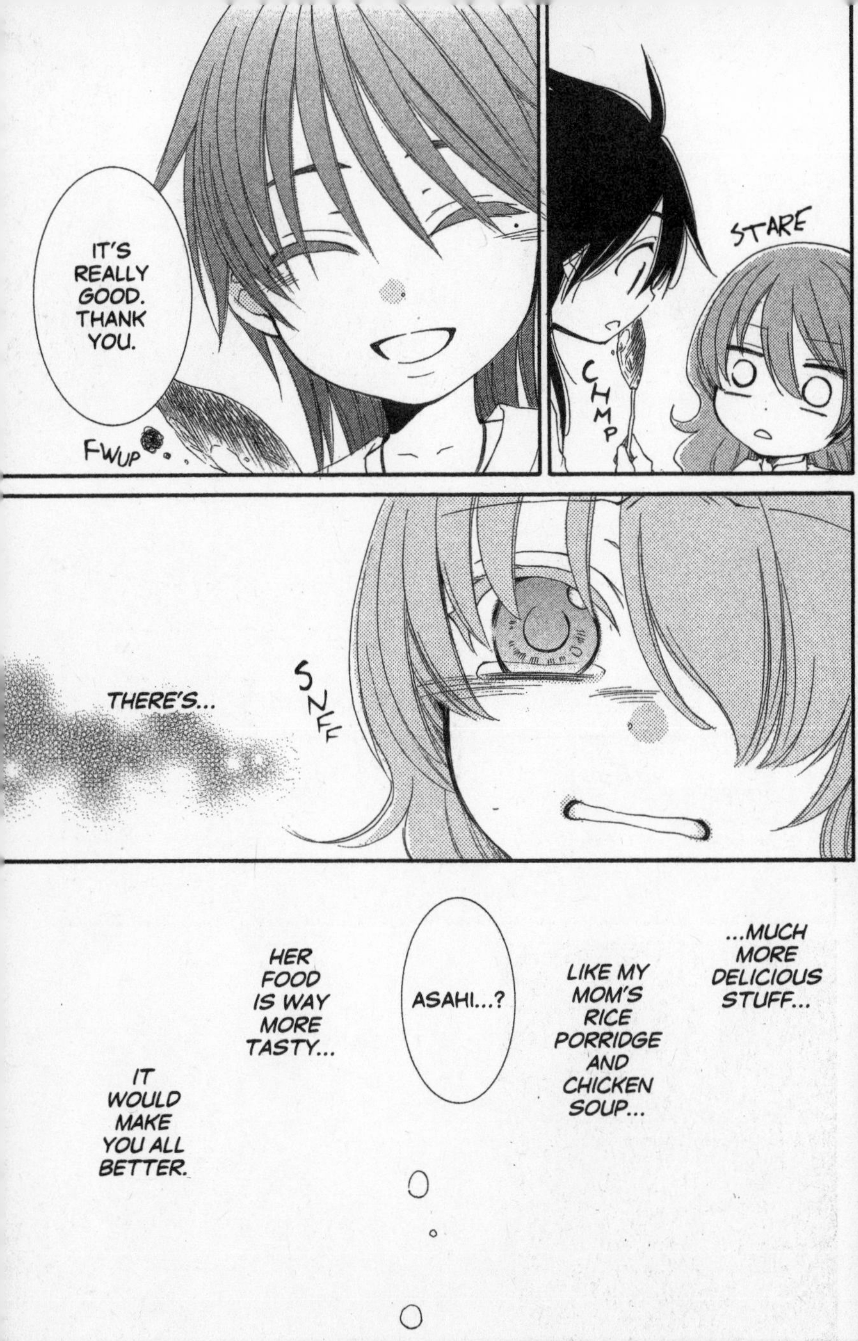
STARE
CHMP
IT'S REALLY GOOD. THANK YOU.
FWUP
SNFF
THERE'S...
...MUCH MORE DELICIOUS STUFF...
LIKE MY MOM'S RICE PORRIDGE AND CHICKEN SOUP...
ASAHI...?
HER FOOD IS WAY MORE TASTY...
IT WOULD MAKE YOU ALL BETTER.

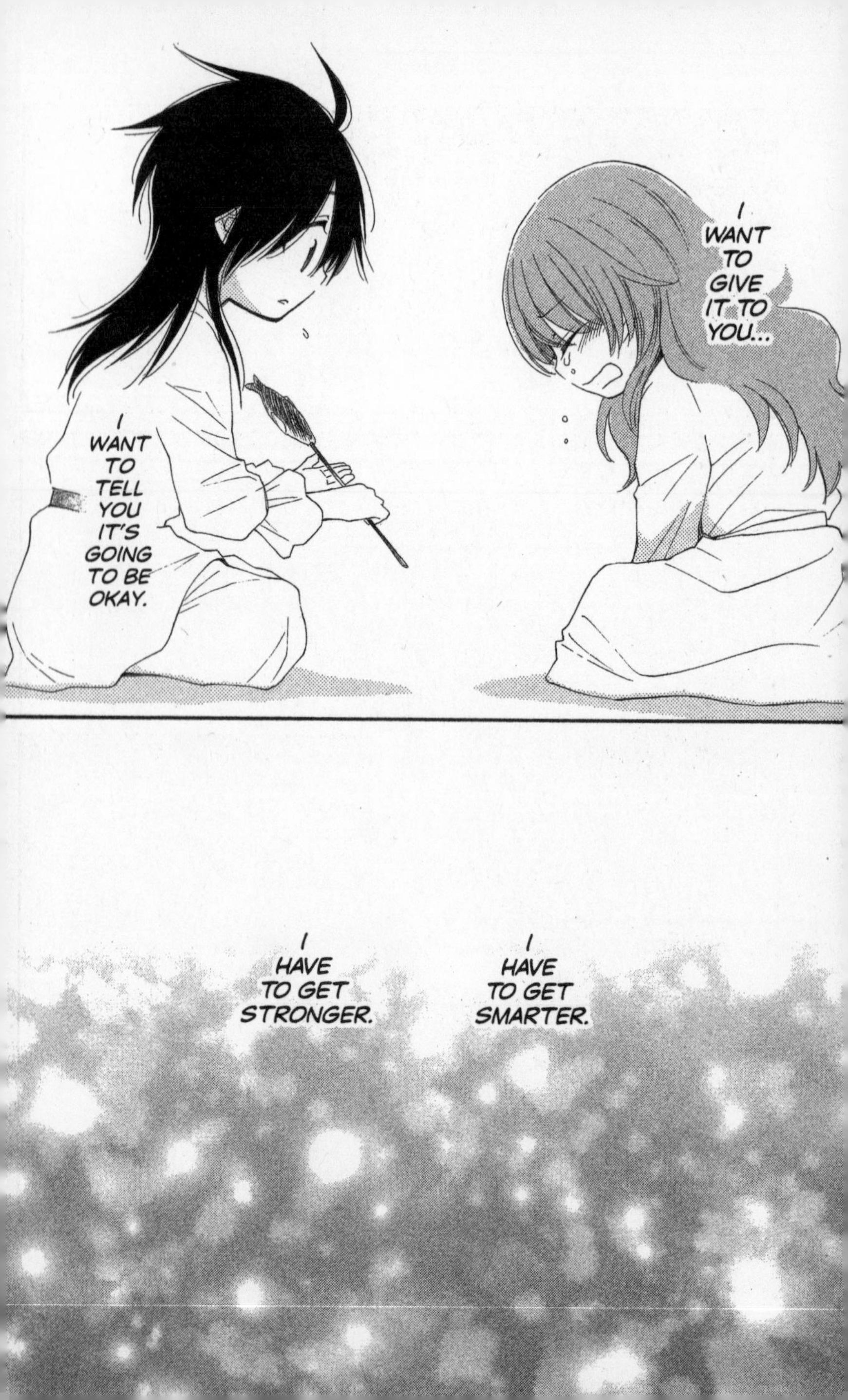
I WANT TO GIVE IT TO YOU...
I WANT TO TELL YOU IT'S GOING TO BE OKAY.
I HAVE TO GET SMARTER.
I HAVE TO GET STRONGER.

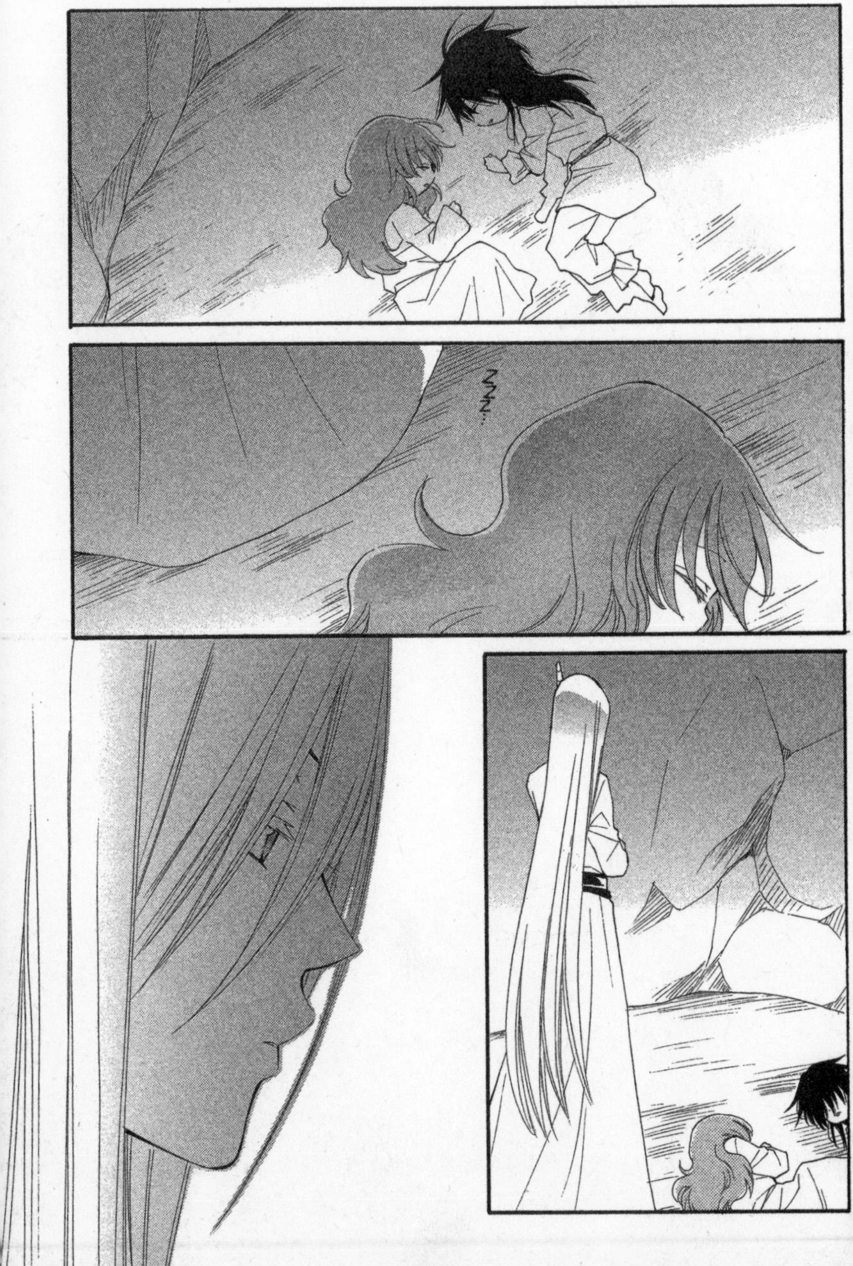
ZZZ...

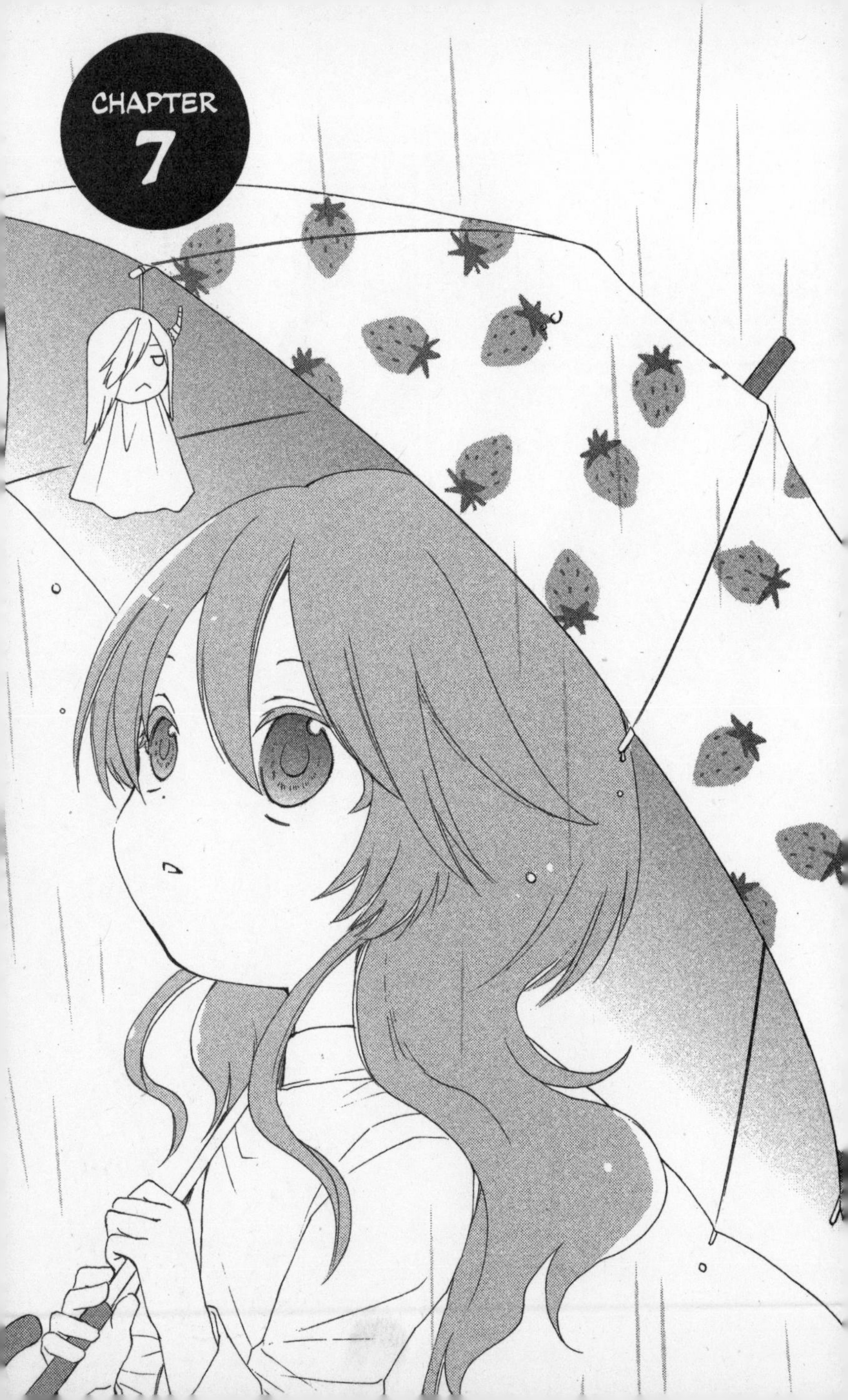
CHAPTER
7

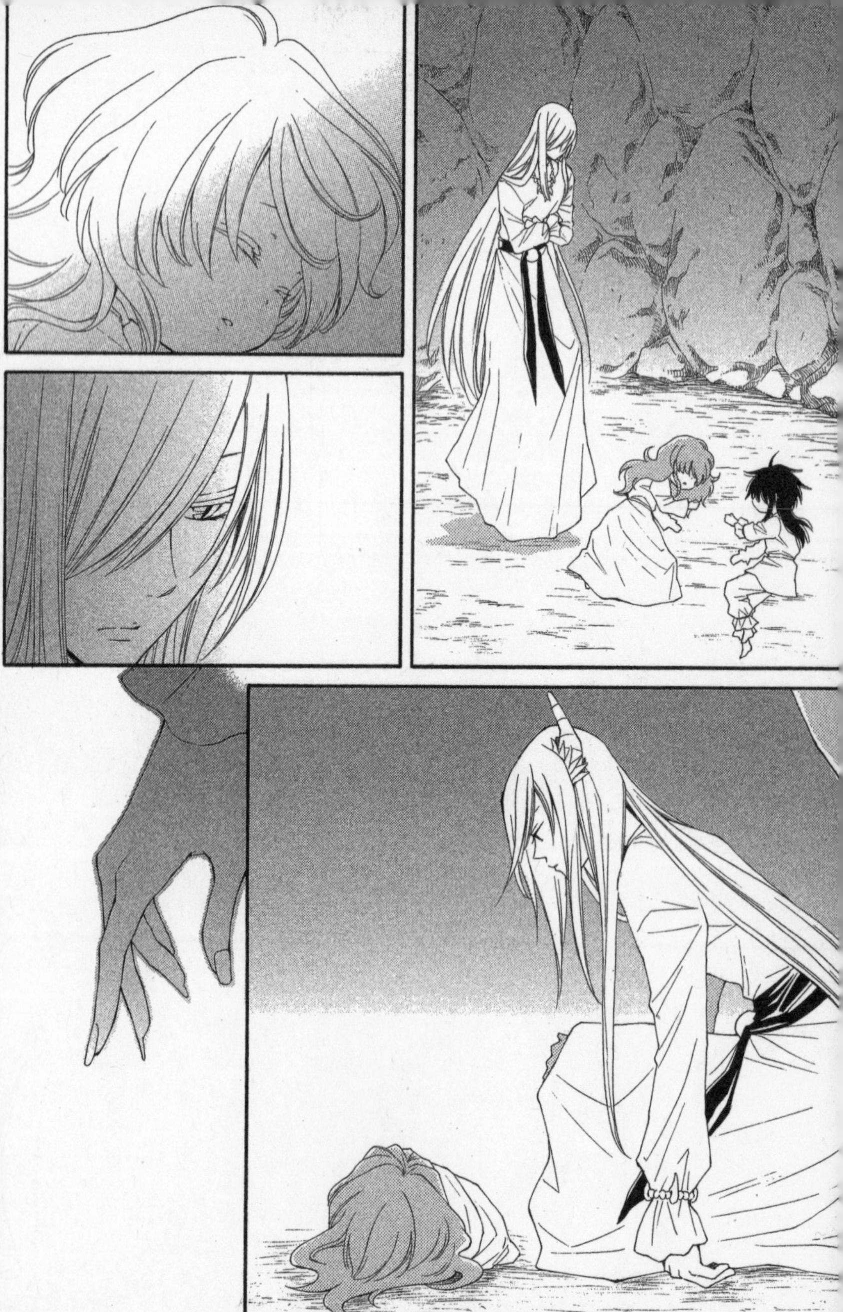

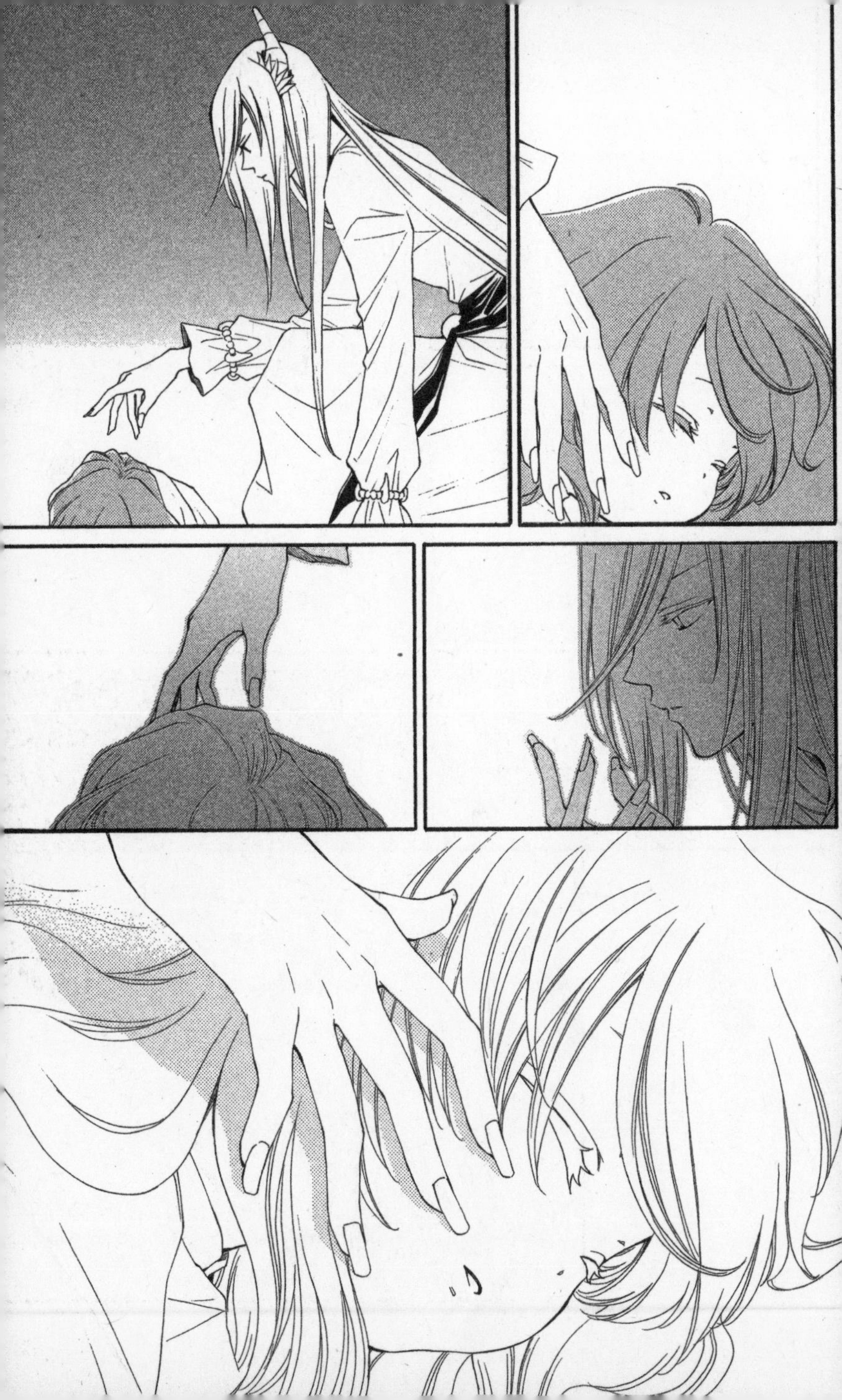

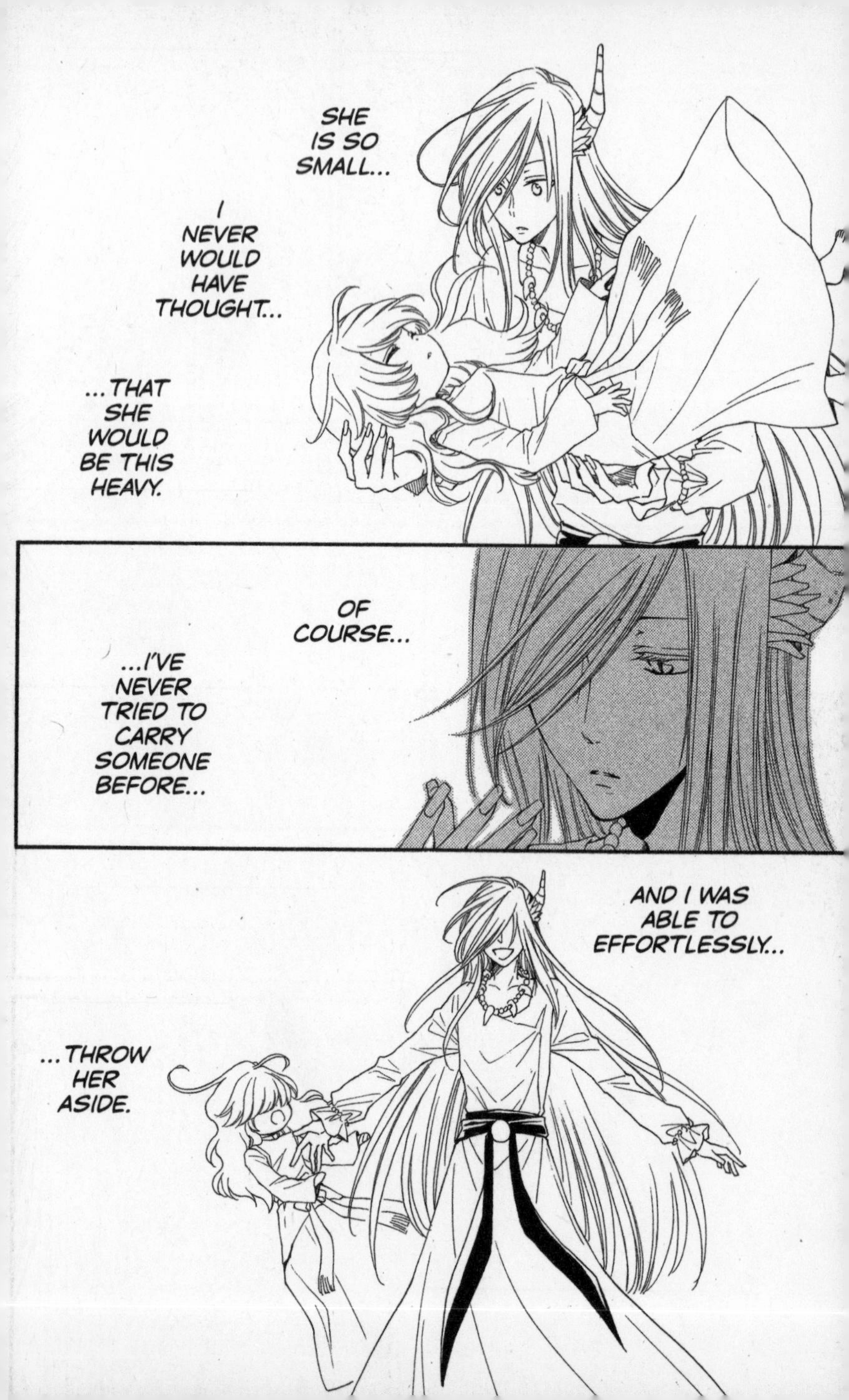
SHE IS SO SMALL...
I NEVER WOULD HAVE THOUGHT...
...THAT SHE WOULD BE THIS HEAVY.
OF COURSE...
...I'VE NEVER TRIED TO CARRY SOMEONE BEFORE...
AND I WAS ABLE TO EFFORTLESSLY...
...THROW HER ASIDE.

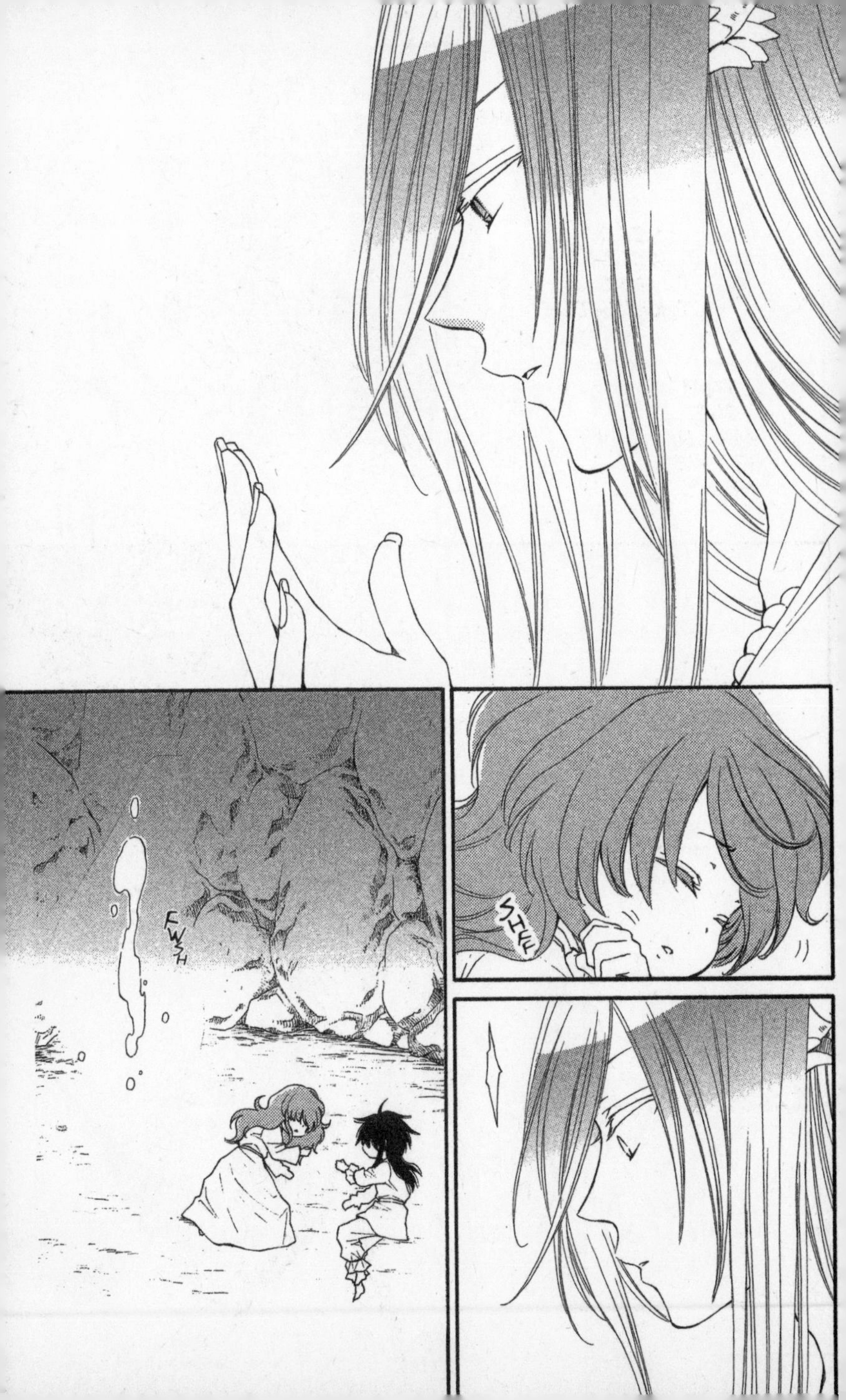
SHFF
FWSH

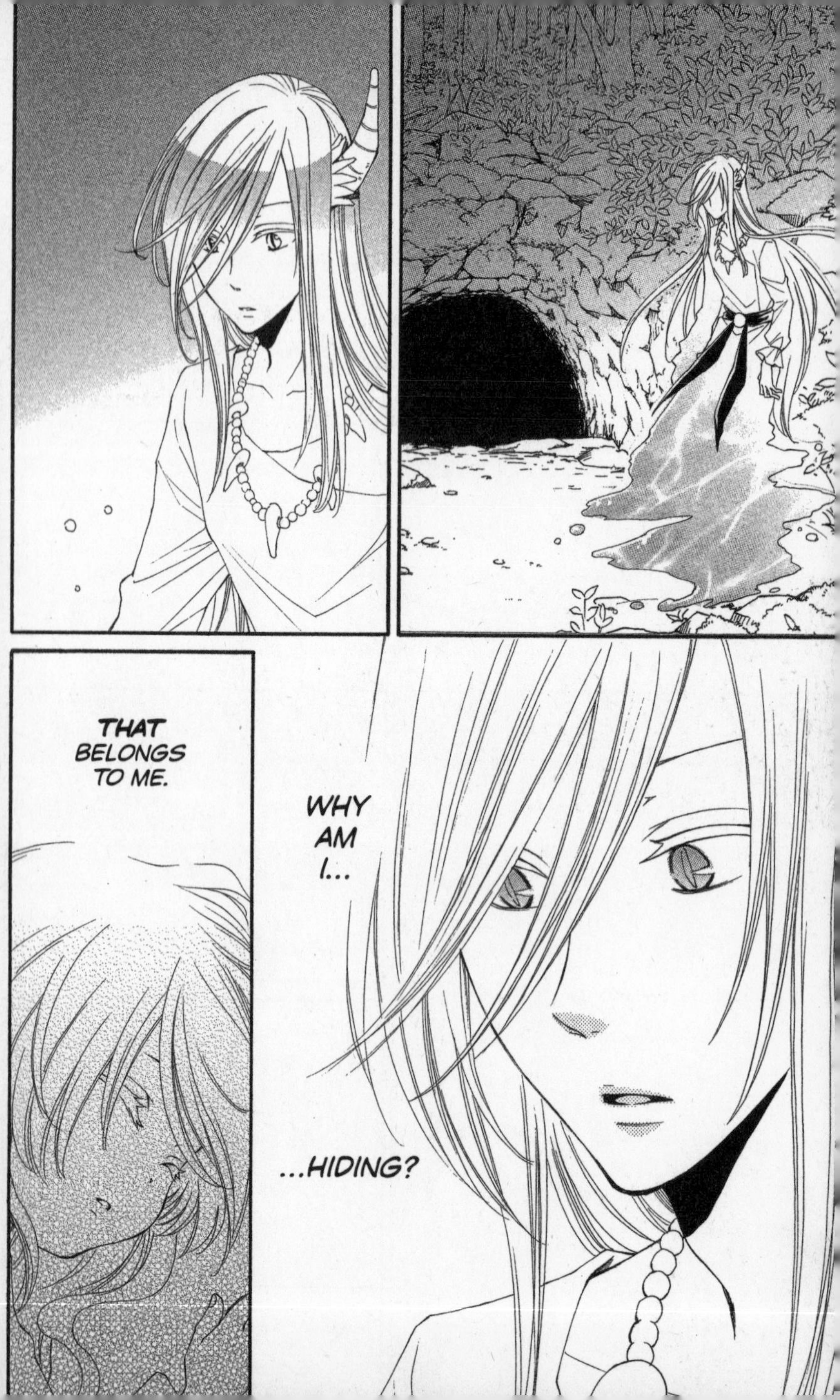
WHY AM I...
...HIDING?
THAT BELONGS TO ME.

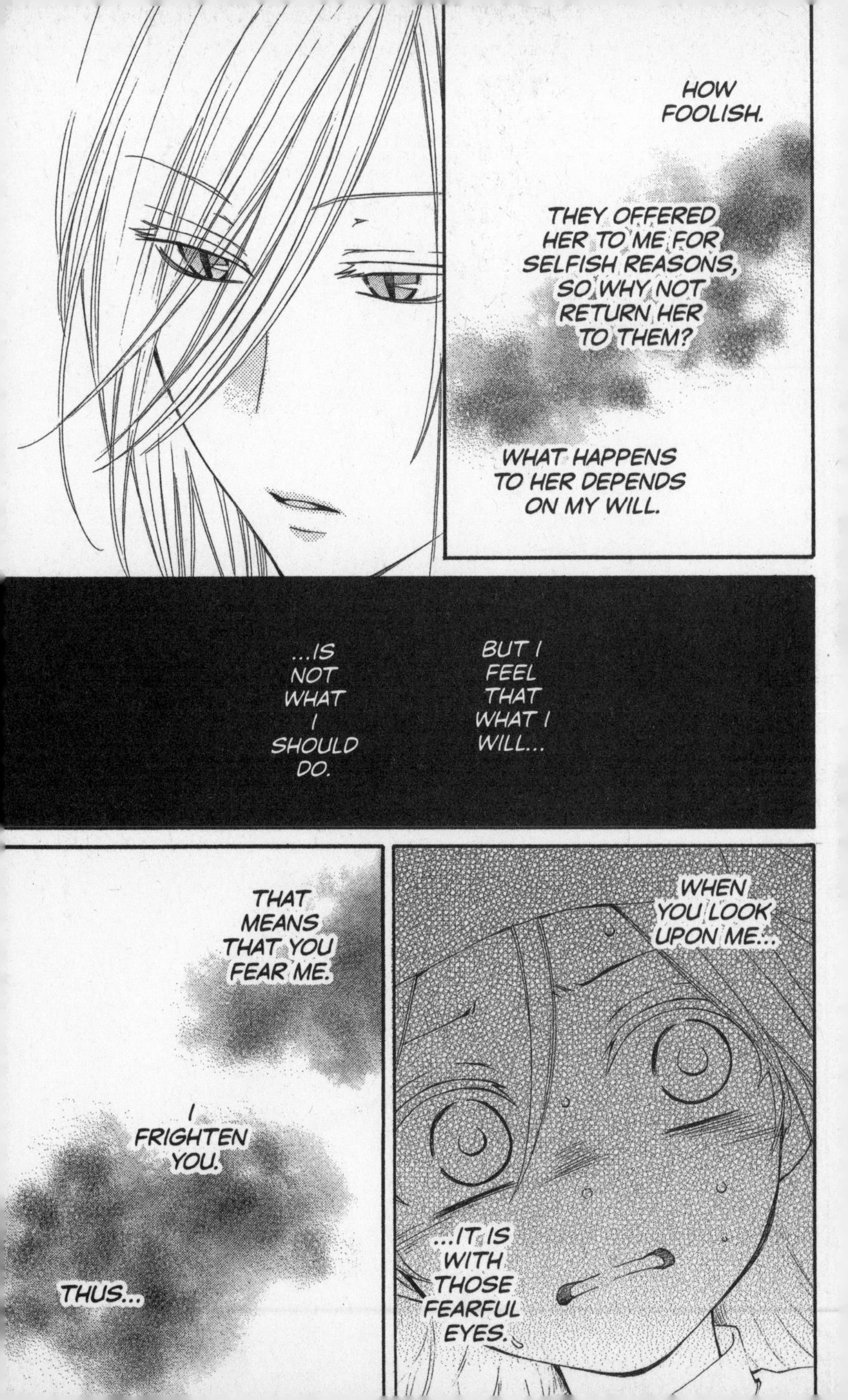
HOW FOOLISH.
THEY OFFERED HER TO ME FOR SELFISH REASONS, SO WHY NOT RETURN HER TO THEM?
WHAT HAPPENS TO HER DEPENDS ON MY WILL.
BUT I FEEL THAT WHAT I WILL...
...IS NOT WHAT I SHOULD DO.
WHEN YOU LOOK UPON ME...
...IT IS WITH THOSE FEARFUL EYES.
THAT MEANS THAT YOU FEAR ME.
I FRIGHTEN YOU.
THUS...

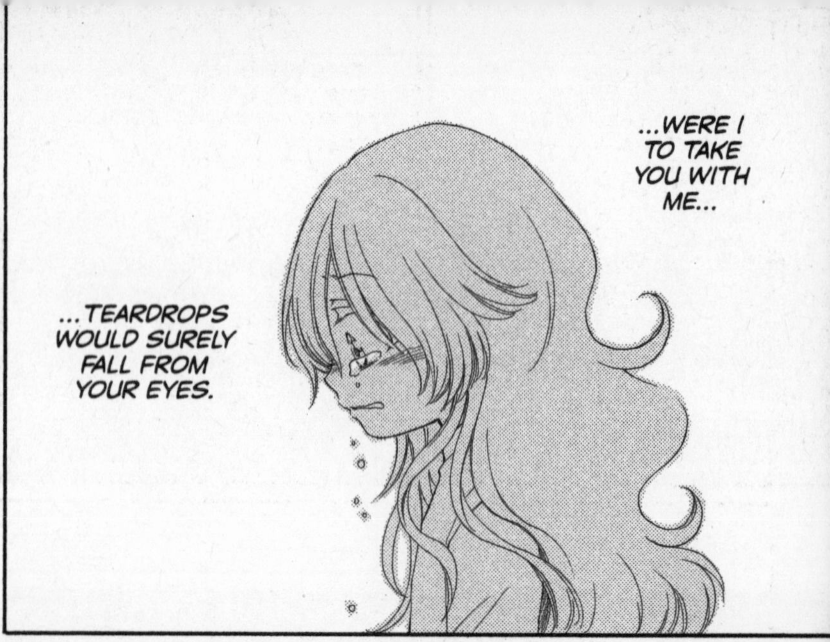
...WERE I TO TAKE YOU WITH ME...
...TEARDROPS WOULD SURELY FALL FROM YOUR EYES.

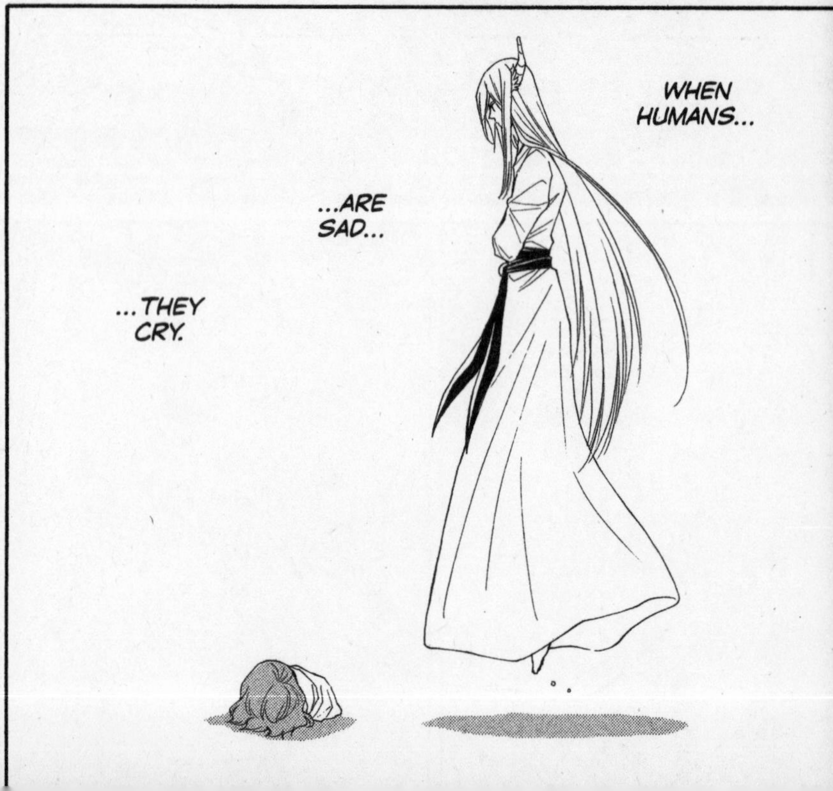
WHEN HUMANS...
...ARE SAD...
...THEY CRY.

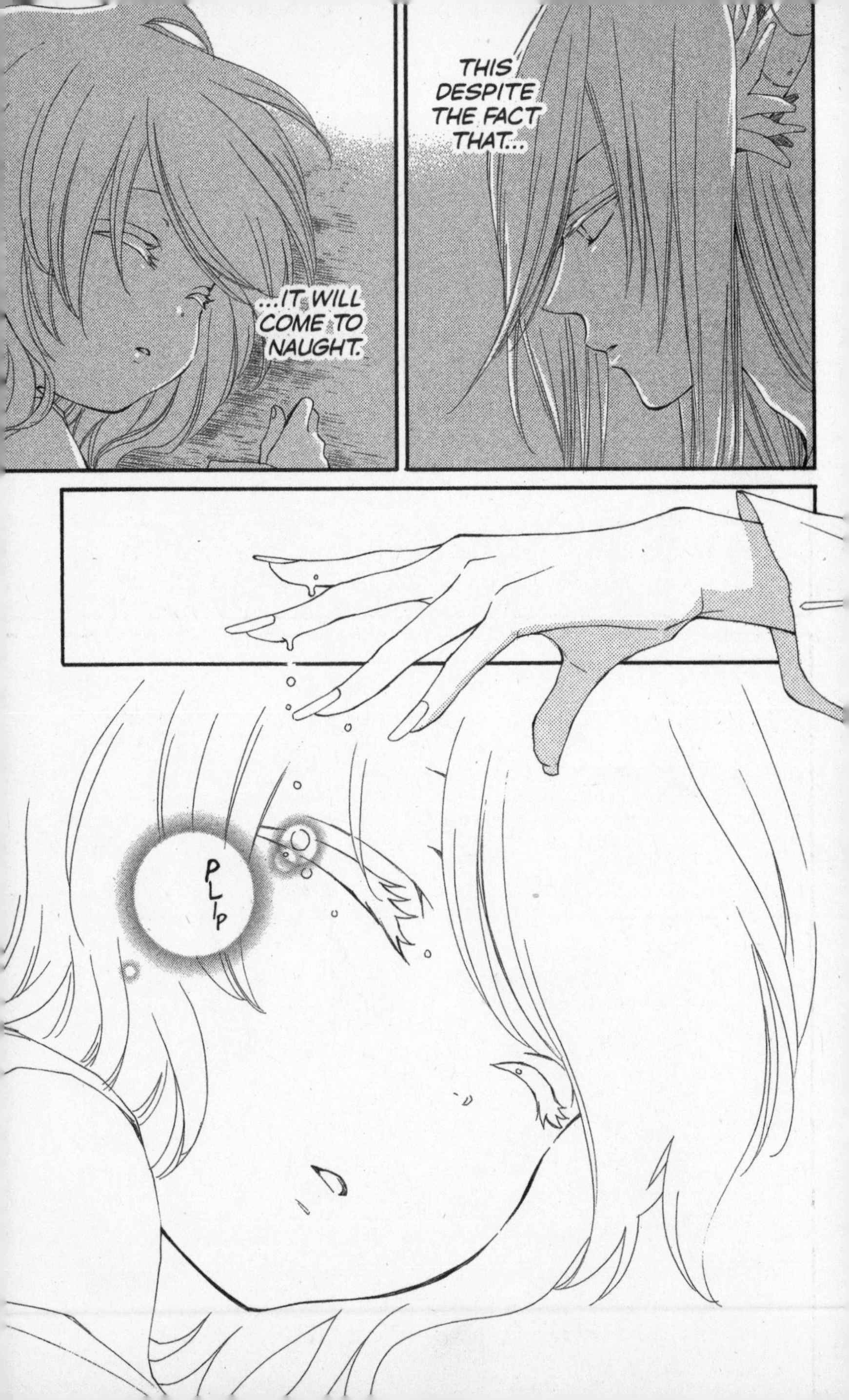
THIS DESPITE THE FACT THAT...
...IT WILL COME TO NAUGHT.
PLIP

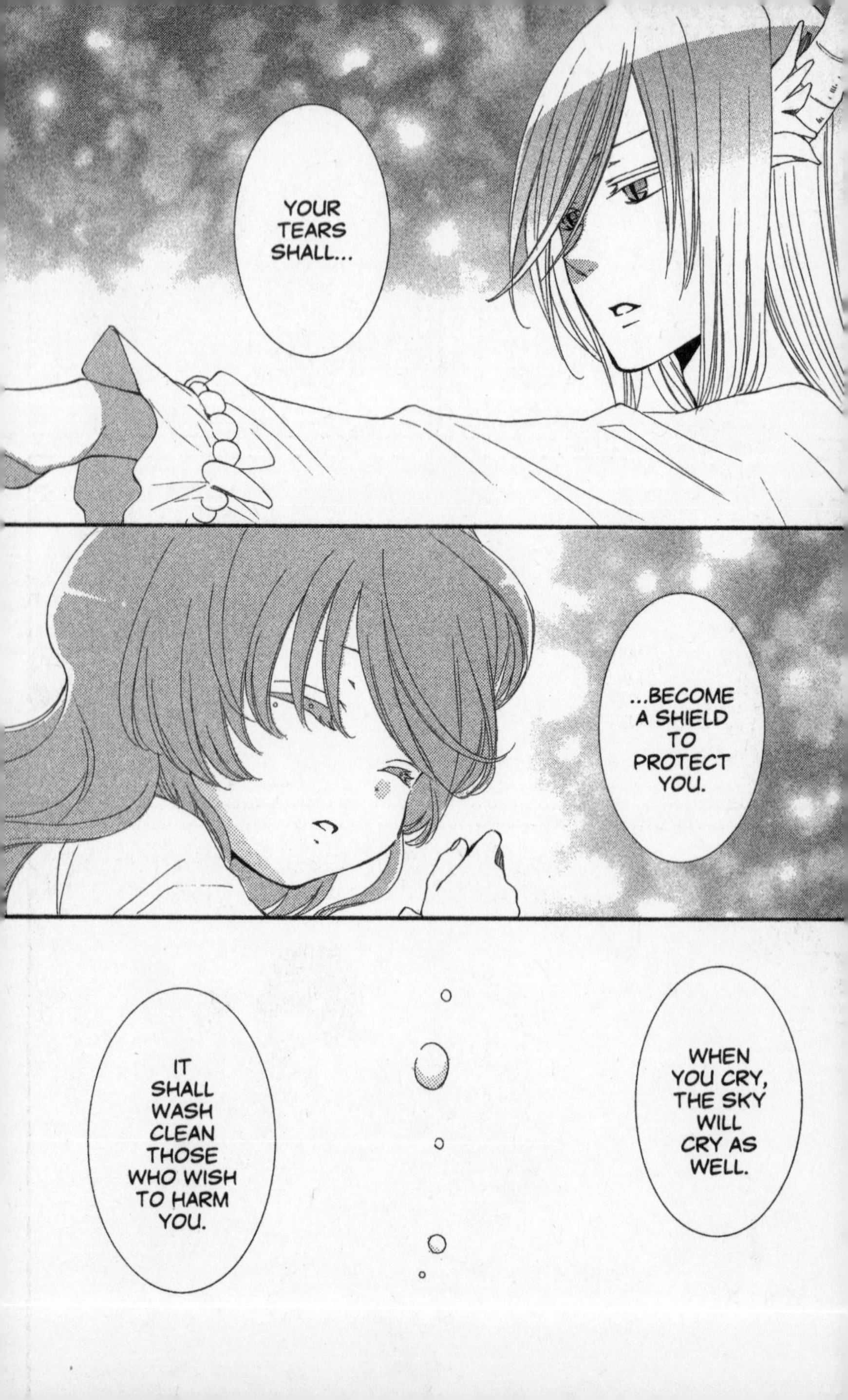
YOUR TEARS SHALL...
...BECOME A SHIELD TO PROTECT YOU.
WHEN YOU CRY, THE SKY WILL CRY AS WELL.
IT SHALL WASH CLEAN THOSE WHO WISH TO HARM YOU.

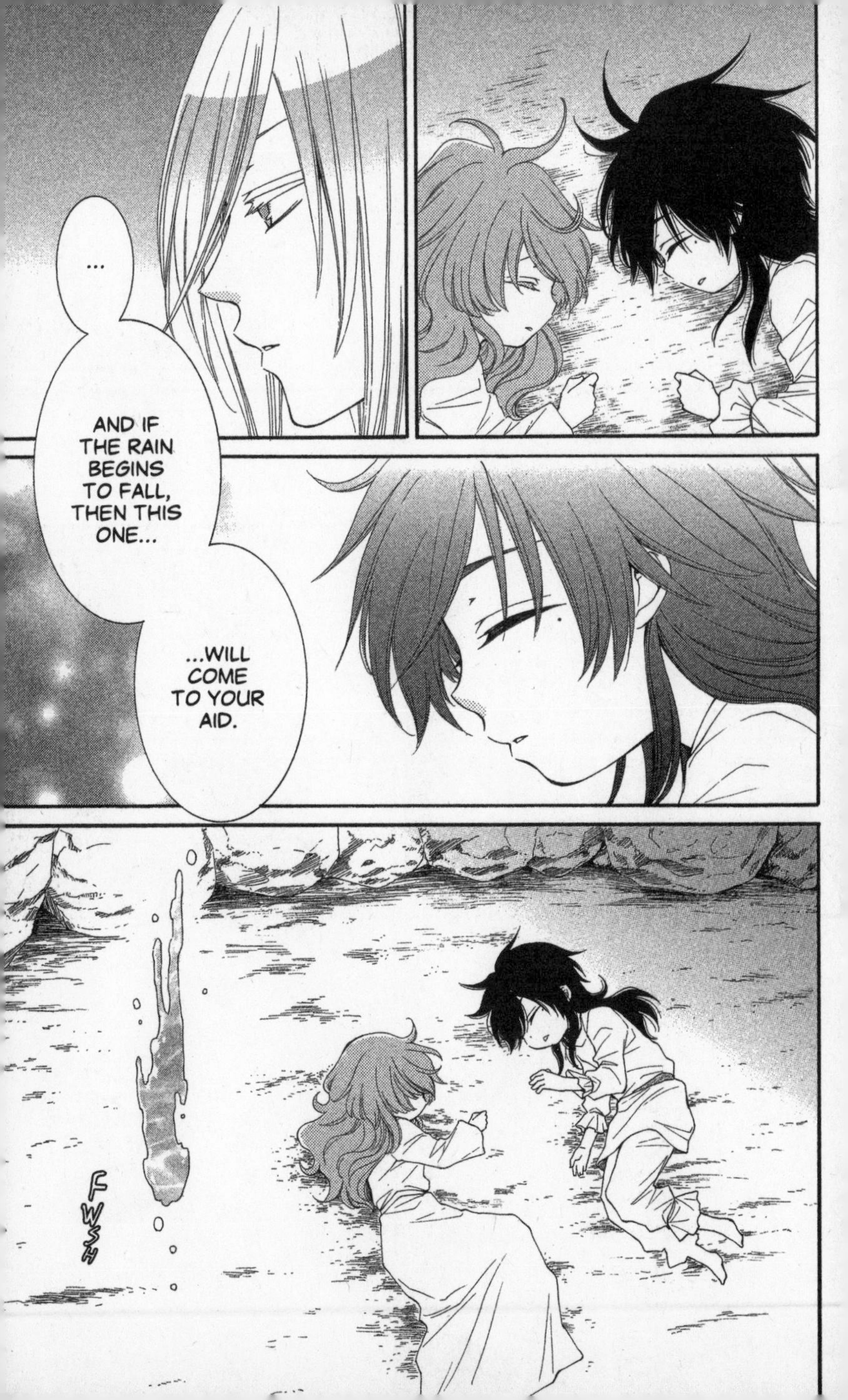
...
AND IF THE RAIN BEGINS TO FALL, THEN THIS ONE...
...WILL COME TO YOUR AID.
FWSH

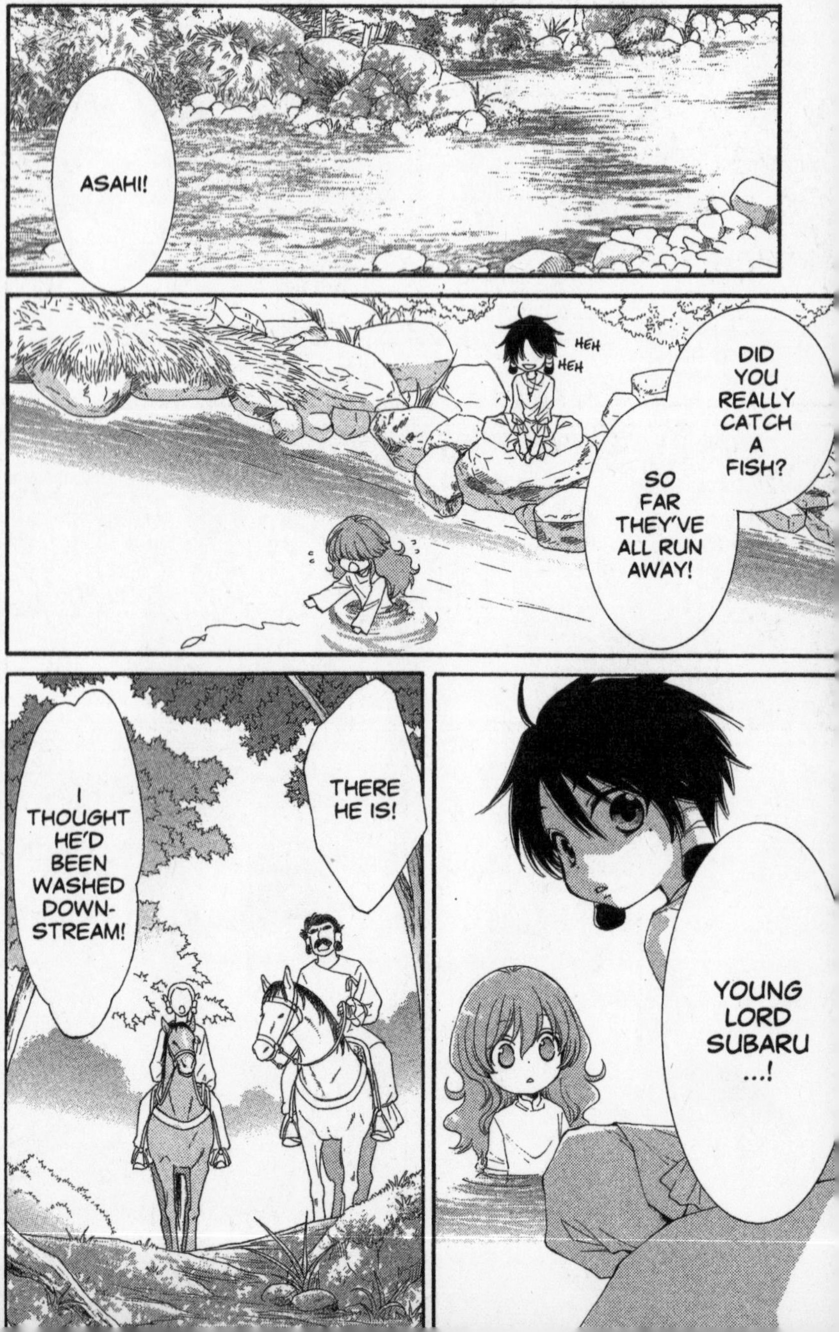
ASAHI!
DID YOU REALLY CATCH A FISH?
HEH HEH
SO FAR THEY'VE ALL RUN AWAY!
YOUNG LORD SUBARU ...!
THERE HE IS!
I THOUGHT HE'D BEEN WASHED DOWN-STREAM!

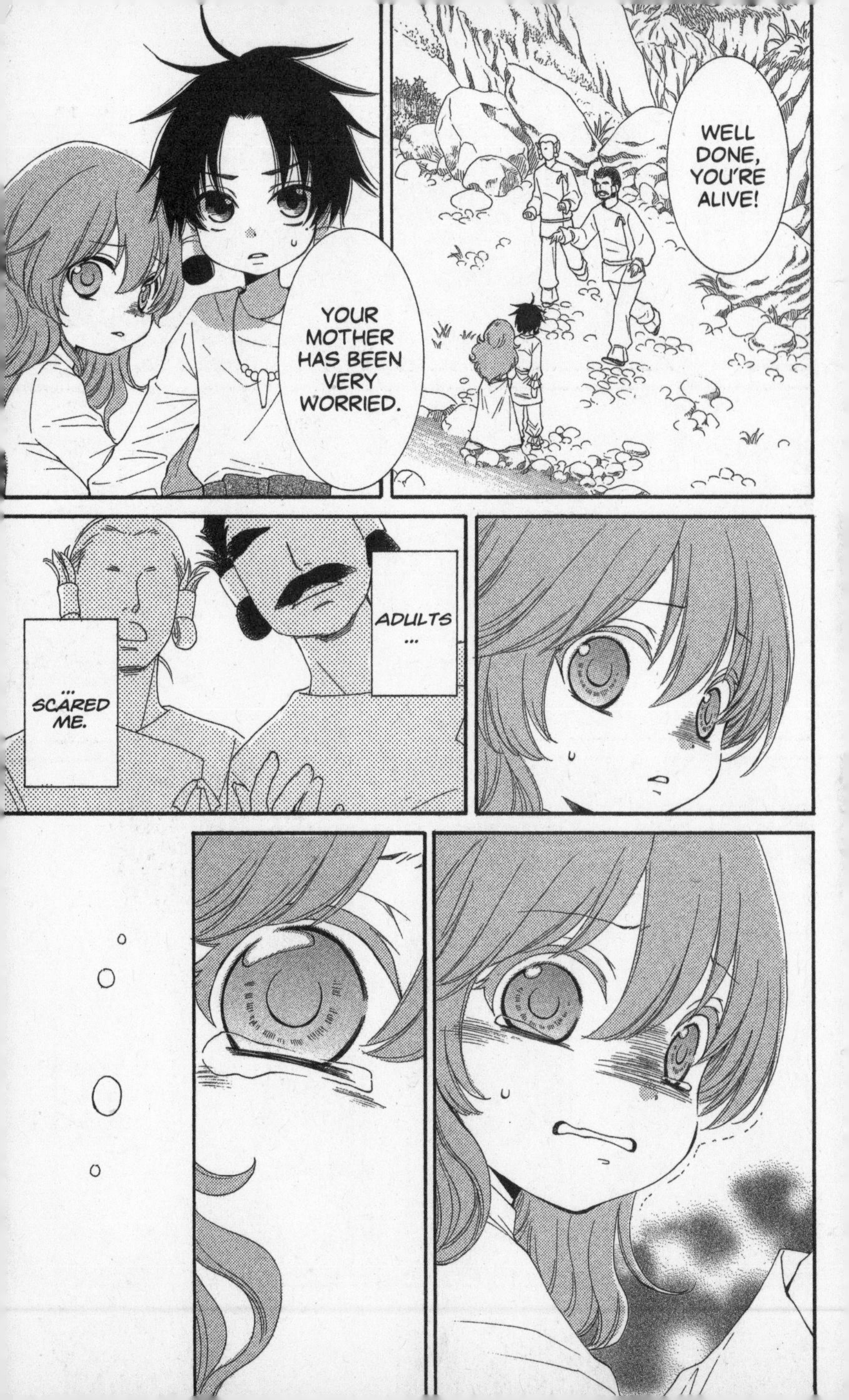
WELL DONE, YOU'RE ALIVE!
YOUR MOTHER HAS BEEN VERY WORRIED.
ADULTS ...
... SCARED ME.

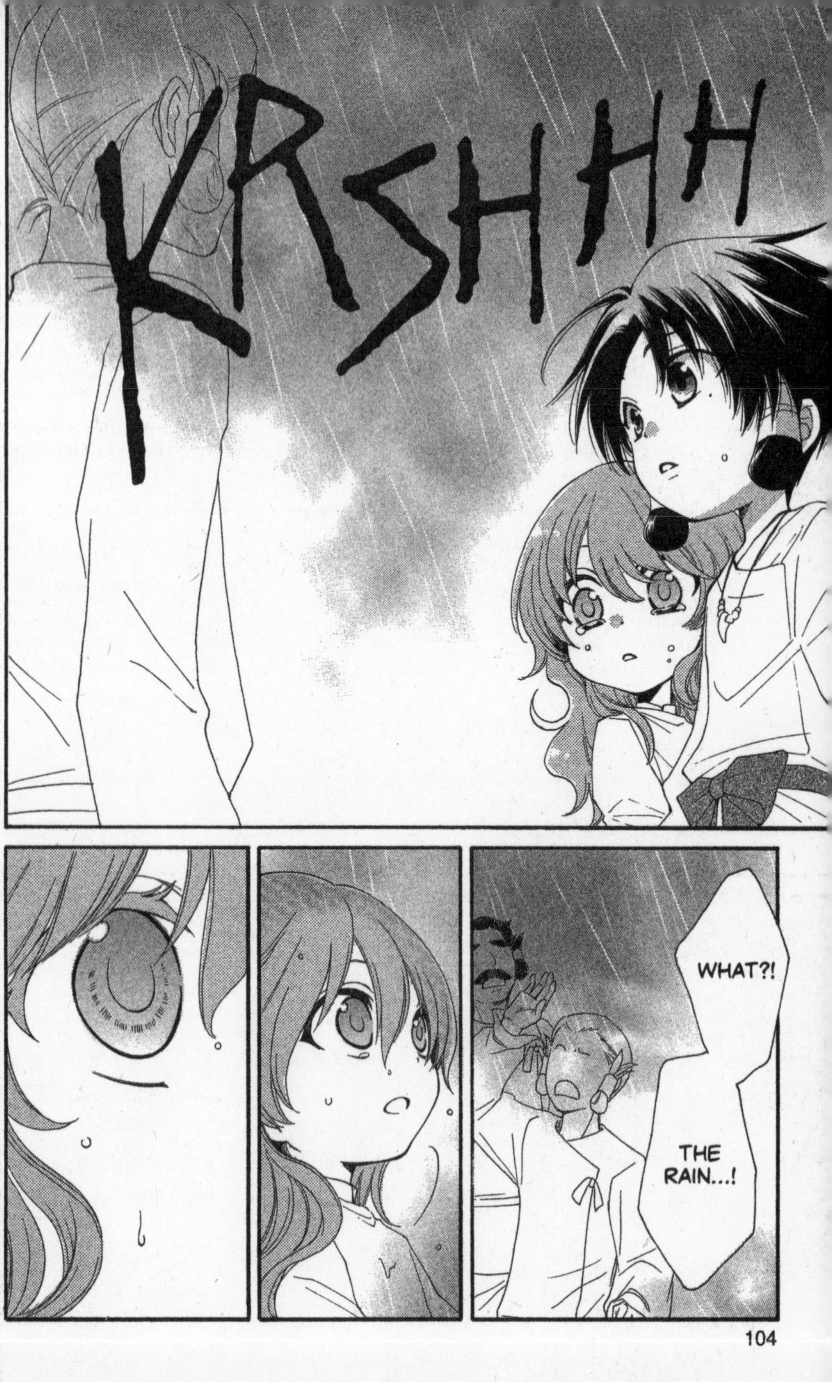
KRSHHH
WHAT?!
THE RAIN...!

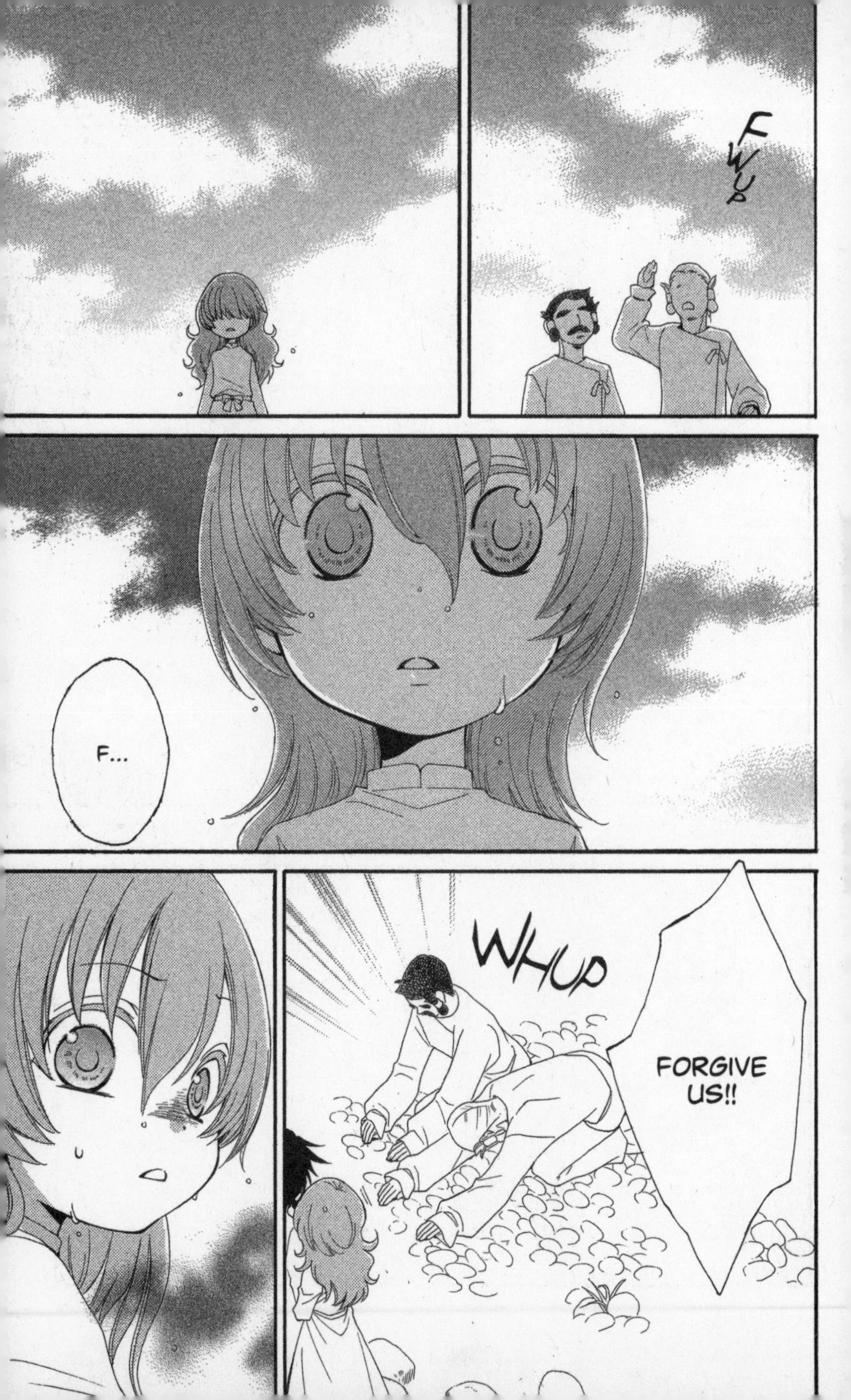
FWUP
F...
WHUP
FORGIVE US!!

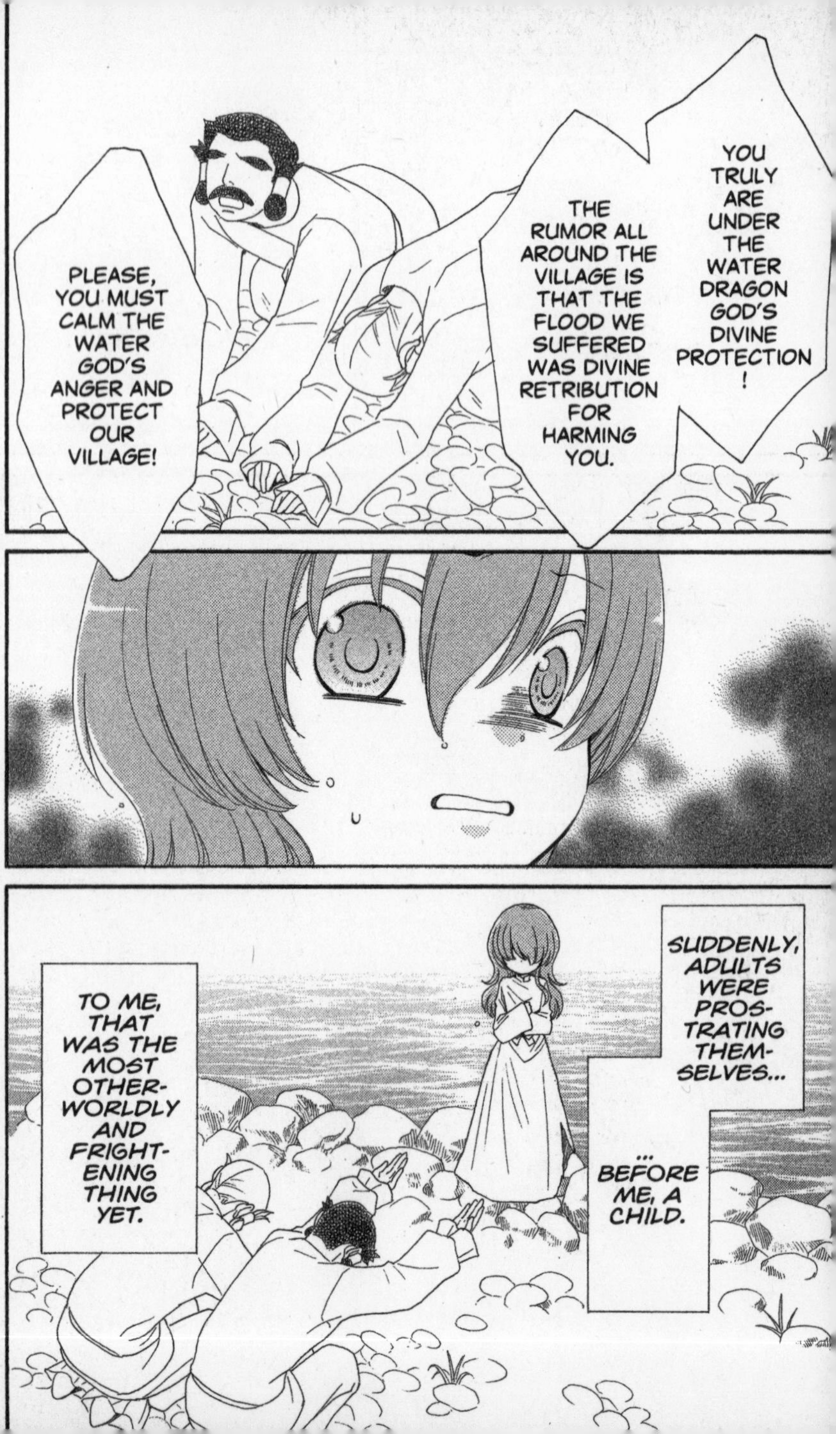
YOU TRULY ARE UNDER THE WATER DRAGON GOD'S DIVINE PROTECTION!
THE RUMOR ALL AROUND THE VILLAGE IS THAT THE FLOOD WE SUFFERED WAS DIVINE RETRIBUTION FOR HARMING YOU.
PLEASE, YOU MUST CALM THE WATER GOD'S ANGER AND PROTECT OUR VILLAGE!
SUDDENLY, ADULTS WERE PROS-TRATING THEM-SELVES...
...BEFORE ME, A CHILD.
TO ME, THAT WAS THE MOST OTHER-WORLDLY AND FRIGHT-ENING THING YET.

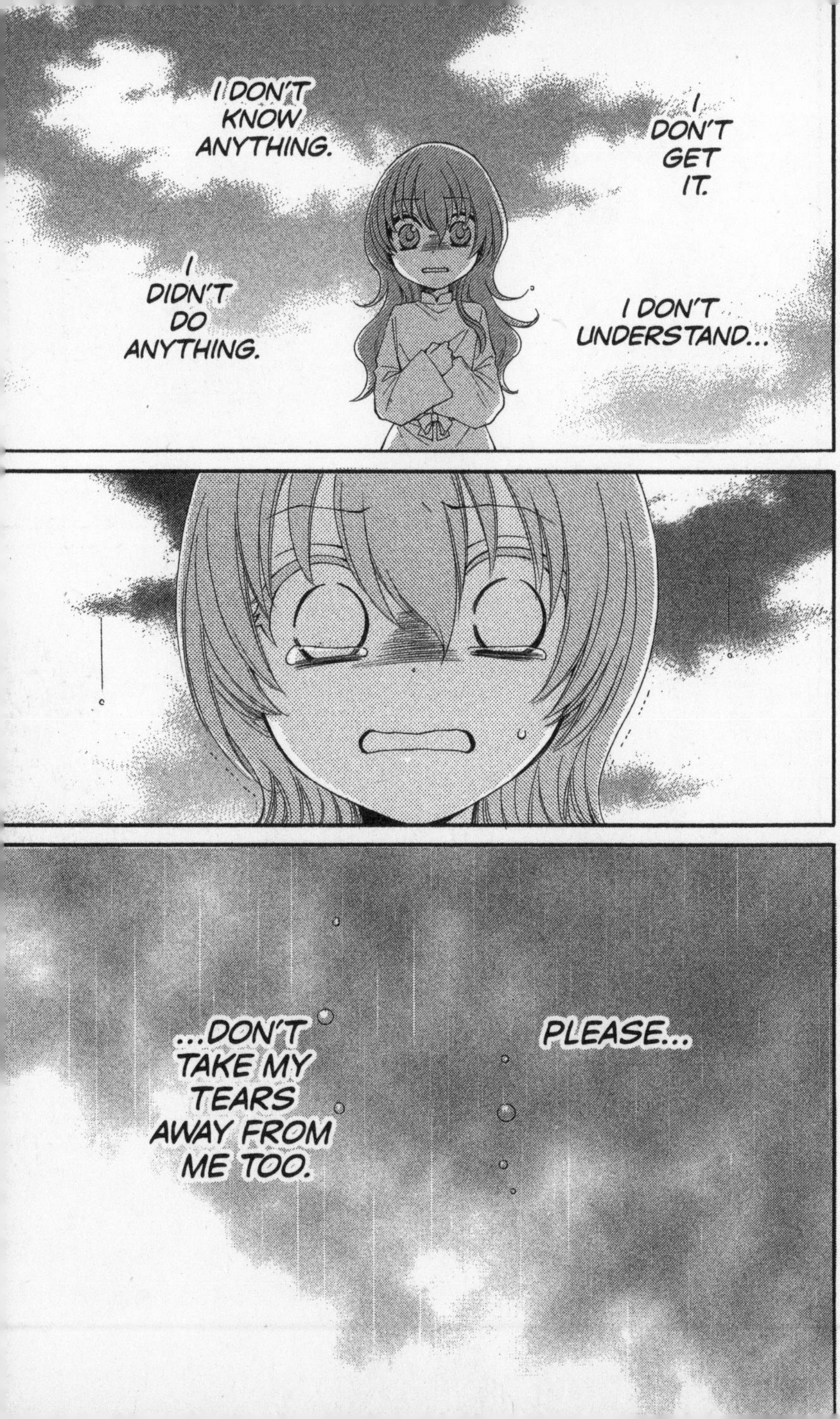
I DON'T GET IT.
I DON'T KNOW ANYTHING.
I DON'T UNDERSTAND...
I DIDN'T DO ANYTHING.
PLEASE...
...DON'T TAKE MY TEARS AWAY FROM ME TOO.

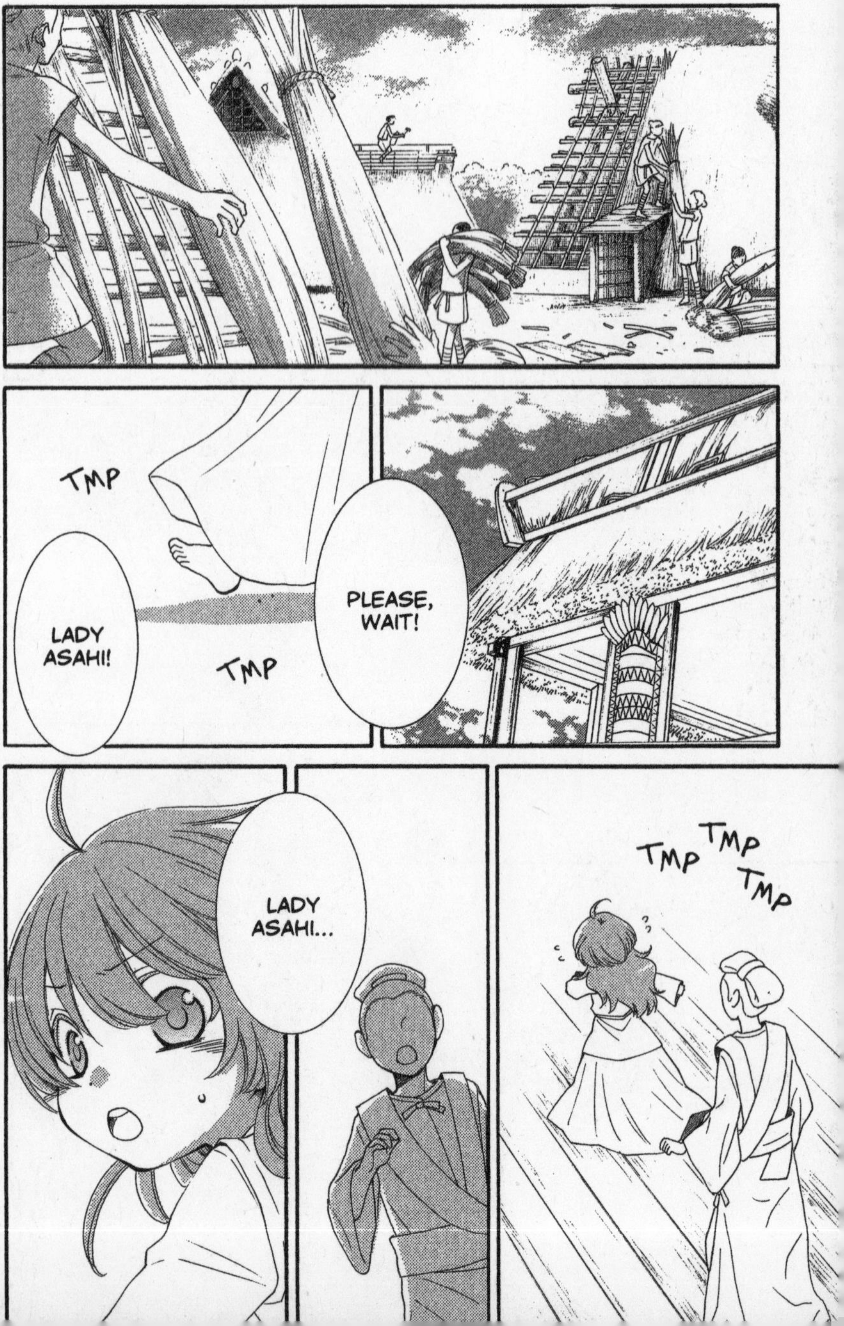
PLEASE, WAIT!
TMP
LADY ASAHI!
TMP
TMP
TMP
TMP
TMP
LADY ASAHI...

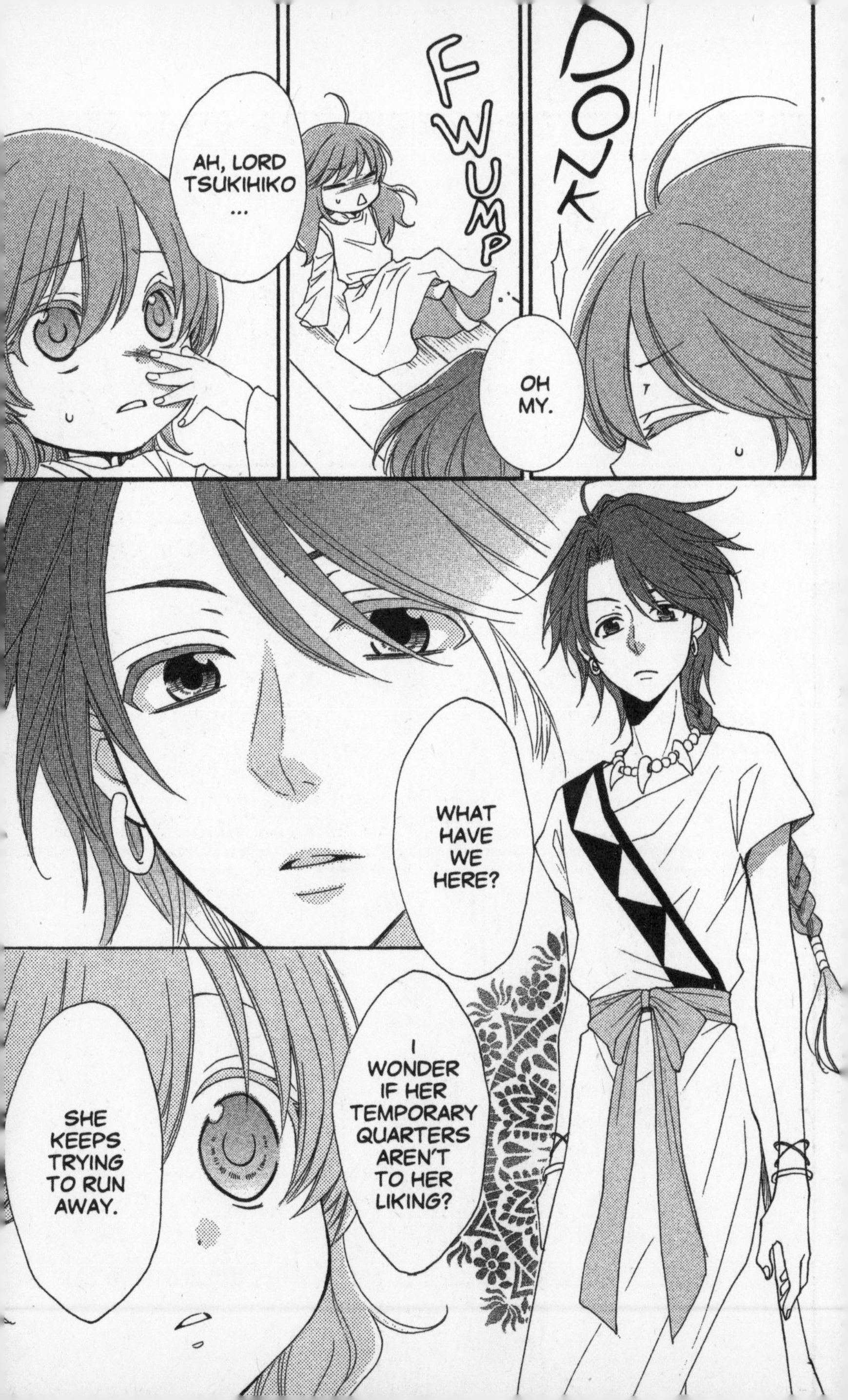
DONK
OH MY.
FWUMP
AH, LORD TSUKIHIKO ...
WHAT HAVE WE HERE?
I WONDER IF HER TEMPORARY QUARTERS AREN'T TO HER LIKING?
SHE KEEPS TRYING TO RUN AWAY.

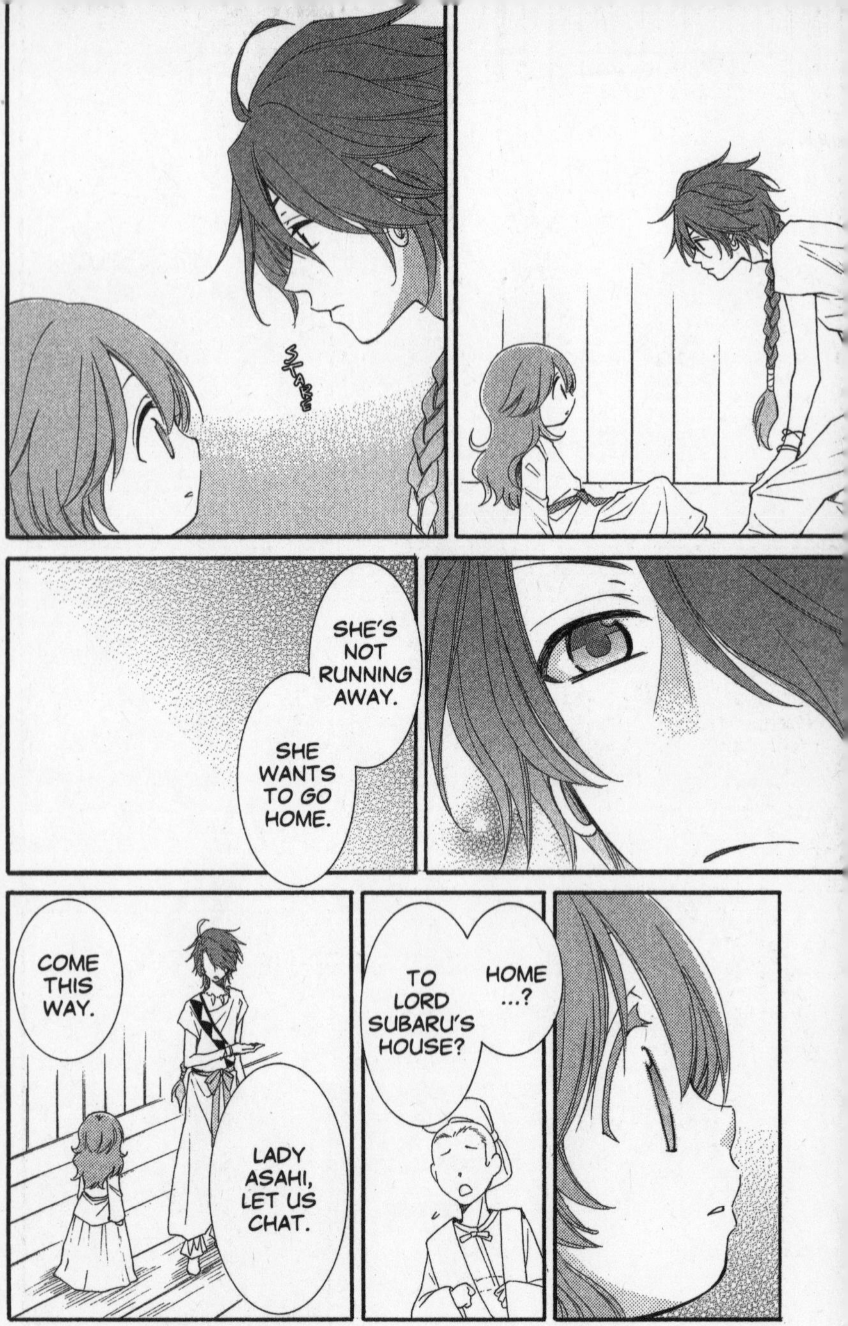
STARE
SHE'S NOT RUNNING AWAY.
SHE WANTS TO GO HOME.
HOME ...?
TO LORD SUBARU'S HOUSE?
COME THIS WAY.
LADY ASAHI, LET US CHAT.

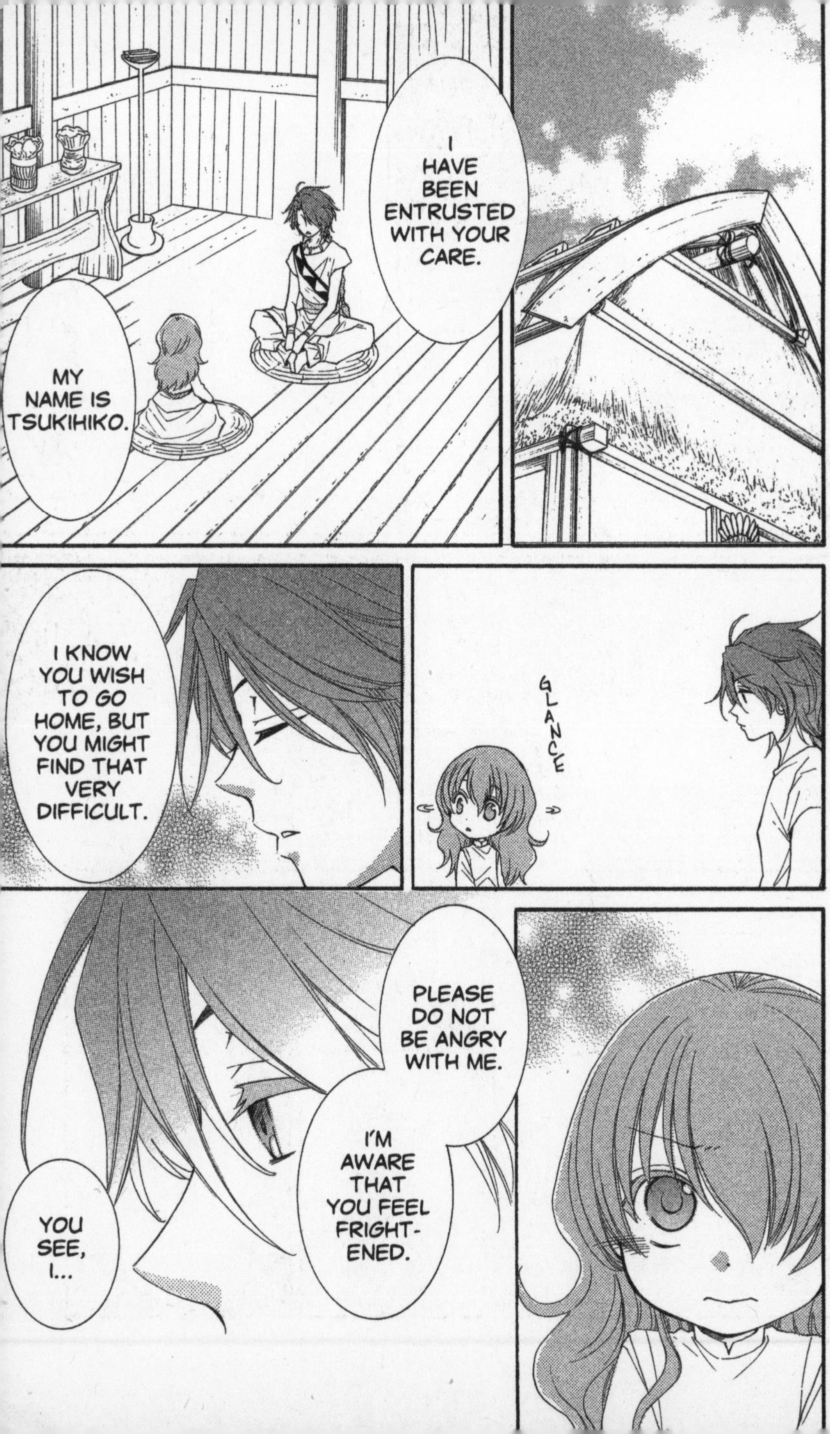
I HAVE BEEN ENTRUSTED WITH YOUR CARE.
MY NAME IS TSUKIHIKO.
GLANCE
I KNOW YOU WISH TO GO HOME, BUT YOU MIGHT FIND THAT VERY DIFFICULT.
PLEASE DO NOT BE ANGRY WITH ME.
I'M AWARE THAT YOU FEEL FRIGHT-ENED.
YOU SEE, I...

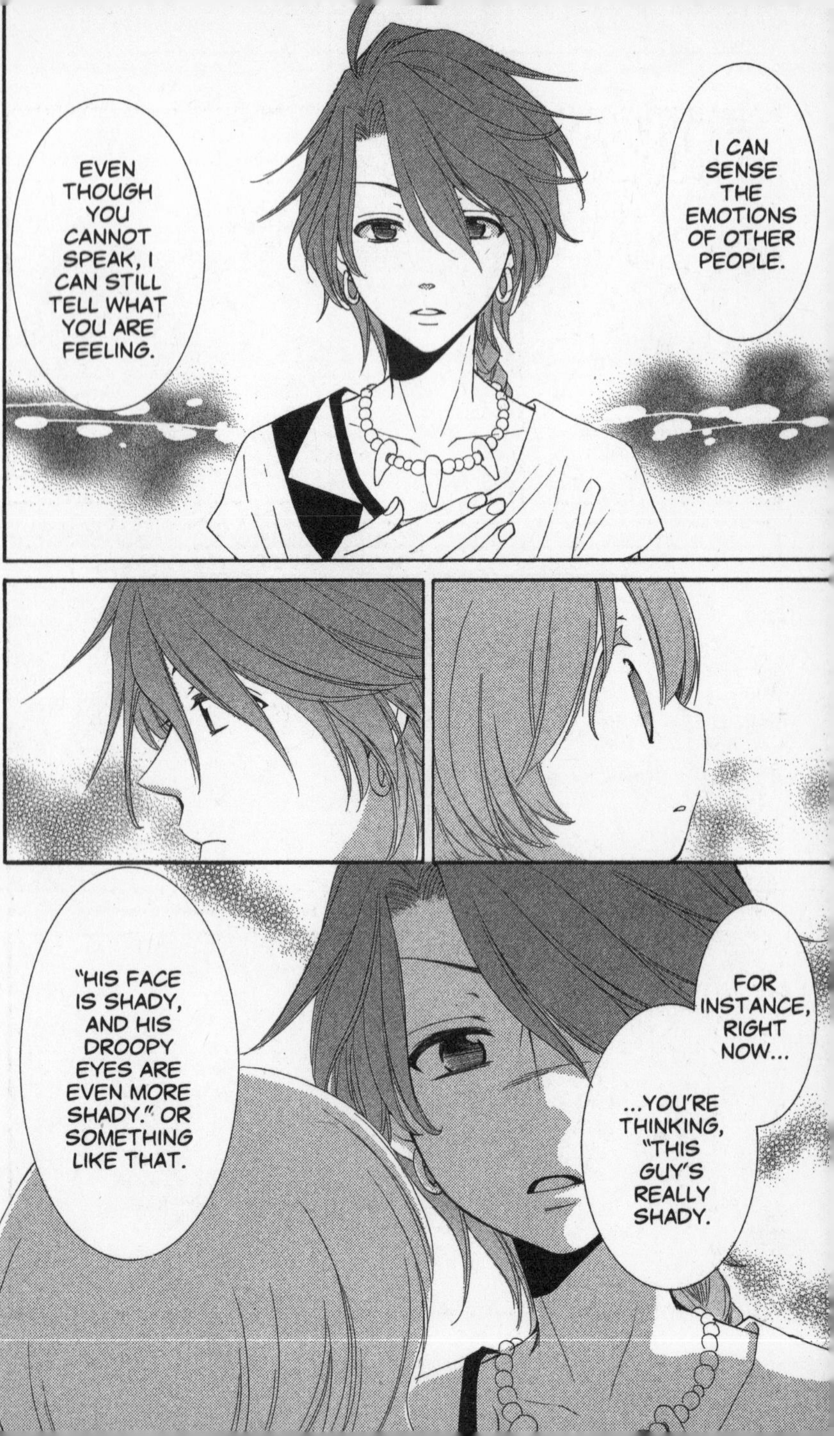
I CAN SENSE THE EMOTIONS OF OTHER PEOPLE.
EVEN THOUGH YOU CANNOT SPEAK, I CAN STILL TELL WHAT YOU ARE FEELING.
FOR INSTANCE, RIGHT NOW...
...YOU'RE THINKING, "THIS GUY'S REALLY SHADY.
"HIS FACE IS SHADY, AND HIS DROOPY EYES ARE EVEN MORE SHADY." OR SOMETHING LIKE THAT.

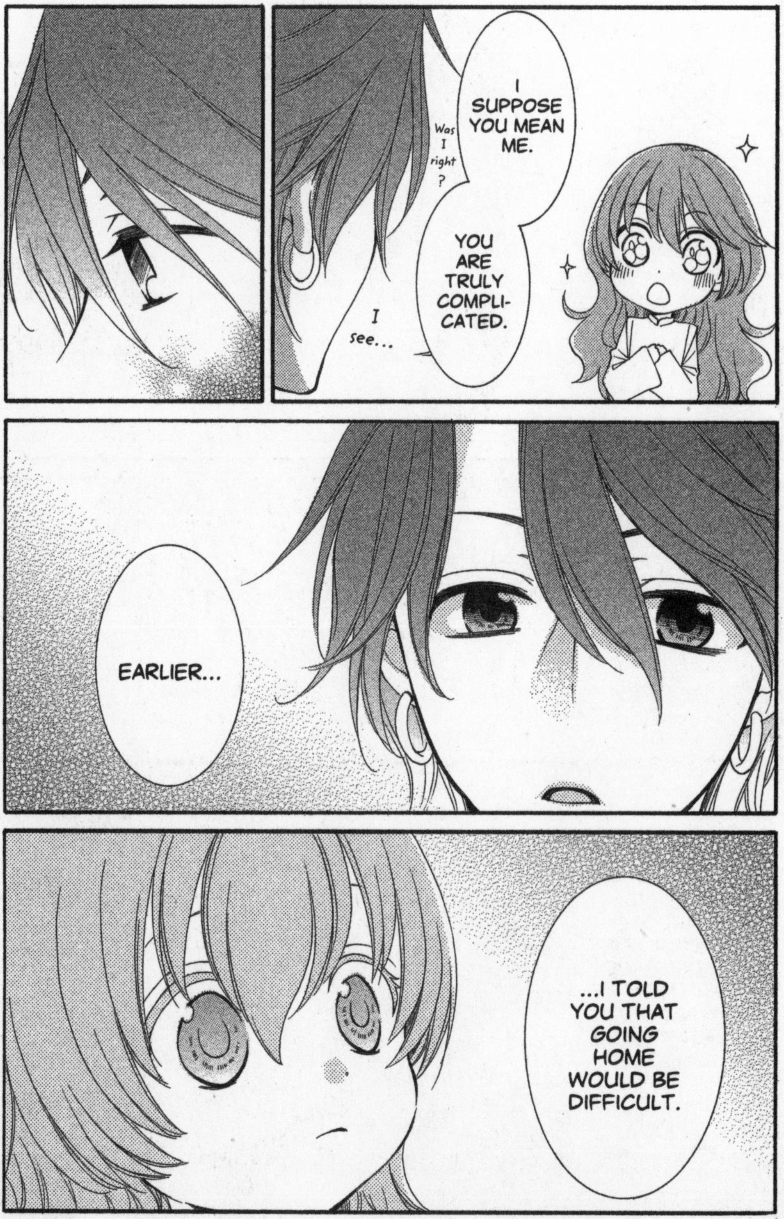
I SUPPOSE YOU MEAN ME.
Was I right?
YOU ARE TRULY COMPLI-CATED.
I see...
EARLIER...
...I TOLD YOU THAT GOING HOME WOULD BE DIFFICULT.

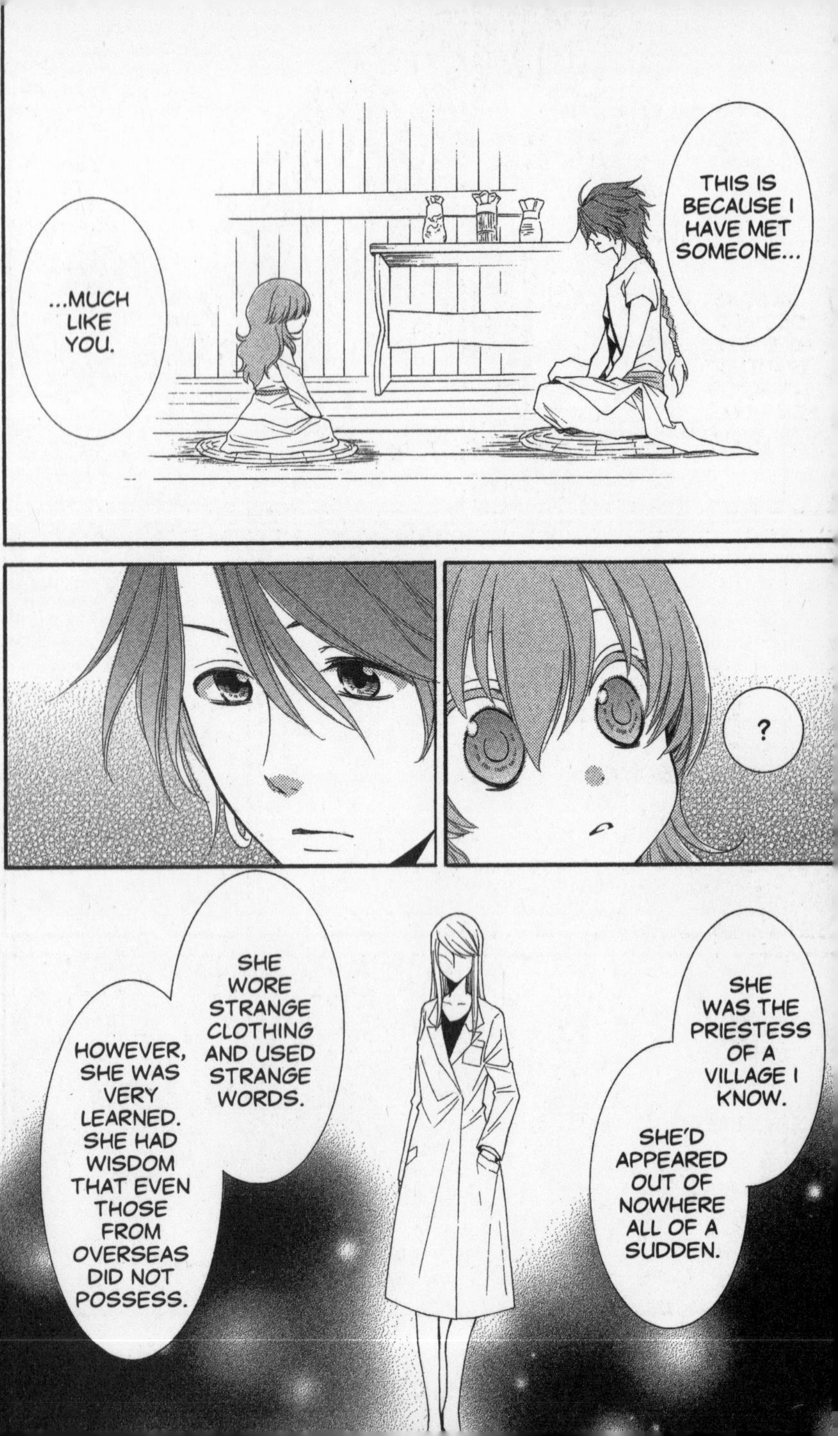
THIS IS BECAUSE I HAVE MET SOMEONE...
...MUCH LIKE YOU.
?
SHE WAS THE PRIESTESS OF A VILLAGE I KNOW.
SHE'D APPEARED OUT OF NOWHERE ALL OF A SUDDEN.
SHE WORE STRANGE CLOTHING AND USED STRANGE WORDS.
HOWEVER, SHE WAS VERY LEARNED. SHE HAD WISDOM THAT EVEN THOSE FROM OVERSEAS DID NOT POSSESS.

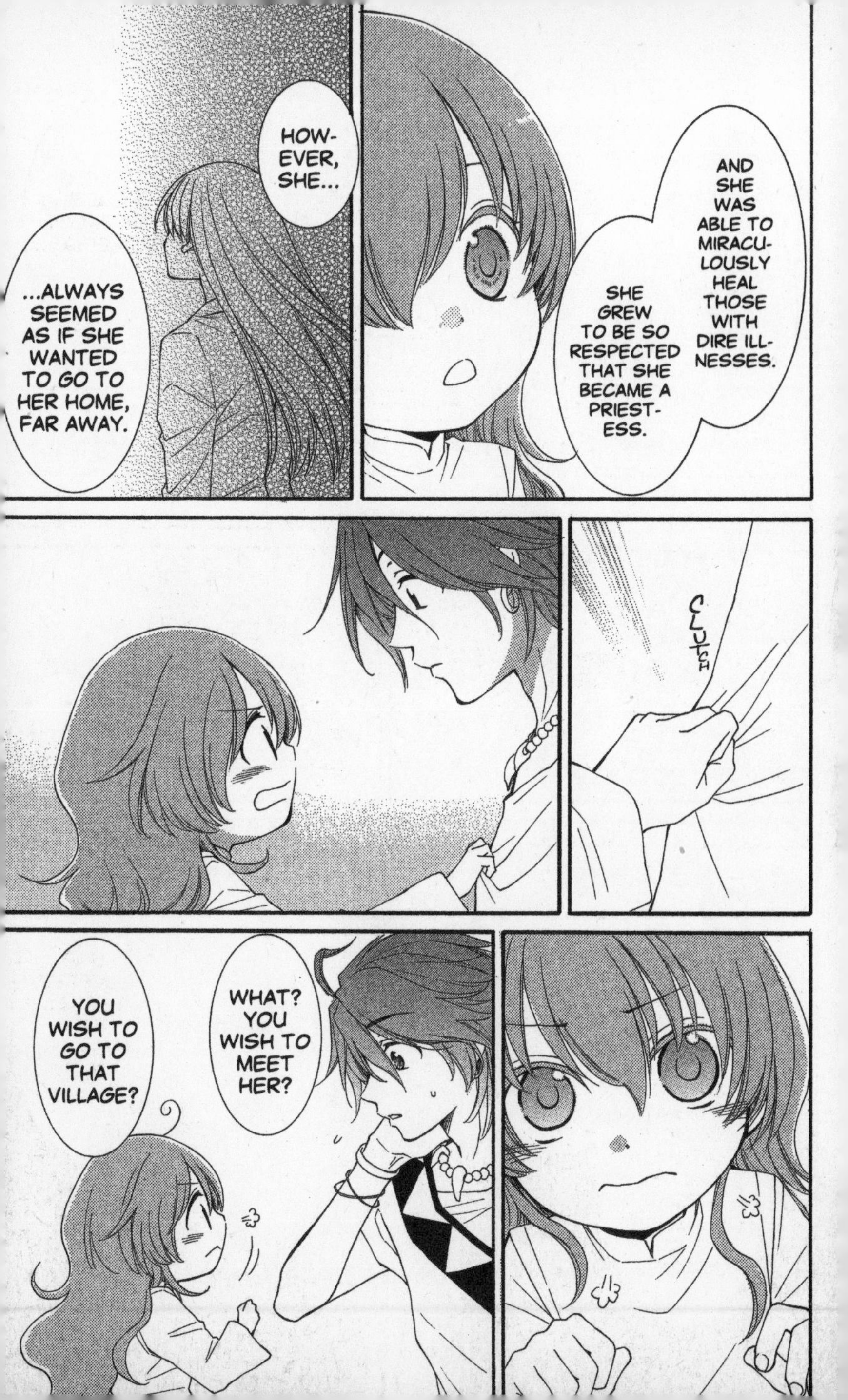
AND SHE WAS ABLE TO MIRACULOUSLY HEAL THOSE WITH DIRE ILLNESSES.
SHE GREW TO BE SO RESPECTED THAT SHE BECAME A PRIESTESS.
HOW-EVER, SHE...
...ALWAYS SEEMED AS IF SHE WANTED TO GO TO HER HOME, FAR AWAY.
CLUTCH
WHAT? YOU WISH TO MEET HER?
YOU WISH TO GO TO THAT VILLAGE?

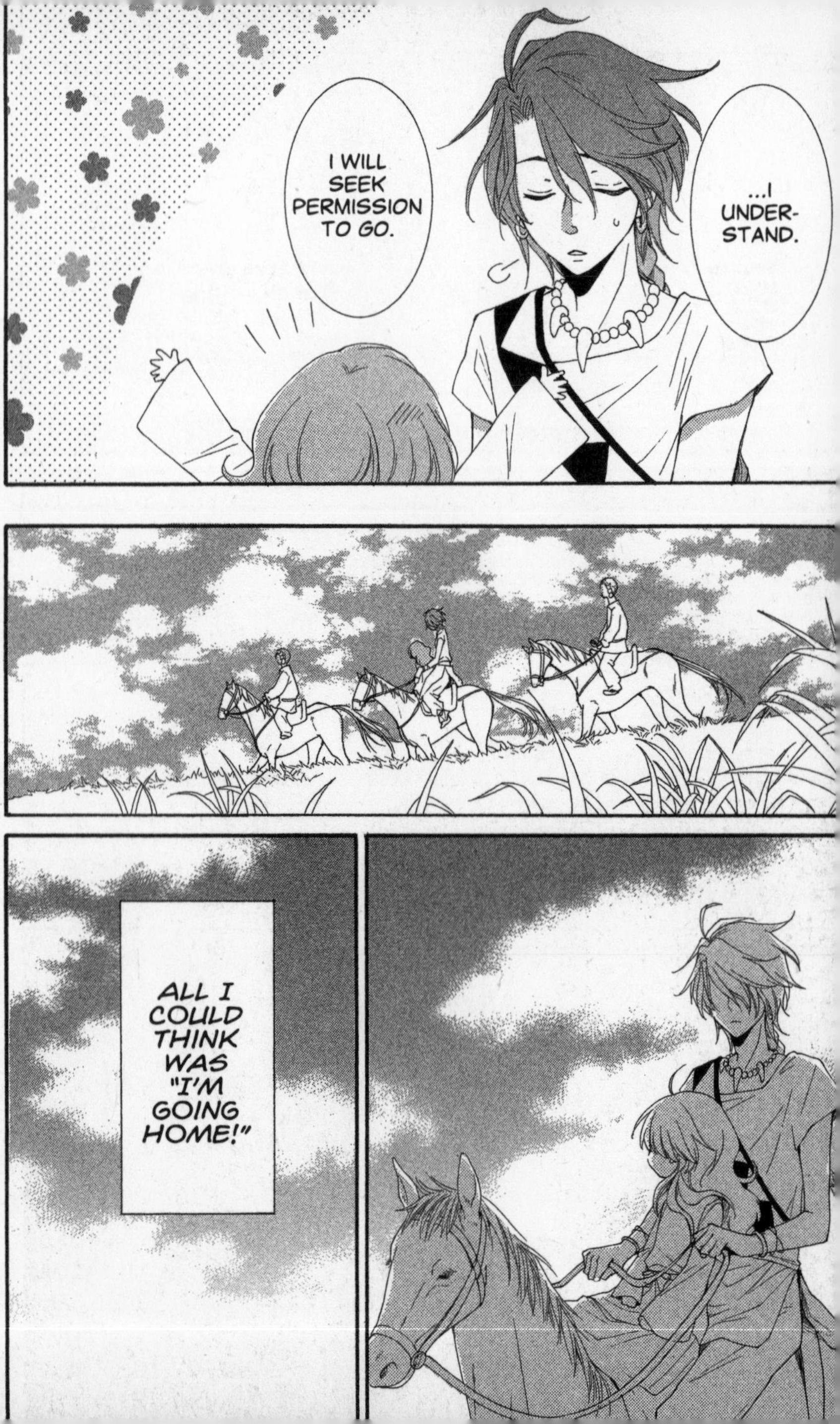
...I UNDER-STAND.
I WILL SEEK PERMISSION TO GO.
ALL I COULD THINK WAS "I'M GOING HOME!"

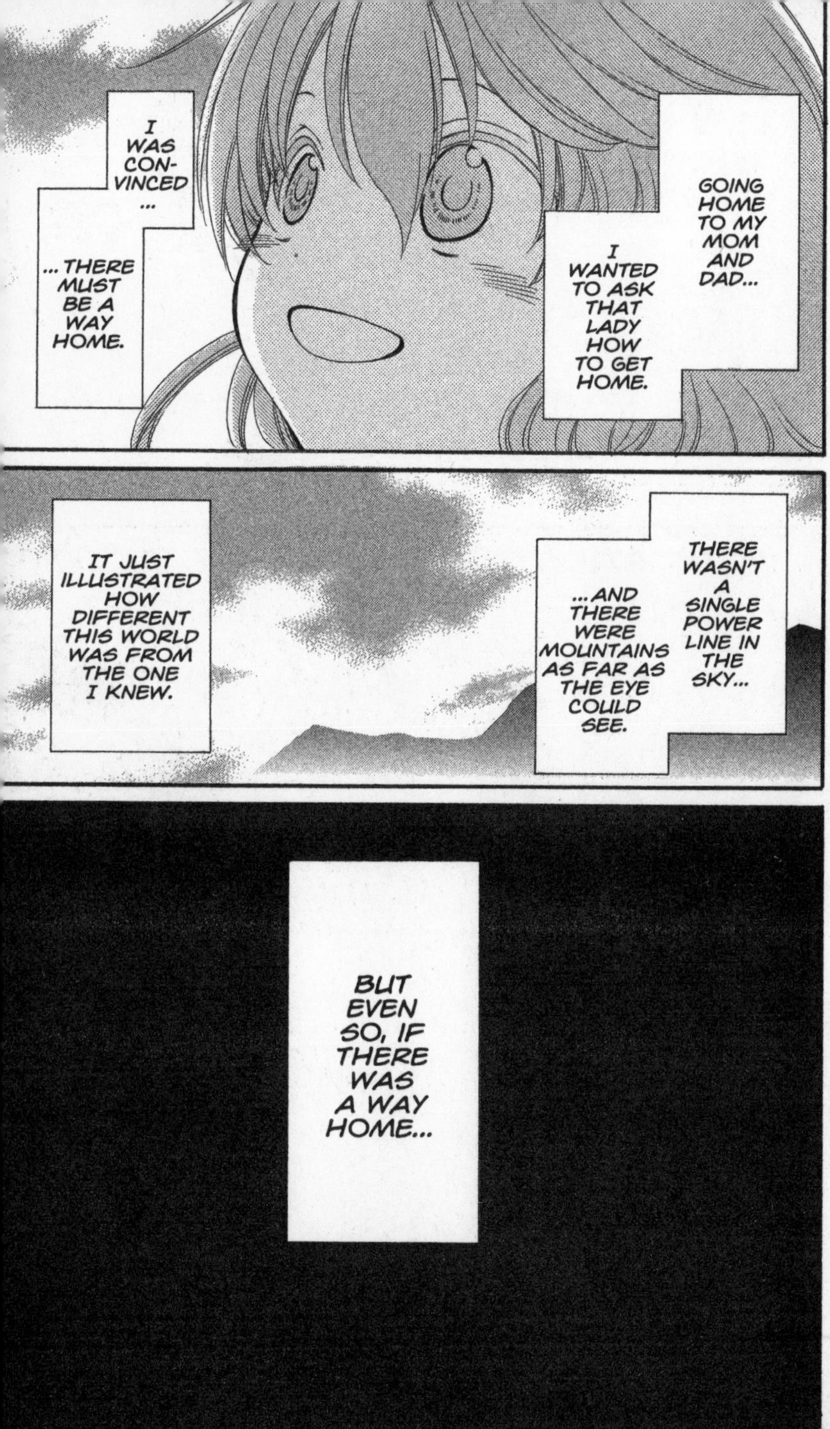
GOING HOME TO MY MOM AND DAD...
I WANTED TO ASK THAT LADY HOW TO GET HOME.
I WAS CON-VINCED...
...THERE MUST BE A WAY HOME.
THERE WASN'T A SINGLE POWER LINE IN THE SKY...
...AND THERE WERE MOUNTAINS AS FAR AS THE EYE COULD SEE.
IT JUST ILLUSTRATED HOW DIFFERENT THIS WORLD WAS FROM THE ONE I KNEW.
BUT EVEN SO, IF THERE WAS A WAY HOME...

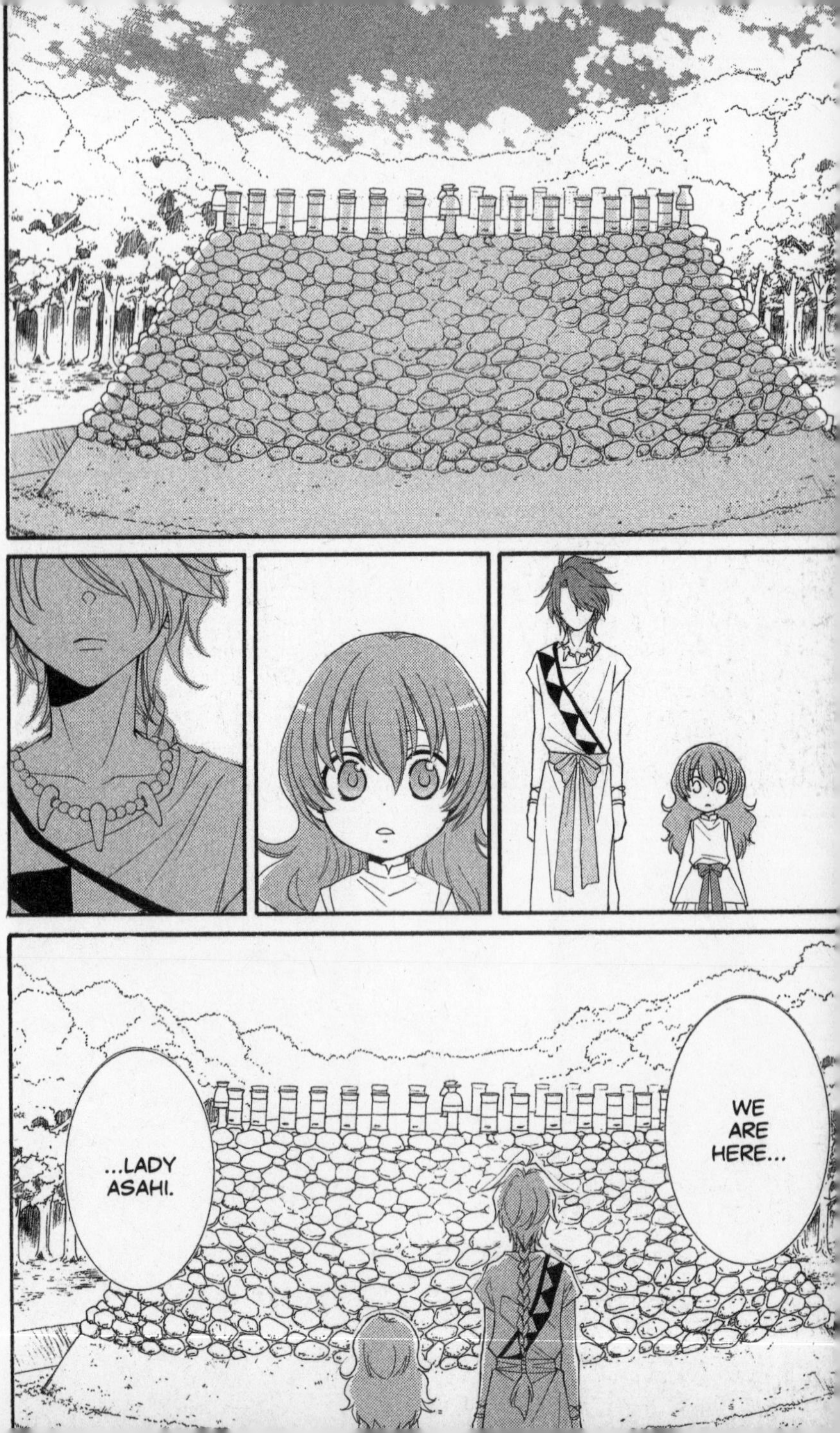
WE ARE HERE...
...LADY ASAHI.

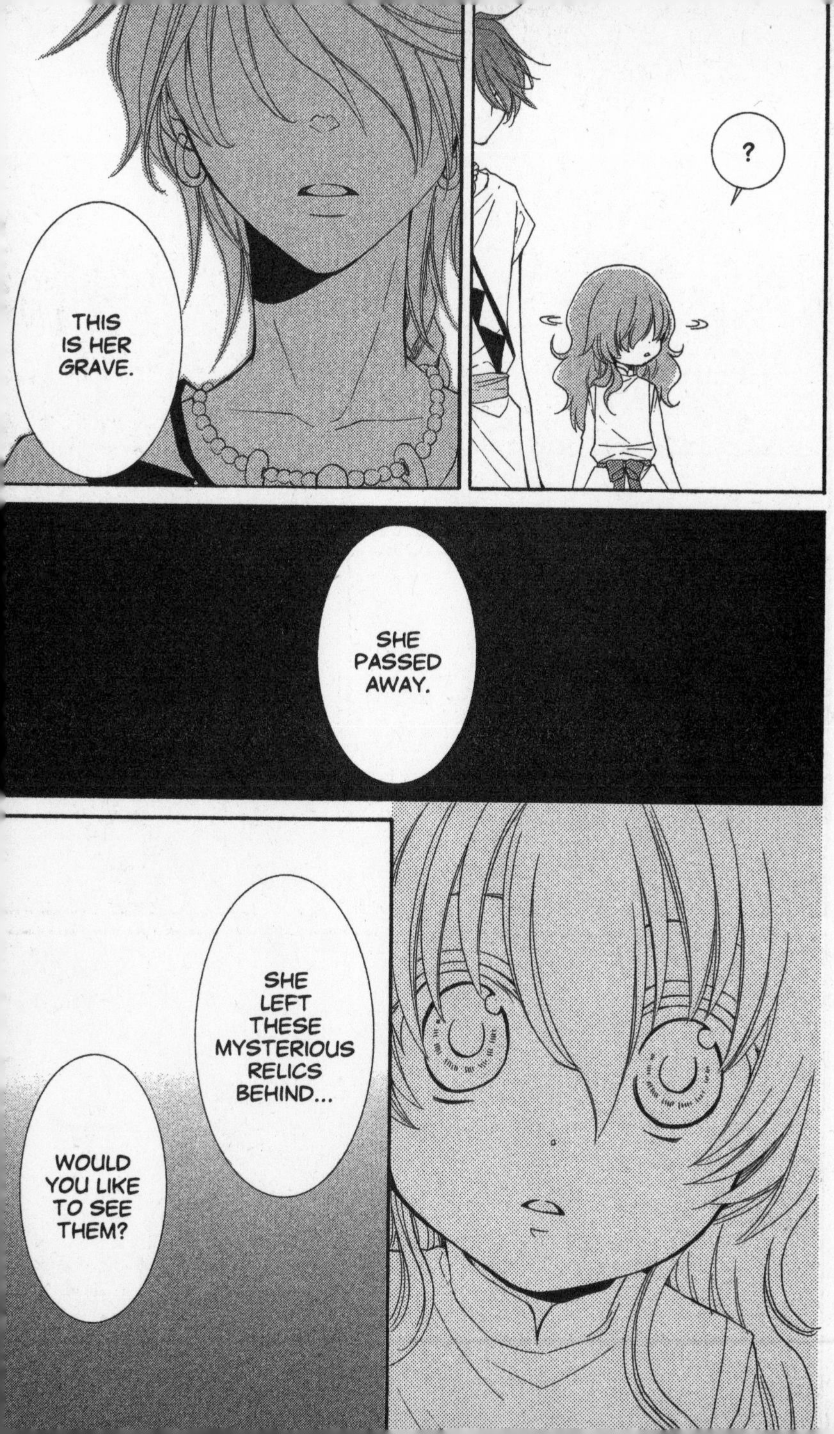
?
THIS IS HER GRAVE.
SHE PASSED AWAY.
SHE LEFT THESE MYSTERIOUS RELICS BEHIND...
WOULD YOU LIKE TO SEE THEM?

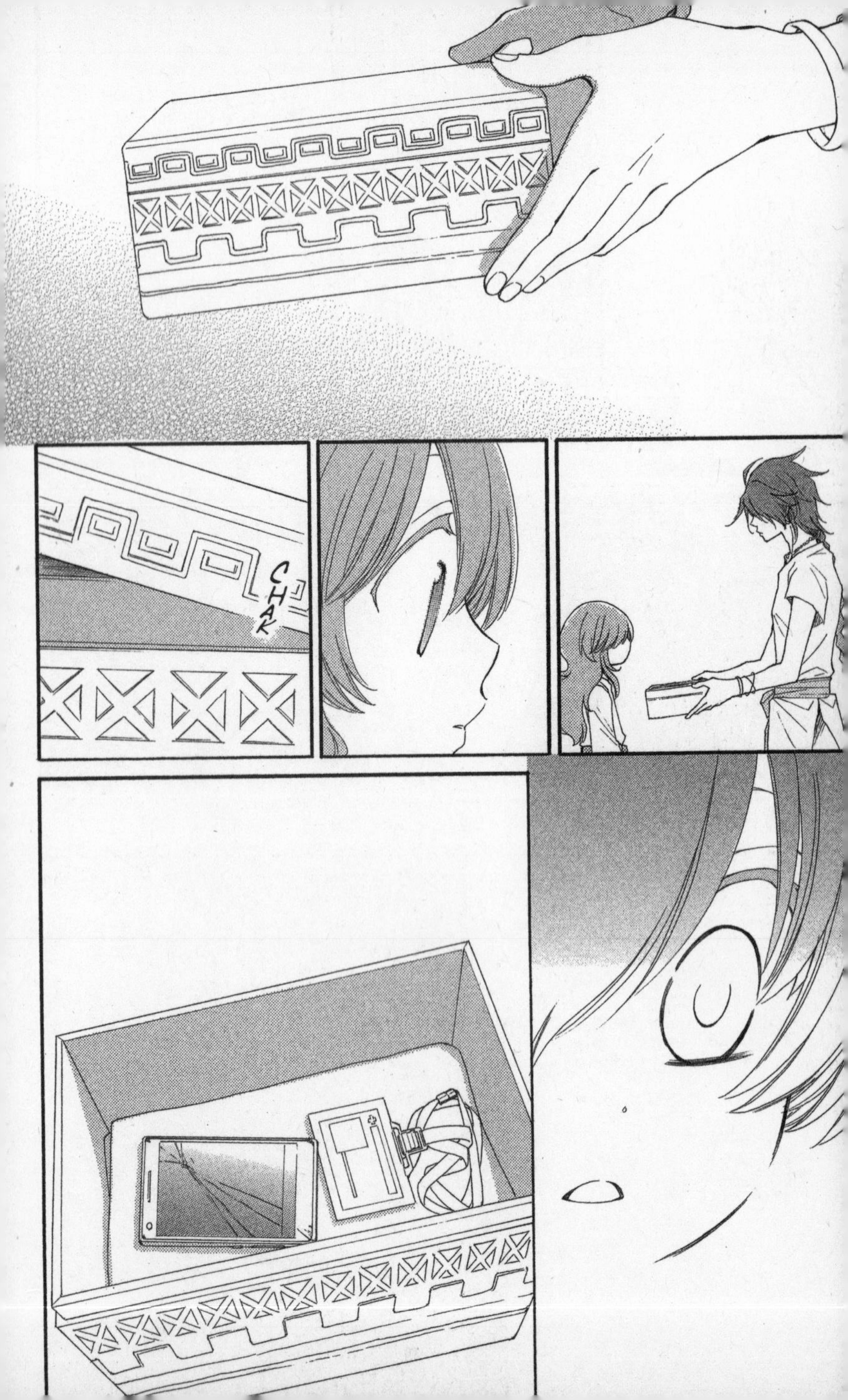
CHAK

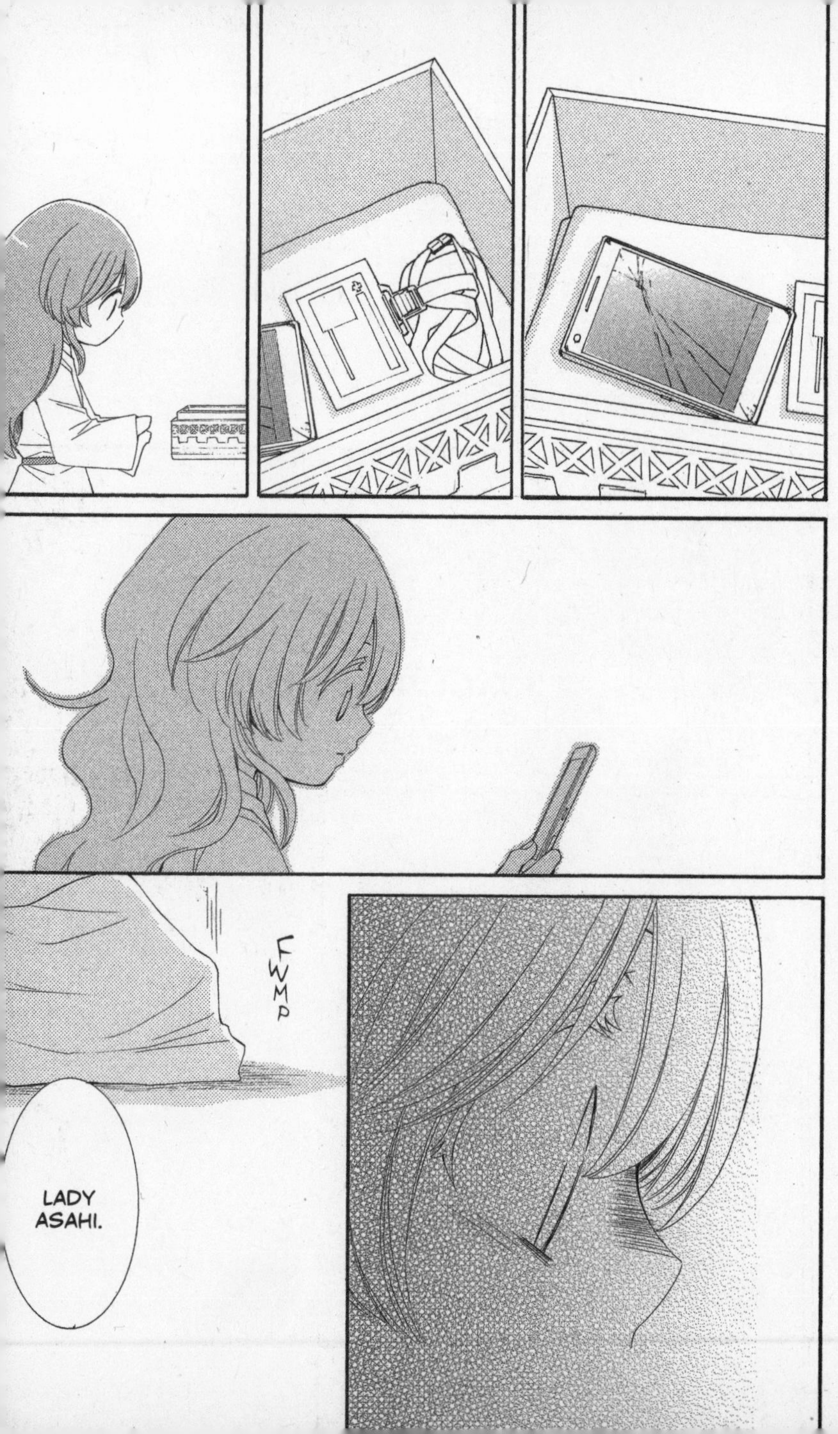
FWMP
LADY ASAHI.

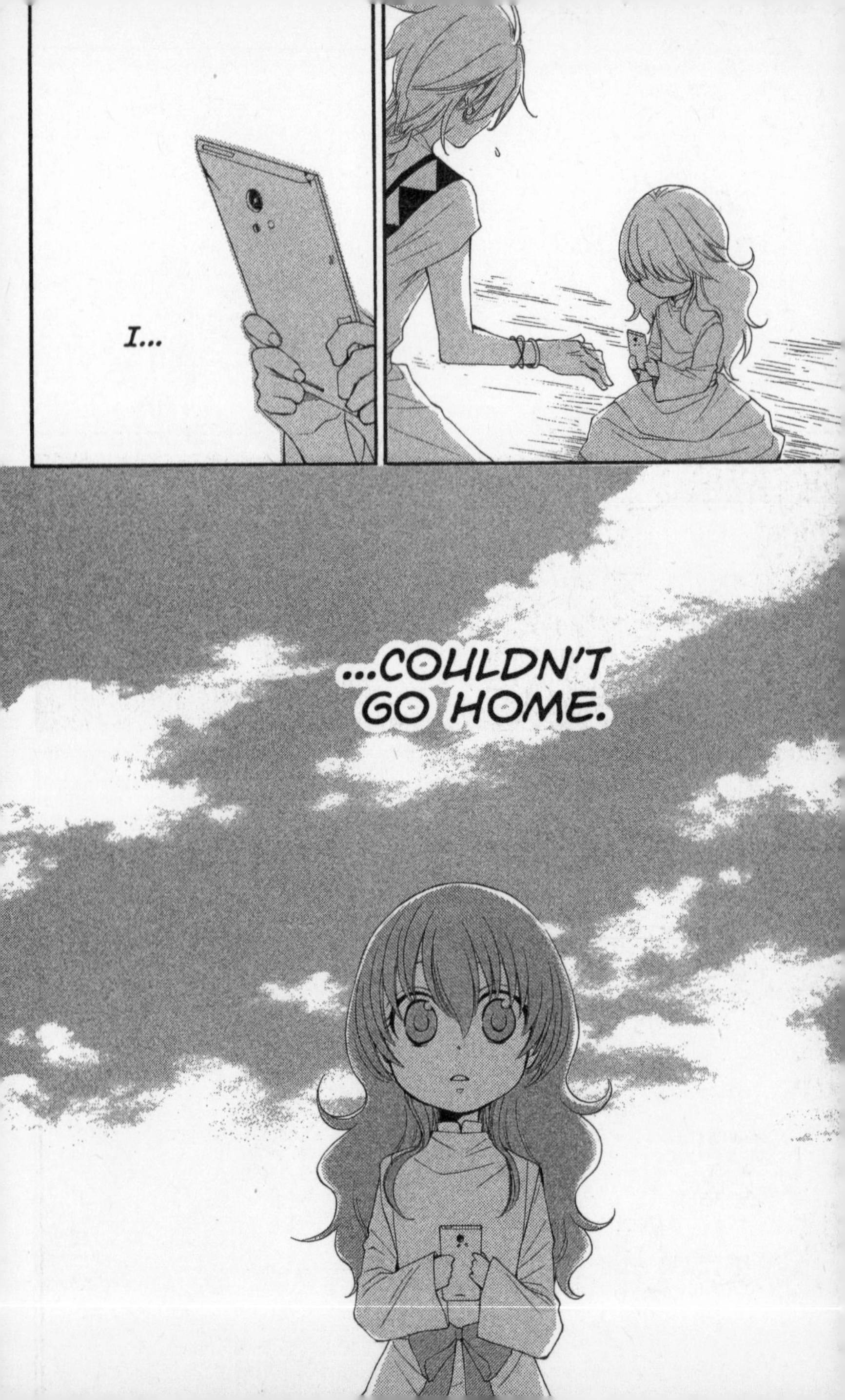
I...
...COULDN'T GO HOME.

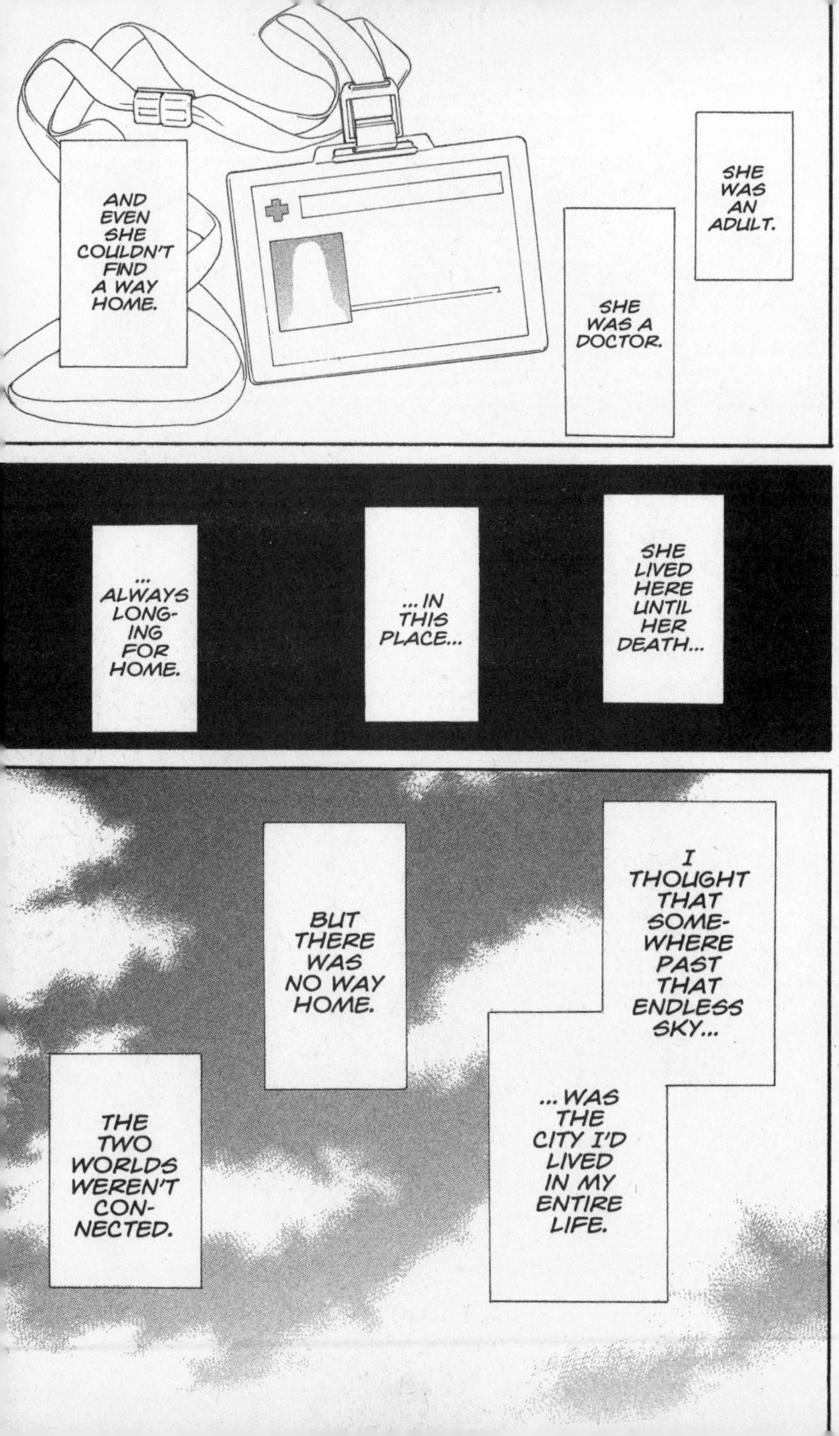
SHE WAS AN ADULT.
SHE WAS A DOCTOR.
AND EVEN SHE COULDN'T FIND A WAY HOME.
SHE LIVED HERE UNTIL HER DEATH...
...IN THIS PLACE...
...ALWAYS LONGING FOR HOME.
I THOUGHT THAT SOMEWHERE PAST THAT ENDLESS SKY...
...WAS THE CITY I'D LIVED IN MY ENTIRE LIFE.
BUT THERE WAS NO WAY HOME.
THE TWO WORLDS WEREN'T CONNECTED.

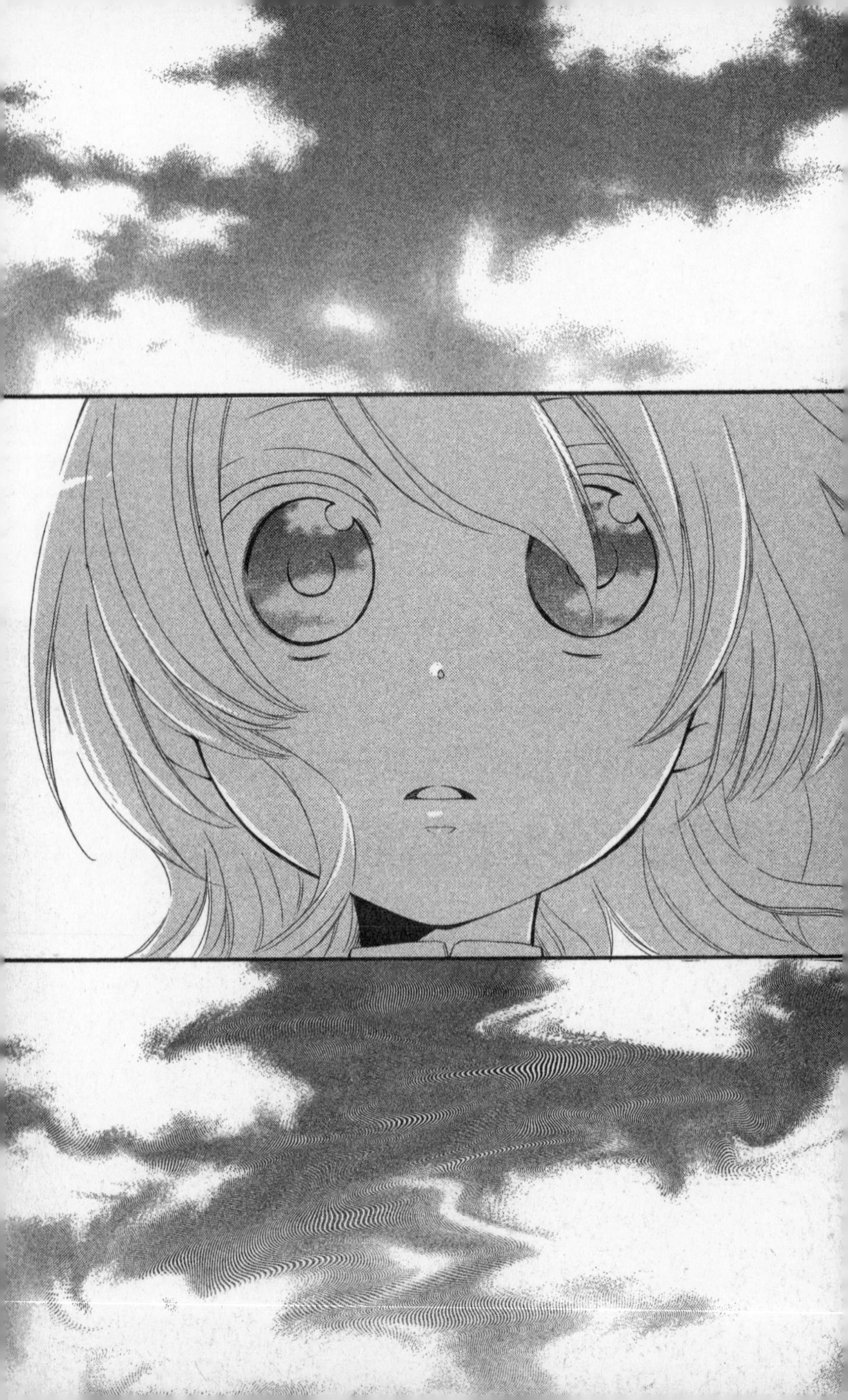

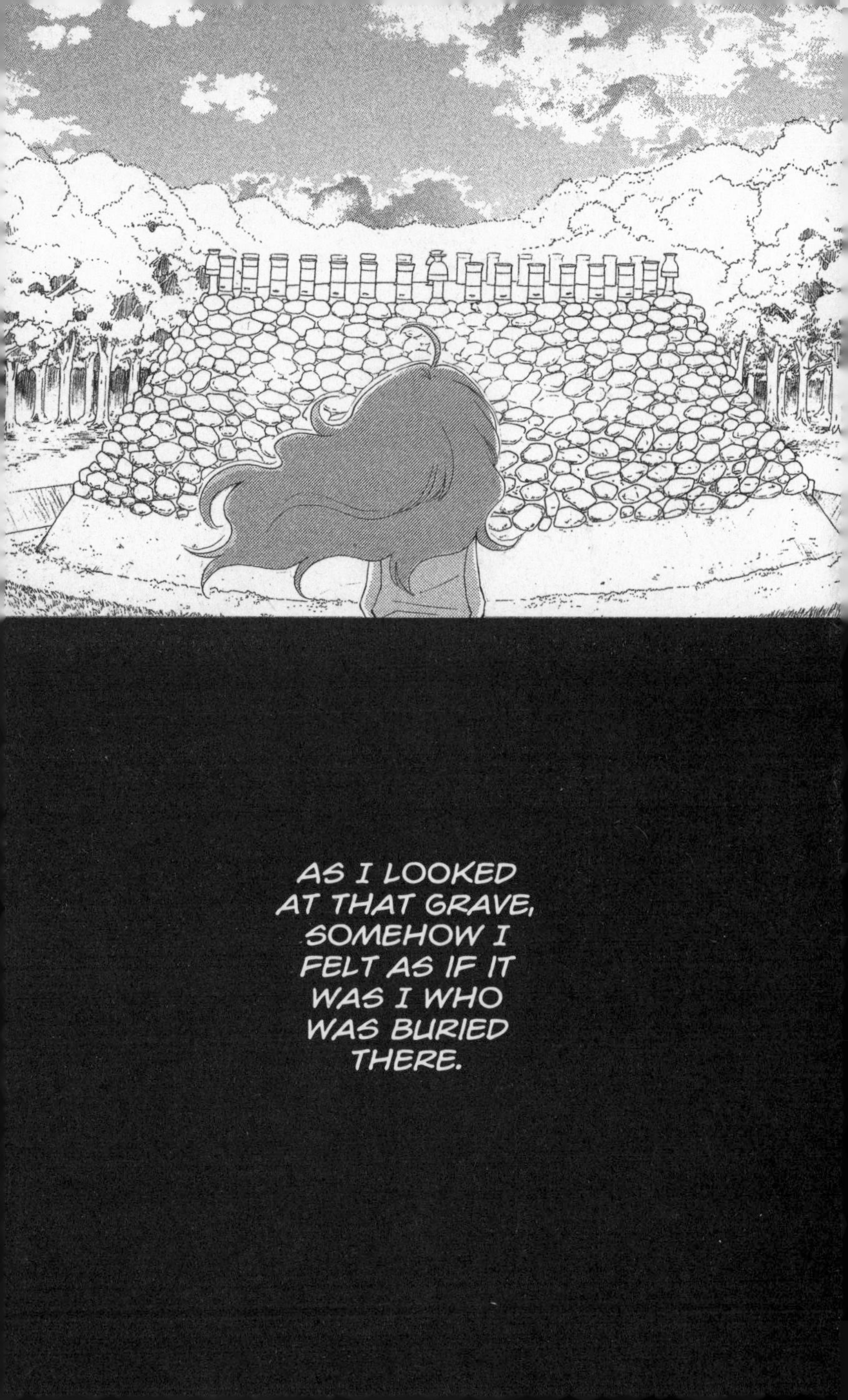
AS I LOOKED AT THAT GRAVE, SOMEHOW I FELT AS IF IT WAS I WHO WAS BURIED THERE.

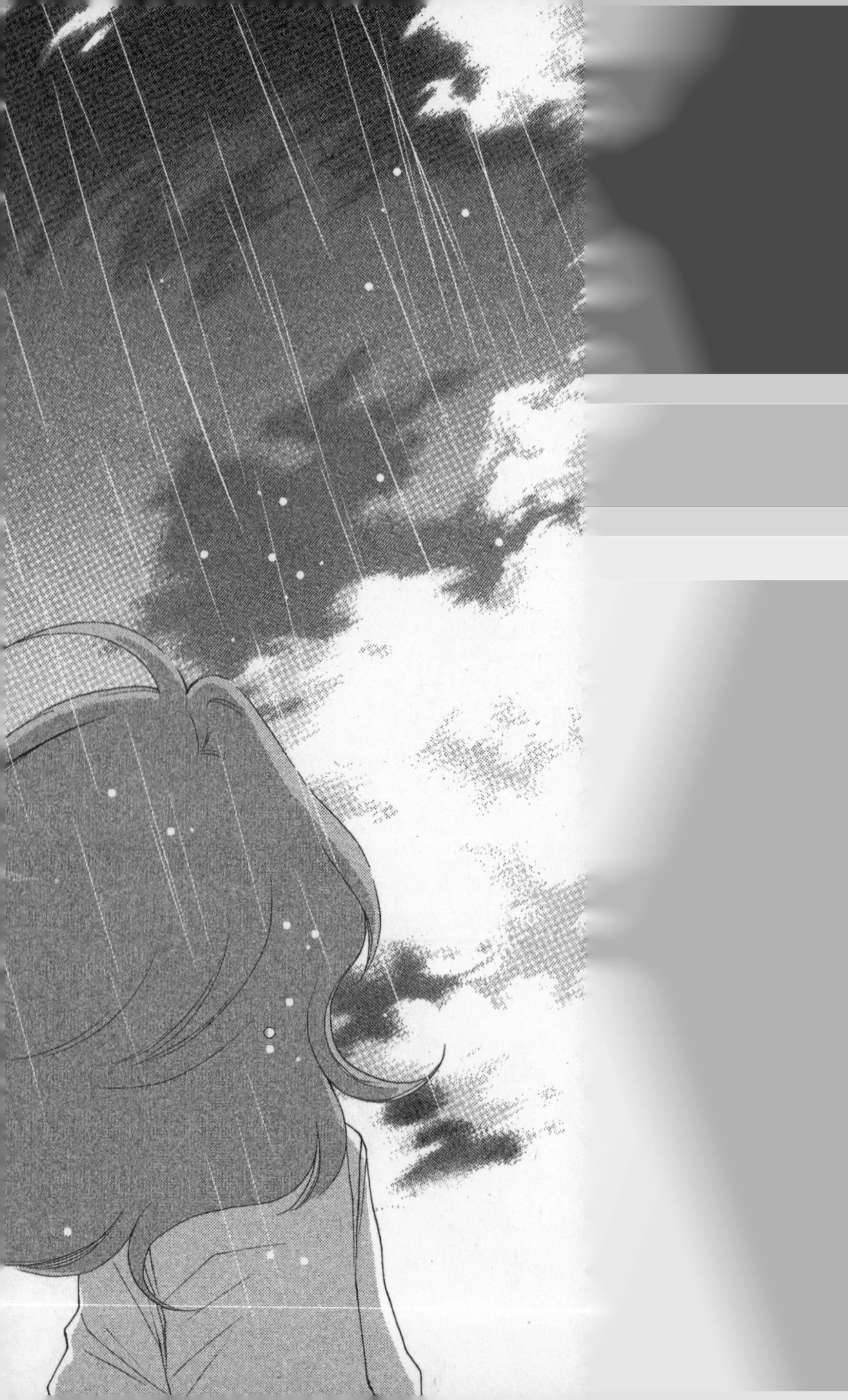

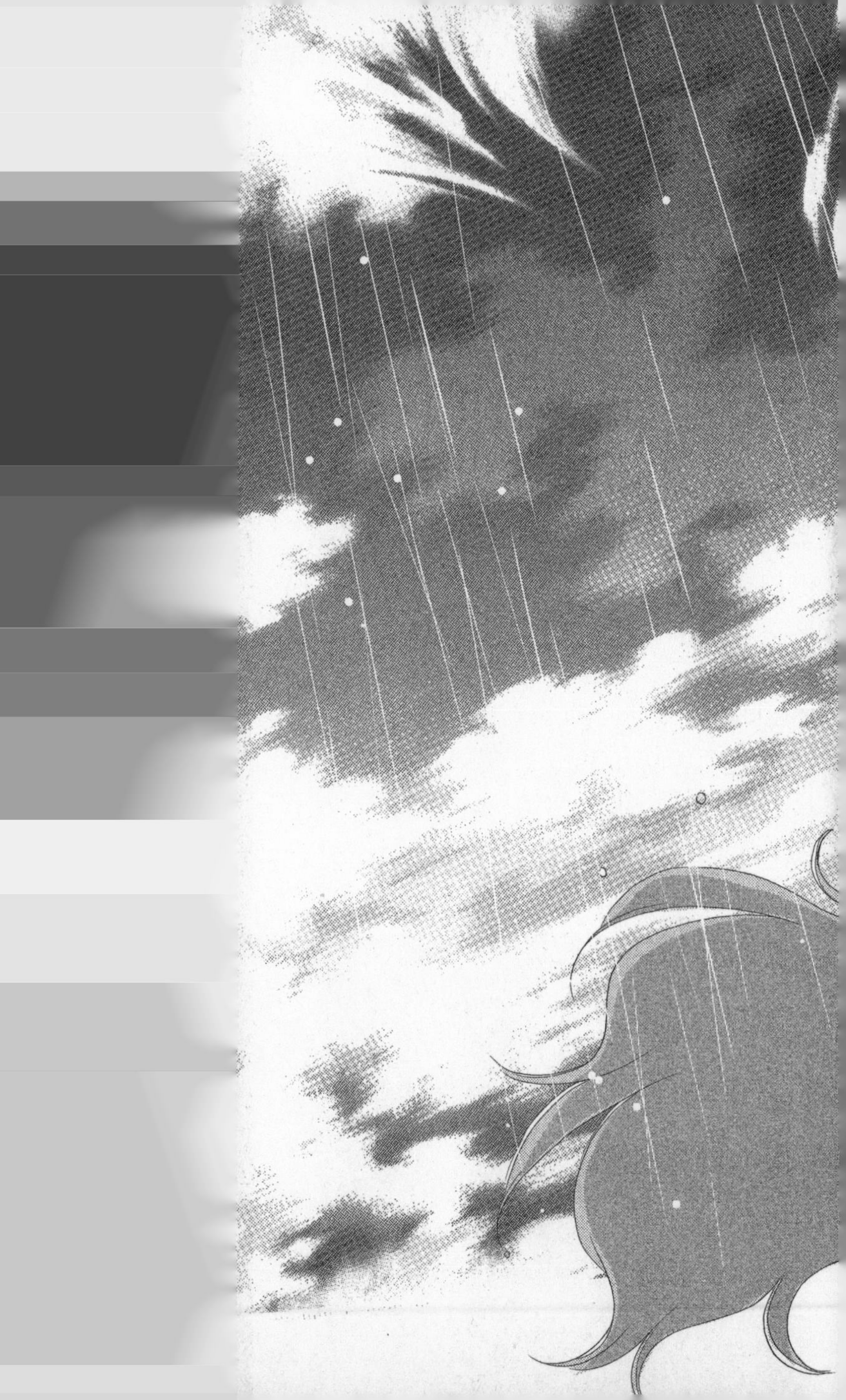

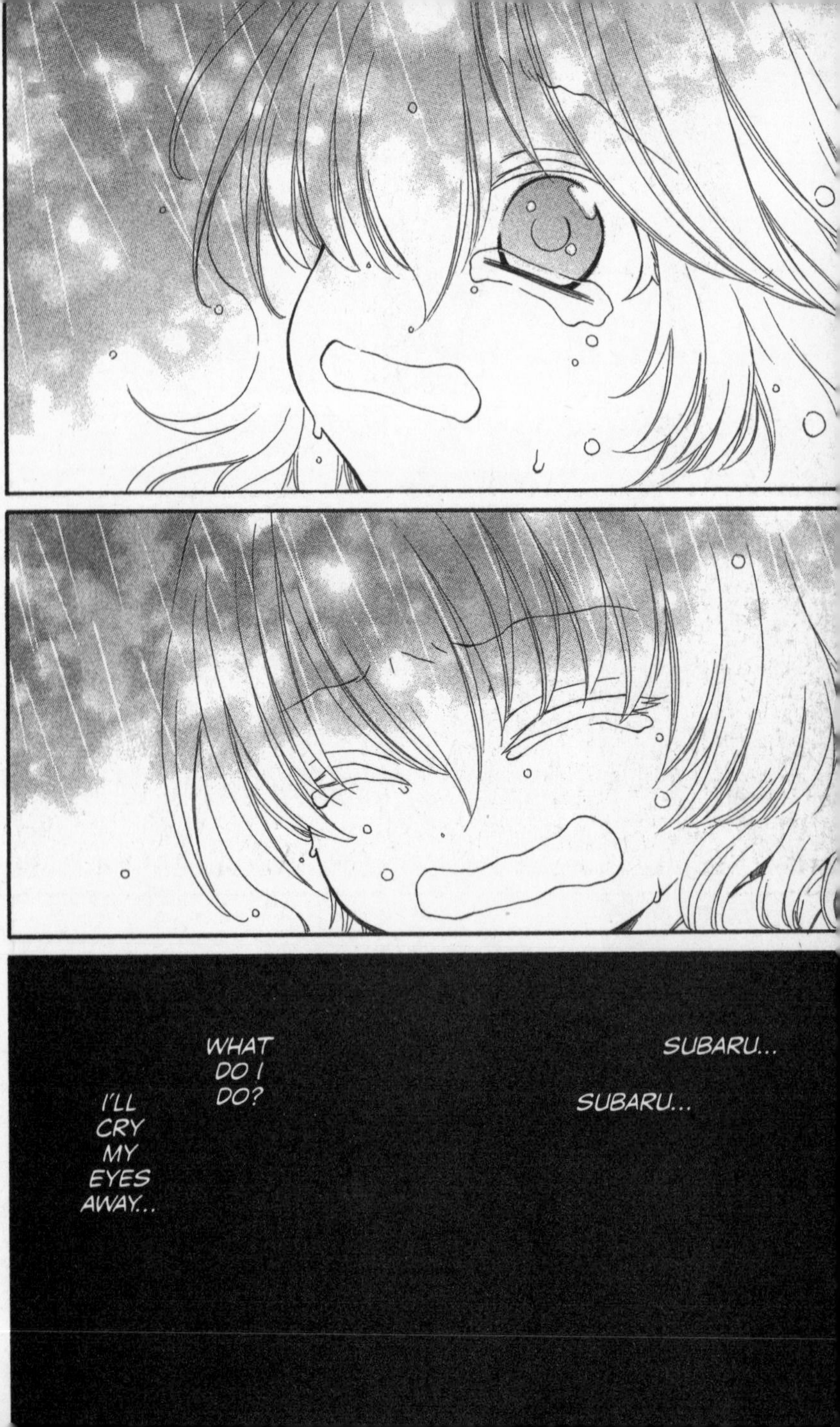
SUBARU...
SUBARU...
WHAT DO I DO?
I'LL CRY MY EYES AWAY...

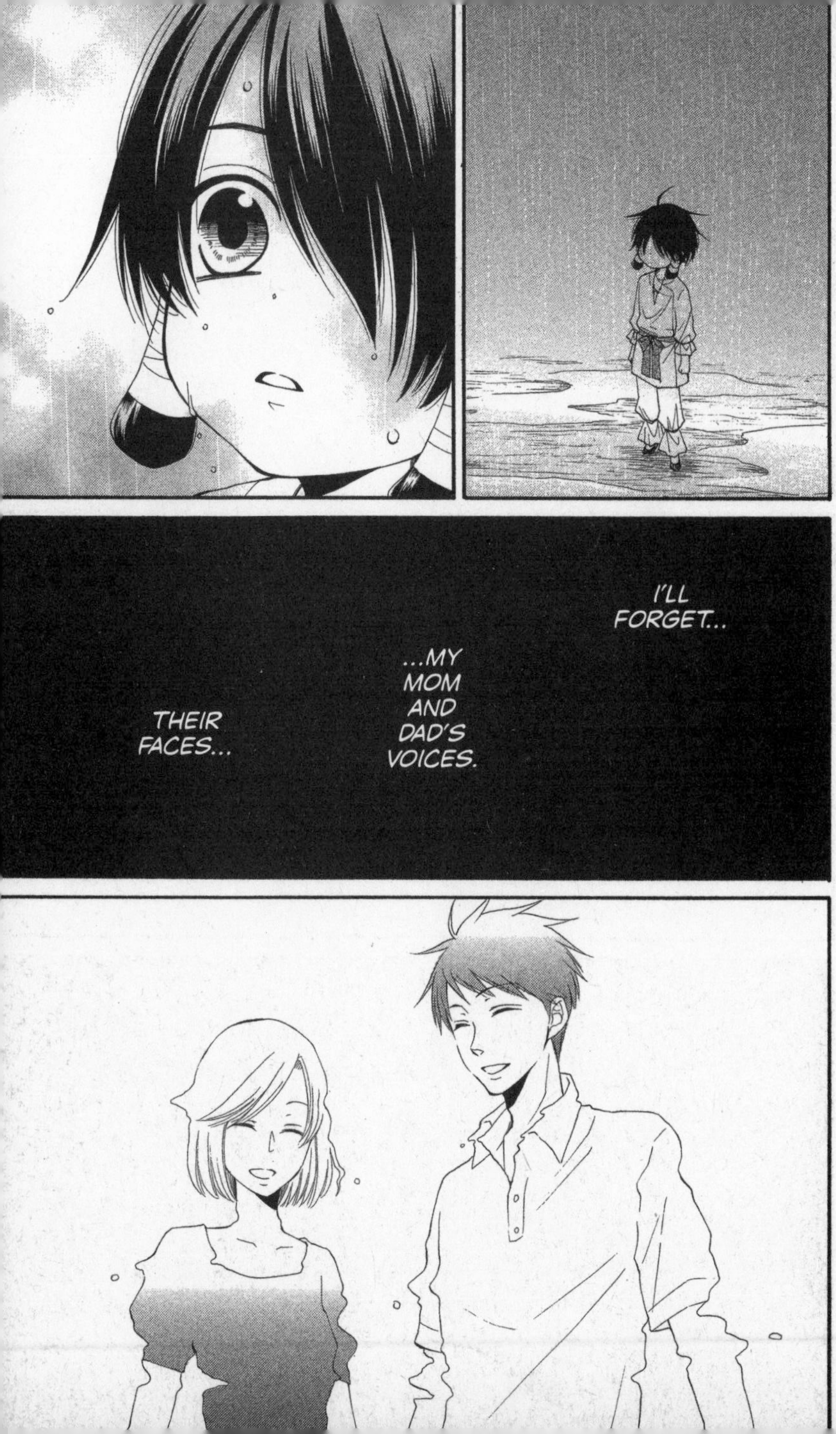
I'LL FORGET...
...MY MOM AND DAD'S VOICES.
THEIR FACES...

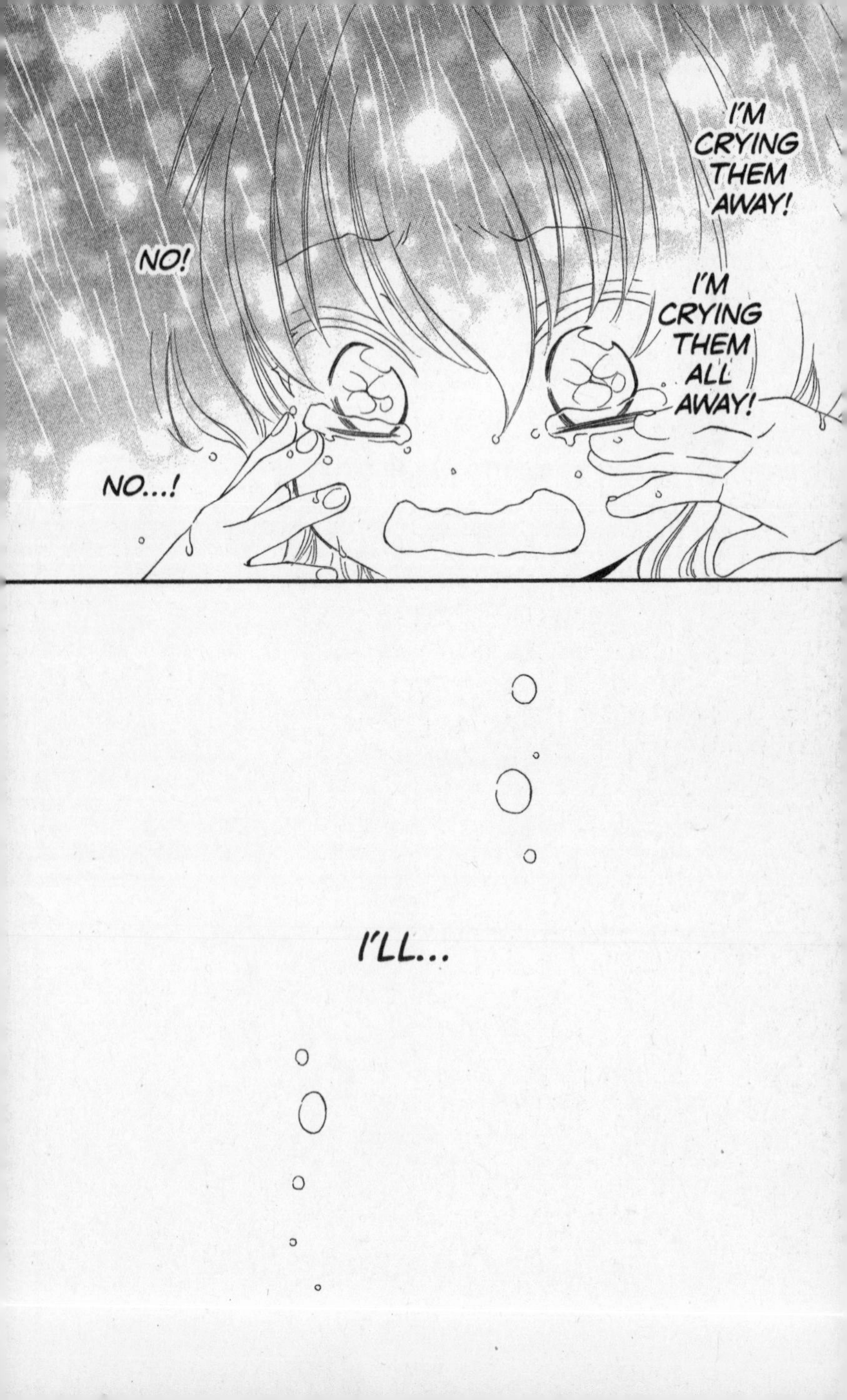
I'M CRYING THEM AWAY!
I'M CRYING THEM ALL AWAY!
NO!
NO...!
I'LL...

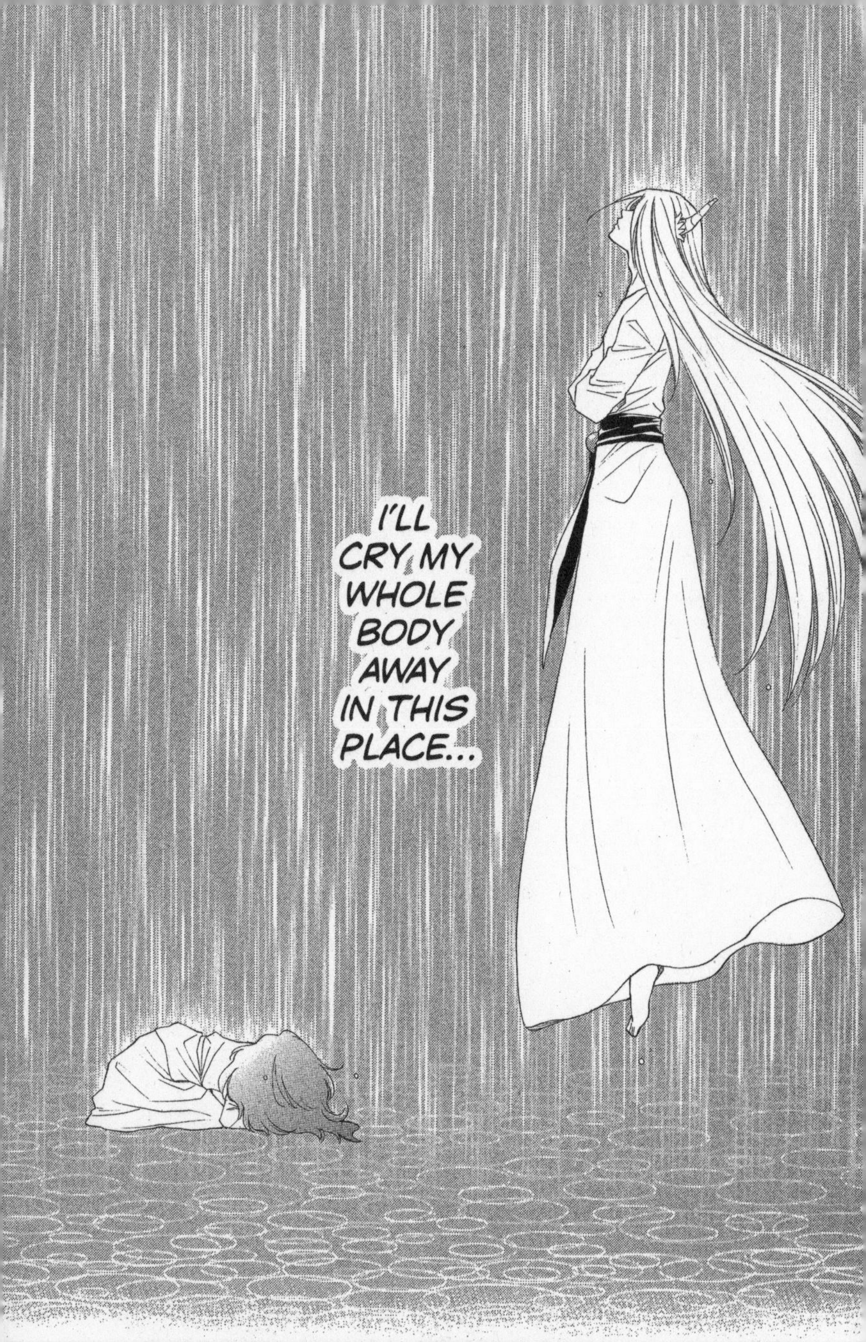
I'LL CRY MY WHOLE BODY AWAY IN THIS PLACE...

LOOM

CHAPTER 8

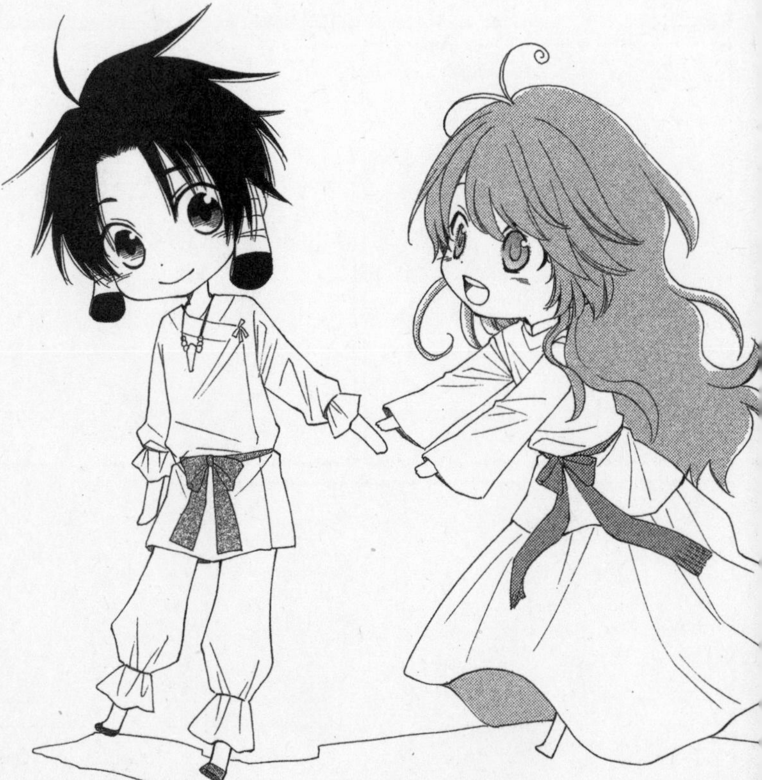

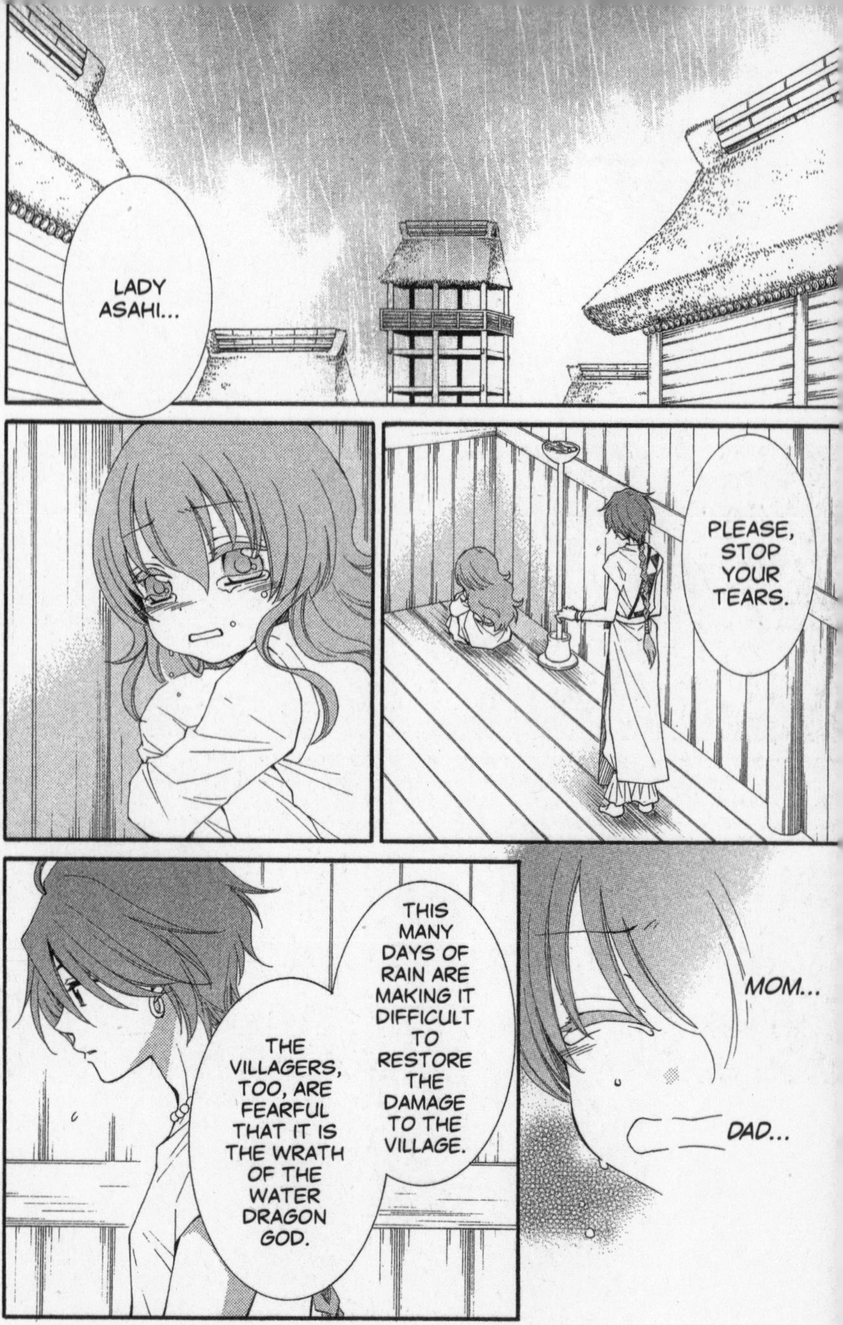
LADY ASAHI...
PLEASE, STOP YOUR TEARS.
MOM...
DAD...
THIS MANY DAYS OF RAIN ARE MAKING IT DIFFICULT TO RESTORE THE DAMAGE TO THE VILLAGE.
THE VILLAGERS, TOO, ARE FEARFUL THAT IT IS THE WRATH OF THE WATER DRAGON GOD.

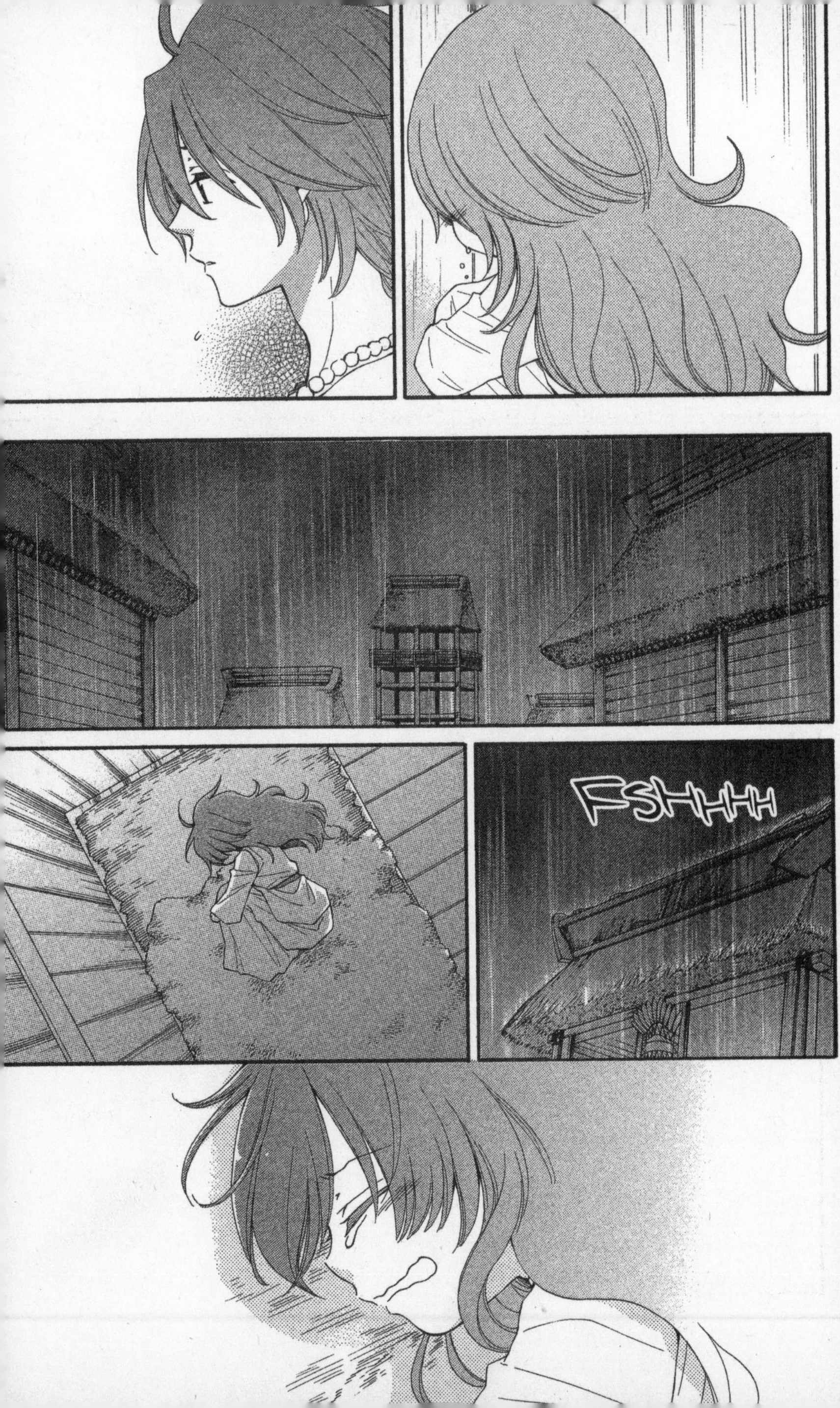
FSHHHH

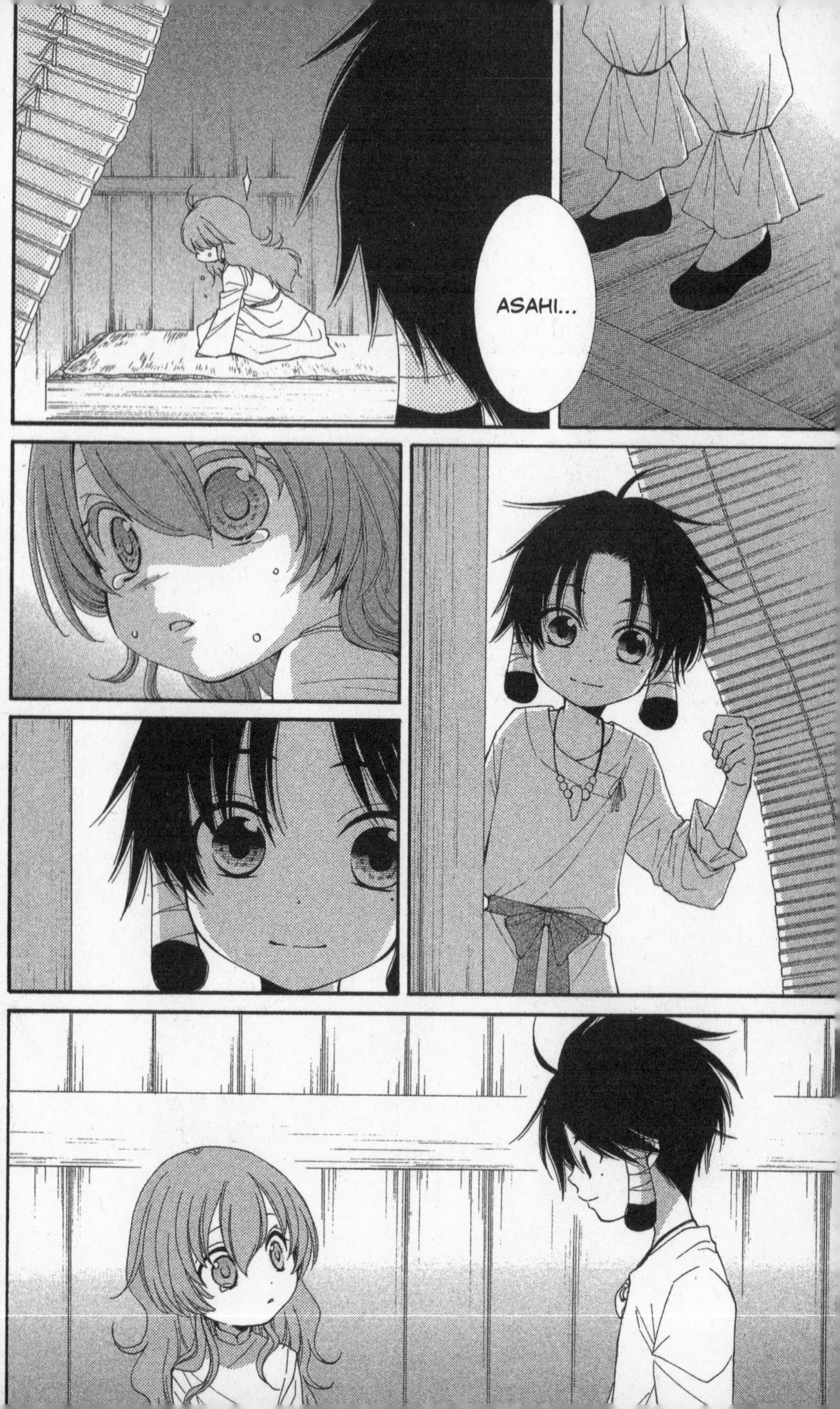
ASAHI...

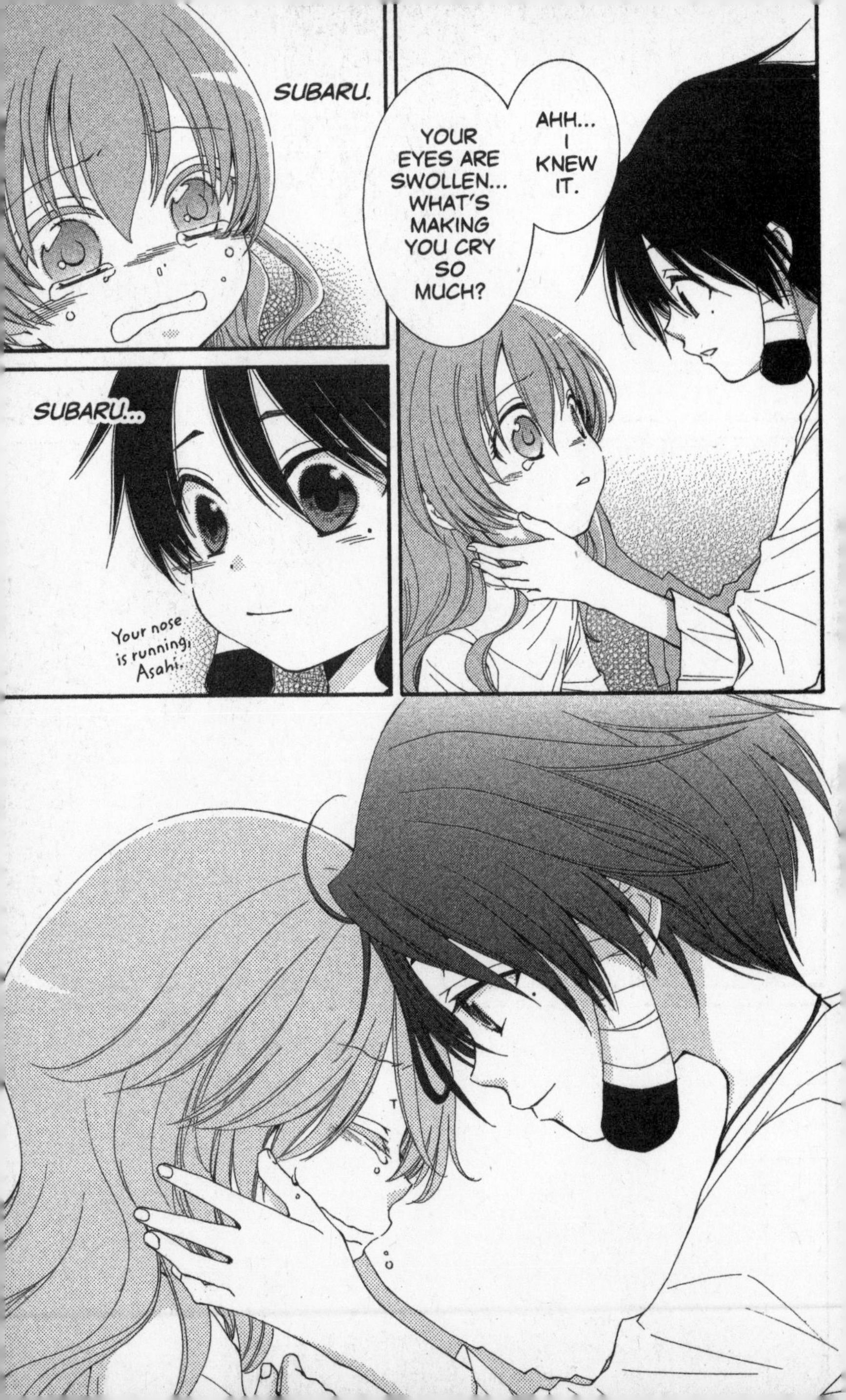
AHH... I KNEW IT.
YOUR EYES ARE SWOLLEN... WHAT'S MAKING YOU CRY SO MUCH?
SUBARU.
SUBARU...
Your nose is running, Asahi.

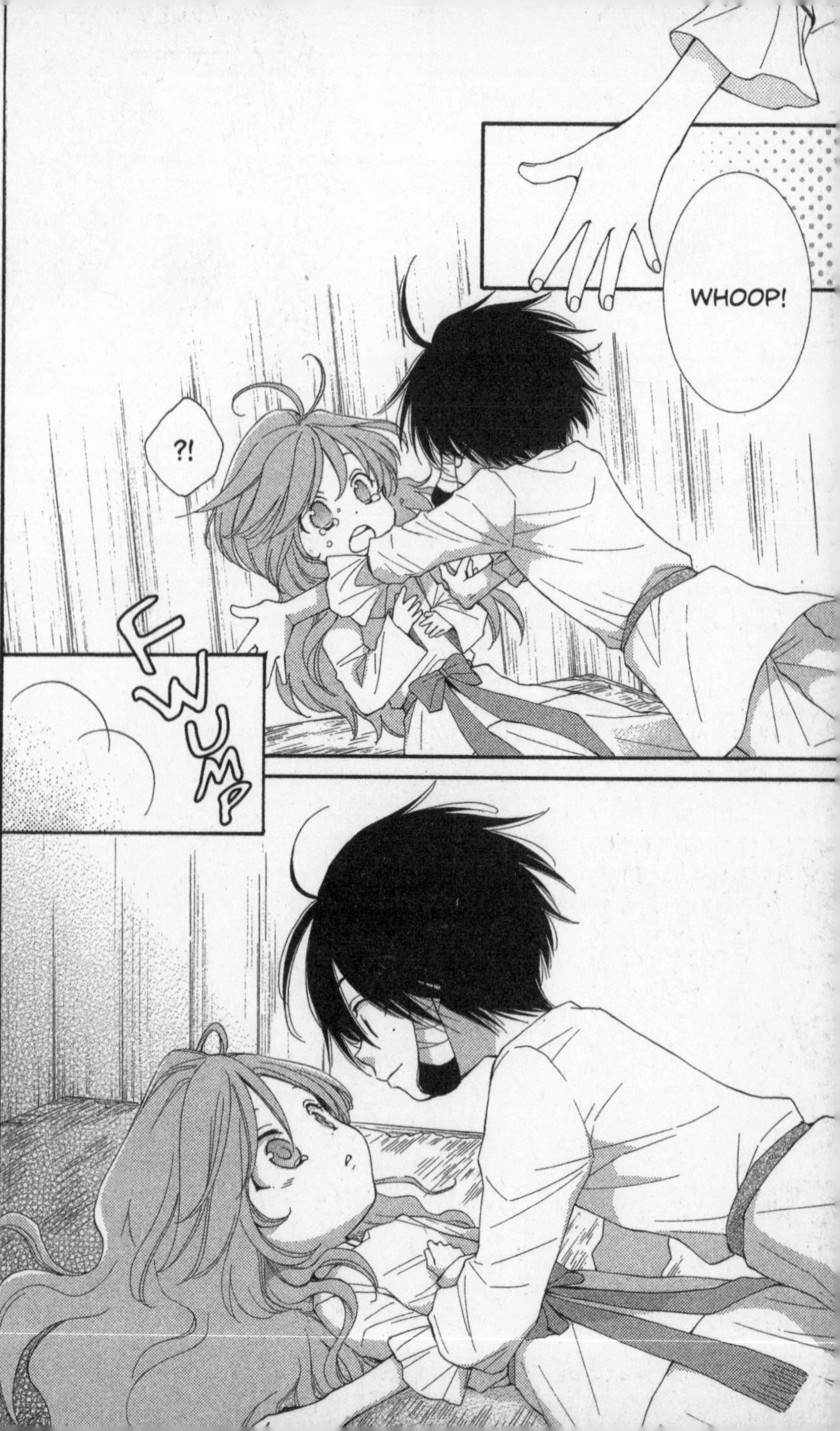
WHOOP!
?!
FWUMP

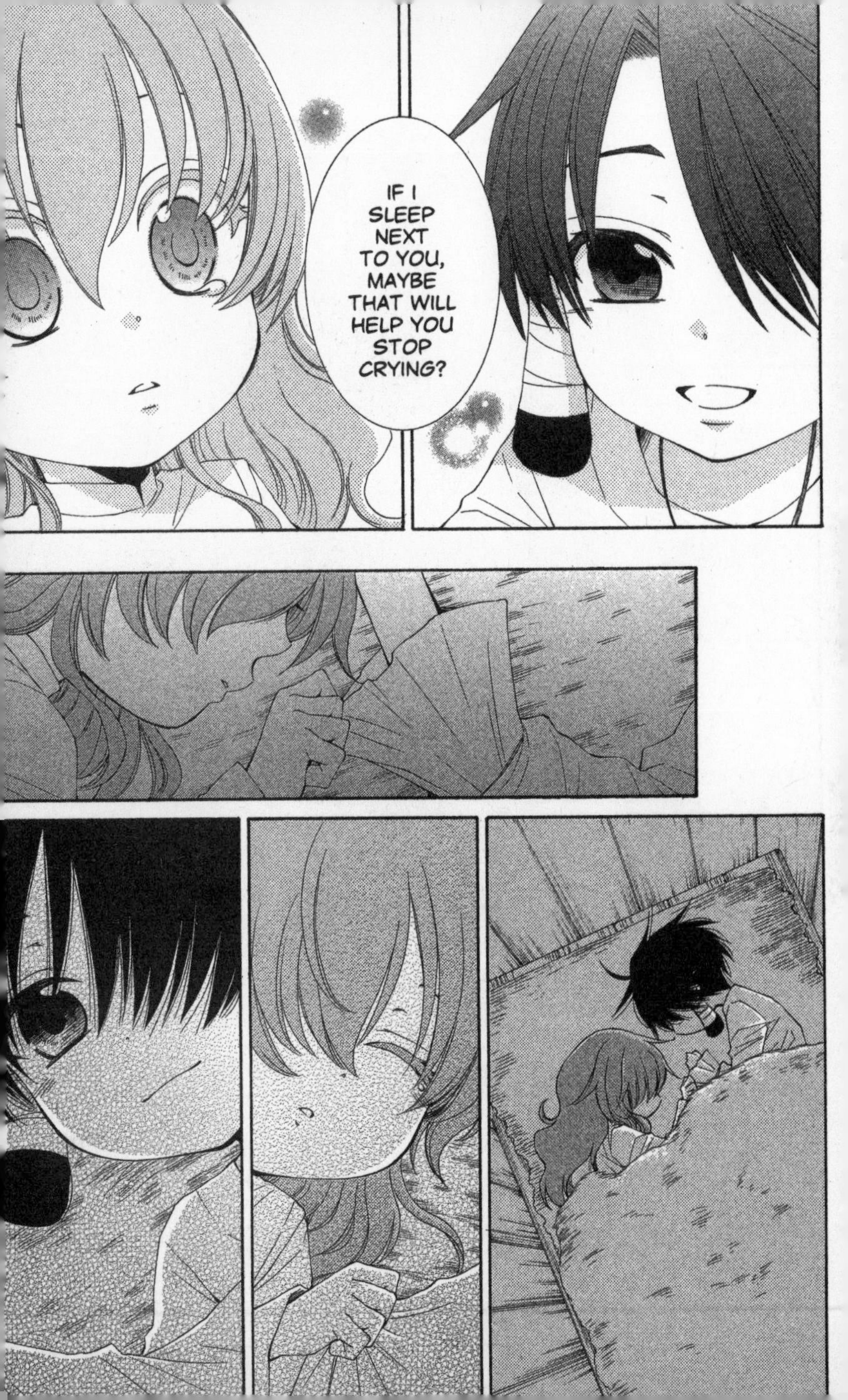
IF I SLEEP NEXT TO YOU, MAYBE THAT WILL HELP YOU STOP CRYING?

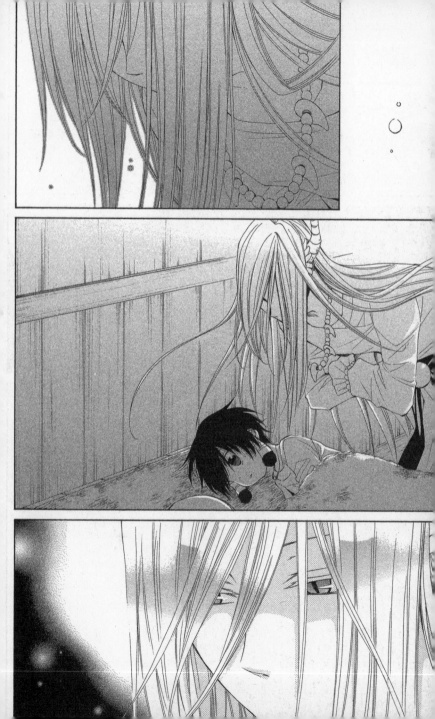

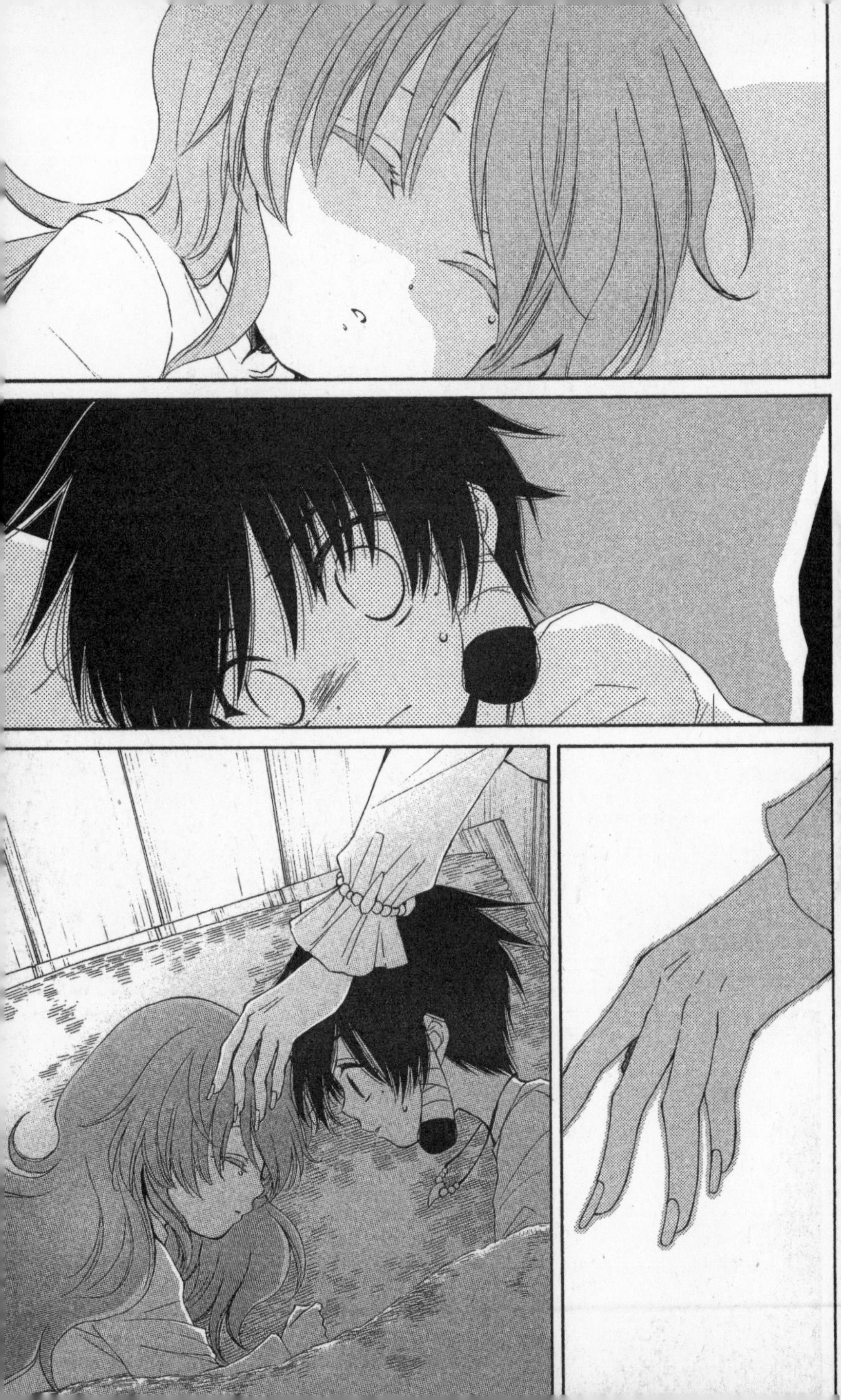

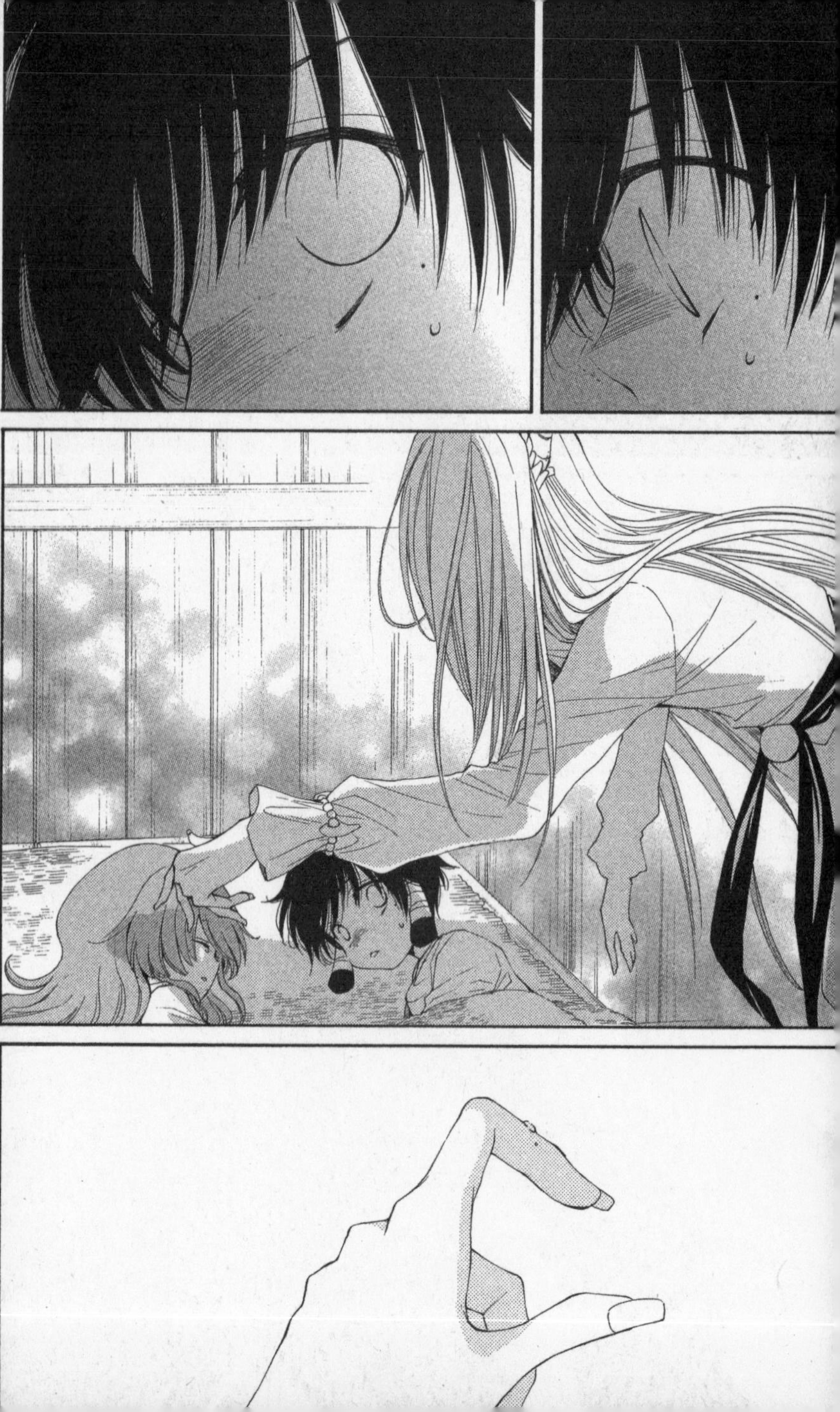

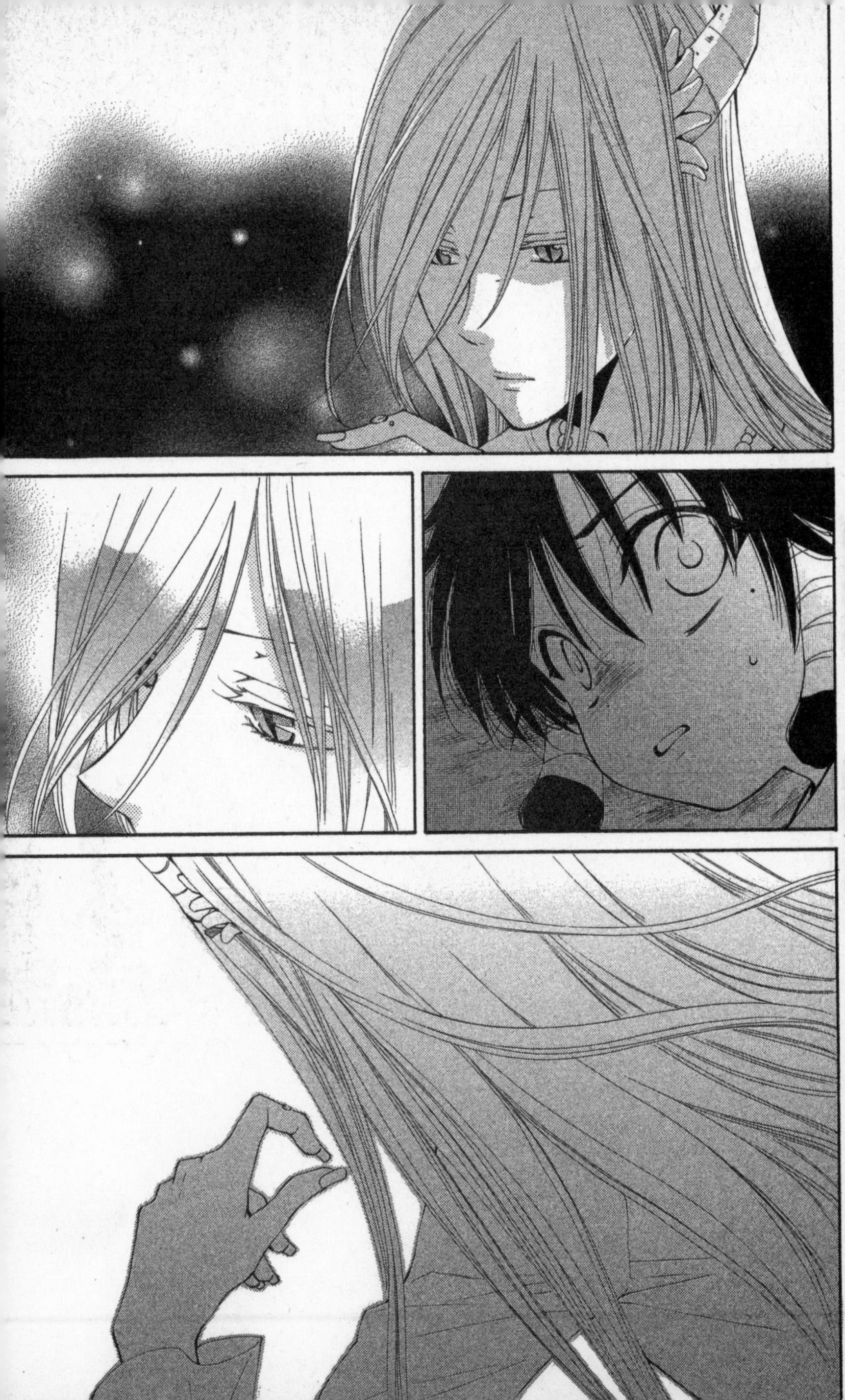

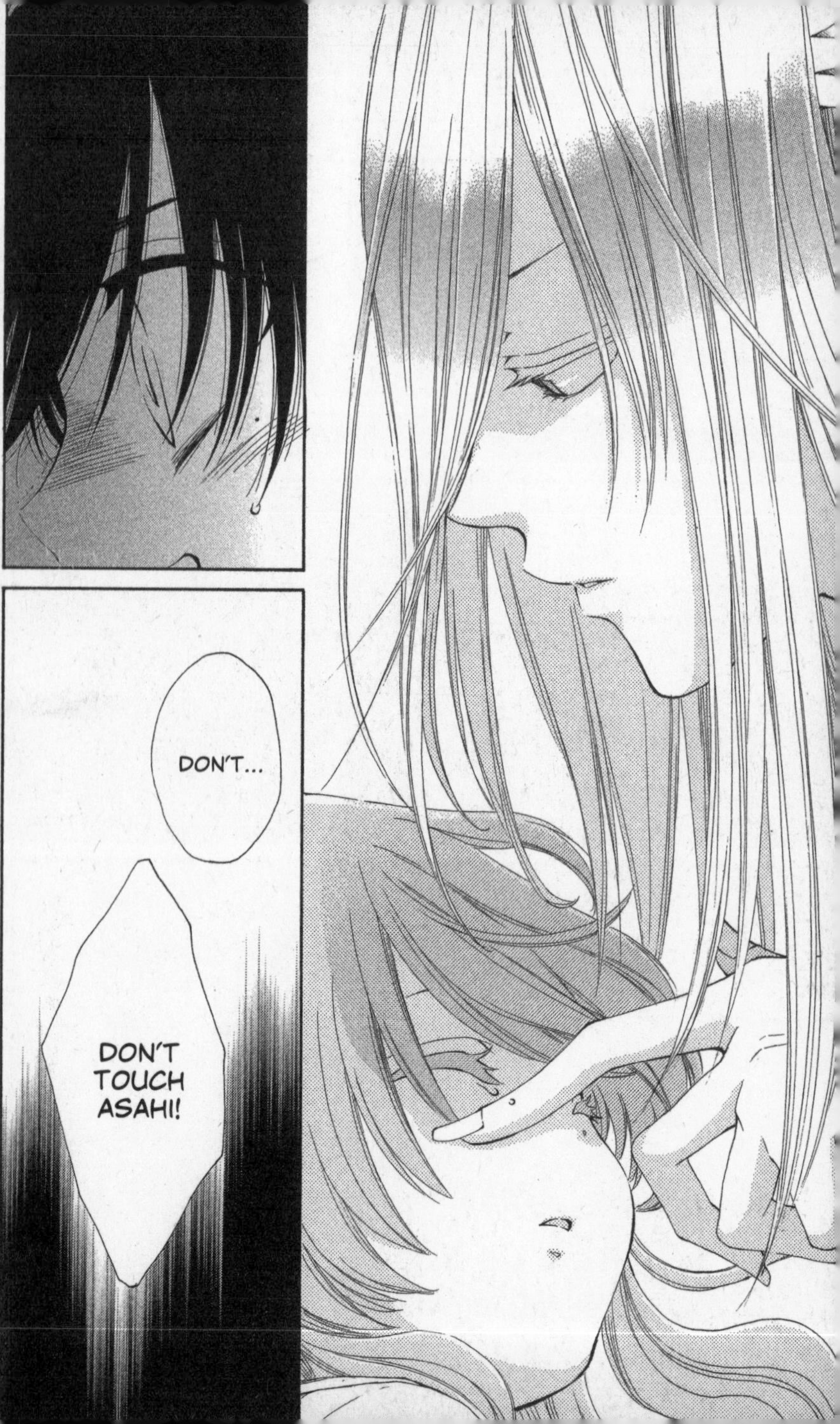
DON'T...
DON'T TOUCH ASAHI!

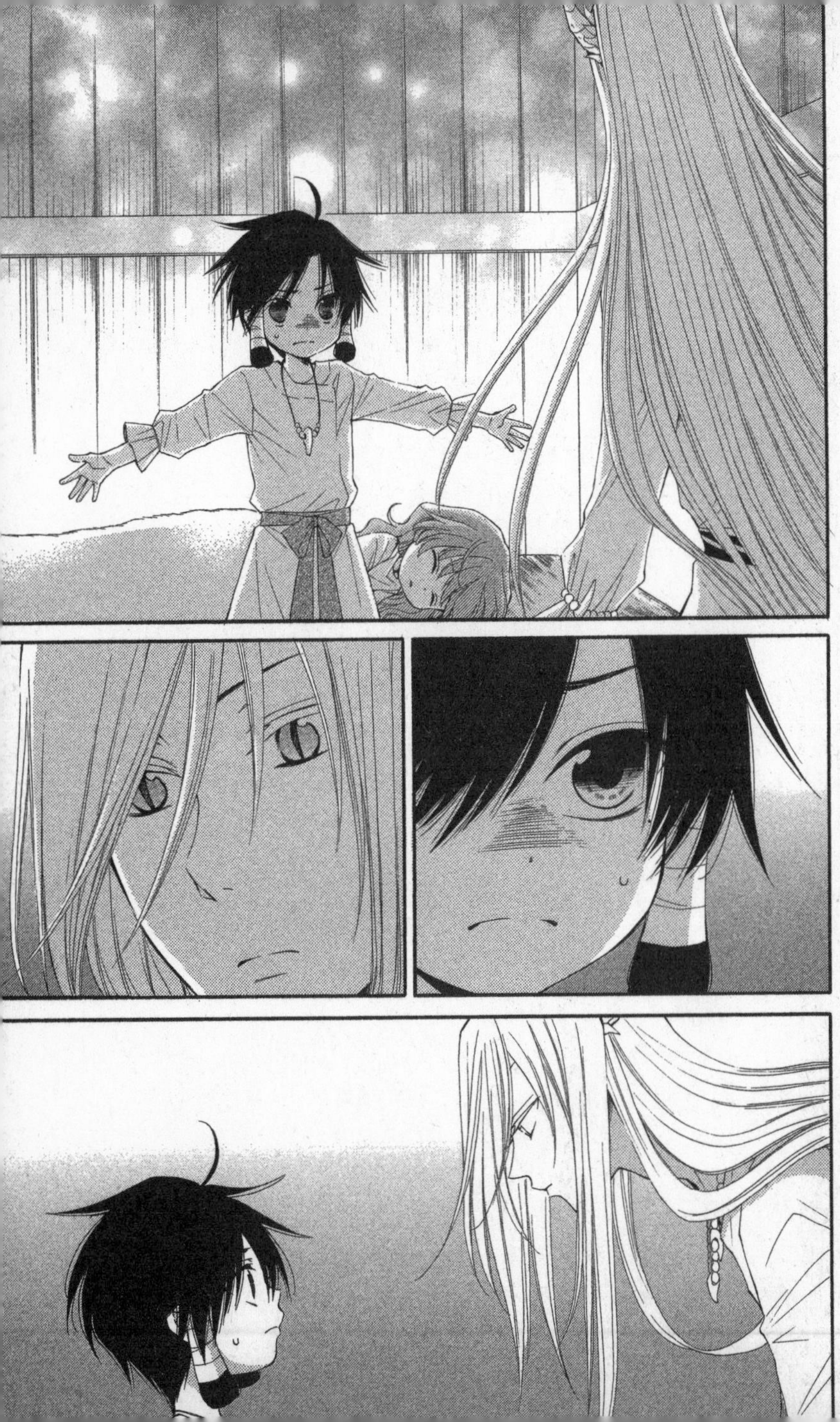

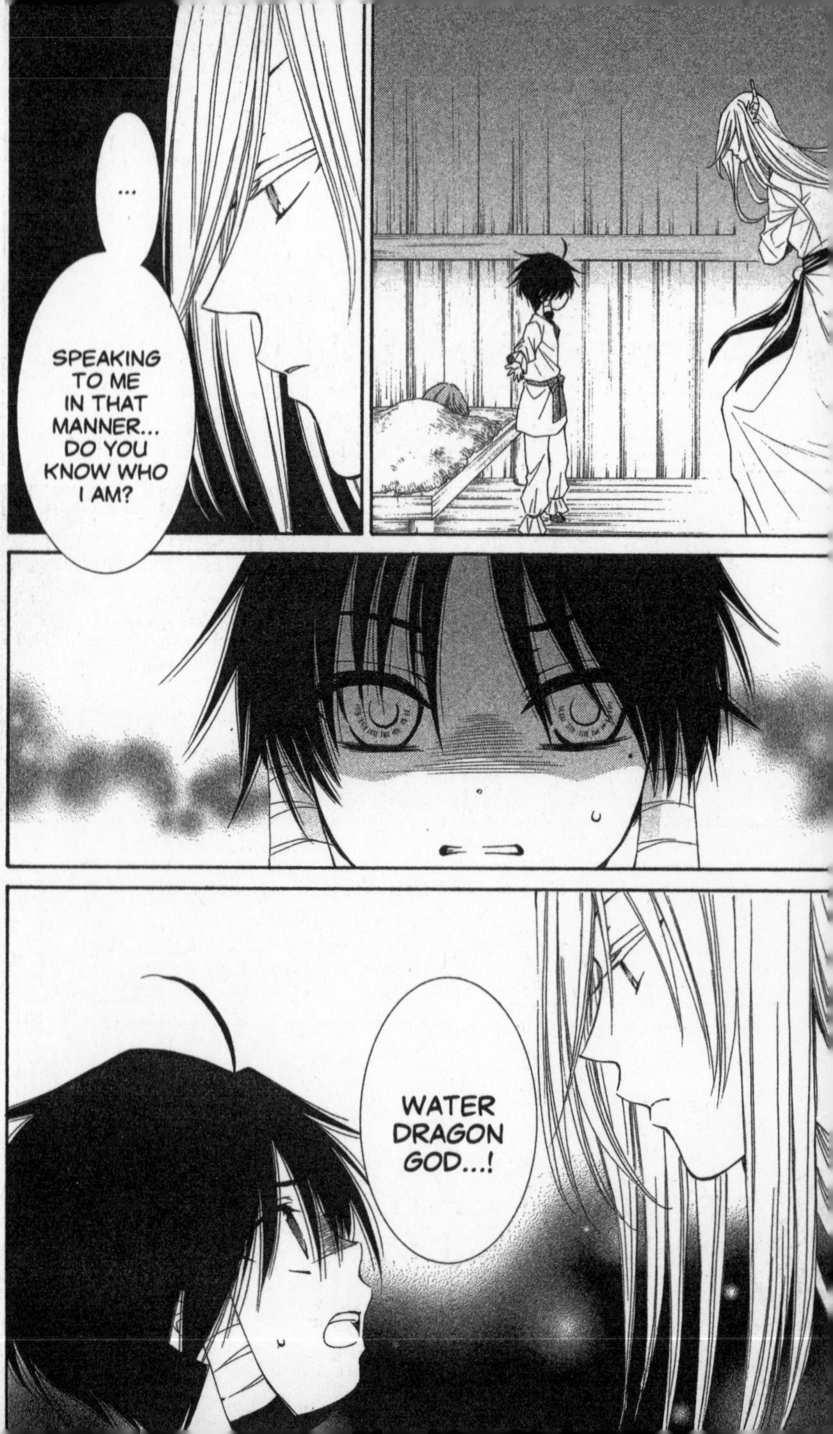
...
SPEAKING TO ME IN THAT MANNER... DO YOU KNOW WHO I AM?
WATER DRAGON GOD...!

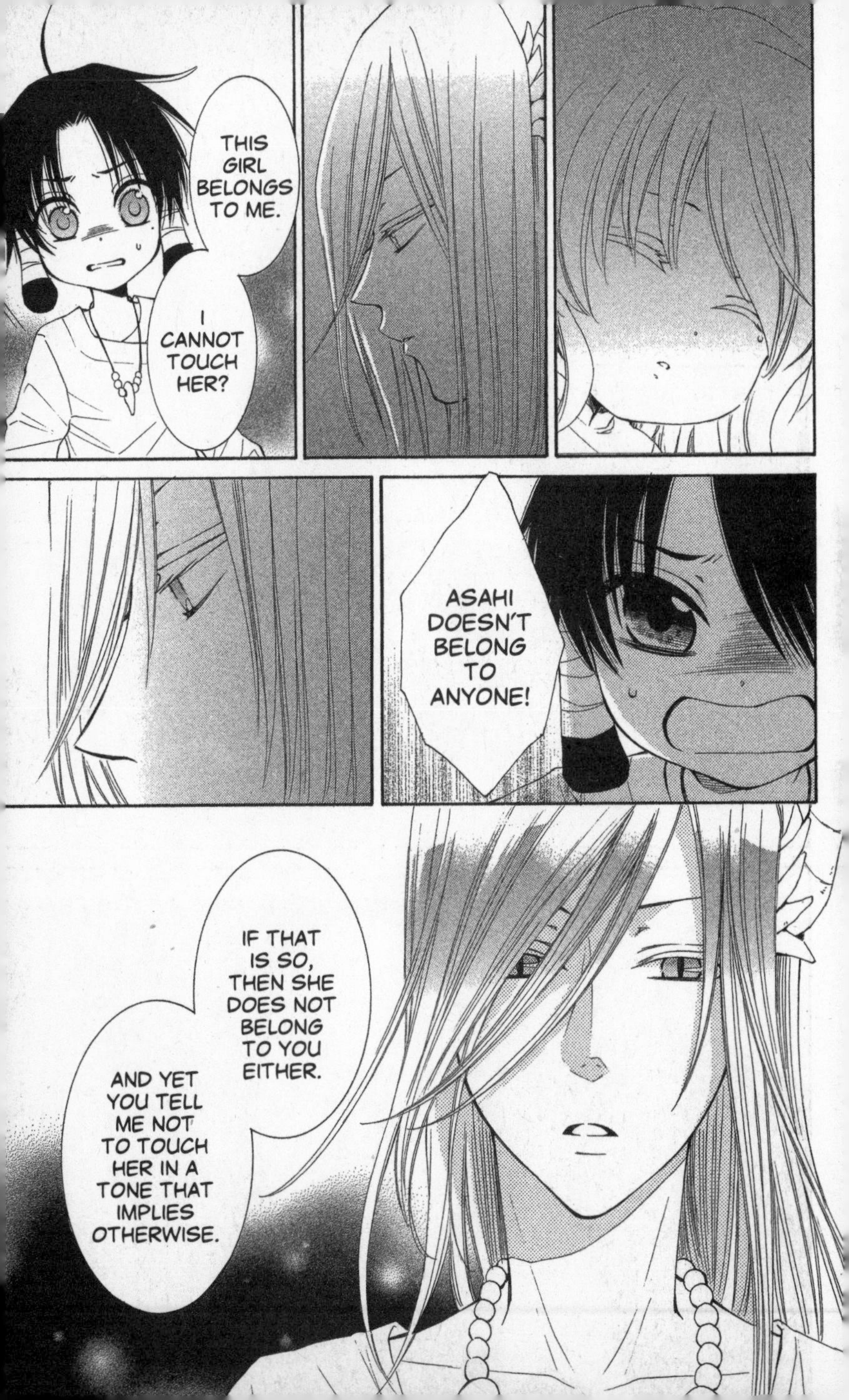
THIS GIRL BELONGS TO ME.
I CANNOT TOUCH HER?
ASAHI DOESN'T BELONG TO ANYONE!
IF THAT IS SO, THEN SHE DOES NOT BELONG TO YOU EITHER.
AND YET YOU TELL ME NOT TO TOUCH HER IN A TONE THAT IMPLIES OTHERWISE.

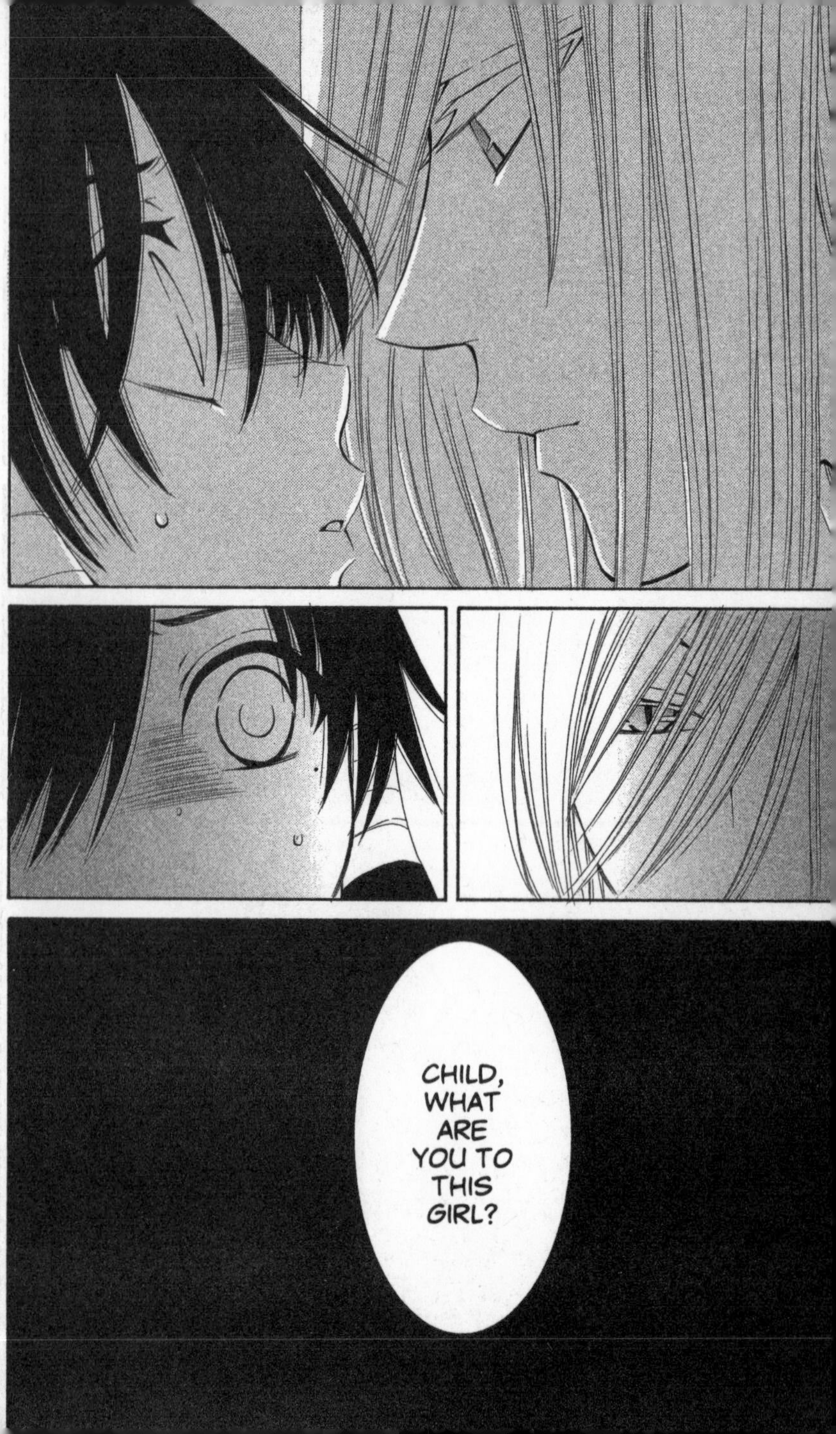
CHILD, WHAT ARE YOU TO THIS GIRL?

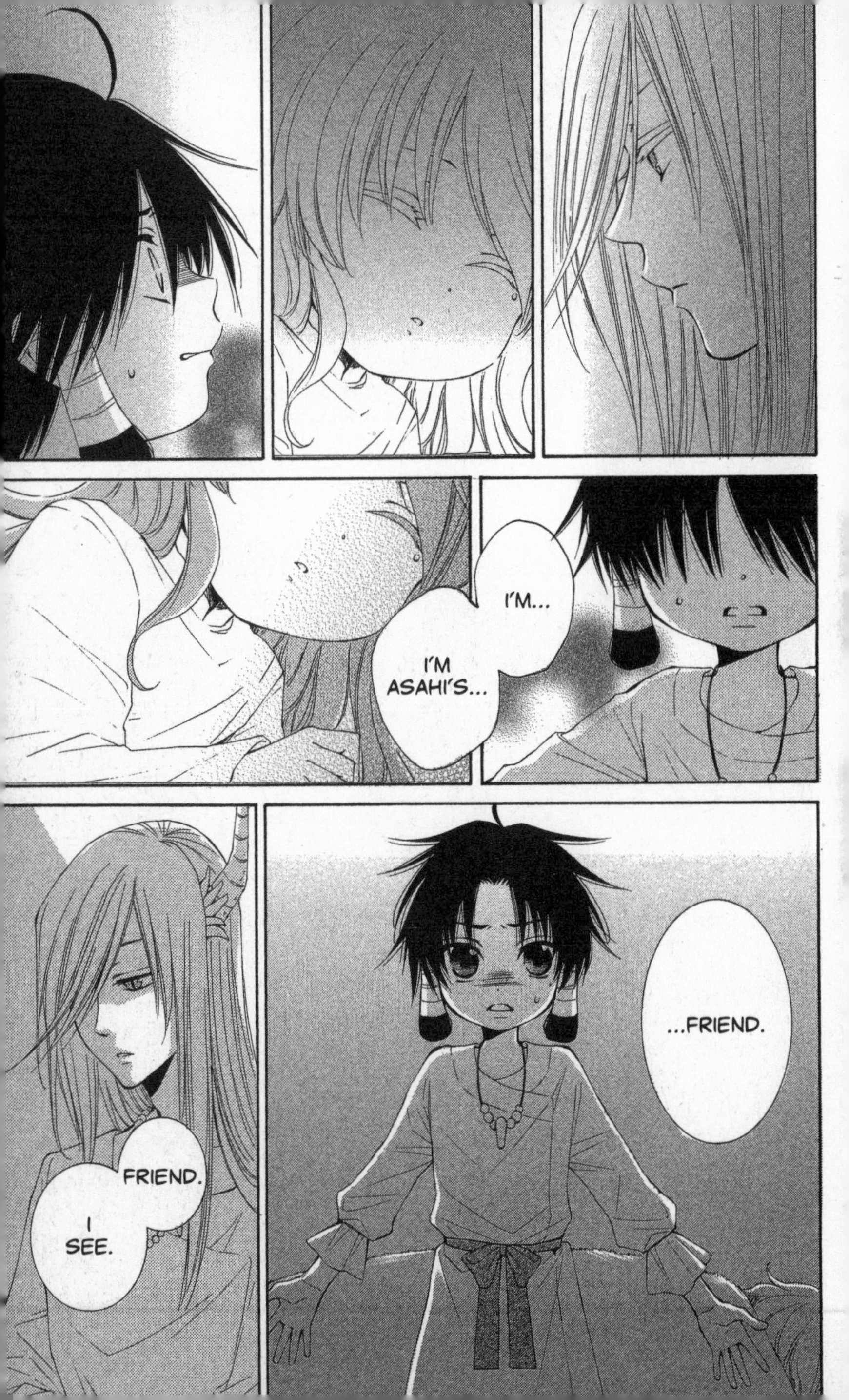
I'M...
I'M ASAHI'S...
...FRIEND.
FRIEND.
I SEE.

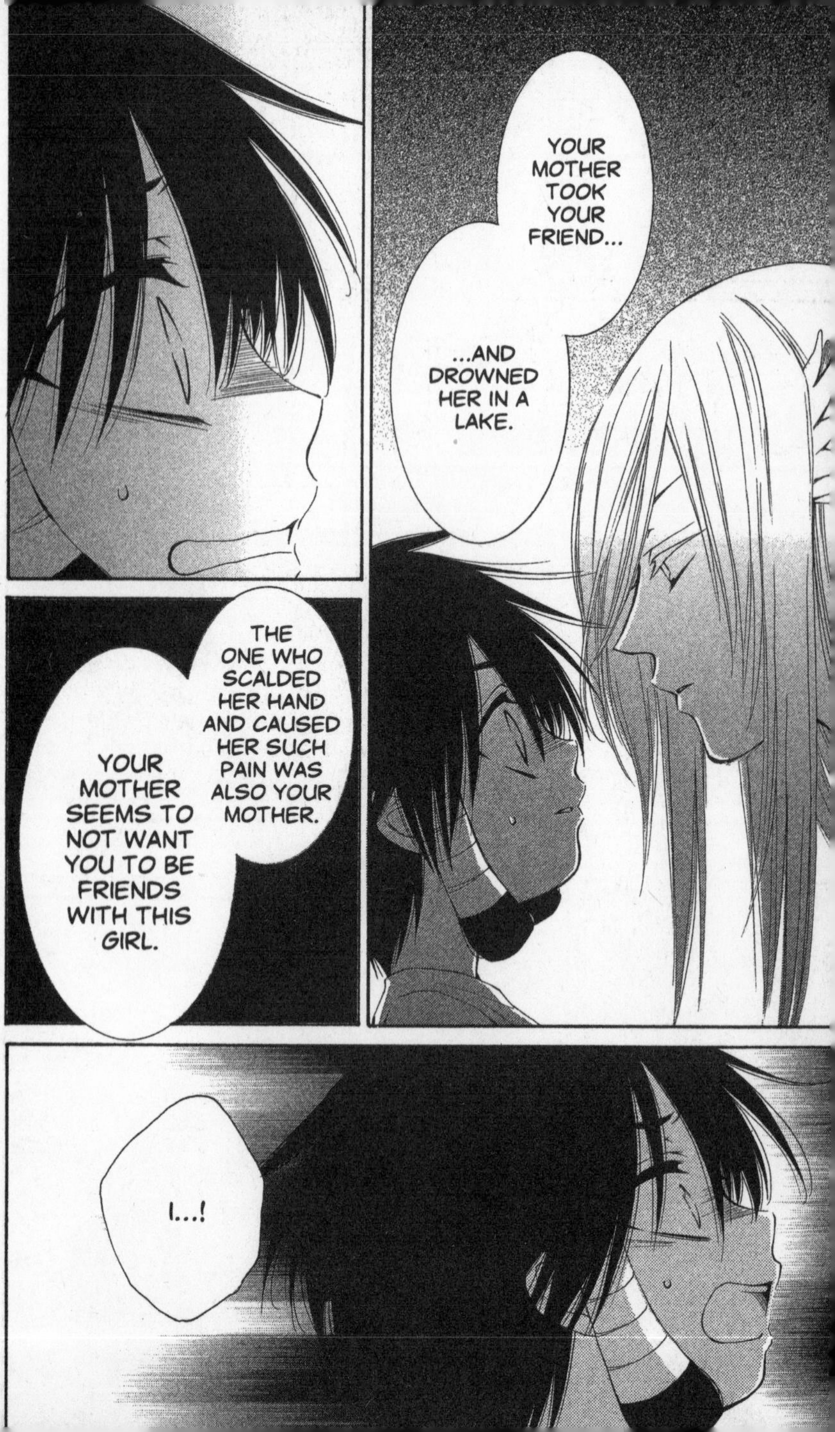
YOUR MOTHER TOOK YOUR FRIEND...
...AND DROWNED HER IN A LAKE.
THE ONE WHO SCALDED HER HAND AND CAUSED HER SUCH PAIN WAS ALSO YOUR MOTHER.
YOUR MOTHER SEEMS TO NOT WANT YOU TO BE FRIENDS WITH THIS GIRL.
I...!

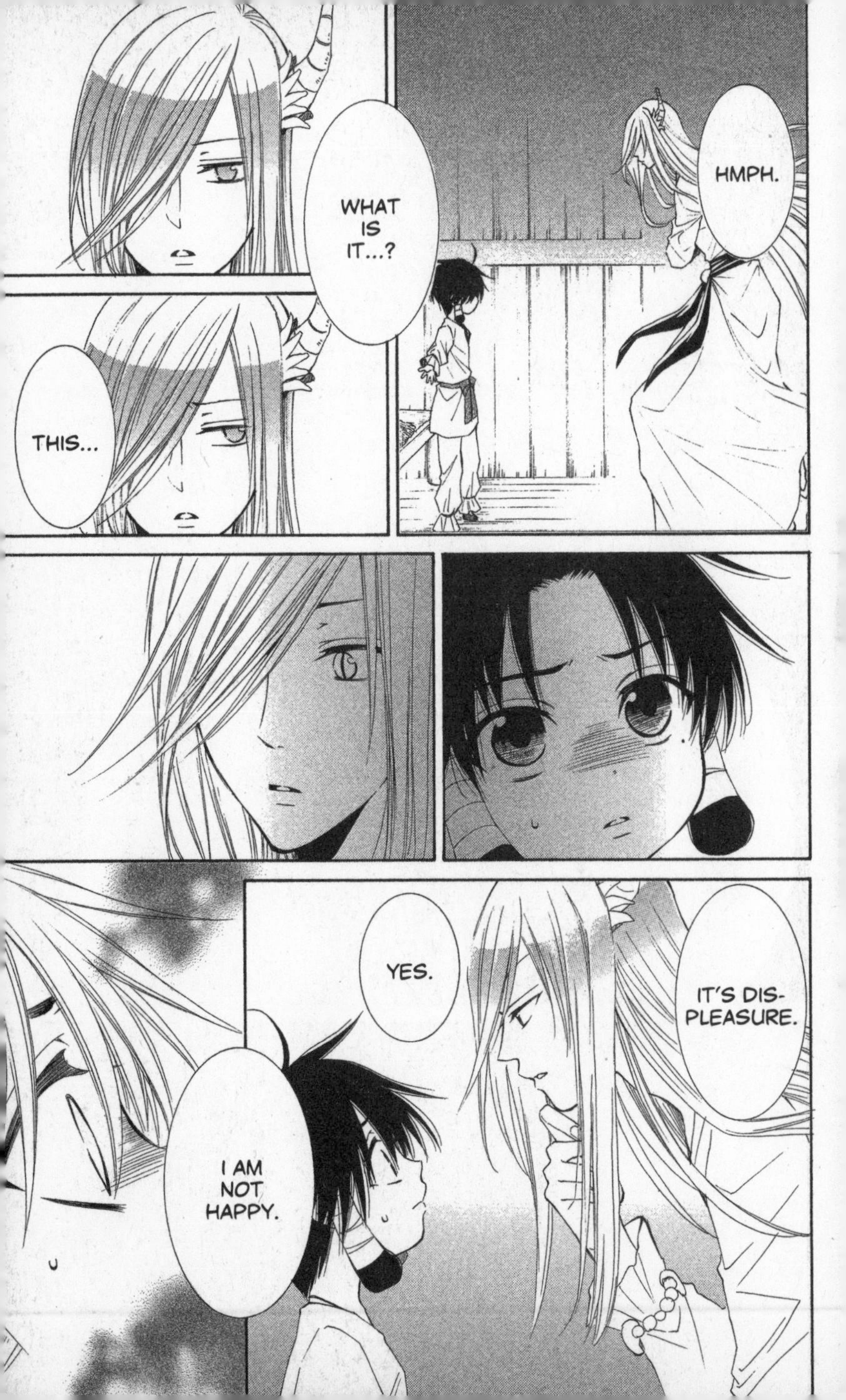
HMPH.
WHAT IS IT...?
THIS...
IT'S DIS-PLEASURE.
YES.
I AM NOT HAPPY.

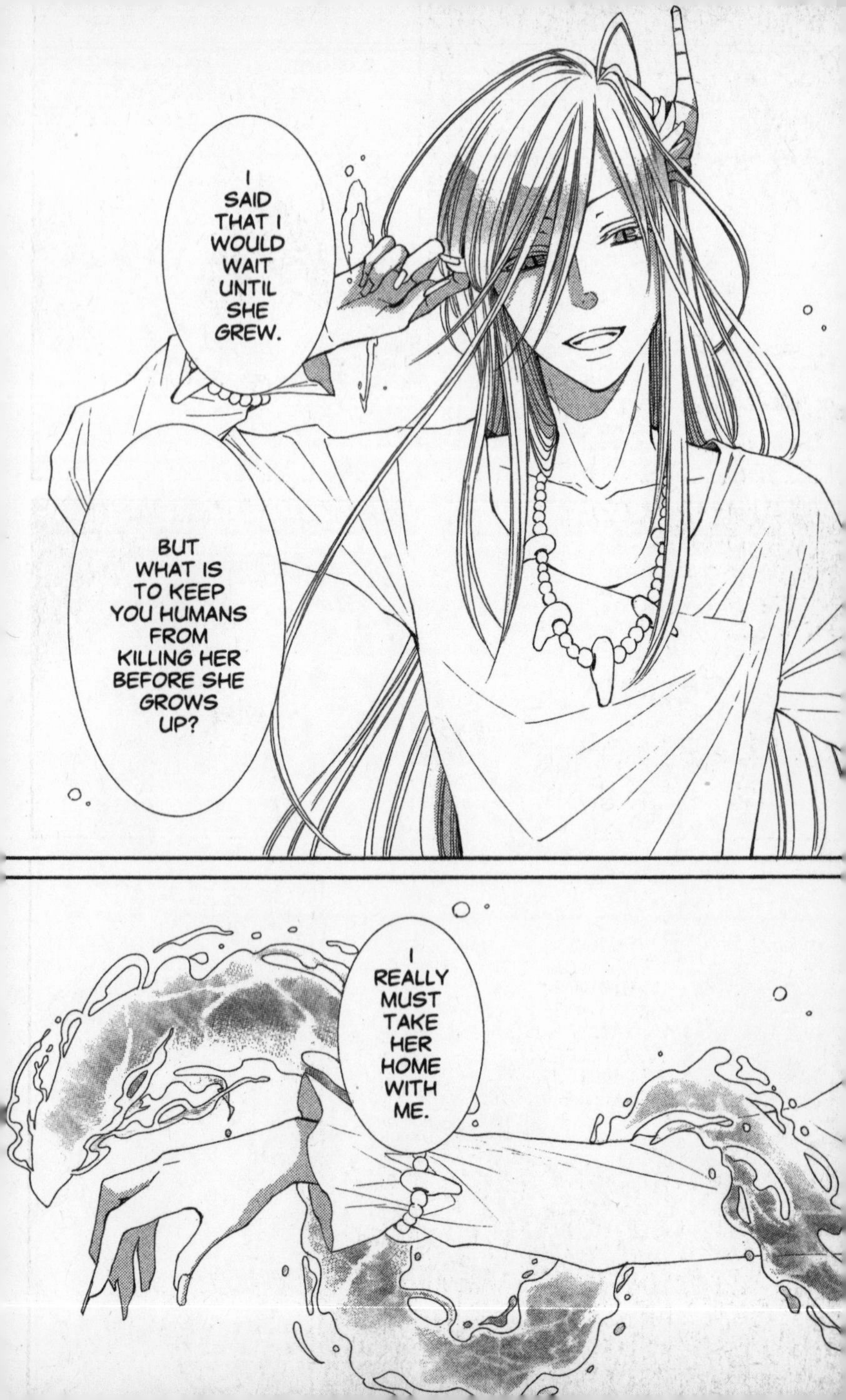
I SAID THAT I WOULD WAIT UNTIL SHE GREW.
BUT WHAT IS TO KEEP YOU HUMANS FROM KILLING HER BEFORE SHE GROWS UP?
I REALLY MUST TAKE HER HOME WITH ME.

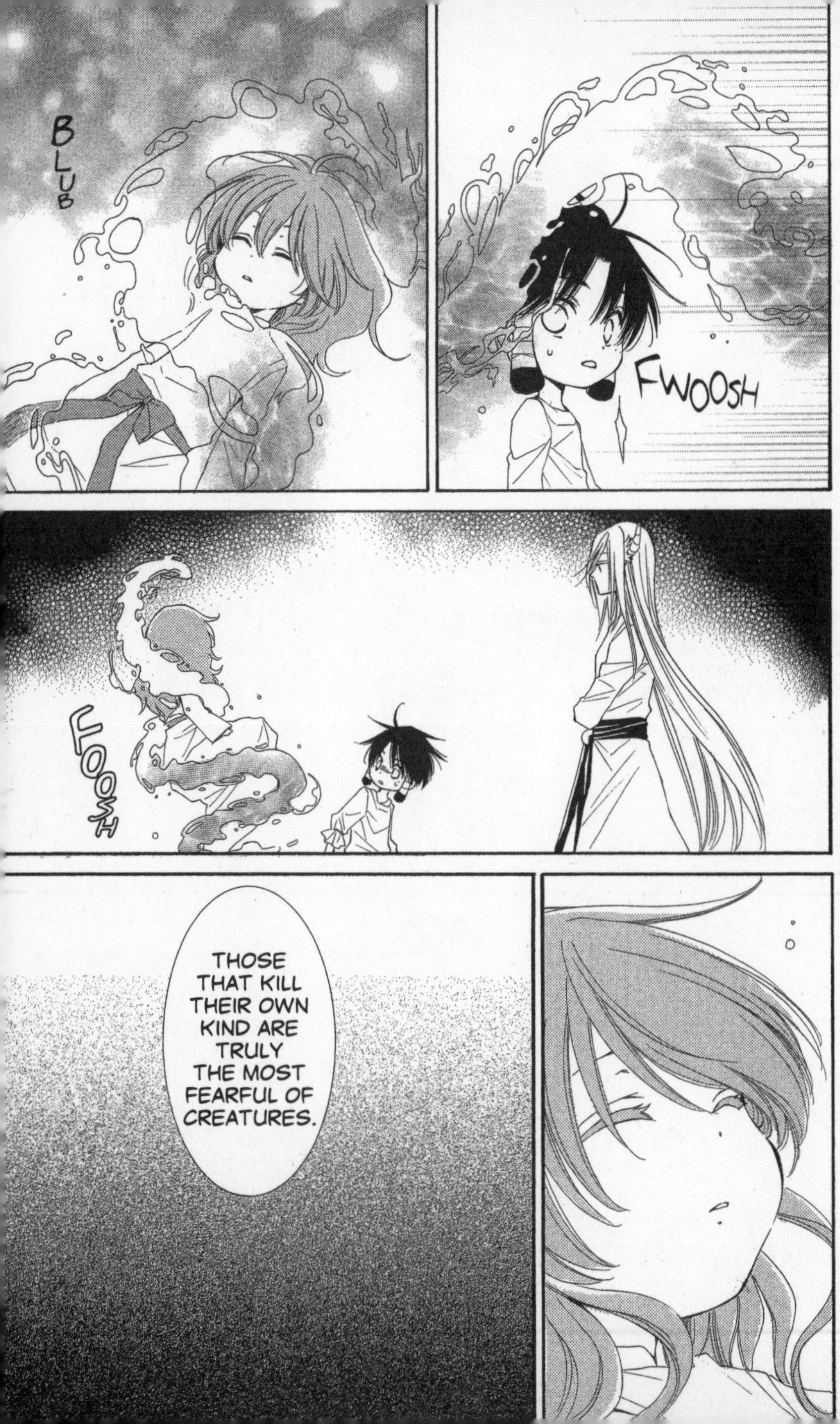
FWOOSH
BLUB
FWOOSH
THOSE THAT KILL THEIR OWN KIND ARE TRULY THE MOST FEARFUL OF CREATURES.

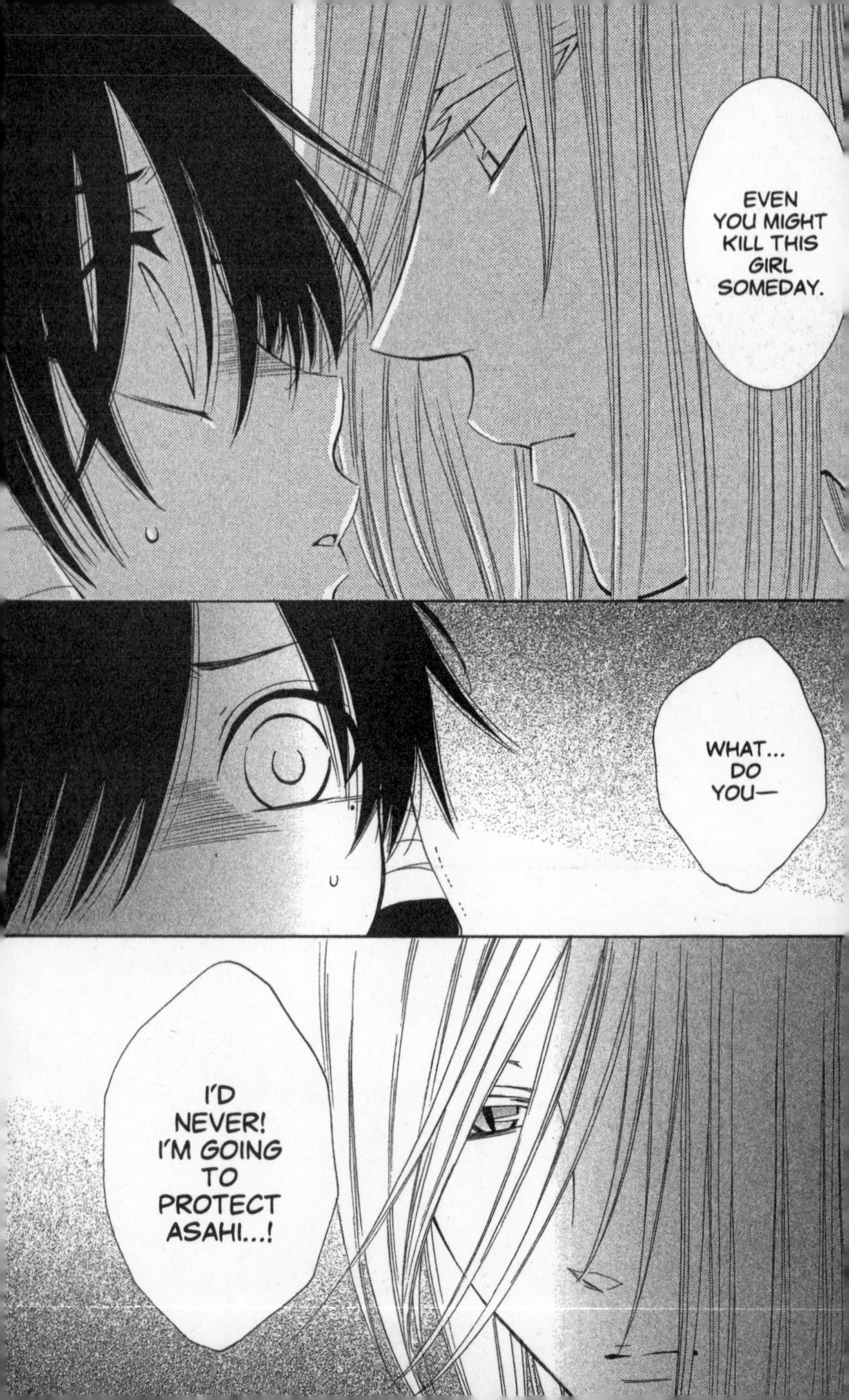
EVEN YOU MIGHT KILL THIS GIRL SOMEDAY.
WHAT... DO YOU—
I'D NEVER! I'M GOING TO PROTECT ASAHI...!

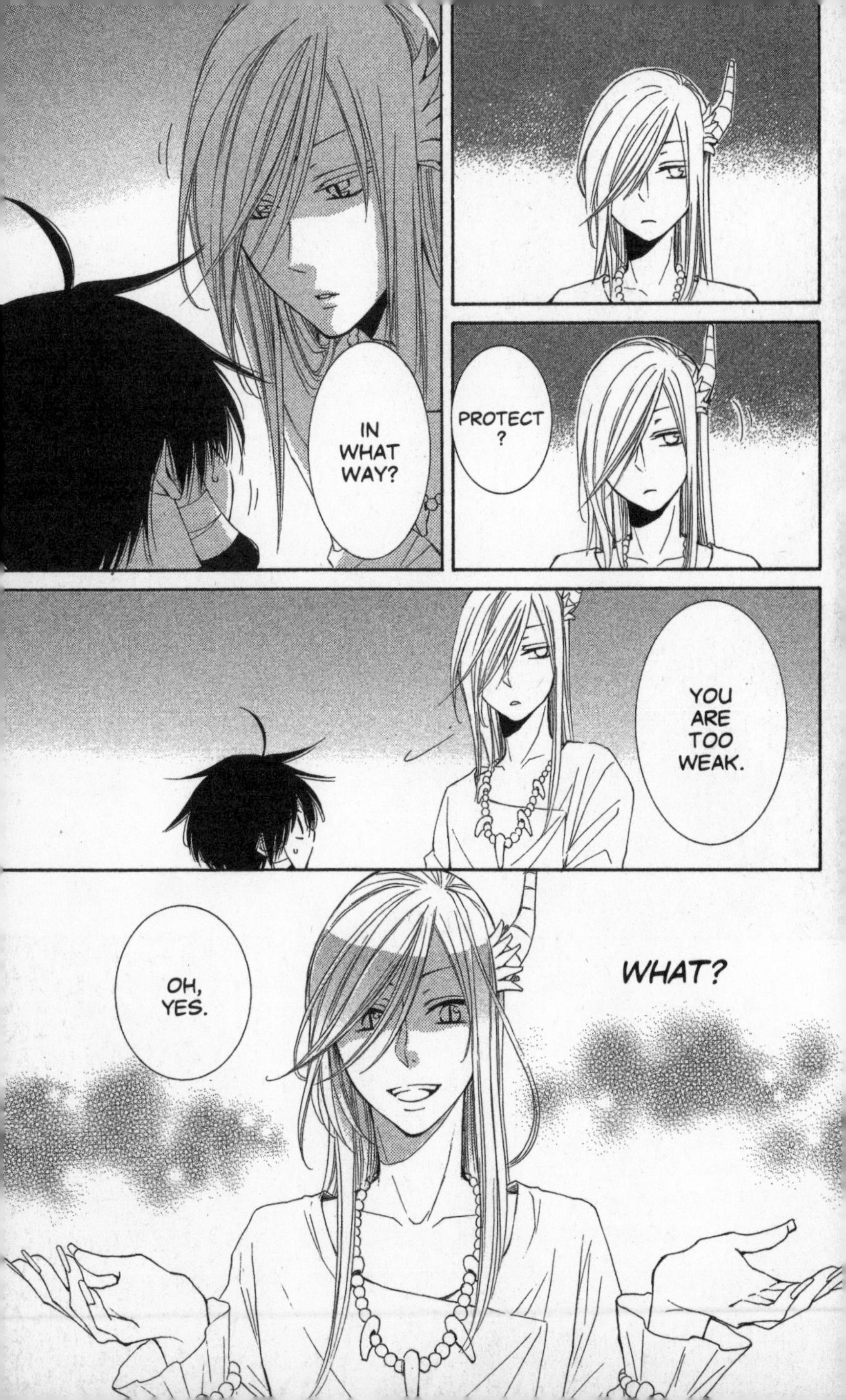
PROTECT ?
IN WHAT WAY?
YOU ARE TOO WEAK.
WHAT?
OH, YES.

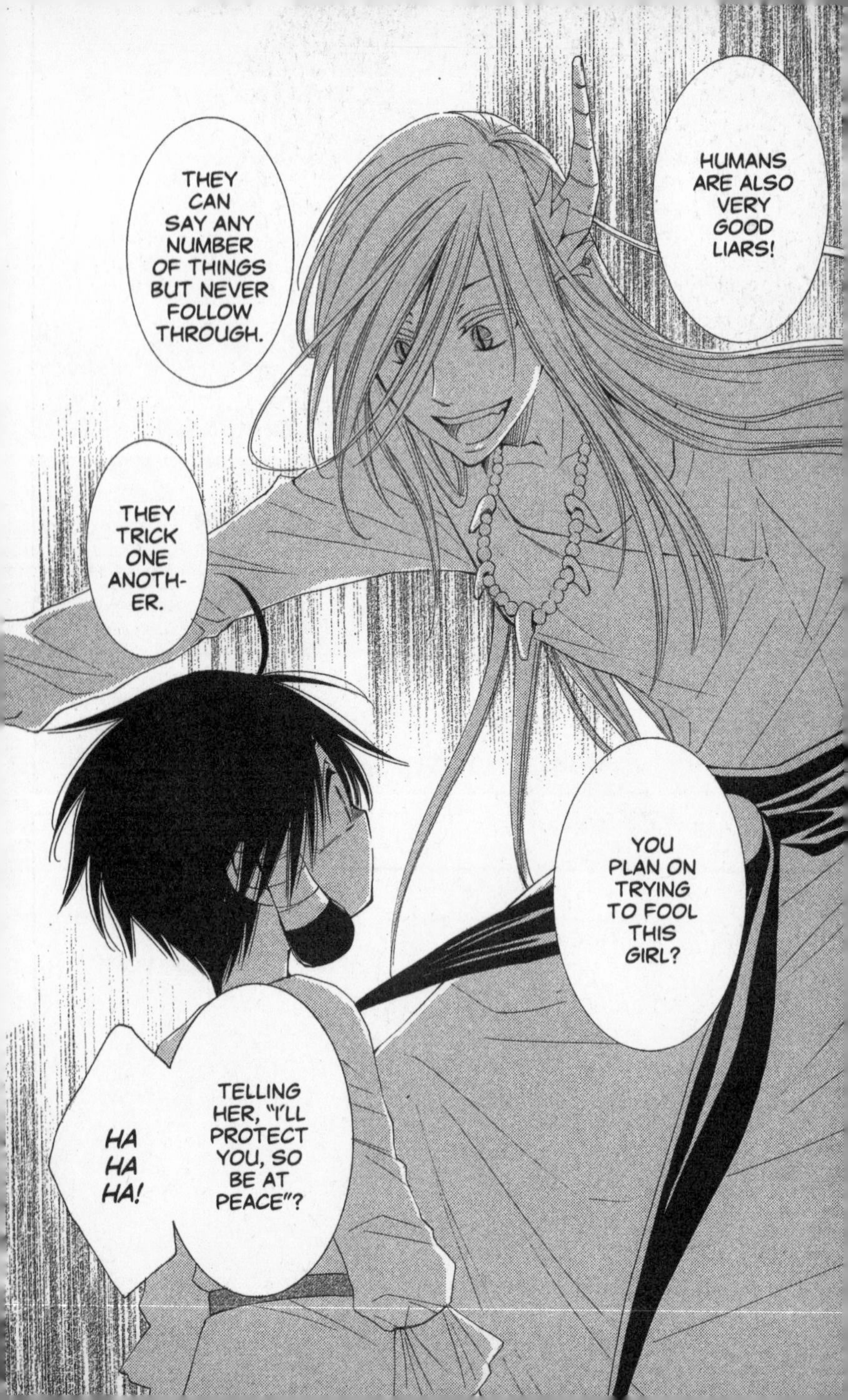
HUMANS ARE ALSO VERY GOOD LIARS!
THEY CAN SAY ANY NUMBER OF THINGS BUT NEVER FOLLOW THROUGH.
THEY TRICK ONE ANOTH-ER.
YOU PLAN ON TRYING TO FOOL THIS GIRL?
TELLING HER, "I'LL PROTECT YOU, SO BE AT PEACE"?
HA HA HA!

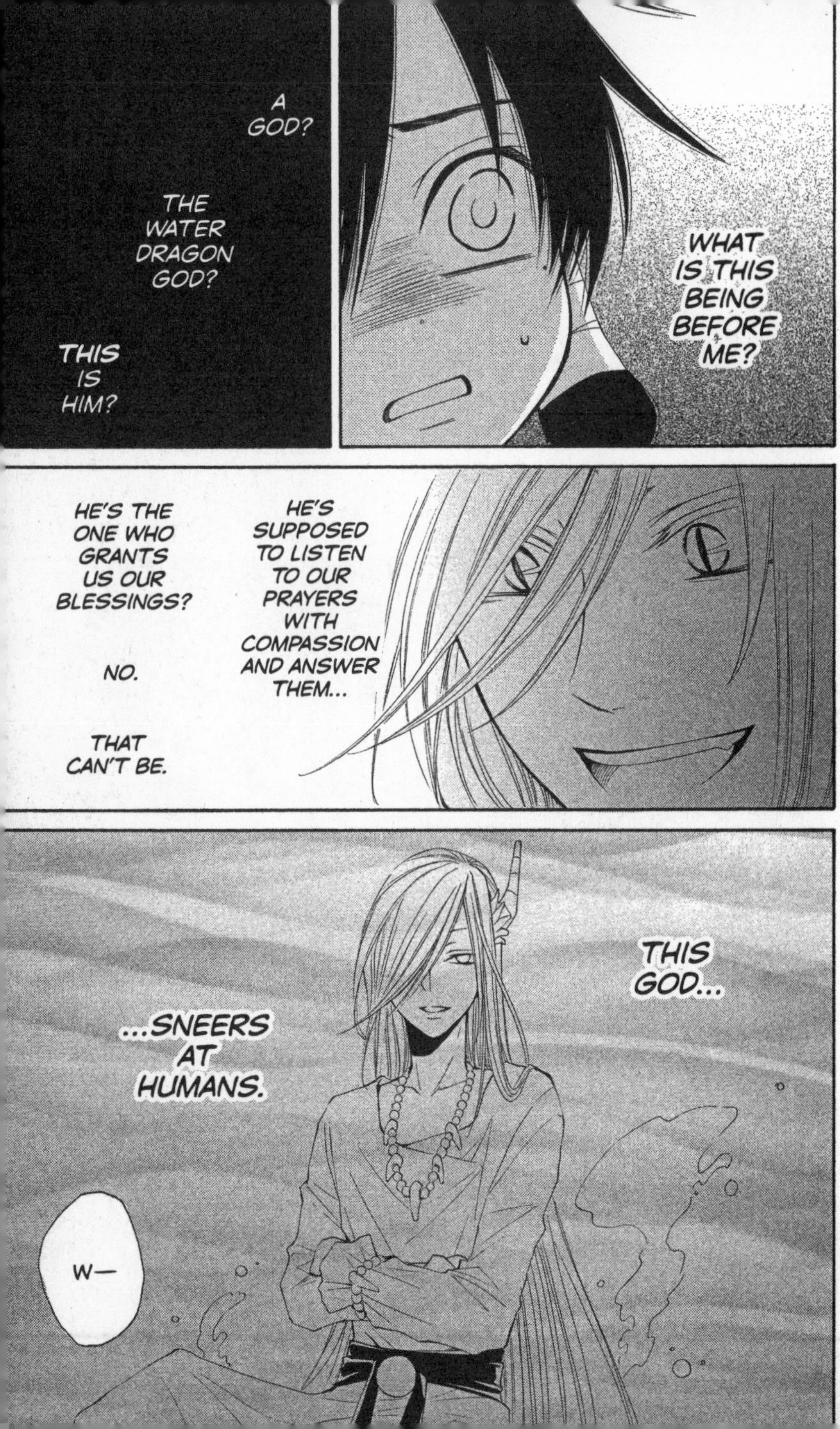
WHAT IS THIS BEING BEFORE ME?
A GOD?
THE WATER DRAGON GOD?
THIS IS HIM?
HE'S SUPPOSED TO LISTEN TO OUR PRAYERS WITH COMPASSION AND ANSWER THEM...
HE'S THE ONE WHO GRANTS US OUR BLESSINGS?
NO.
THAT CAN'T BE.
THIS GOD...
...SNEERS AT HUMANS.
W—

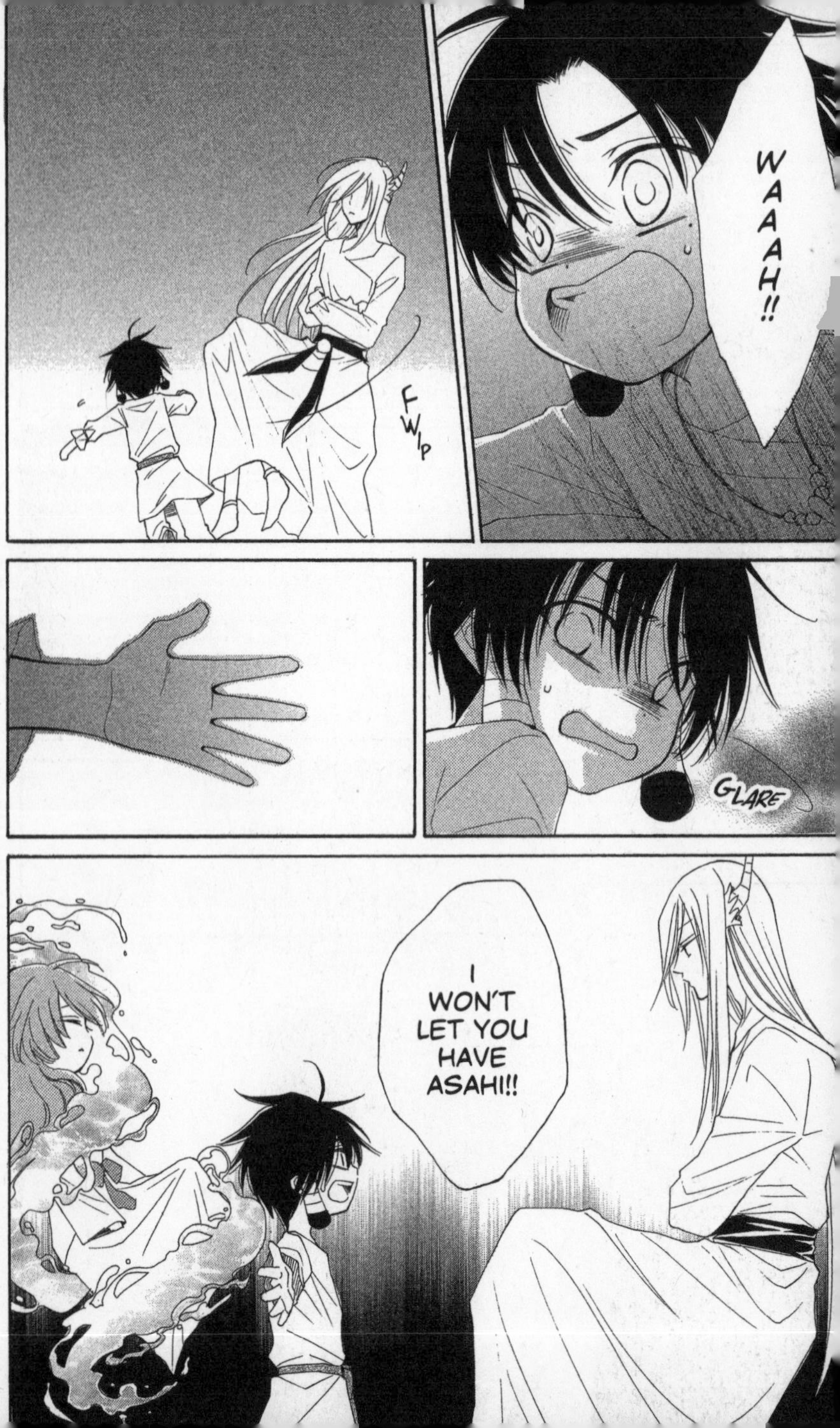
WAAAAH!!
FWIP
GLARE
I WON'T LET YOU HAVE ASAHI!!

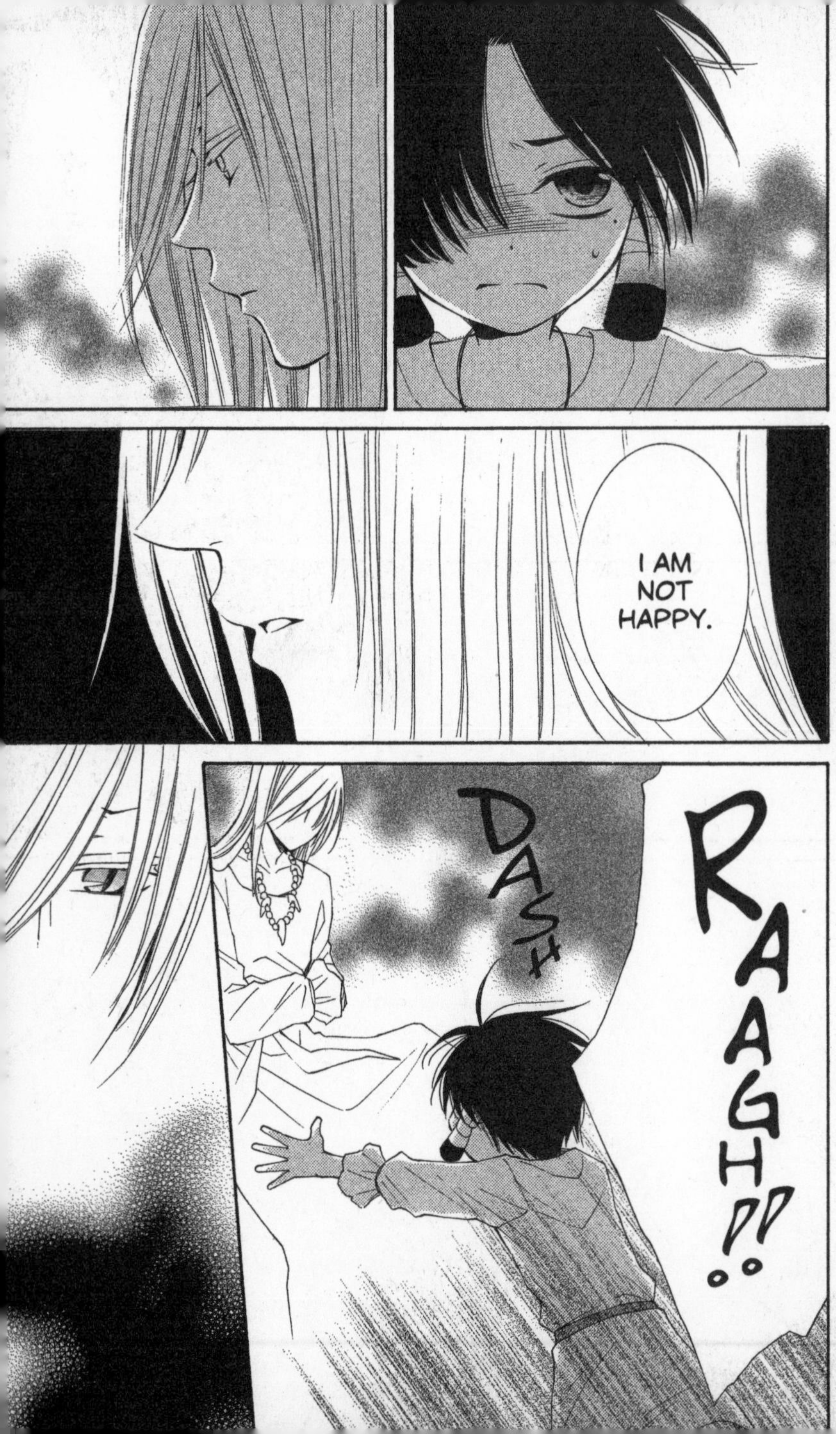
I AM NOT HAPPY.
RAAGH!!
DASH

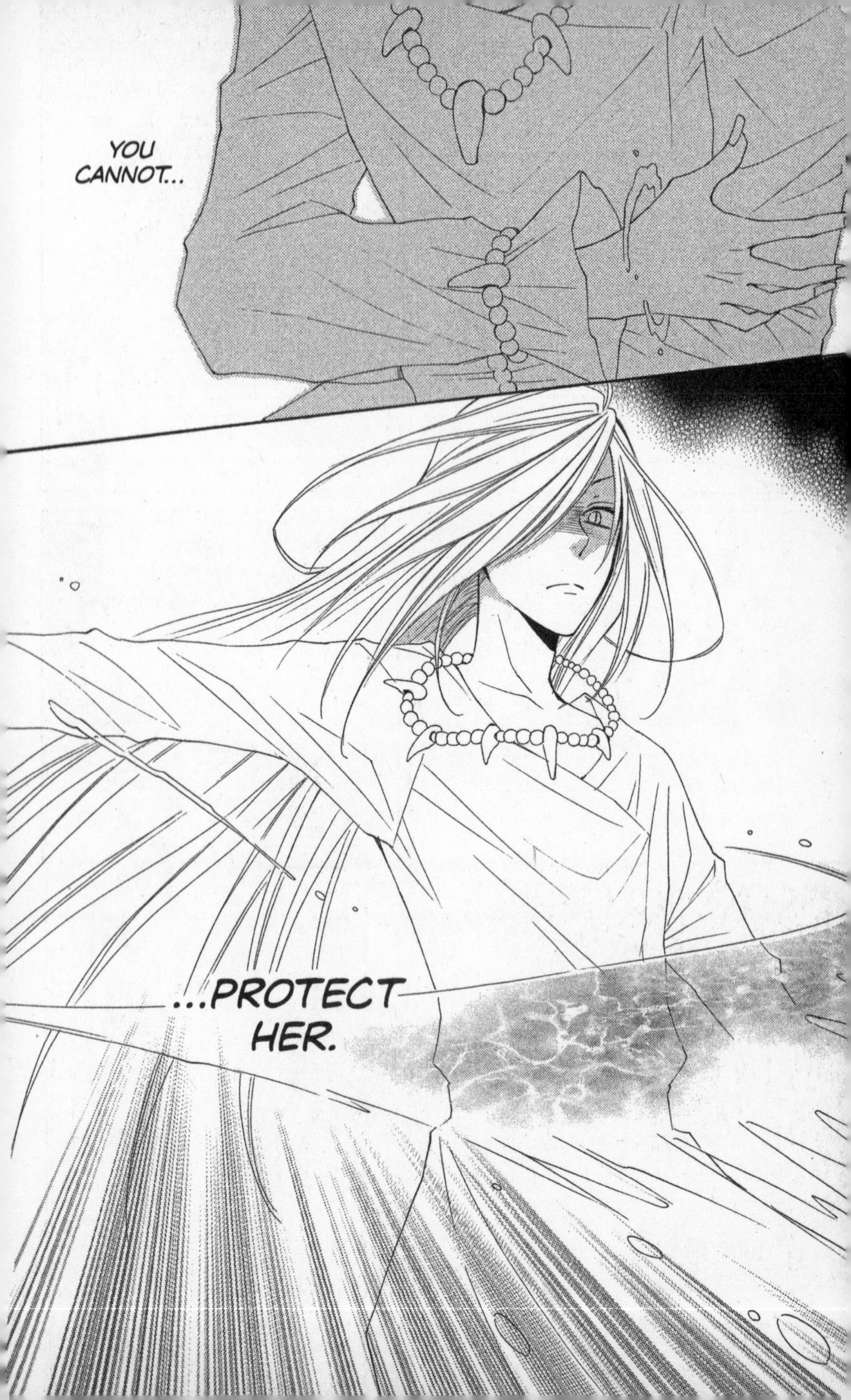
YOU CANNOT...
...PROTECT HER.

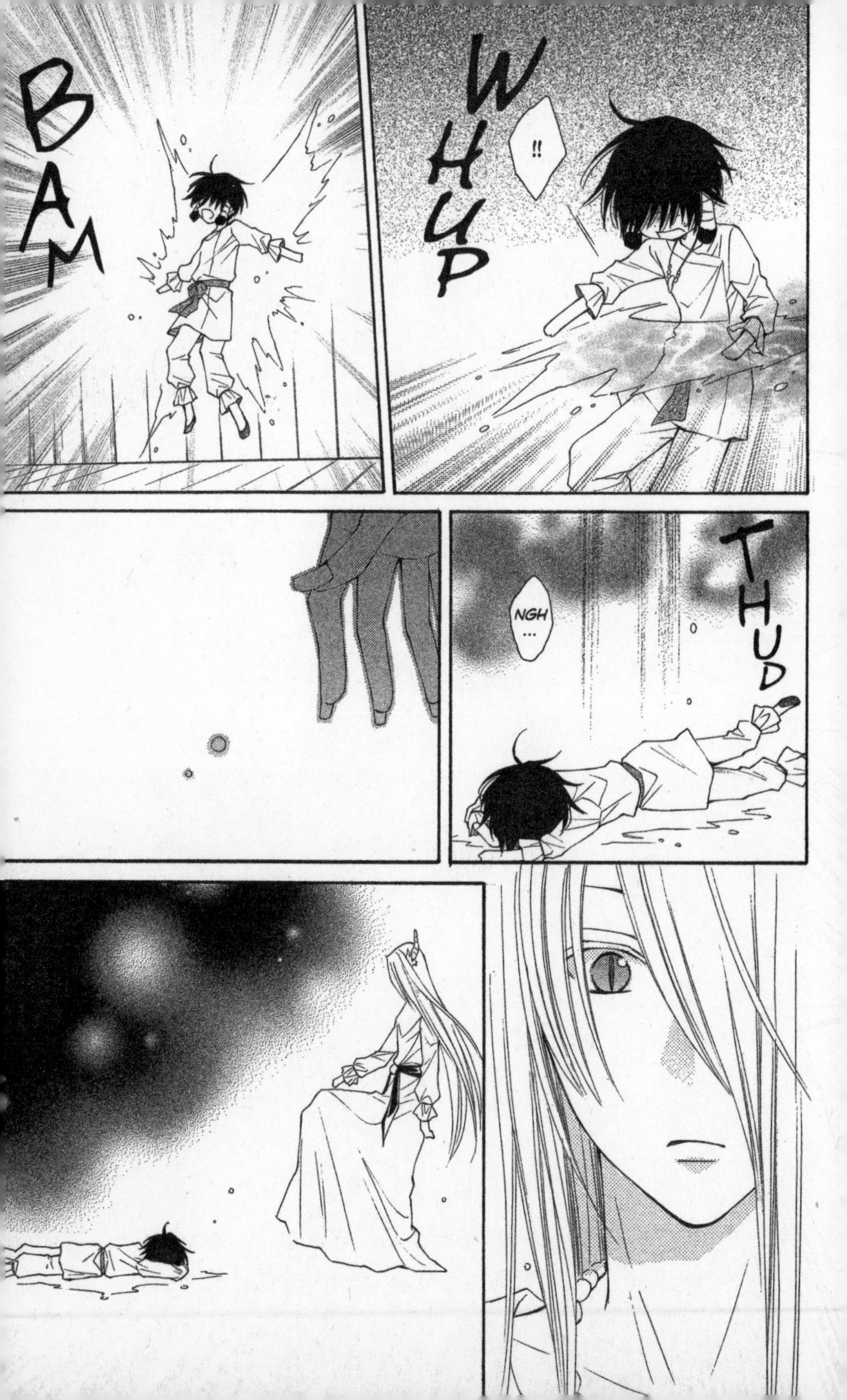
WHUP
!!
BAM
THUD
NGH...

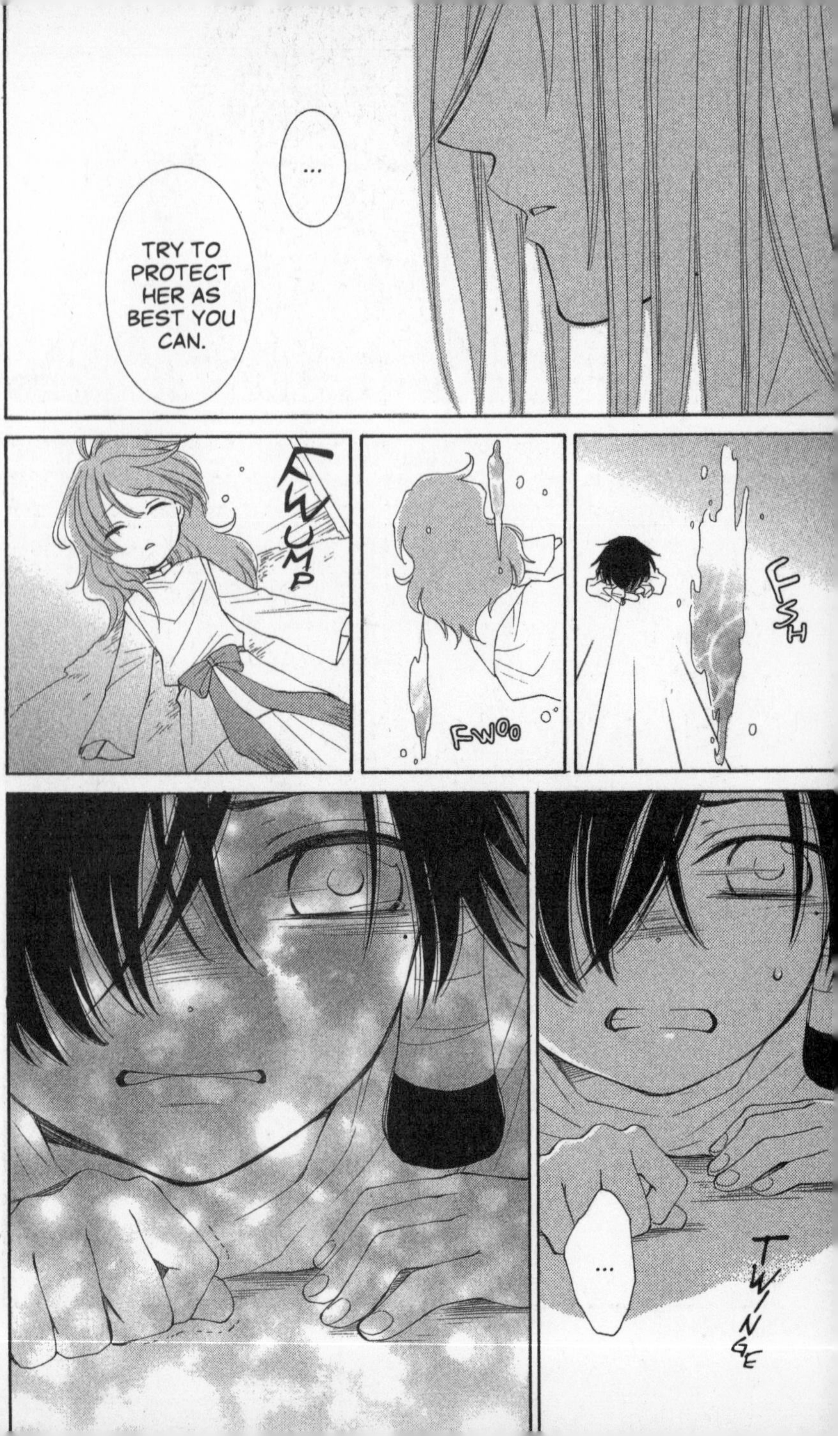
...
TRY TO PROTECT HER AS BEST YOU CAN.
FSH
FWOO
KWUMP
...
TWINGE

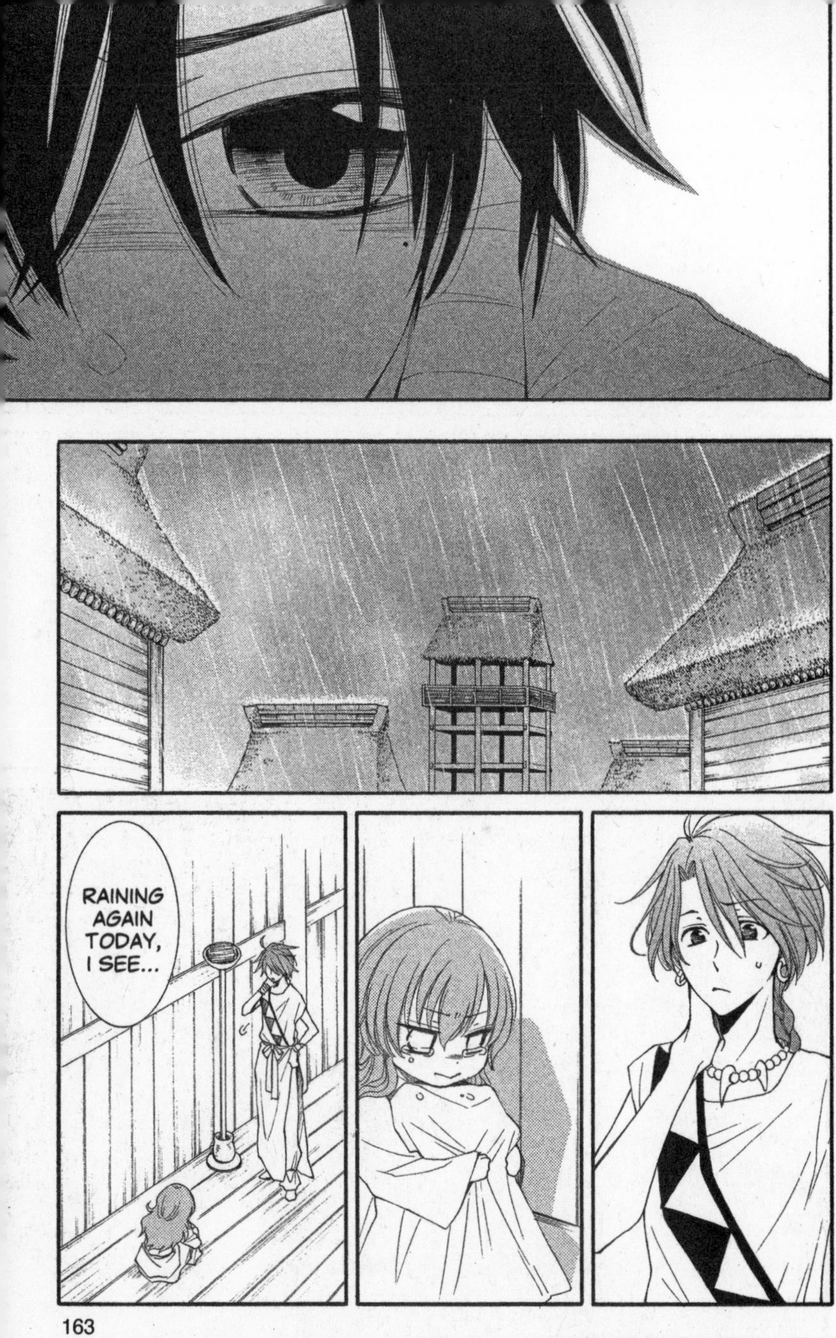
RAINING AGAIN TODAY, I SEE...

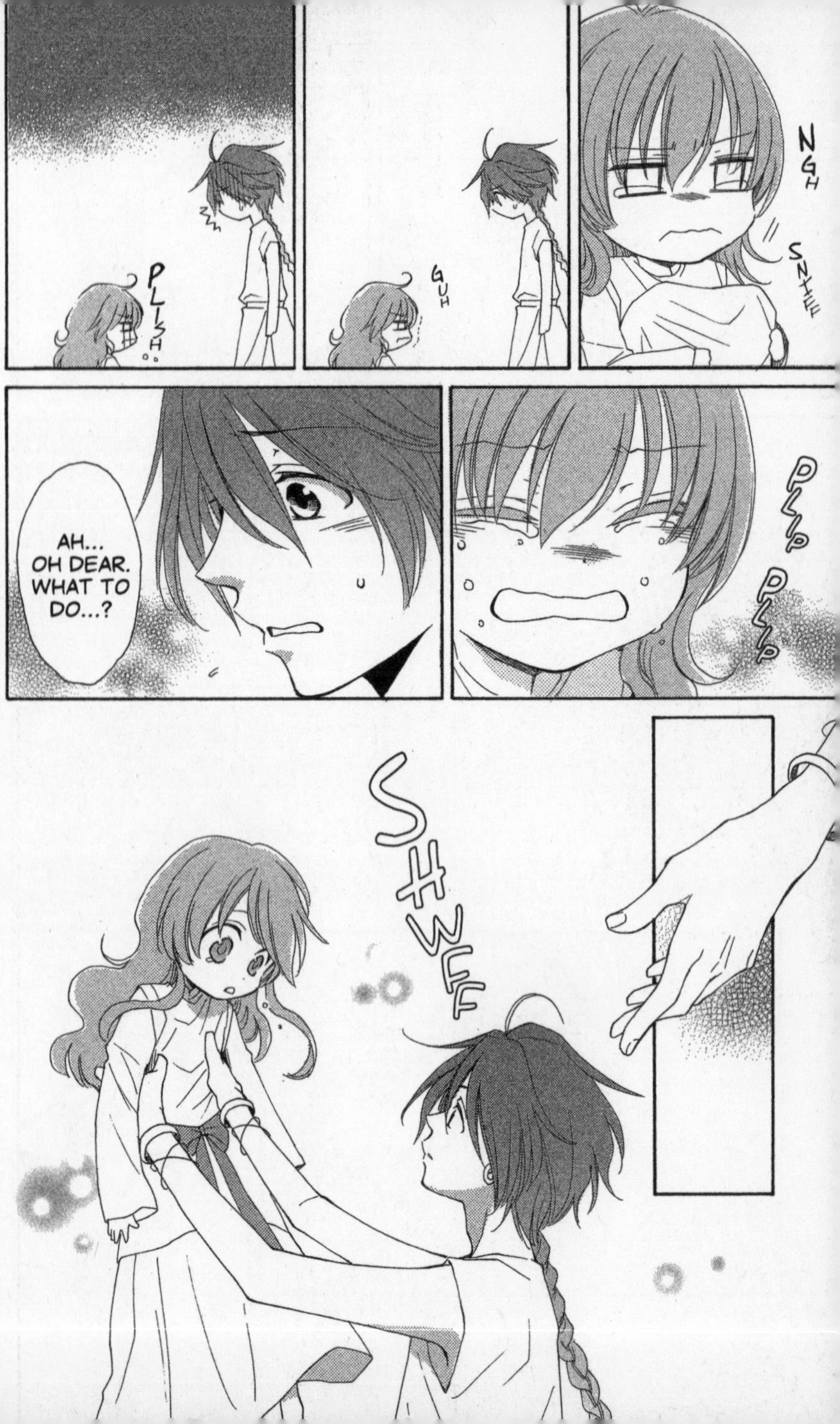
NGH
SNIFF
GUH
PLISH
PLIP PLIP
AH... OH DEAR. WHAT TO DO...?
SHWFF

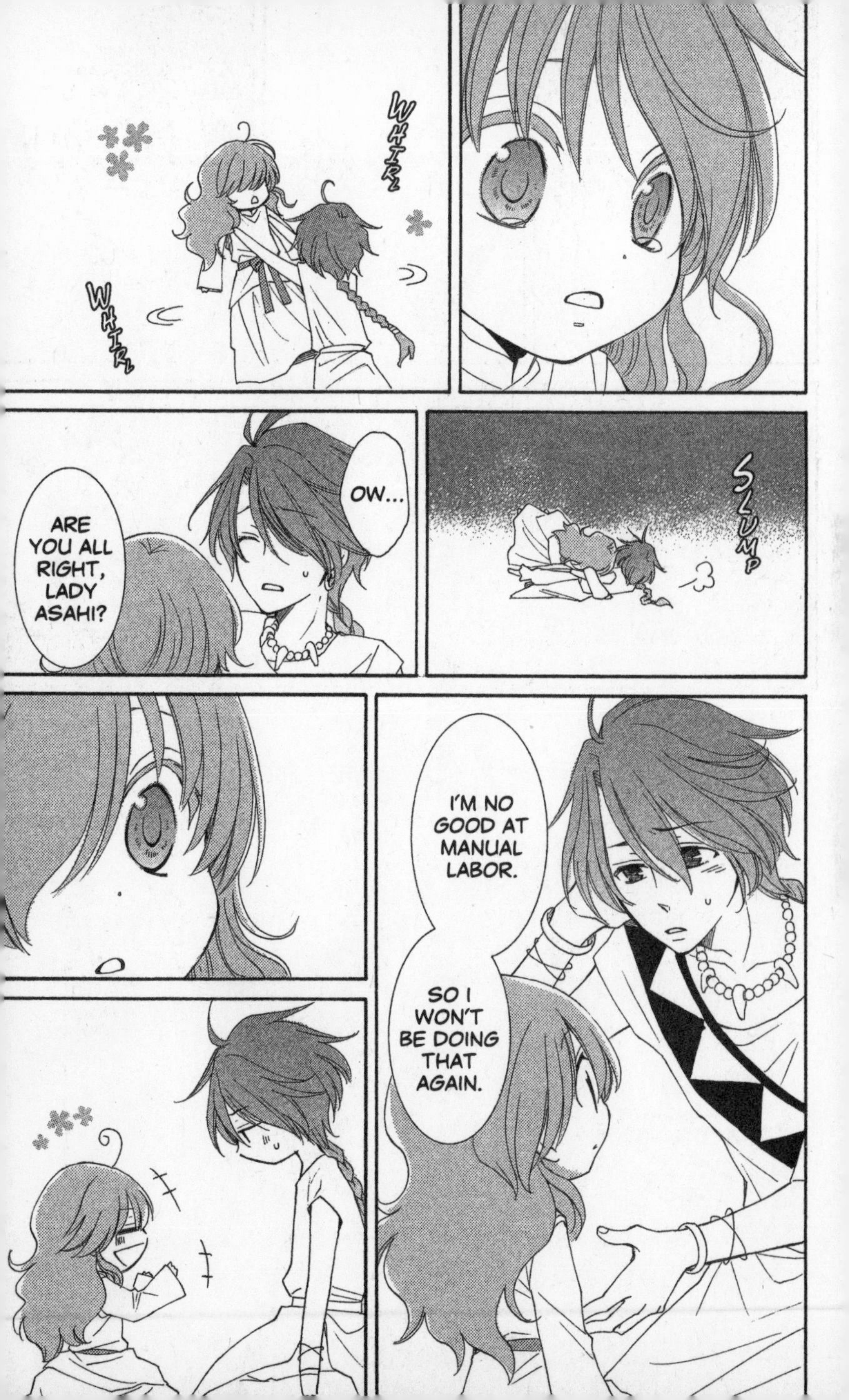
WHIRL
WHIRL
SLUMP
OW...
ARE YOU ALL RIGHT, LADY ASAHI?
I'M NO GOOD AT MANUAL LABOR.
SO I WON'T BE DOING THAT AGAIN.

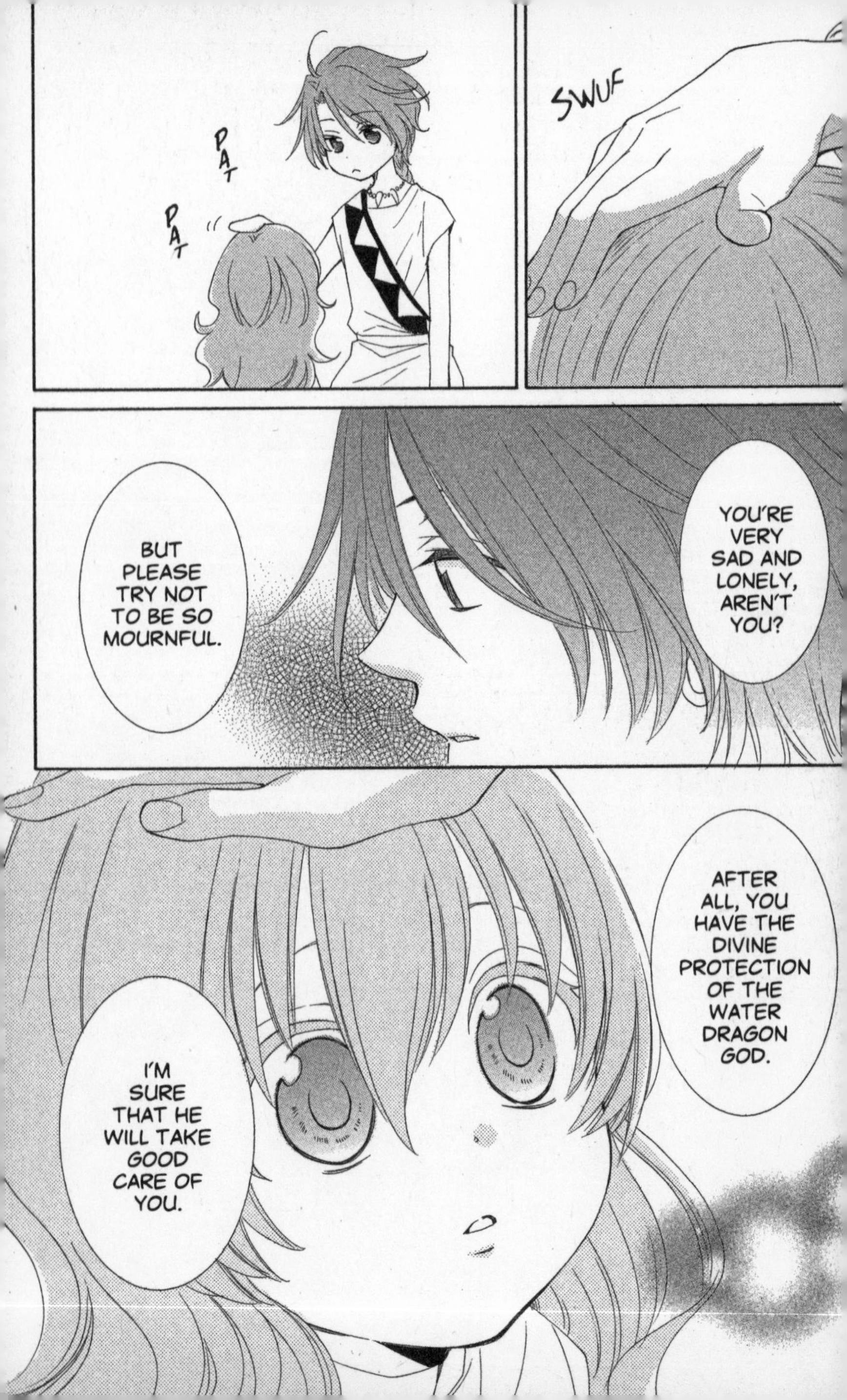
SWUF
PAT PAT
YOU'RE VERY SAD AND LONELY, AREN'T YOU?
BUT PLEASE TRY NOT TO BE SO MOURNFUL.
AFTER ALL, YOU HAVE THE DIVINE PROTECTION OF THE WATER DRAGON GOD.
I'M SURE THAT HE WILL TAKE GOOD CARE OF YOU.

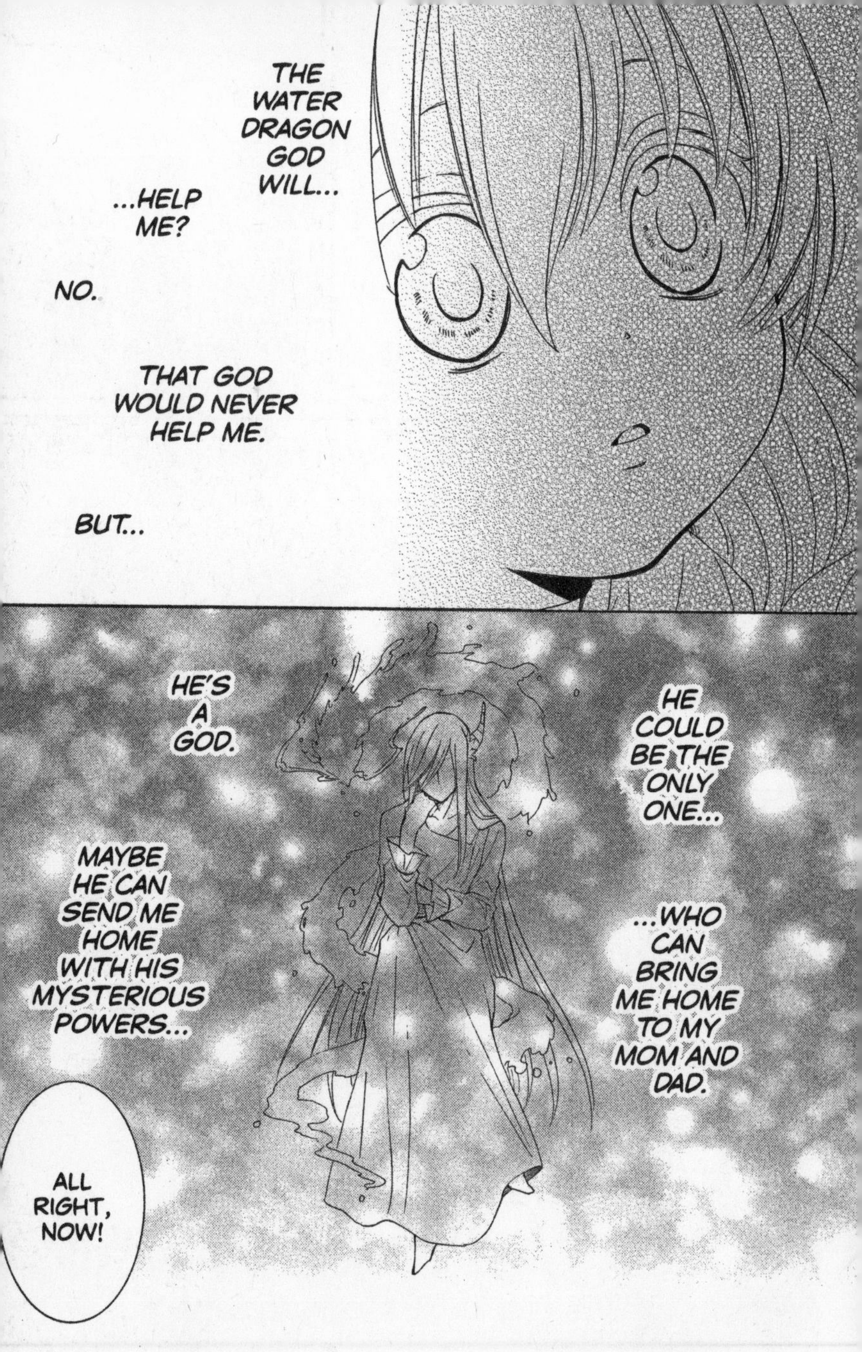
THE WATER DRAGON GOD WILL...
...HELP ME?
NO.
THAT GOD WOULD NEVER HELP ME.
BUT...
HE COULD BE THE ONLY ONE...
...WHO CAN BRING ME HOME TO MY MOM AND DAD.
HE'S A GOD.
MAYBE HE CAN SEND ME HOME WITH HIS MYSTERIOUS POWERS...
ALL RIGHT, NOW!

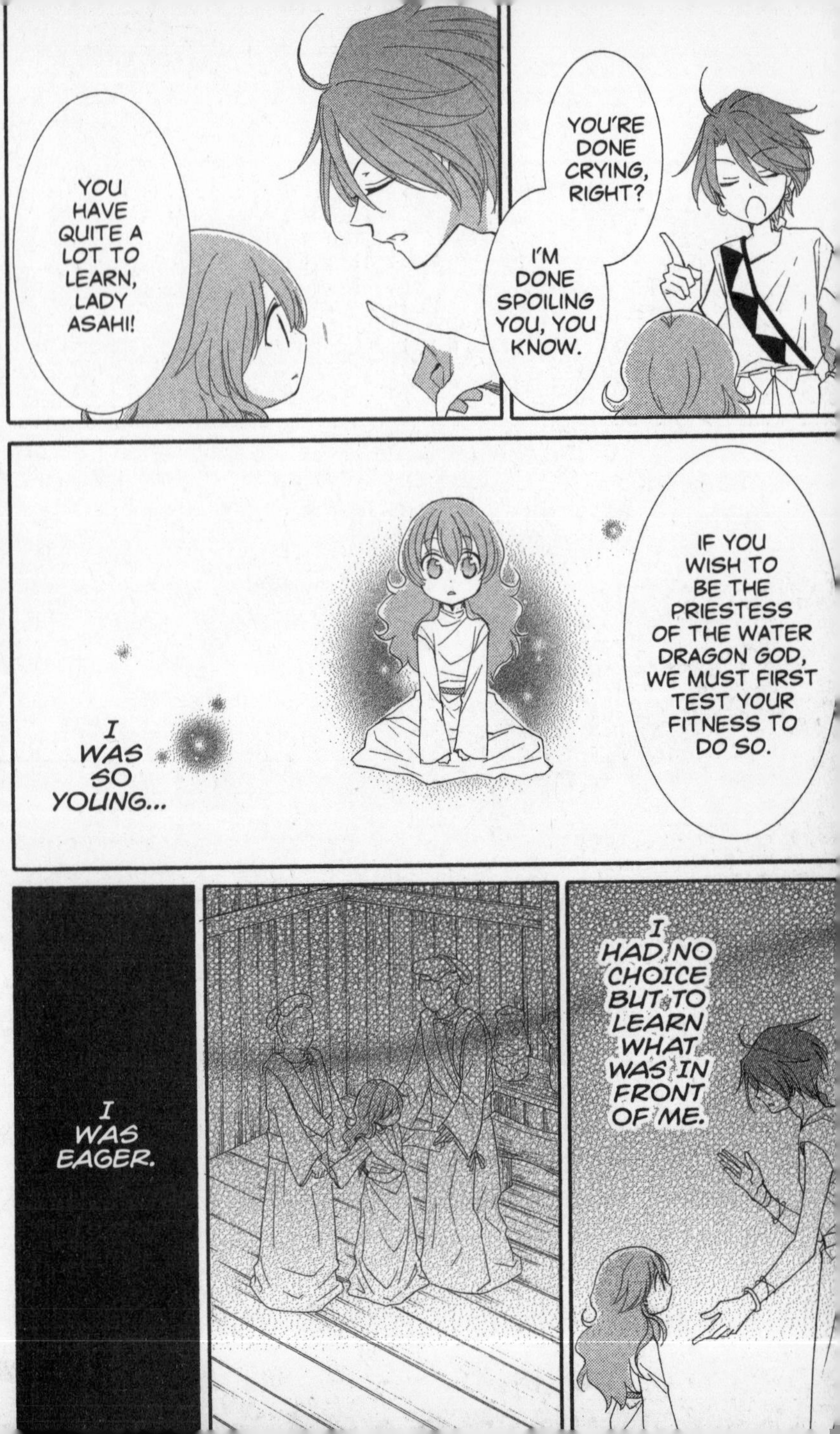
YOU'RE DONE CRYING, RIGHT?
I'M DONE SPOILING YOU, YOU KNOW.
YOU HAVE QUITE A LOT TO LEARN, LADY ASAHI!
IF YOU WISH TO BE THE PRIESTESS OF THE WATER DRAGON GOD, WE MUST FIRST TEST YOUR FITNESS TO DO SO.
I WAS SO YOUNG...
I HAD NO CHOICE BUT TO LEARN WHAT WAS IN FRONT OF ME.
I WAS EAGER.

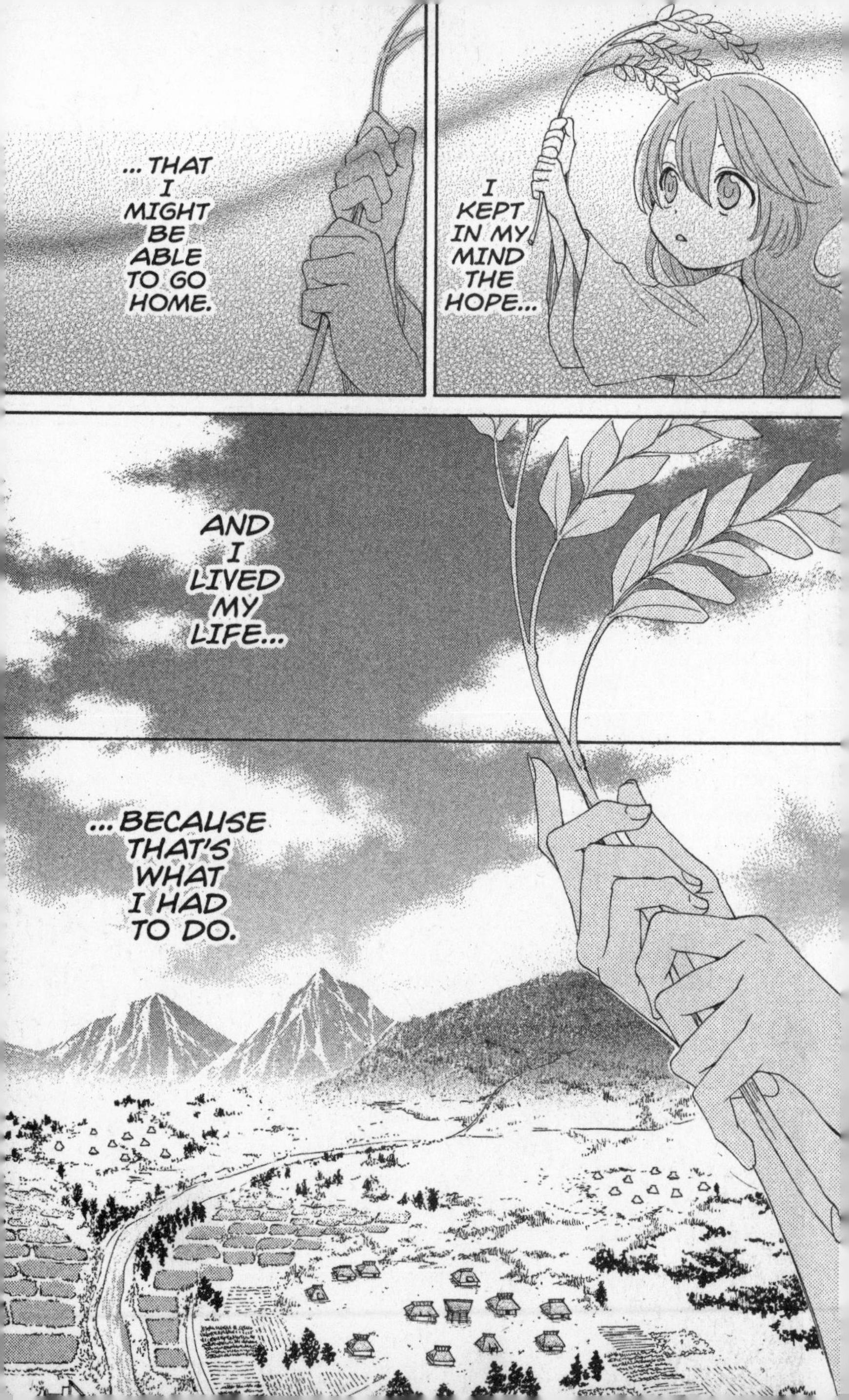
I KEPT IN MY MIND THE HOPE...
...THAT I MIGHT BE ABLE TO GO HOME.
AND I LIVED MY LIFE...
...BECAUSE THAT'S WHAT I HAD TO DO.

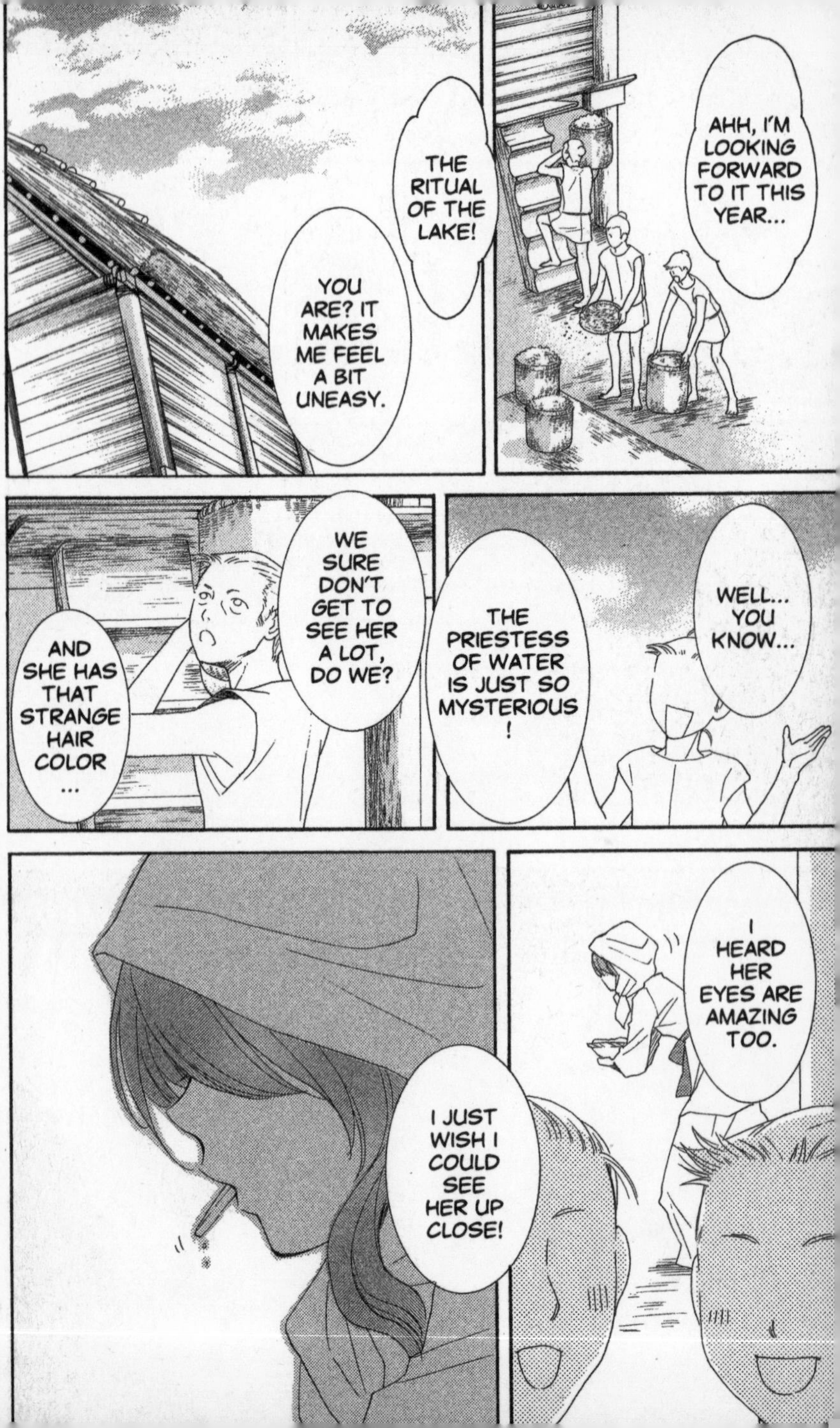
AHH, I'M LOOKING FORWARD TO IT THIS YEAR...
THE RITUAL OF THE LAKE!
YOU ARE? IT MAKES ME FEEL A BIT UNEASY.
WELL... YOU KNOW...
THE PRIESTESS OF WATER IS JUST SO MYSTERIOUS!
WE SURE DON'T GET TO SEE HER A LOT, DO WE?
AND SHE HAS THAT STRANGE HAIR COLOR...
I HEARD HER EYES ARE AMAZING TOO.
I JUST WISH I COULD SEE HER UP CLOSE!

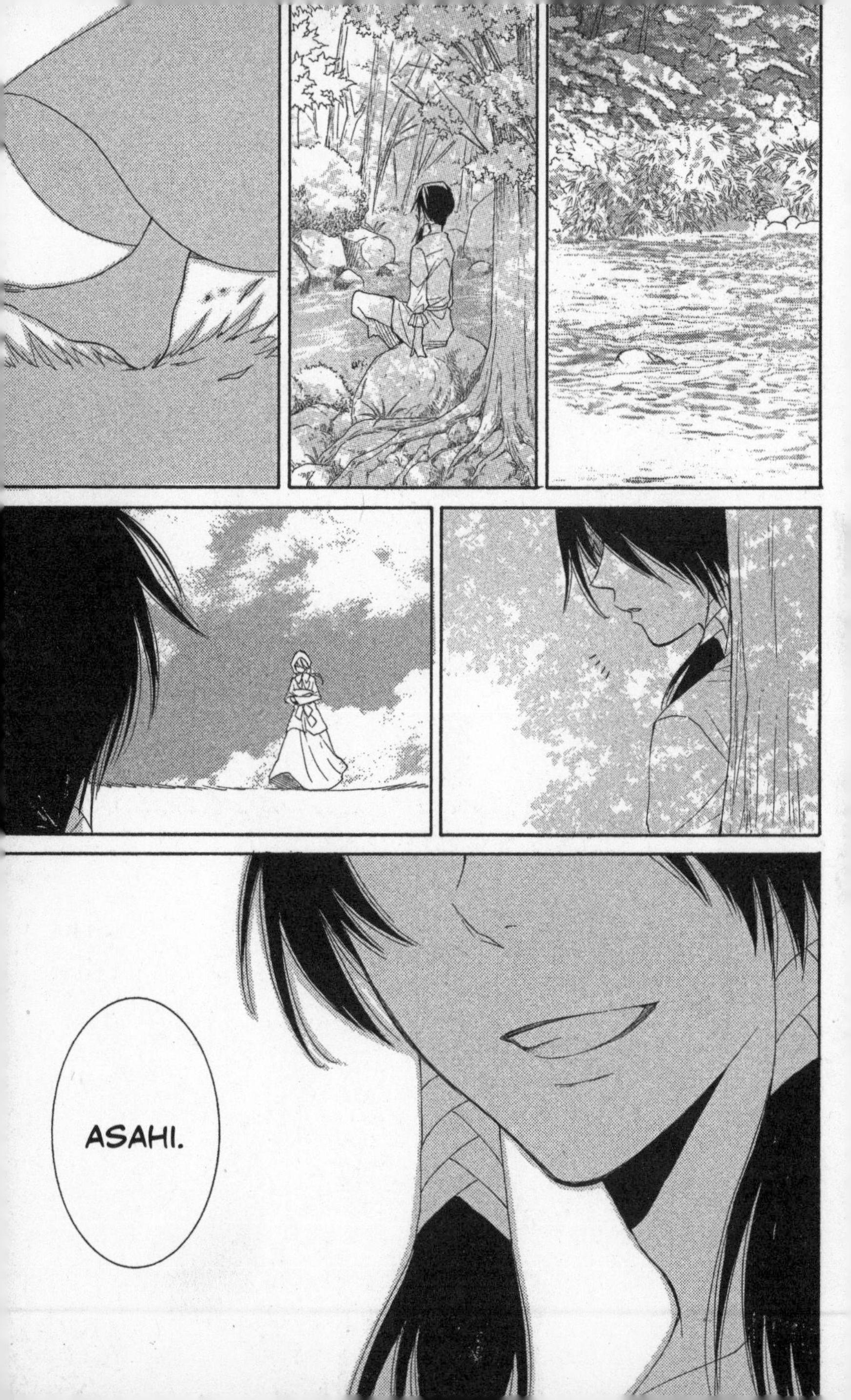
ASAHI.

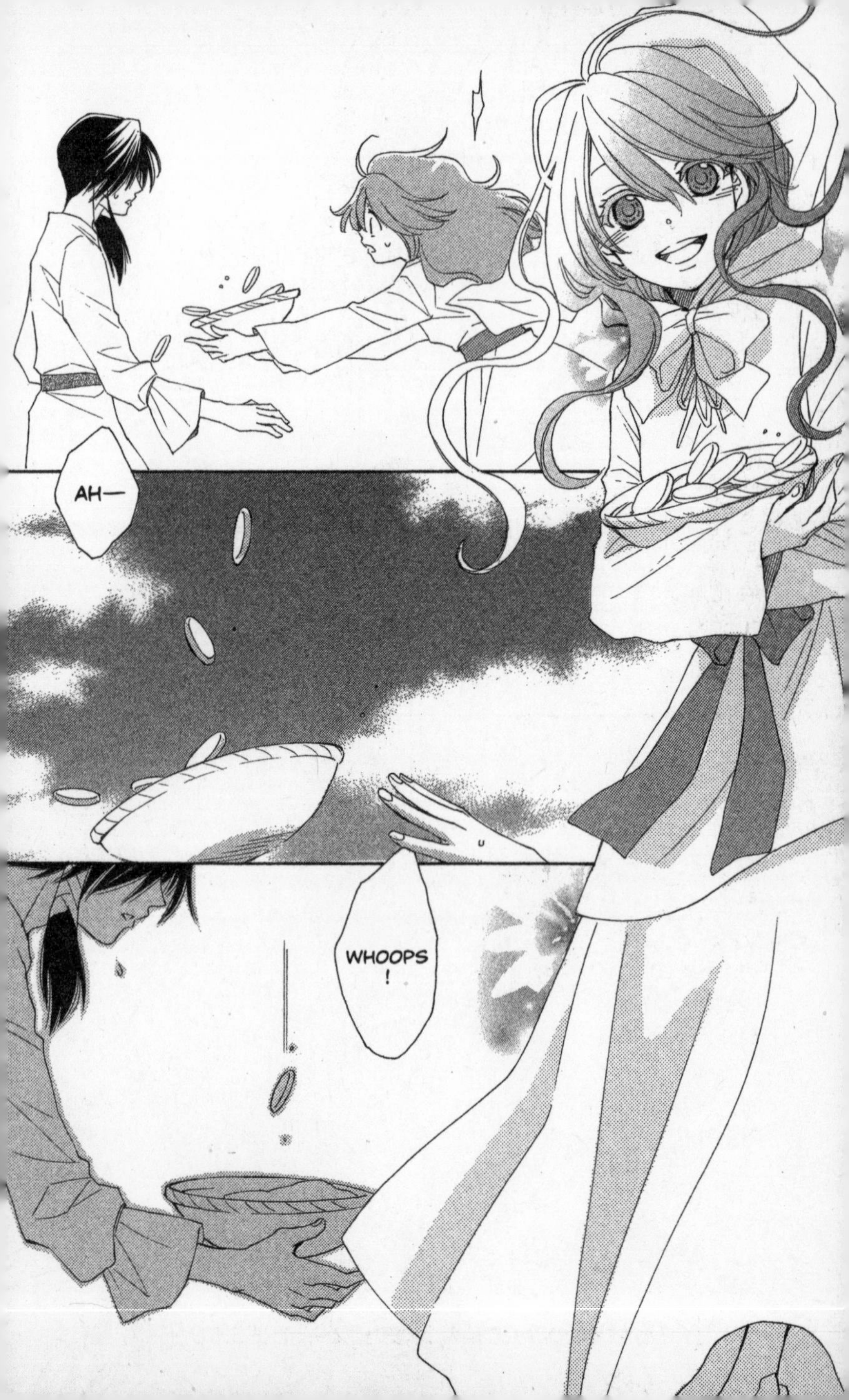
AH—
WHOOPS!

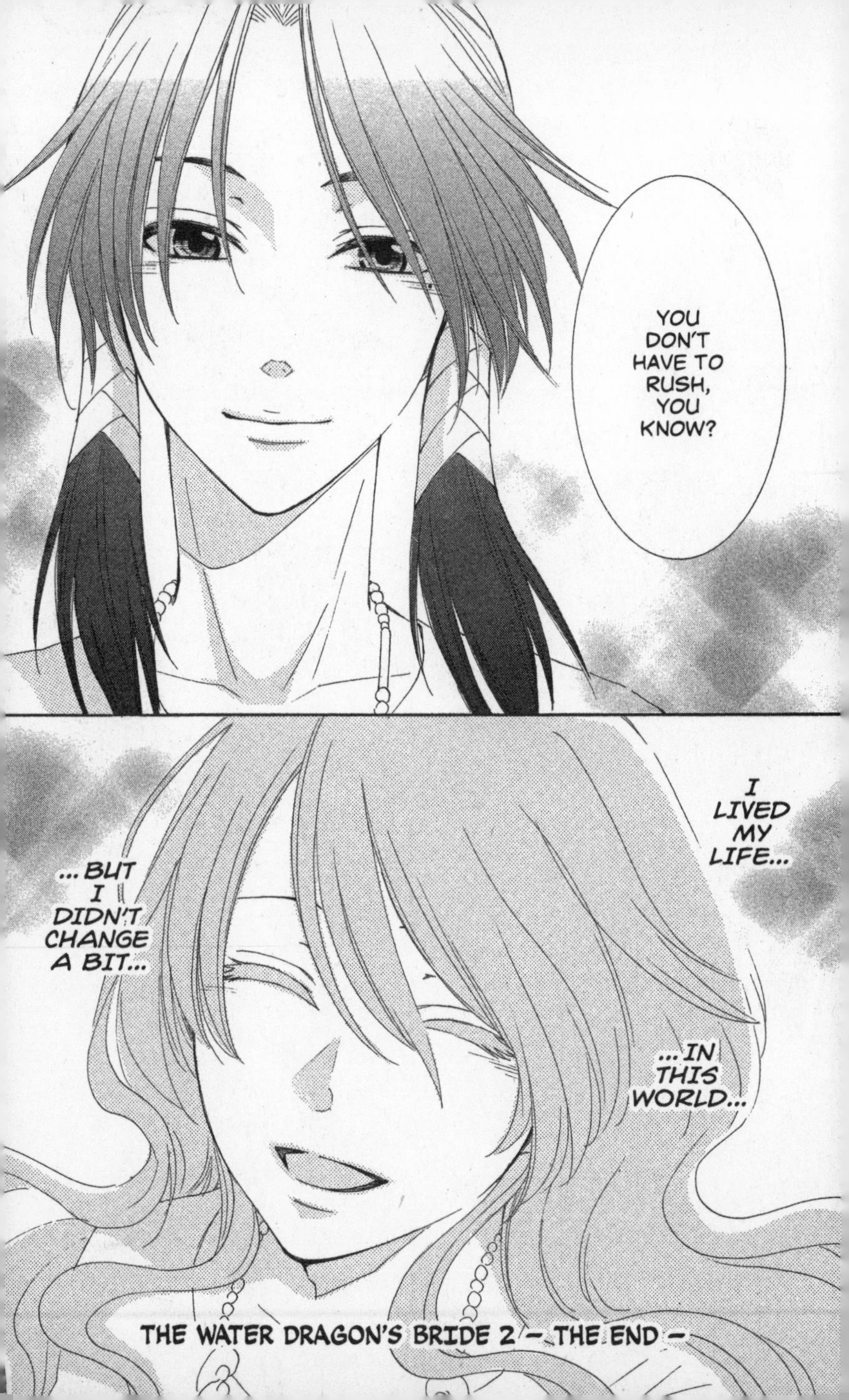
YOU DON'T HAVE TO RUSH, YOU KNOW?
I LIVED MY LIFE...
...IN THIS WORLD...
...BUT I DIDN'T CHANGE A BIT...
THE WATER DRAGON'S BRIDE 2 – THE END –

The Water Dragon's Bride

Bonus Comics 1

The Water Dragon God's Daily Life

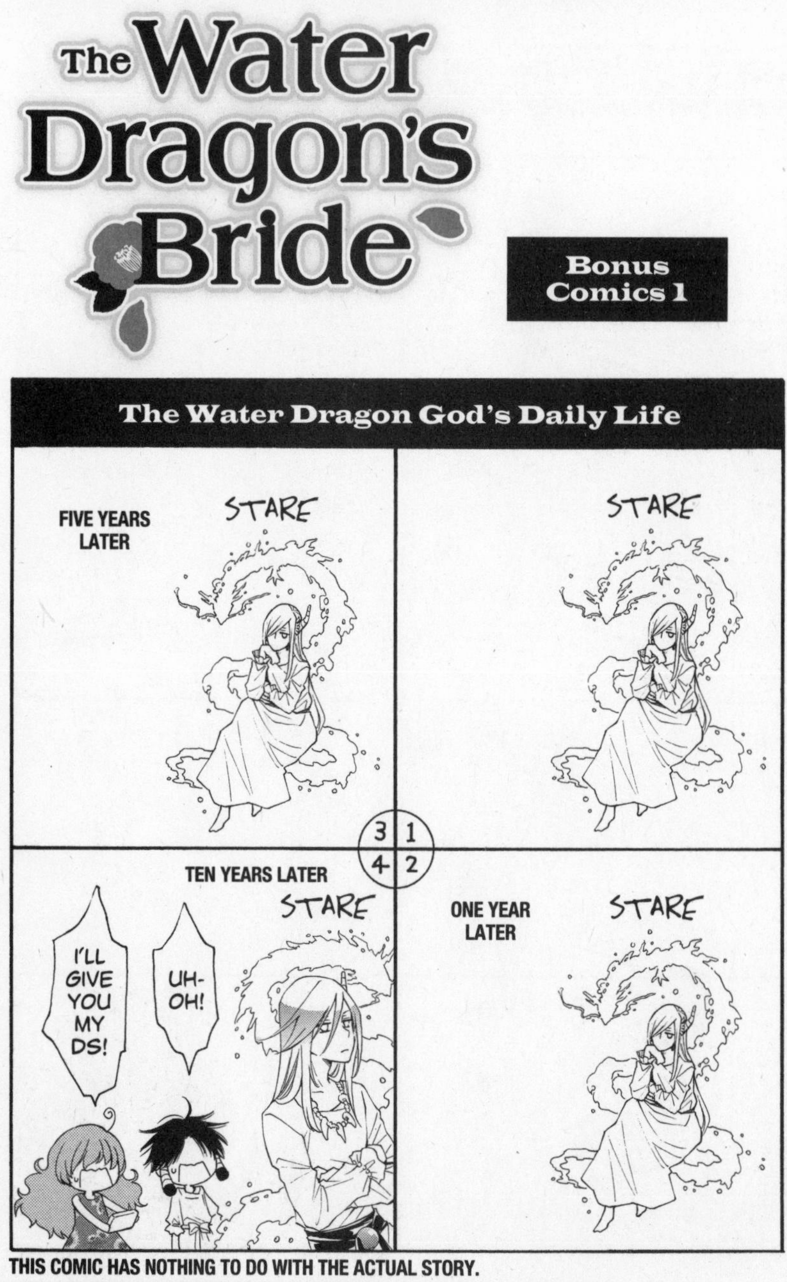
STARE
ONE YEAR LATER
STARE
FIVE YEARS LATER
STARE
TEN YEARS LATER
STARE
UH-OH!
I'LL GIVE YOU MY DS!

THIS COMIC HAS NOTHING TO DO WITH THE ACTUAL STORY.

The Water Dragon God Plays DS

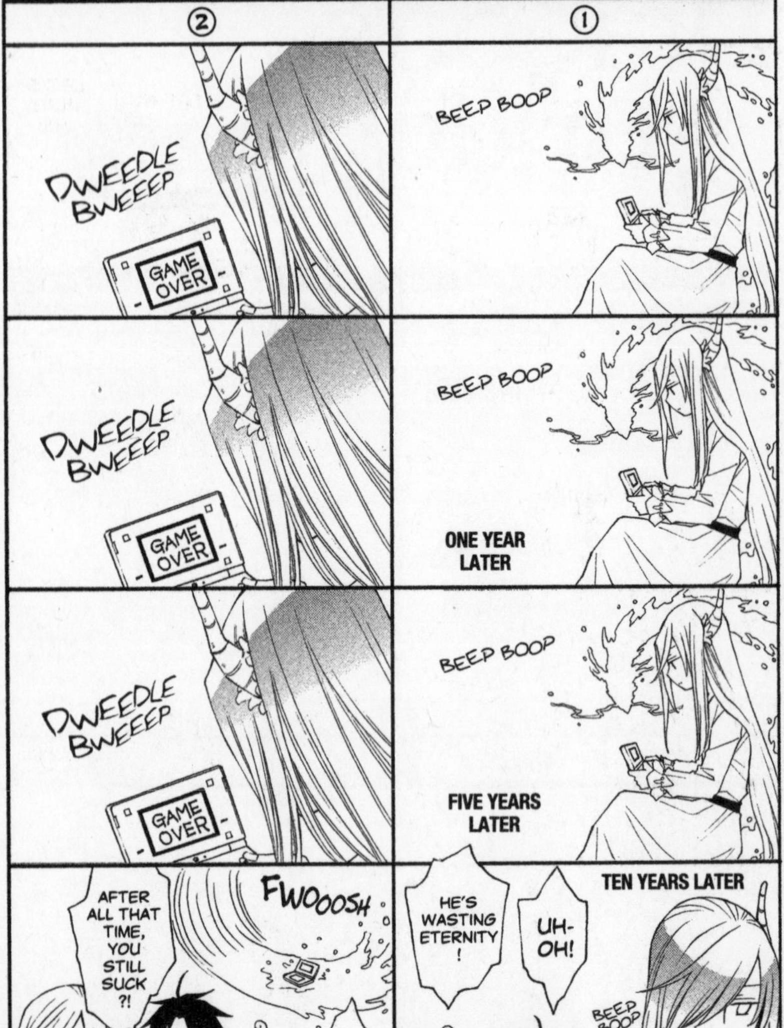
①
BEEP BOOP
BEEP BOOP
ONE YEAR LATER
BEEP BOOP
FIVE YEARS LATER
TEN YEARS LATER
UH-OH!
HE'S WASTING ETERNITY!
BEEP BOOP
②
DWEEDLE BWEEEP
GAME OVER
DWEEDLE BWEEEP
GAME OVER
DWEEDLE BWEEEP
GAME OVER
FWOOOSH
AFTER ALL THAT TIME, YOU STILL SUCK?!
MY DS!

The Water Dragon God Plays Wii

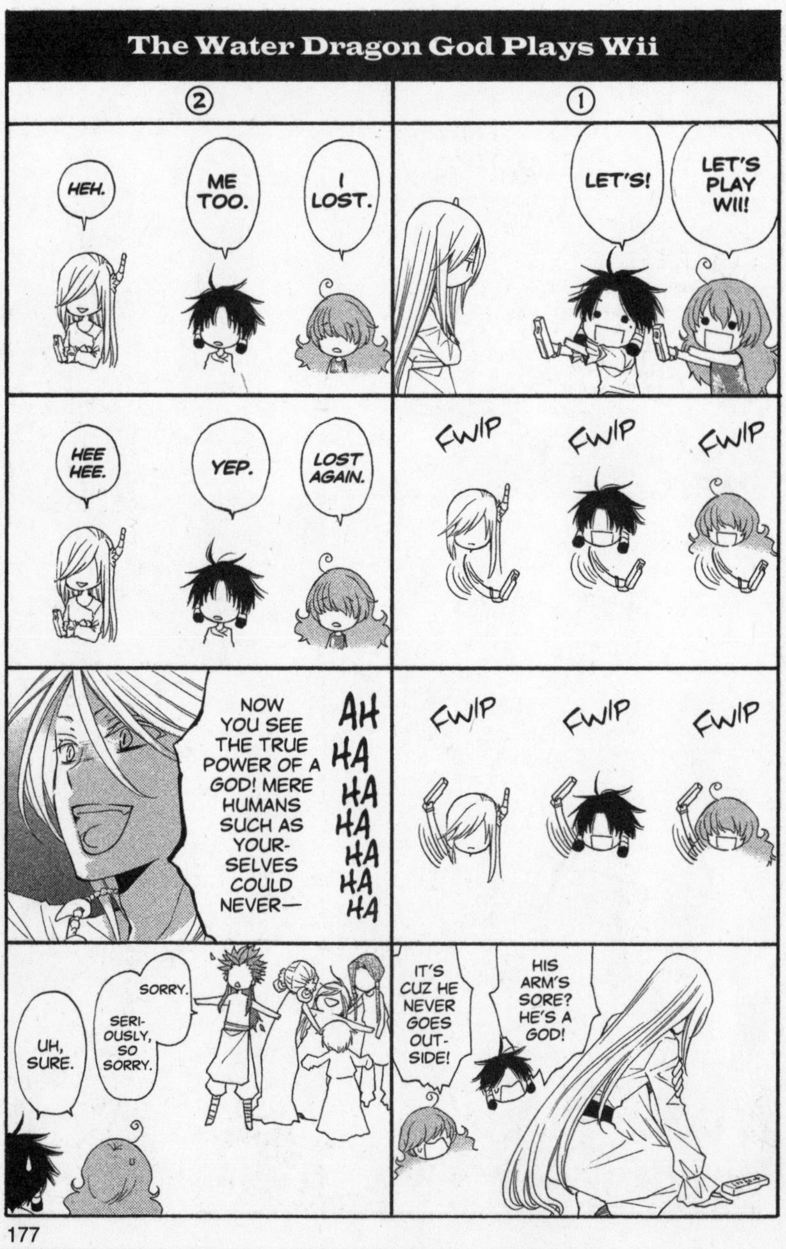
①
LET'S PLAY WII!
LET'S!
FWIP
FWIP
FWIP
FWIP
FWIP
FWIP
HIS ARM'S SORE? HE'S A GOD!
IT'S CUZ HE NEVER GOES OUT-SIDE!
②
I LOST.
ME TOO.
HEH.
LOST AGAIN.
YEP.
HEE HEE.
AH HA HA HA HA HA HA HA
NOW YOU SEE THE TRUE POWER OF A GOD! MERE HUMANS SUCH AS YOUR-SELVES COULD NEVER—
SORRY. SERI-OUSLY, SO SORRY.
UH, SURE.

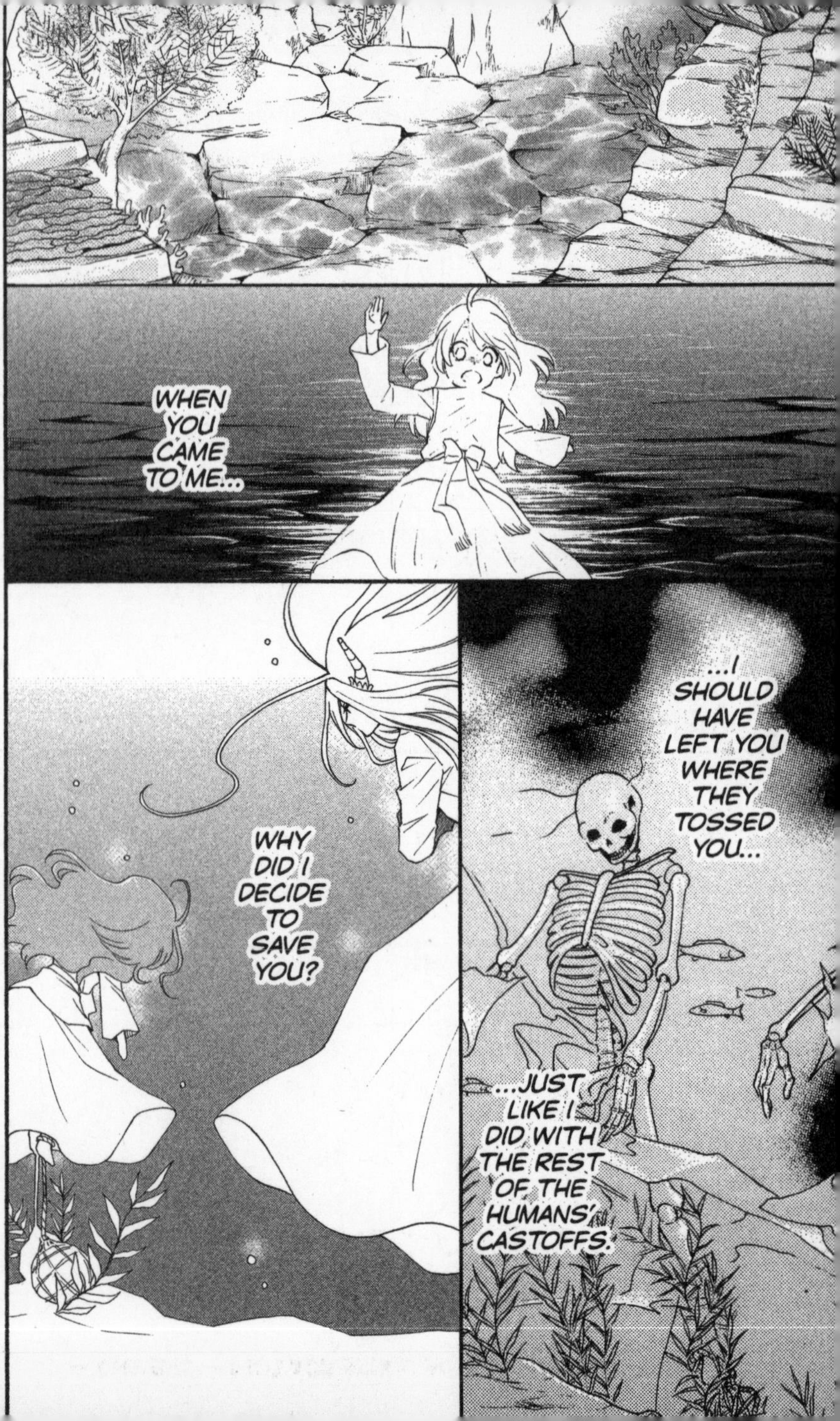
WHEN YOU CAME TO ME...
...I SHOULD HAVE LEFT YOU WHERE THEY TOSSED YOU...
...JUST LIKE I DID WITH THE REST OF THE HUMANS' CASTOFFS.
WHY DID I DECIDE TO SAVE YOU?

GOD
ONLY
KNOWS?

NO...

I HAVE
YET TO
FIGURE
IT OUT,
ACTUALLY.

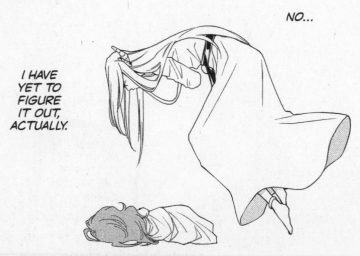

THE WATER DRAGON'S BRIDE BONUS COMICS 1 – THE END –

In honor of volumes 1 and 2 being released in just two months in Japan, they made a promotional video of ***The Water Dragon's Bride***. I can't believe I got to hear Asahi's, Subaru's and the water dragon god's voices! The water dragon god and the narrator were voiced by Ryohei Kimura, Asahi was voiced by Konomi Fujimura and Subaru was voiced by Megumi Satou!!! Really!!!

The first video was basically just a condensed version, but the scene where Subaru calls out Asahi's name was my favorite. Asahi's voice in the scenes where she's narrating as her mature future self were perfect and just as I'd imagined. The cadence of the speech was perfect. And the water dragon god! Ohh, he was so cool. Though most of his water dragon god lines were very short...

(That darn water dragon god doesn't really talk very much, which is a huge problem! I really want him to talk more, that pain-in-the-butt brat! I'm not gonna be nice about it anymore! For no reason, I just had a ton of scenes where the water god is peeking out of the surface of the water, but I really feel like I should have made that a little less obvious! I'm so dumb!!)

Not too short, not too tall, refreshing yet blunt. That's the water dragon god. His accent was just as moderated as I'd imagined, and with just one line, I knew he was perfect. The next line left an echoing impression. That was lovely as well. I felt like that one line could have crushed ten *magatama*.

The promotional video was made to play in bookstores, so it's pretty short, but watch it if you get a chance! I'd like to thank the people who created the video and the voice actors for broadening the world of ***The Water Dragon's Bride***.

Well, see you in volume 3!

Rei Toma

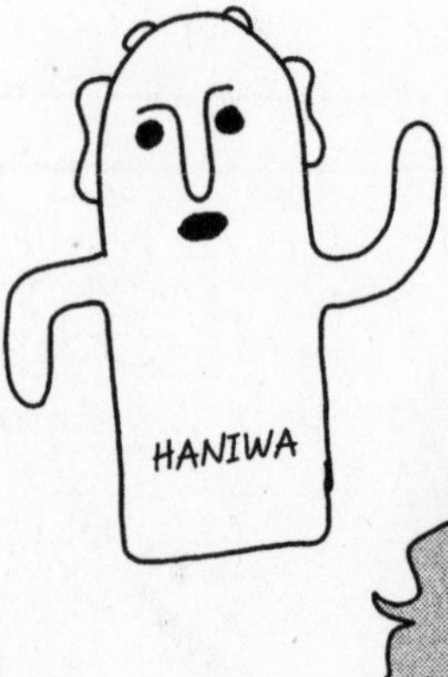
HANIWA

Please send your letters here! ↓
Rei Toma
c/o The Water Dragon's Bride Editor
VIZ Media
P.O. Box 77010
San Francisco, CA 94107

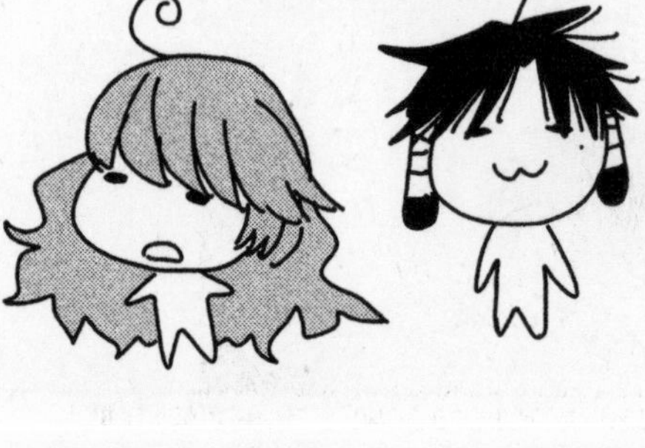

The Water Dragon's Bride

Bonus Comics 2

The Water Dragon God's Meals

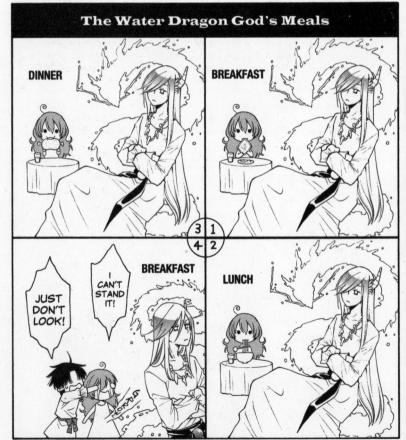

THIS COMIC HAS NOTHING TO DO WITH THE ACTUAL STORY.

The Water Dragon God's Three-Minute Cooking

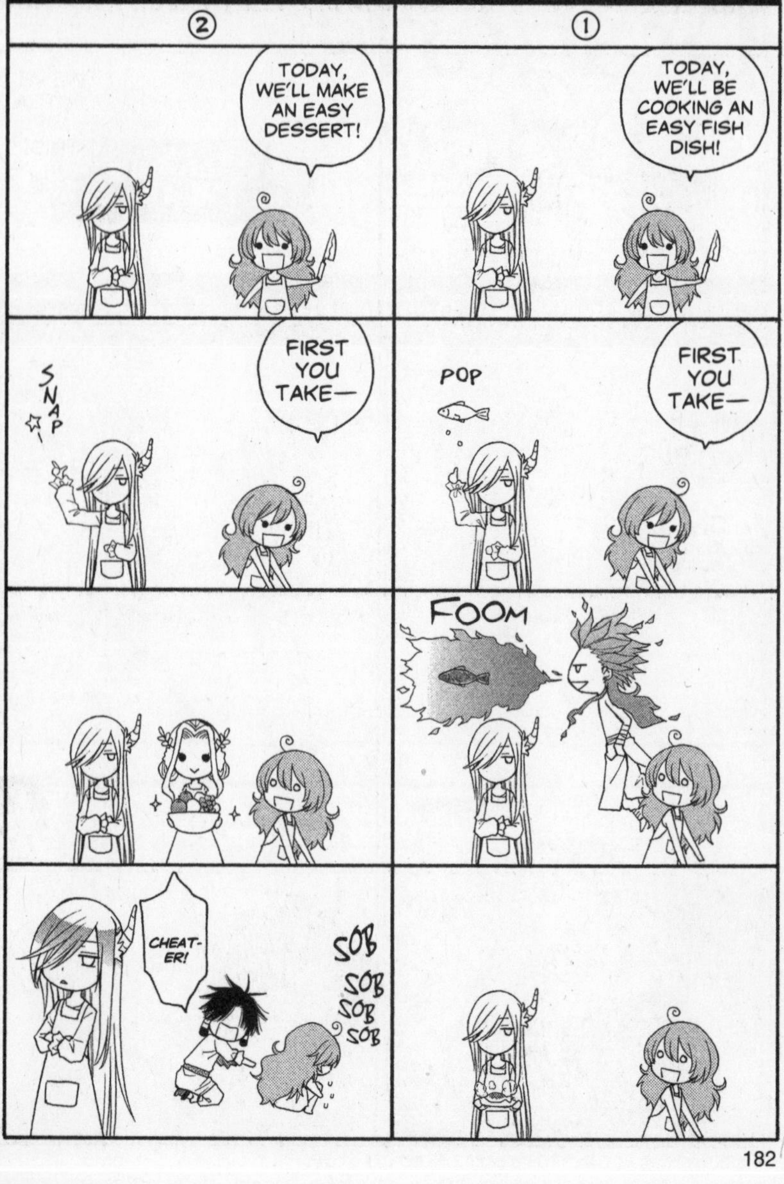

①
TODAY, WE'LL BE COOKING AN EASY FISH DISH!
FIRST YOU TAKE—
POP
FOOM
②
TODAY, WE'LL MAKE AN EASY DESSERT!
FIRST YOU TAKE—
SNAP
SOB SOB SOB SOB
CHEAT-ER!

The Water Dragon God's First Time Cooking

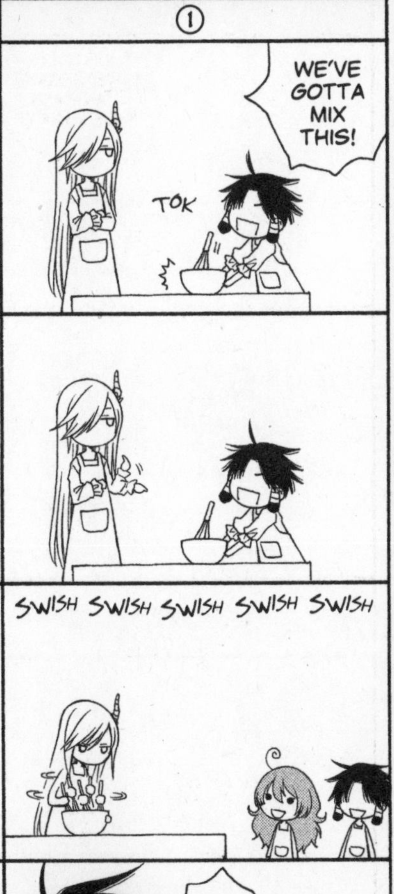
①
WE'VE GOTTA MIX THIS!
TOK
SWISH SWISH SWISH SWISH SWISH
THE SORE ARM RETURNS!
You're a god!
SMIRK

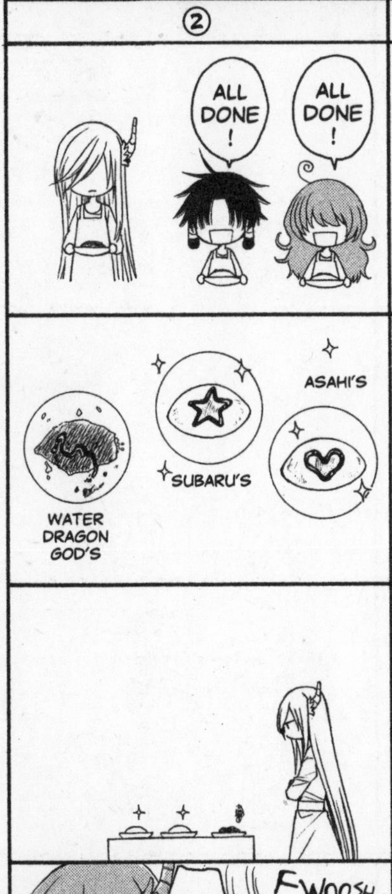
②
ALL DONE!
ALL DONE!
ASAHI'S
SUBARU'S
WATER DRAGON GOD'S
FWOOSH
I THOUGHT YOU'D DO THAT!
SWEPT AWAY!
UGH

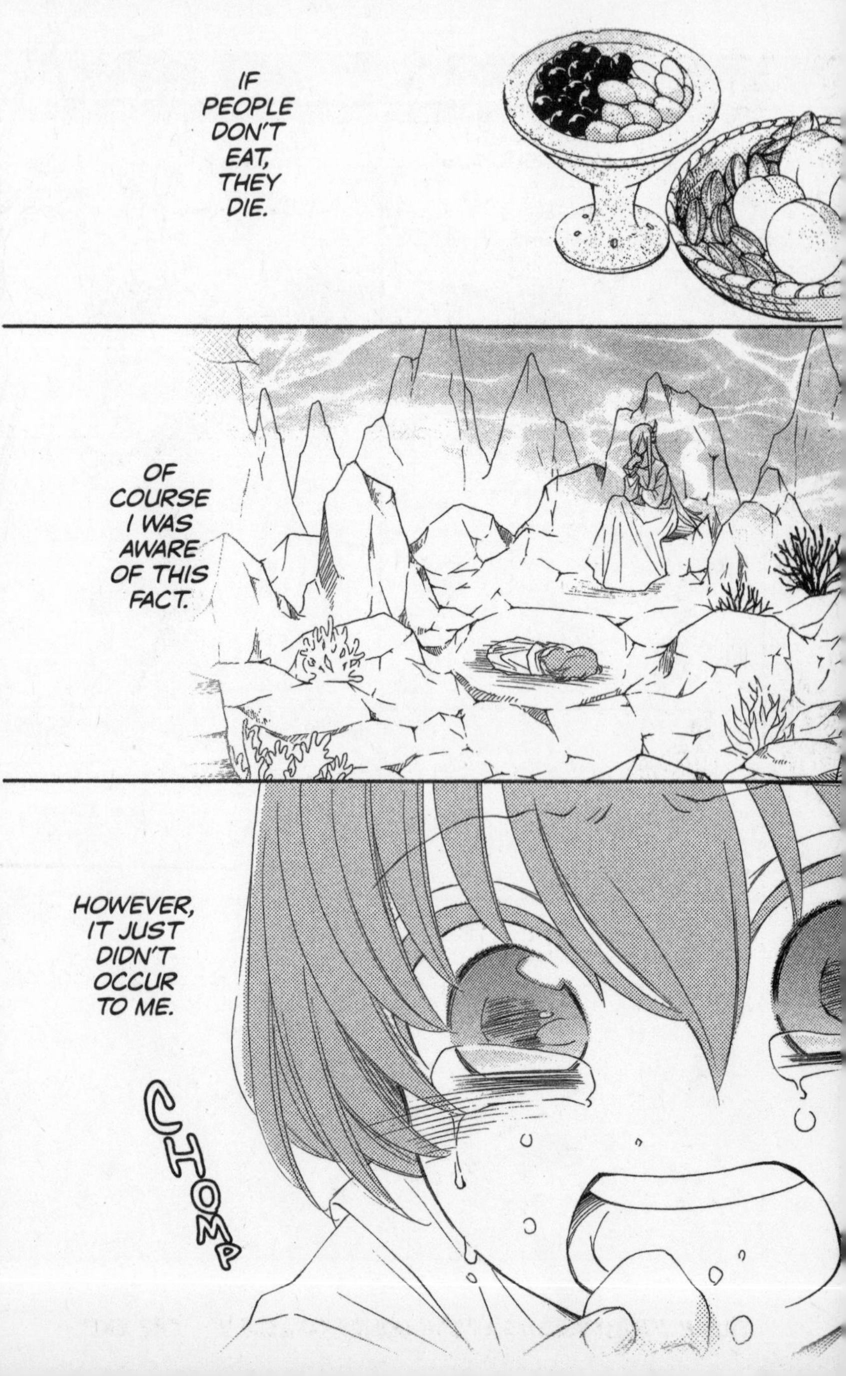
IF PEOPLE DON'T EAT, THEY DIE.
OF COURSE I WAS AWARE OF THIS FACT.
HOWEVER, IT JUST DIDN'T OCCUR TO ME.
CHOMP

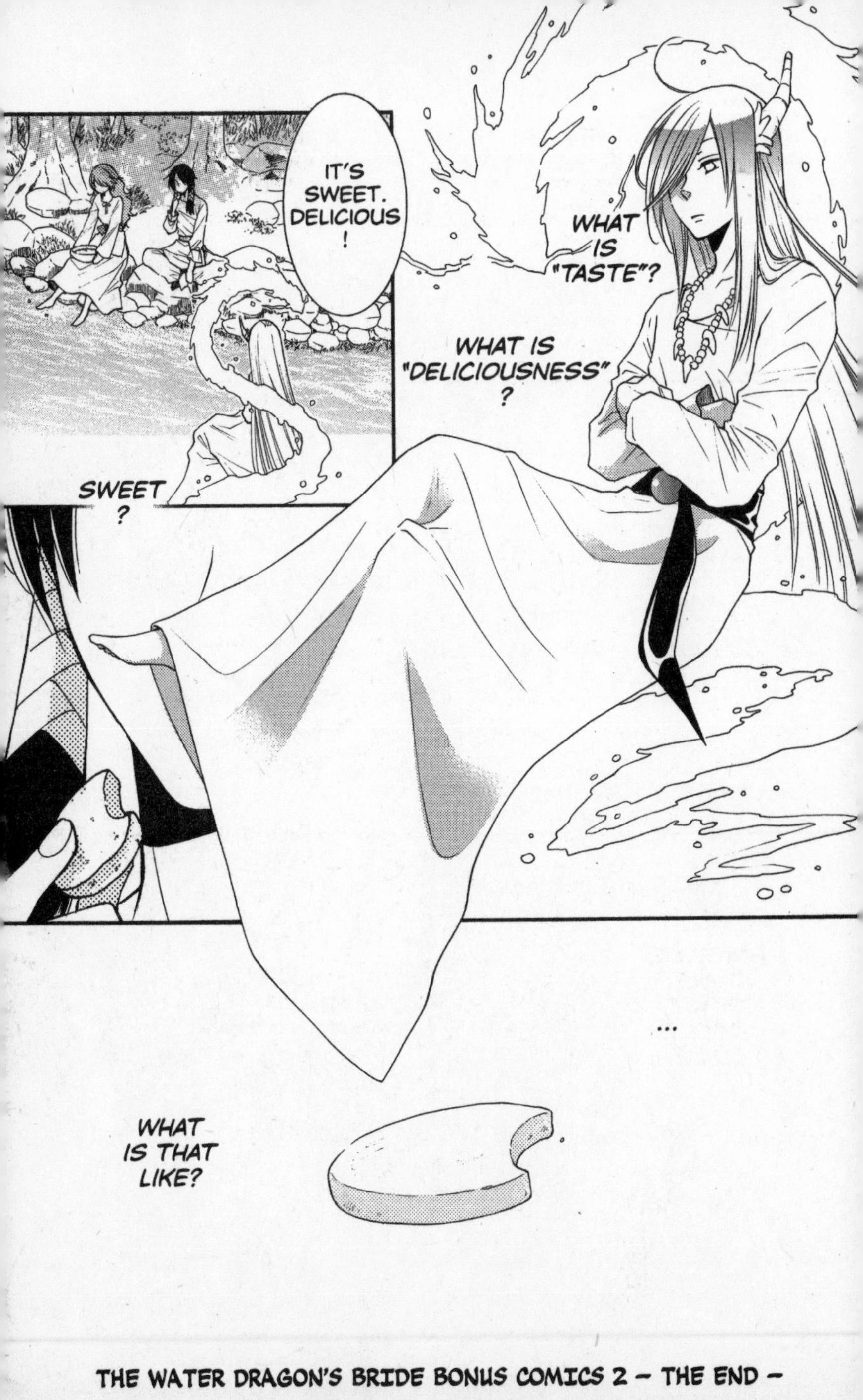
IT'S SWEET. DELICIOUS!
SWEET?
WHAT IS "TASTE"?
WHAT IS "DELICIOUSNESS"?
...
WHAT IS THAT LIKE?

THE WATER DRAGON'S BRIDE BONUS COMICS 2 – THE END –

This is volume 2. My favorite part is
the bonus comics, which I created
for the extra issue of the magazine that
The Water Dragon's Bride is serialized in.

– REI TOMA

Rei Toma has been drawing since childhood, and she
created her first complete manga for a graduation project
in design school. When she drew the short story manga
"Help Me, Dentist," it attracted a publisher's attention and
she made her debut right away. After she found success
as a manga artist, acclaim in other art fields started to
follow as she did illustrations for novels and video game
character designs. She is also the creator of *Dawn of the
Arcana*, available in North America from VIZ Media.

The Water Dragon's Bride
VOL. 2
Shojo Beat Edition

Story and Art by
Rei Toma

SUIJIN NO HANAYOME Vol.2
by Rei TOMA
© 2015 Rei TOMA
All rights reserved.
Original Japanese edition published by SHOGAKUKAN.
English translation rights in the United States of America,
Canada, the United Kingdom, Ireland, Australia and New
Zealand arranged with SHOGAKUKAN.

ORIGINAL COVER DESIGN/Hibiki CHIKADA (fireworks.vc)

English Translation & Adaptation **Abby Lehrke**
Touch-Up Art & Lettering **Monalisa de Asis**
Design **Alice Lewis**
Editor **Amy Yu**

Printed in Canada

Published by VIZ Media, LLC
P.O. Box 77010
San Francisco, CA 94107

10 9 8 7 6 5 4 3 2 1
First printing, July 2017

viz.com
shojobeat.com

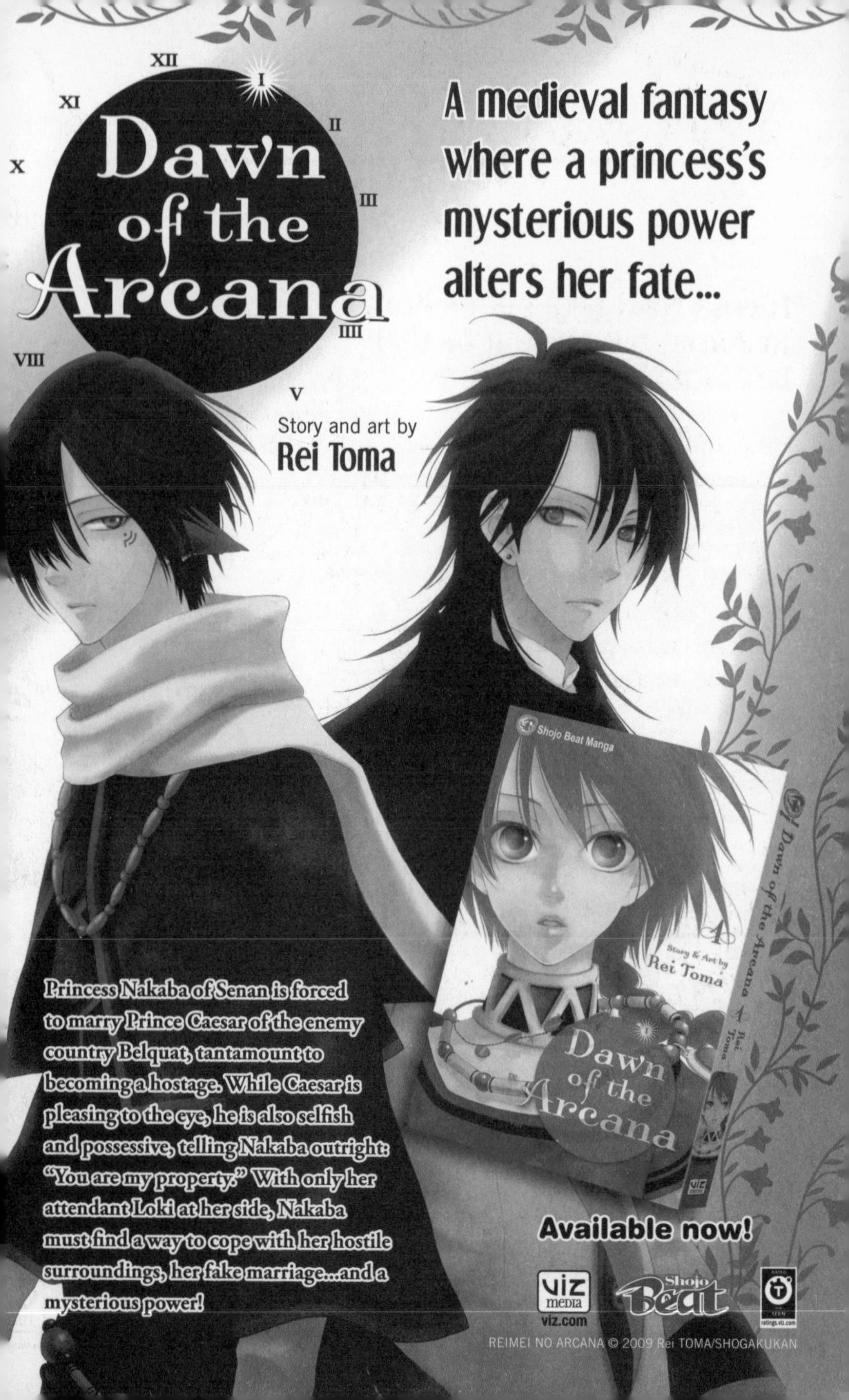
XII
I
XI
II
X
III
Dawn of the Arcana
IIII
VIII
V
A medieval fantasy where a princess's mysterious power alters her fate...
Story and art by
Rei Toma
Shojo Beat Manga
Dawn of the Arcana 1 Rei Toma
Story & Art by Rei Toma
1
Dawn of the Arcana
Princess Nakaba of Senan is forced to marry Prince Caesar of the enemy country Belquat, tantamount to becoming a hostage. While Caesar is pleasing to the eye, he is also selfish and possessive, telling Nakaba outright: "You are my property." With only her attendant Loki at her side, Nakaba must find a way to cope with her hostile surroundings, her fake marriage...and a mysterious power!
Available now!
viz media
viz.com
Shojo Beat
ratings.viz.com
REIMEI NO ARCANA © 2009 Rei TOMA/SHOGAKUKAN

Honey Blood

Story & Art by *Miko Mitsuki*

Hinata can't help but be drawn to Junya, but could it be that he's actually a vampire?

When a girl at her school is attacked by what seems to be a vampire, high school student Hinata Sorazono refuses to believe that vampires even exist. But then she meets her new neighbor, Junya Tokinaga, the author of an incredibly popular vampire romance novel… Could it be that Junya's actually a vampire—and worse yet, the culprit?!

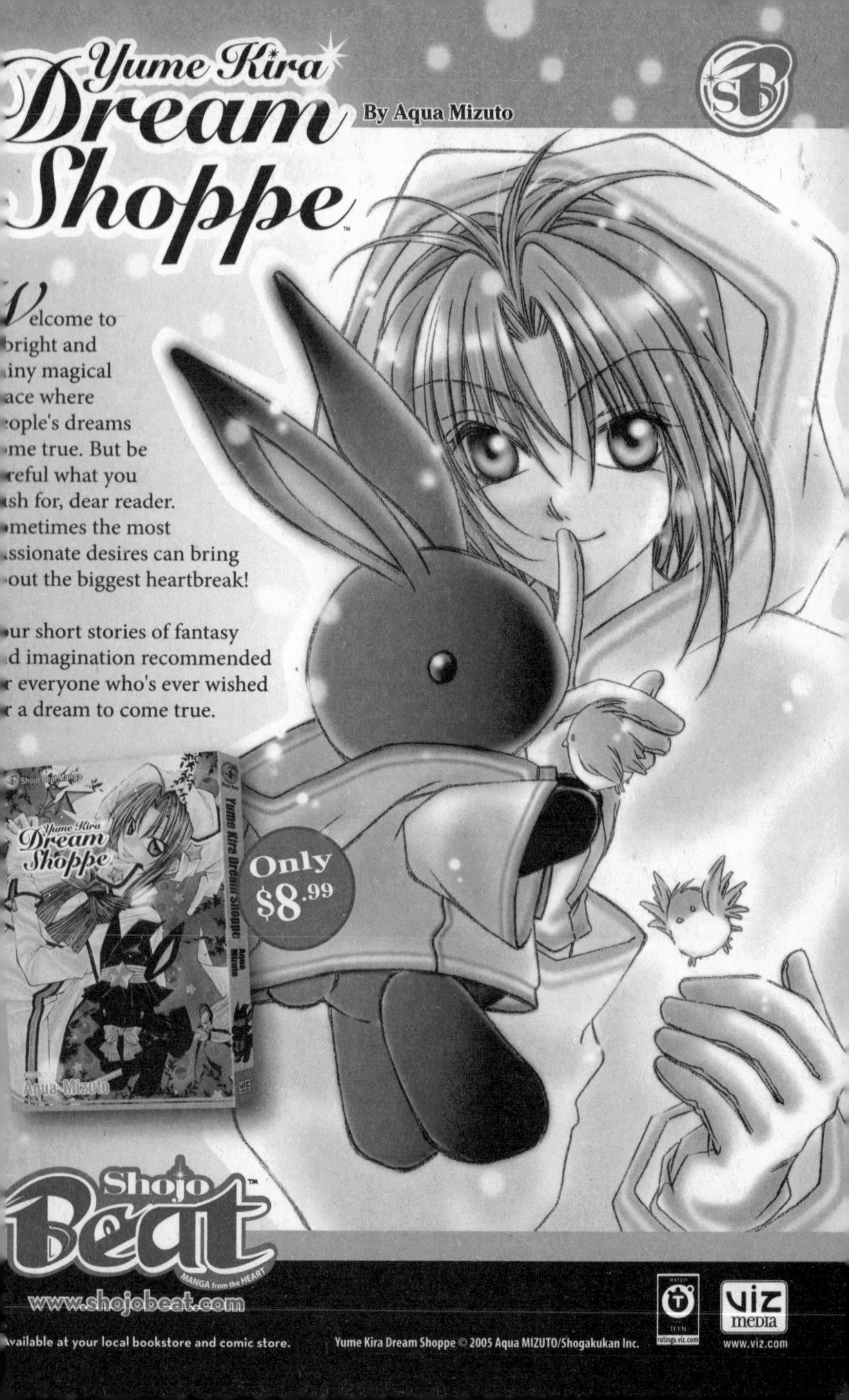
Yume Kira Dream Shoppe™
By Aqua Mizuto
Velcome to
bright and
iny magical
ace where
ople's dreams
me true. But be
reful what you
sh for, dear reader.
metimes the most
ssionate desires can bring
out the biggest heartbreak!
ur short stories of fantasy
d imagination recommended
r everyone who's ever wished
r a dream to come true.
Shojo Beat Manga
Yume Kira Dream Shoppe
Aqua Mizuto
Only $8.99
Shojo Beat™
MANGA from the HEART
www.shojobeat.com
vailable at your local bookstore and comic store.
Yume Kira Dream Shoppe © 2005 Aqua MIZUTO/Shogakukan Inc.
RATED T TEEN
ratings.viz.com
VIZ media
www.viz.com